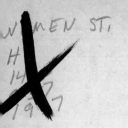

Just as in America there is no Negro problem, but rather a
white problem; just as "antisemitism is not a Jewish problem: it is our problem," so the woman problem has always
been a man's problem.

Simone de Beauvoir

CONTRIBUTORS

ELIZABETH M. ALMQUIST, Ph.D., Sociology, University of Kansas, 1968. Currently Associate Professor at North Texas State University. Her publications include *Careers and Contingencies: How College Women Juggle with Gender Roles* and, forthcoming, *Women, Men and Society* and *Sex Roles: Tradition and Change.*

JOEL ARONOFF, Ph.D., Personality and Cross-cultural Social Psychology, Brandeis University, 1965. Currently Professor of Psychology at Michigan State University, East Lansing, Michigan.

ROBERT F. BALES, Ph.D., Sociology, Harvard University, 1945. Currently Professor of Social Relations and Research Associate at the Laboratory of Social Relations at Harvard. A pioneer in the study of small group behavior, he has written numerous articles and books including *Personality and Inter-personal Behavior.*

NANCY S. BARRETT, Ph.D., Economics, Harvard University, 1968. Currently on leave from American University in Washington, D.C., she is Deputy Assistant Director for Fiscal Analysis of the Congressional Budget Office. She is the author of several books on economic policy.

CAROLYN SHAW BELL, Ph.D., Economics, London University, 1949. Currently the Katharine Coman Professor of Economics at Wellesley College. She chairs the Federal Advisory Council on Unemployment Insurance and serves on the Executive Committee of the American Economic Association.

MARGARET L. BENSTON, Ph.D., Chemistry, University of Washington, 1964. Currently teaching Chemistry at Simon Fraser University in Canada. She has done research and theoretical studies in molecular and atomic quantum mechanics as well as having written on women's issues.

PETER L. BERGER, Ph.D., Sociology, University of London, 1954. Currently

WOMAN IN A MAN-MADE WORLD

SECOND EDITION

A SOCIOECONOMIC HANDBOOK

Nona Glazer
Helen Youngelson Waehrer Editors

both of Portland State University

Rand McNally
College Publishing Company
Chicago

teaching at Rutgers University in New Jersey. He has written numerous books including *Invitation to Sociology* and *The Social Construction of Reality.*

LEIGH BIENEN is an attorney who has done research on sex offenses and homicide. She is a former editor of the *Womens' Rights Reporter,* and is currently doing research on incest. She is on the faculty of the School of Law, University of California, Berkeley.

FRANCINE D. BLAU, Ph.D., Economics, Harvard University, 1975. Currently Assistant Professor of Economics, and Labor and Industrial Relations at the University of Illinois. Her dissertation is entitled *Pay Differentials and Differences in the Distribution of Employment of Male and Female Office Workers.*

RUTH BRANDWEIN is completing her Ph.D. at the Florence Heller Graduate School of Social Welfare, Brandeis University. Currently Assistant Professor at Boston University School of Social Work, she is chairperson of Community Organization and Administration. She is also cofounder and member of the Women's Research Center of Boston. She is interested in policy issues affecting female-headed families.

CAROL A. BROWN. Currently a member of the Women's Research Center of Boston and Associate Professor of Sociology, University of Massachusetts at Lowell. Her research interests are the health professions, the labor force, and women under capitalism.

JUDITH K. BROWN, Ph.D., Harvard Graduate School of Education. She holds a certificate in Child Development from the Institute of Education, University of London, and has held a postdoctoral fellowship at the Radcliffe Institute. She is currently an Associate Professor of Anthropology at Oakland University.

ALAN CRADDOCK, B.A. (Sydney, 1968), M.A.Ps.S., is Principal Tutor in the Department of Psychology at the University of Sydney, and is currently completing a Ph.D. thesis involving a longitudinal study of premarital power and value expectations as factors in subsequent marital adjustment.

WILLIAM D. CRANO, Ph.D., Psychology, Northwestern University, 1968. Currently Professor of Psychology at Michigan State University, Lansing.

KATHERYN THOMAS DIETRICH, M.A., Sociology, University of Kentucky. Currently a Research Associate at Texas A. & M. University.

RICHARD C. EDWARDS, Ph.D., Economics, Harvard University, 1972. Currently Assistant Professor of Economics at the University of Massachusetts at Amherst.

ROSLYN FELDBERG, Ph.D., Sociology, University of Michigan. She teaches Sociology at Boston University and is working with Janet Kohen and other members of the Women's Research Center on a book about single parent families. She is also doing research on clerical workers.

ELIZABETH M. FOX, Clinical Psychology, Yale University. She is a founding member of the Women's Research Center of Boston. Currently an Associate in Pediatrics in the Child Development Unit of the Boston Children's Hospital, she teaches child development to pediatricians and is doing research on the impact of day care and single parenting on early childhood growth and development.

VICTOR R. FUCHS, Ph.D., Economics, Columbia University, 1955. Currently Professor of Economics at Stanford University and Vice President of the National Bureau of Economic Research, where he directs the Center for Economic Analysis of Human Behavior and Social Institutions. He is the author of many articles and books, his latest being *Who Shall Live? Health, Economics and Social Choice.*

NONA GLAZER, Ph.D., Sociology, Cornell University, 1965. Currently Professor at Portland State University in Oregon. She has published on women's position and the family, including *Old Family/New Family.* During 1976–78, she is serving as President of Sociologists for Women in Society, and is chair-elect (1976–77) of the Sex Role section of the American Sociological Association.

DAVID M. GORDON, Ph.D., Economics, Harvard University, 1971. Currently Assistant Professor of Economics in the Graduate Faculty of the New School for Social Research.

KATHLEEN GOUGH, Ph.D., Anthropology, Girton College, Cambridge, 1950. She is a Research Associate in Anthropology at the University of British Columbia, Vancouver, Canada. She spent a number of years in southern India doing field work in the villages and has published widely on comparative kinship and on the social institutions of India. She spent 1976 studying changing agrarian relations in southeast India.

BETTY MACMORRAN GRAY is currently with the Word Guild, a professional association of free-lance writers, researchers, designers, artists, translators, editors, proof readers, and indexers that is based in Cambridge, Massachusetts.

ROBERT F. E. GUBBELS is on the faculty of the University of Brussels. He is Professor of Labor Organization and Research Director of the Institute of Sociology, where he chairs a working group on "Family Roles." His areas of interest are organization, role theory, and the condition of women workers. His latest English-language publication is "The Female Labour Force in Western Europe" in *Women in the World.*

HELEN MAYER HACKER, Ph.D., Sociology, Columbia University. Currently Professor of Sociology at Adelphi University. She pioneered courses on gender roles, nonethnic minorities, and sexuality. Recent publications include *The Social Roles of Women and Men: A Sociological Approach.* She is currently replicating her 1960 study of the attitudes of Americans toward working wives.

HEIDI HARTMANN, Ph.D., Economics, Yale University, 1974. Currently researching the sex and race typing of jobs at the U.S. Commission on Civil Rights. Her doctoral dissertation is "An Economic History of Housework in the Early 20th Century in the United States." She has taught in the graduate political economy program at the New School for Social Research.

AGNES HELLER studied with George Lukacs in Budapest, Hungary. She has written extensively in the fields of Marxism, ethics, value theory and history. She is currently employed by the Hungarian government as a researcher.

CAROL L. JUSENIUS, Ph.D., Economics, New York University, 1973. Currently a Brookings Economic Policy Fellow at the Economic Development Administration, U.S. Department of Commerce, on leave of absence from the City and Regional Planning Department, Ohio State University.

HANSFRIED KELLNER has taught Sociology at the University of Frankfurt in Germany.

JANET KOHEN is Assistant Professor at the University of Massachusetts in Boston. She is a member of the Women's Research Center, which is studying divorced mothers. She is also involved in research on children's social role in the United States.

ROBERT J. LAMPMAN, Ph.D., University of Wisconsin, 1950. Currently William F. Vilas Professor of Economics, University of Wisconsin, and a fellow of the Institute for Research on Poverty. He has published widely, including *Top Wealth-Holders' Share of National Wealth* and *Ends and Means of Reducing Income Poverty.*

JACOB MINCER, Ph.D., Economics, Columbia University, 1957. Currently Professor of Economics at Columbia University and Senior Research Staff, National Bureau of Economic Research. He has written numerous works including *Schooling, Experience and Earnings,* and *Distribution of Labor Incomes.*

JULIET MITCHELL is currently a free-lance writer and University Lecturer in Womens' Studies and English Literature. She also works as a community psychotherapist and is in training as a psychoanalyst at the London Institute of Psychoanalysis.

ALBERT W. NIEMI, JR., Ph.D., Economics, University of Connecticut, 1969. Currently Professor of Economics and Director of the Division of Research of the College of Business and Administration at the University of Georgia.

ALICIA OSTRIKER studied at Brandeis University and the University of Wisconsin. She is a poet and Professor of English Literature at Rutgers University.

J. P. OSTRIKER studied at Harvard University and the University of Chicago. He is currently Professor of Astrophysics at Princeton University.

TALCOTT PARSONS, Ph.D., Philosophy, University of Heidelberg, 1927. Currently Professor Emeritus of Sociology at Harvard University. He is the author of many books, including *The Structure of Social Action* and *Family Socialization and Interaction.*

MICHAEL REICH, Ph.D., Economics, Harvard University, 1973. Currently Assistant Professor of Economics at the University of California, Berkeley.

DOROTHY E. SMITH, Ph.D., University of California at Berkeley, 1963. Currently teaches in the Department of Anthropology and Sociology at the University of British Columbia, Canada. She specializes in the sociology of knowledge and women's studies in sociology.

JUDITH STACEY, Ph.D. candidate in Sociology, Brandeis University, is writing her dissertation on Thermadorean reaction to family revolution. Currently a collective member and teacher at the Women's School in Cambridge Massachusetts, she has taught at Richmond College of City University of New York and at the University of California, Berkeley.

DAVID TRESEMER, Ph.D., Social Psychology, Harvard University. Currently a therapist and consultant in Brattleboro, Vermont. His interest in misconceptions about gender roles has led him to introduce statistical methods to avoid the assumption traps described in his article. His works include *Fear of Success*.

MIHALY VAJDA is a student of Georg Lukacs. He has written on problems of phenomenology, Marxism, aesthetics and fascism. He is currently employed as a researcher in Hungary.

HELEN YOUNGELSON WAEHRER, Ph.D., Economics, Columbia University, 1966. Currently Associate Professor of Economics at Portland State University in Oregon. She is a member of the Committee on the Status of Women in the Economics Profession of the American Economic Association.

LENORE WEITZMAN, Ph.D., Sociology, Columbia University. Currently Associate Professor of Sociology at the University of California, Davis. She was a fellow at Yale Law School for two years, and is presently Principal Investigator, California Divorce Law Research Project, which is exploring the effects of the no-fault divorce law in that state.

ELI ZARETSKY, Ph.D., American History, University of Maryland. Currently research historian at the Childhood and Government Project, University of California Law School, Berkeley. He is coauthor of a book on government policy toward children, and is preparing a separate work on the twentieth-century American family. He has also published studies on psychoanalysis and psychotherapy.

PREFACE

Why this enlarged and considerably revised edition? Since the preparation of the first edition in 1971, a prodigious increase in scholarly writings about women means there is a rich source of new materials. By drawing from these works, we are able to present, first, a more multifaceted and much strengthened collection of articles, two-thirds of which are new to the book. New essays on basic methodological issues, on women's history, and on a broader spectrum of sociological and economic issues enrich the book. These articles raise important issues neglected in the first edition of the handbook either because of our oversight or because of the absence of suitable materials. Second, empirical materials are updated, thereby providing the reader with many recent analyses of hypotheses about the family and work roles of women. Updated descriptive statistics on women are also included, a modicum of dreary reality for those who believe that women's situation "must have" changed dramatically in the decade since the women's movement re-emerged. Third, the increased size of the book allows us to include articles on new topics such as housework, patriarchy, and the aftermath of the end of marriage for women and their children, and allows us to include more materials about black women. Our publisher's understandable refusal to respond to our constantly escalating demand for "just another thirty or so pages" means that not all neglected or omitted topics are now in the volume. Since we selected in favor of articles that confront women's social position in the United States and that emphasize a structural approach in sociology, we apologize to the many scholars whose articles we reviewed but did not include here. Fourth, the selection of articles in this edition benefits from a greater sensitivity to contrasting sociological approaches. Articles have been chosen to mirror the contrasts in sociological focuses. Thus we have answered, we hope, the demands voiced over the past five years by students in the Sociology of Women course at Portland State University who have searched for the many sides of each issue. Future students will benefit from this comparative presentation. The increase in literature on women by economists also means that the handbook can consider variations in approach to understanding women's experiences in the economy.

The handbook is organized into five parts. The first three parts have several subsections, each of which is prefaced by an introduction providing the reader with a historical or conceptual background for understanding and evaluating the selections. Part One is divided into two sections. Readings in the first section consider some of the methodological issues that sociologists and economists are now considering. Readings in the second section are historical. They examine variations in views about the family and the impact of patriarchy on capitalism, as well as present an overview of women's status in the labor force. Part Two is divided into two sections also. First, there is a discussion of four major sociological approaches to sex stratification—sex differences, gender roles, minority group theory, and caste/class theory—followed by articles that use each of these approaches. Second, the major economic approaches, including the neoclassical, institutional, and radical, are discussed. The articles that follow, which illustrate these three approaches, deal with labor force participation, labor market differences, and nonmarket activity. The readings in Part Three present theoretical and empirical studies of the family, the economy, and the interrelationships between these as lived by women before, during, and after marriage. Part Four includes documentation that may dispel myths perpetuating women's subordinate position. Finally, in Part Five, the selections consider alternatives for women in total societies, examining the status of women in Sweden, in the People's Republic of China, and in a utopian communist state. Whether or not our society has been moving toward solutions to sex stratification we leave to the reader to judge—and, we hope, to move toward developing new solutions for "the longest revolution."

This new edition is intended for use in undergraduate courses, workshops, or institutes that are concerned with the social and economic experiences of women; it may also serve to inform the generally curious reader. In either case, this edition will be useful to those who seek a sturdy base of information from which to confront the reluctance of friends, lovers, and husbands as well as other powerholders in society who refuse to take seriously the contemporary plight of women. There appears to be nothing like a "fact" for disarming the skeptic, although disarming powerholders of their power is yet another issue. The book is not easy: those who seek a "Mickey Mouse course" or the immediately understood are in for a disappointment. However, students will be relieved to know that the selections become easier to understand as the book progresses both because the materials are usually less abstract and because the reader has gotten a foundation from the preceding selections. Our belief is that the analysis of women's condition, while it must start with the everyday lives of women rather than with a picture as filtered through patriarchical attitudes, must move rapidly to careful scholarship.

The continued collaboration of a sociologist and an economist, in spite of our different points of view and the quite different approaches of our disciplines, emphasizes our belief in the critical importance of understanding women's social position in a hardheaded way, and in the need to assess the status of women through an interdisciplinary approach. One of us has been much influenced by the theoretical and empirical work derived from Freud and Marx, and by a sociology of knowledge perspective; the other is especially interested in theoretical and empirical analyses derived from mainstream neoclassical economics. Our differences have not abated. However, the new introductory comments reflect our realization that students would benefit from a more explicit statement of the differences within our respective disciplines and thus be able to select more explicitly, themselves, between the differing perspectives that we hold.

Many colleagues, students, and friends must be thanked for their direct and indirect contributions to this new edition. Special thanks to the hundreds of students who, taking part in Sociology of Women classes, have shared their misgivings, criticisms, and delights about various selections. In preparing, often with considerable agony, an assigned journal that was to embody C. Wright Mills' ideal of using sociology as well as history to illuminate personal life, these women and men made the sociologist editor acutely aware of the pitfalls of the first edition. We hope the new edition remedies these. Sharon Massey, an honors student in sociology, helped search the sociological literature for pertinent articles. Linda Majka, Department of Sociology, Portland State University, made helpful suggestions of articles to include in the new edition. Catherine Lynde read sections of the introductory comments to economic perspectives. Lori Fox, Deborah Perkins, and Christy Newton gracefully handled the deluge of correspondence, collated the articles for the manuscript, and maintained their composure in the face of lost pages and misplaced letters. Helen Youngelson Waehrer assumed responsibility for selecting and editing the materials by economists and for writing the introductory comments to these materials. Nona Glazer was responsible for materials about women from a historical, sociological, and social psychological perspective, and assumed the major responsibility for writing the introductory comments. We share responsibility for the limitations of the book and for errors of omission as well as commission. We gratefully acknowledge the permission of authors and publishers to reprint the selections in this reader.

Finally, we wish to express our appreciation to the editors at Rand McNally, Martha Urban and Marge Boberschmidt, who saw the second edition to press. We also fondly remember Laurette Hupman, the editor of the first edition, and her struggles with a man typesetter who got hung up on one article. The problem was finally resolved by reassigning the material to the sole woman typesetter. It is a small sign of progress that at least in the second edition there has been no such hassle.

Portland State University
Portland, Oregon
January 1977

NONA GLAZER
Department of Sociology

HELEN YOUNGELSON WAEHRER
Department of Economics

CONTENTS

PART ONE
General Perspectives

Political Man: The Social Bases of Politics by Seymour
   Martin Lipset
Man Alone: Alienation in Modern Society by Eric and
   Mary Josephson
Man Against Poverty: World War III by Arthur Blau-
   stein and Robert Woock
Man and Society in an Age of Reconstruction by Karl
   Mannheim

THE INVISIBILITY OF WOMAN

Woman's exclusion from the man-made world is not altered by the
contention that the word *man* is generic, meant to include both sexes.
We must consider the following. First, sex identity (our belief that we
are female or male) is learned very early in life, before there is an
awareness of race, religion, nationality, or social class. By three years or
so, a girl "knows" she is a girl and will become a woman, a boy "knows"
he is a boy and will become a man.[1] Second, beyond a certain point in

---

[1]Sex identity, it should be noted, may run counter to biology: children with erroneously announced
sex believe themselves to be a member of the sex to which they are socially assigned; transsexuals
believe they are the sex to which they have assigned themselves, regardless of chromosomes and
hormones. Money and Erhardt suggest that only hermaphrodites who already have an unsure sex
identity can change their sex identity easily after puberty. John Money and Anke A. Erhardt, *Man
and Woman, Boy and Girl* (Baltimore: Johns Hopkins Press, 1972).

psychosexual development, sex identity is sufficiently tenacious that it appears easier to change physical and hormonal characteristics (through surgery and hormone therapy) than to bring a person's social sex into accord with biology.[2] Third, a successful sex identity includes learning the correct language—"I am a girl, you are a boy." One major approach to gender-role socialization (the cognitive developmental theory) views the learning of the appropriate sex label for the self as a necessary basis for future learning of sex-typed behavior.[3] Both sexes must learn to know when *man* as well as other supposedly generic words (*adults, children, workers,* etc.) apply to females.

Language is an elementary form of women's exclusion from much of the world, a way of "ignoring the existence of women outside the domestic, sexual, and service realms [which] relegate women to the sidelines of life."[4] To whom does the phrase "man is becoming urban" refer? And, are women included in "all men are created equal"? Both sexes learn the many nuances of language; but just because there is considerable ambiguity about woman's place in society, neither sex inevitably considers both women and men to be included in generic terms. For example, women and men students were asked to bring illustrations for a supposed sociology text whose table of contents included chapters on "Urban Man," "Economic Man," "Industrial Man," "Family," etc. The majority of students failed to see *man* as referring consistently to both sexes.[5] Furthermore, Graham found that only 32 of 490 citations of *he* in school textbooks referred to both sexes, that *mother* occurred more often than *father,* although children were more often referred to as the offspring of the male than of the female parent—Bob's daughter, Gary's son, rather than Mary's daughter, Sally's son.[6]

The newspaper confirms the exclusion of women from a man's world. The existence of a woman's page suggests that editors and publishers apparently believe that the interests of women differ, to a substantial degree, from the interests of men.[7] It is not only that recipes, household

[2]Money and Erhardt, *Man and Woman,* p. 23.

[3]L. Kohlberg, "A Cognitive-developmental Analysis of Children's Sex-role Concepts and Attitudes," in Eleanor E. Maccoby (ed.), *The Development of Sex Differences* (Stanford, Calif.: Stanford University Press, 1966).

[4]Jean Lipman-Blumen, "Toward a Homosocial Theory of Sex Roles: An Explanation of the Sex Segregation of Social Institutions." *Signs: Journal of Women in Culture and Society* 1, no. 3, pt. 2(Spring 1976):15–31.

[5]Joseph W. Schneider and Sally L. Hacker, "Sex Role Imagery and the Use of Generic 'Man' in Introductory Texts." *The American Sociologist* 8(February 1973):12–18.

[6]Alma Graham, "The Making of a Non-Sexist Dictionary," in Barrie Thorne and Nancy Henley (eds.) *Language and Sex* (Rowley, Mass.: Newsbury House Publishers, 1975), p. 58.

[7]Women, too, sometimes believe that there is or ought to be a separate "women's culture." Ann Battle-Sister, "Conjectures on the Female Culture Question." *Journal of Marriage and the Family* 33(August 1971):411–420; Berit Ås, "On Female Culture." *Acta Sociologica* 18, no. 2–3 (1975): 142–161. Radical feminism—one approach within the current women's movement—supports the notion

hints, and fashion news delineate the outlines of woman's lives, but the news about women scientists, college presidents, and other notables is similarly relegated to the section reserved for the female sex. The media thus discourage men from becoming aware of women's myriad interests and accomplishments. (Women, in turn, may be discouraged from learning about "men's affairs," by the placement of business news in the "sports" section—which is mainly about men's sport!)

The Invisibility of Women in Science. Science is a way of reporting about the world and is prone to distortions similar to those in the mass media. The overwhelming majority of scientists are men; hence the overwhelming majority of those who set scientific problems, award research grants, select papers for conference presentations, and otherwise carry on scientific activity are men. In the social sciences, women have been peripheral in universities and colleges where, as Ph.D.'s, they have been concentrated in nontenured positions,[8] in the less prestigious universities and colleges, and in the lower academic ranks. Until recent pressure by women's caucuses forced some change, women participated to a limited extent in national professional associations as session organizers and presenters of papers and through committee appointments and elected office.[9] While women social scientists publish, proportionately, as much as men,[10] historically women have remained invisible because:

—Men develop professional ties during graduate school and tend to help each other to publish, move to better academic jobs, etc.[11] This "old boy" network has excluded women in the past and usually continues to exclude them.

—A woman's dual role often limits her continuing employment as she leaves to take care of children and because of other family responsibilities.[12]

—Outright discrimination is practiced through the application of more stringent standards to the qualifications and work of women than of men.[13]

---

of separatism; this approach sees women's developing a separate culture as a precursor of their liberation.

[8]The awarding of tenure guarantees the job indefinitely rather than on a year-by-year basis.

[9]Helen MacGill Hughes, *The Status of Women in Sociology, 1968-1972* (Washington, D.C.: American Sociological Association, 1973); Barbara B. Reagan, "Committee on the Status of Women in Economic Professions," *American Economic Review* 65(May 1975):100–107.

[10]See the article by Bienen et al. in Part Four of this reader.

[11]Thomas Sowell, " 'Affirmative Action' Reconsidered." *The Public Interest* no. 42(Winter 1976): 47–65.

[12]Sowell, " 'Affirmative Action' Reconsidered," pp. 53–54.

[13]Letters of application for jobs and vita, identical except for the sex of the applicant, yielded many more job offers in academia for men than for women. L. S. Fidell, "Empirical Verification of Sex Discrimination in Hiring Procedures in Psychology," in Rhoda Kesler Unger and Florence L. Denmark (eds.), *Woman: Dependent or Independent Variable* (New York: Psychological Dimensions, 1975), pp. 774–785.

Including Women in Science.   To speed the movement of women into jobs, including those in science, the federal government developed a series of guidelines (Affirmative Action) that require employers, admission officers, and others to give women the *opportunity* for access to training and jobs. Administrators are required to demonstrate that fully qualified women were *not* available for jobs, promotions, and admission to training programs in industry and to colleges and universities. Under these guidelines, women (and minorities) are to be given preferential hiring *if*—and only *if*—they are equally qualified compared with white male candidates. (Unfortunately, there has been a wide misunderstanding and, sometimes, a misapplication of the guidelines, which have been interpreted erroneously to mean that women and minority group members, regardless of qualifications, should be given preference over *more* qualified white males.)

Affirmative Action has had only a minimal impact on the pay, employment, or promotions of women in academe, in spite of wide publicity and much criticism of its supposed lowering of quality. In 1968–1969, women were 19.1 percent of academics compared with 20.0 percent in 1972–1973, hardly, as Sowell notes, "revolutionary changes." Similarly, continually employed women doctorates in the natural and social sciences earned the same percentage of the income of men doctorates in both 1970 and 1973.[14] What has changed is hiring *procedures* (not hiring), which includes recruiting, screening, and evaluating candidates to demonstrate to federal agencies that the universities are acting in "good faith." Thus, while women may figure more prominently in professional activities than ever before, they are still marginal to the social science disciplines as members of faculties of major universities and in earnings.[15]

Experience and Scientific Knowledge.   Who is involved in scientific activity is important since men (sic) of science have long been aware of how everyday experience shapes what one thinks. Marx observed:

> It is not the consciousness of men that determines their existence, but, on the contrary, their social existence determines their consciousness.

The essential problem is this: Can those who are located in the centers of power or who work as intellectuals (scientists, policy advisors, artists, writers) for the powerful overcome their own intellectual blindness that comes from the limits of their own location in society? Hence, studies

---

[14]Sowell, " 'Affirmative Action' Reconsidered," p. 57.

[15]The establishment of special sections in professional associations (e.g., Sex Role, Marxist Sociology) serves both to draw critical thinkers into the association and to isolate them, intellectually, within the association.

of the poor, of blacks, and of the working class need to be examined for ideas that are shaped by the social experience of the knowers, for the taken-for-grantedness that comes from researchers *not* being among those who are marginal to society. (The other side of the coin is that researchers may take for granted the "naturalness" and inevitability of the organization of power.) These ideas may be built into the conduct of inquiry: into the selection of certain scientific topics rather than others (e.g., petty robberies rather than corporate crime, male rather than female sexuality), into the development of concepts and research techniques as well as into the logic of the organization of scientific thinking.

While these issues have been given attention by several generations of social thinkers,[16] as Daniels notes, the discourse has been limited to men—to how men are influenced by their location, and to whether men can grasp the meanings and structure of the social worlds of other men.[17] Numerous sexist biases characterize social science. The founding fathers of sociology have been called "sexist to a man."[18] The psychologists' models of healthy adults and of healthy women have been shown to be contradictory.[19] Historians have ignored women's role in history[20] while, until recently, economists have ignored the work of women in the home as a contribution to the standard of living of the family.[21] Even the writings of women themselves, such as Hannah Arendt's *The Human Condition,* have been called sexist.[22]

Sociological research on leisure provides a specific example of the effect of taking-for-granted assumptions about society on the *formulation* of a scientific issue.[23] The early researchers on leisure in the United States considered the study of women's leisure to be difficult because housewives were considered to have *only* leisure. Yet most women, and

---

[16]Marx, Mannheim, Durkheim, Weber, Veblen, Boulding, to name a few, have considered the issues.

[17]Arlene Daniels, "Feminist Perspectives in Sociological Research," in Marcia Millman and Rosabeth Moss Kanter (eds.), *Another Voice* (New York: Doubleday, 1975), pp. 340–380.

[18]Julia Schwendinger and Herman Schwendinger, "Sociology's Founding Fathers: Sexists to a Man," *Journal of Marriage and the Family* 33(November 1971):783–799.

[19]Inge Broverman, Donald Broverman, Frank E. Clarkson, Paul Rosenkrantz and Susan R. Vogel, "Sex Role Stereotypes and Clinical Judgements about Mental Health." *Journal of Consulting and Clinical Psychology* 34: 1–7.

[20]Ruth Rosen, "Sexism in History or, Writing Women's History is a Tricky Business," *Journal of Marriage and the Family* 33 (August 1971): 541–544.

[21]Sylvia M. Gelber, "The Labor Force, the GNP, and Unpaid Housekeeping Services." An address delivered at the North American Conference on Labor Statistics, June 8, 1970.

[22]Hannah Arendt, *The Human Condition* (Chicago: University of Chicago Press, 1958); Clarice Stasz Stoll, *Female and Male: Socialization, Social Roles, and Social Structure* (Dubuque, Ia.: Wm. C. Brown, 1974), p. 68.

[23]The contention that the scientific method prevents social biases does not answer the criticism that (*a*) the formulation of social science problems, (*b*) the development of concepts, (*c*) the selections of certain techniques rather than others, and (*d*) the organization of the research procedures are all themselves subject to social influences that have nothing to do with the imminent development of knowledge.

some men, know quite well that housework is *work,* that the problem for the housewife may be that she is denied leisure rather than that she has only leisure.[24] The neoclassical economist's analysis of *leisure* retains some of that meaning when housewives are considered to be choosing between *leisure* and *paid work.* Economists' research takes other social biases for granted. Accepting the existing sex division of labor, economists' study of the economy became synonymous with the study of goods and services produced in the market by men. Thus, not only was the study of women's household production left to home economists until recently, but even the analysis of women's economic role in the market was ignored.[25] Furthermore, omitting an estimate of the monetary value of housework from the gross national product reinforces further the belief that most women make no economic contribution.[26]

THE IMPACT OF FEMINISM ON SCHOLARSHIP

Feminism has affected scholarship as well as raised a variety of issues about methodology, theories and concepts, and topics. First, feminists have questioned the effect of being a woman on the perception of social reality and on the development of social science. The issue here is not that women have been ignored in theories and research. Rather, the issue is whether women as women have unique experiences in society that would lead (as implied by a sociology of knowledge perspective) to theories and methodologies different from those developed by men. To understand how this would be the case, we need to examine briefly the theoretical stance developed by Peter Berger and Thomas Luckman. This stance moves the focus of the sociology of knowledge from understanding the problem of the development of humanistic, scientific, and historical knowledge to the problem of how people know their everyday world.[27] People, going about their daily activities, interacting with others, construct a social reality that consists of shared meanings. This symbolic world is not visible to the outside observer, although social scientists (as well as others) attempt to infer the meanings and the structure of these social worlds from their observations of visible activity. Yet, from the perspective of symbolic interaction, the way to

[24]Joann Vanek, "Time Spent in Housework." *Scientific American* 231 (November 1974):14, 116–120.

[25]Cynthia B. Lloyd, "The Division of Labor Between the Sexes: A Review," in Cynthia B. Lloyd (ed.), *Sex, Discrimination and the Division of Labor* (New York: Columbia University Press, 1975).

[26]Colin Clark, "The Economics of Housework." *Bulletin in the Oxford Institute of Statistics* 20 (May 1958): 205–211.

[27]Peter Berger and Thomas Luckmann, *The Social Construction of Reality* (Garden City, N.Y.. Doubleday, 1966).

understand such social realities is to ask people what their own unique world of meanings is, for social scientists are seen as situated in their own unique world of meanings, distinct from those whom they study. Men, too, are situated in their own unique world of meanings, distinct from women's worlds. Regardless of how sympathetic or empathetic men may be, they can never, except perhaps as transsexuals, be women and, therefore, can never comprehend the world of women as women do. For social scientists to understand women's social position fully, it follows that they need to start with the experiences of women, as Dorothy Smith urges be done in the first selection following these introductory comments.

Second, feminist scholars have made explicit the sexism involved in many concepts and theories. For example, Joan Acker notes how wives' status-creating resources (their education and occupations) are ignored in studies of social stratification, as if these had no effect on the family's status.[28] Millman questions theories of female deviance that explain women's behaviors in sexually stereotyped terms, e.g., seeing prostitution as a sexual act rather than as an occupation.[29] Cynthia Lloyd notes that economists take the division of labor by sex for granted rather than examine the basis for the differentiation.[30] Bell, whose article is the second selection in Part One, explores the stereotyping of women in neoclassical microeconomics.[31]

Third, the range of topics in which women are included has been expanded in sociology from a narrow focus on the family and family-related topics. In economics, there has been a shift from concern with the labor force activities of men to those of women as well. A dearth of research still characterizes many areas of scholarship, however. Thus while some serious attention is given to the sociological study of women in work organizations,[32] the two roles of employed married women,[33] and mental illness,[34] many topics remain virtually untouched: women's political activities, women as single parents, single women's life-styles, women intellectuals, and so on. Labor economists have expanded the

---

[28]Joan Acker, "Women and Social Stratification: A Case of Intellectual Sexism." *American Journal of Sociology* 78 (January 1973): 936–945.

[29]Marcia Millman, "She Did It All for Love: A Feminist View of the Sociology of Deviance," in Millman and Kanter, *Another Voice,* pp. 251–279.

[30]Lloyd, "Division of Labor Between Sexes," pp. 1–7.

[31]See article by Carolyn Bell, Part One.

[32]See, for example, Cynthia Epstein, *Woman's Place* (Berkeley: University of California Press, 1970); Pamela Roby, *The Conditions of Women in Blue-Collar and Service Jobs: A Review of Research and Proposals for Research, Action and Policy* (New York: Russell Sage Foundation, forthcoming).

[33]See, for example, Michael P. Fogarty, Rhona Rapoport, and Robert N. Rapoport, *Sex, Career and Family* (London: George Allen & Unwin, 1971).

[34]See, for example, Pauline Bart, "Depression in Middle-Aged Women," in Vivian Gornick and B. K. Moran (eds.), *Woman in Sexist Society* (New York: Signet, 1972), pp. 163–186; Kevin Clancy and Walter Gove, "Sex Differences in Mental Illness." *American Journal of Sociology* 80(July 1974):205–216.

study of women to include the participation of women in the work force,[35] wage differentials,[36] and women's occupational distribution,[37] although very little has been done by scholars in other fields of economics.

Four, social scientists have begun to ask questions about women as women, apart from their inclusion in the usual range of topics in existing theories. For example, motherhood, which has been intensively studied from the perspective of asking how mothers affect children's well-being,[38] has now begun to be explored as it affects the mothers themselves.[39] The theory of allocation of time first developed by Becker has been extended to the examination of nonmarket activities[40] and the family.[41] Even though the model has been extended to nonmarket behavior, men's family activities in the home are still neglected—as if only women as family members have activities in the home.

---

[35]T. Aldrich Finegan, "Participation of Married Women in the Labor Force," in Lloyd, *Sex, Discrimination, and Division of Labor,* pp. 27–54.

[36]Janice Madden, *The Economics of Sex Discrimination* (Lexington, Mass.: D.C. Heath, 1973).

[37]Barbara R. Bergmann, "Occupational Segregation, Wages, and Profits, When Employers Discriminate by Race or Sex." *Eastern Economic Journal* 1(April/July 1974):103–110.

[38]F. Ivan Nye and Lois W. Hoffman, *The Employed Mother in America* (Chicago: Rand McNally, 1963).

[39]Jessie Bernard, *The Future of Motherhood* (New York: Dial Press 1974); Rochelle Paul Wortis, "The Acceptance of the Concept of the Maternal Role by Behavioral Scientists: Its Effect on Women." *American Journal of Orthopsychiatry* 41, no. 5(1971):733–746.

[40]Gary S. Becker, "A Theory of the Allocation of Time." *Economic Journal* 70(September 1965):493–517.

[41]Arleen Leibowitz, "Education and Home Production." *American Economic Review* 64(May 1974):243–250; Shirley B. Johnson, "The Impact of Women's Liberation on Marriage, Divorce and Family Lifestyle," in Lloyd, *Sex, Discrimination, and Division of Labor,* pp. 401–426; Heather L. Ross and Isabel V. Sawhill, *Time of Transition: The Growth of Families Headed by Women* (Washington, D.C.: Urban Institute, 1975).

Feminist Scholarship

Introduction The Editors

The first two selections in this reader—by Dorothy E. Smith, a sociologist, and by Carolyn Shaw Bell, an economist—are discussions of some broad issues raised by feminist scholars.[1] In a sense, most of the selections in this reader are feminist scholarship or are compatible with feminist concerns. These two articles are distinct because each examines some basic issues of scholarship rather than a particular substantive topic or social science theory.

A NOTE ON THEORY

Many articles in this reader are theoretical, complementing those articles that are purely descriptive. The theoretical selections attempt (from diverse points of view) to explain the social world, sometimes by examining assumptions and concepts and suggesting relationships, and sometimes by actually testing theories themselves, using empirical data. The descriptive articles, in contrast, provide information about the frequency of certain characteristics (e.g., earnings by sex, income, marital status, educational attainment over several decades, etc.) but do not attempt to account for these characteristics, to explain the frequencies.

Sometimes students (and social scientists, too) are uneasy with theory since it may conjure up vague, often incoherent statements about the

[1]Carolyn Shaw Bell, "Economics, Sex, and Gender." *Social Science Quarterly* 55(December 1974):615–631. Other critiques by feminist scholars can be found in Cynthia B. Lloyd, "The Division of Labor Between the Sexes: A Review," in Cynthia B. Lloyd (ed.), *Sex, Discrimination and the Division of Labor* (New York: Columbia University Press, 1975).

social world. Such suspicions about theory may arise from a language problem—"to theorize" is understood sometimes to mean "to speculate without any empirical basis," without reference to what goes on in the world. Theory is certainly abstract, selecting only some characteristics and then stating how these characteristics are related to each other, though the theorists may be well aware that other relevant factors are being ignored. The theorist believes, hopefully, that the most important characteristics have been included in the theory. Theory is supposed to make explicit the assumptions that its writer holds about the nature of people, human behavior, how people relate to each other, etc. Some of the problems that students may have in understanding theory come from writers themselves not always being sure about their assumptions or concepts, or being clear about how variables are related to each other.

Yet theory, the result of an innovative imagination, has enormous value. It provides a summary statement (the level of abstraction is, therefore, high) about experience, which means that we need not try to understand every instance by piecing together an explanation event by event. Rather, we have a way of understanding classes of events and, thus, of understanding a specific event (e.g., women's low wages) by using the theory, which sometimes has been empirically tested and sometimes still awaits testing. Thus, theory is not an ivory-tower enterprise but a practical activity that pulls together and makes sense of apparently disparate occurrences.

Only those who believe that there are *no* common characteristics among people or among other natural phenomena should be disturbed by the level of abstraction, once it is realized that theory searches for commonalities, and that scientists are well aware that no two events, persons, laboratory animals, or falling objects are ever identical in all respects. We act "as if" events are the same because it gives us more power to understand and to control than if we approach each event as if it were completely unique—which is just how we act in our relationships with people.

READINGS

The first two selections in the reader consider issues in sociology and economics that arise in attempts to construct theory, and from the recognition of the influence of the location of people in society to their scientific interpretation of the world.

The article by Dorothy E. Smith is quite abstract and difficult to understand at first reading. She begins with the belief that the everyday worlds experienced and described by women are vastly different from the everyday worlds experienced and described by men. Furthermore, she believes these different worlds to be the basis for the development of diverse social science frameworks. The very orderly theories of men —a "rational-administrative framework" is her label for these theories— derive from their everyday experiences that occur in the world of work organized in supposedly rational ways. Bureaucratic rules, regular production procedures, patterns of promotion, yearly schedules exemplify such supposed rationality. Although many parts of men's world are disorderly (unemployment, inflation, promotions and raises, work evaluation by employers and co-workers, retirement, etc.), the experts who study the world of work both experience their own world as orderly and share with owners and managers a belief in the basic orderliness of the world. This belief is actually a mixture of what *is* and what *ought* to be, as most men social scientists (and most men owners and managers) miss entirely the tenuousness and disorder in the everyday world of people unlike themselves.

While one perspective in Smith's framework is microsociology, using a phenomenological approach to the world, the other perspective is macrosociology, using a Marxian analysis of the political economy. Sociologists have been markedly unsuccessful in developing theories that explain both the microlevels and macrolevels, that explain how the personal autobiographies and mental life of people are connected to the broader social structure within which people live. Hence Mead, Berger and Kellner, Garfinkle, Goffman give us theories of face-to-face interaction as well as an understanding of some of the underlying psychological processes. Marx, Weber, Dahrendorf, Lenski, Merton, Parsons, and a host of others provide theories about large-scale institutions (the family, the political economy, religion, etc.) but little insight into the connection between psychological processes and society. For these latter theorists (Marx is an exception), society seems to exist without living, loving, feeling people.

Smith's intent is to link some of the particulars of the two worlds, using theories from each domain. To provide an understanding of persons who are marginal to the centers of power in society, she believes, it is necessary to *start* with the everyday life of people—in this case, women—as the world is actually experienced and known by them. This is in sharp contrast to understanding women's world by starting with a description or framework developed by outsiders (men, women sociologists), who use a framework based on *their own* worlds. Smith is arguing, therefore, that the world as "known" by the women who experience it has a reality that is not grasped, and is indeed impossible to grasp, by those who have not experienced it.

Yet people do not necessarily recognize the oppression of their own social worlds. For instance, "false consciousness" may exist among workers who do not realize that their interests are in conflict with the interests of capitalists. Thus we would need to study "submerged consciousness"[2] as found among those women who succumbed to what Betty Friedan called "the feminine mystique."[3] Before such women began to be dissatisfied with their gender roles and family lives, before Friedan began to write about "the problem that has no name," they appear to have embraced their own oppression. In spite of the unease and frustration some college-educated, white, suburban housewives felt, most women were apparently telling themselves that they were enjoying the best of all possible worlds and trying to ignore their feelings of discontent. The degree of awareness of oppression and frustration particularly needs investigation when studying women, who, trained to be subordinate, turn their anger about the world inward against themselves.[4] An interesting perspective about the gap between behaving, and feeling and believing is suggested by Warner, Wellman, and Weitzman: oppressed persons may play out their socially designated role with ostensible signs of acceptance, while actually rejecting the role, psychologically and morally.[5] If this is the case with women, then studying women by starting with their own descriptions of their lives may provide a complex picture of women's world that stands in sharp contrast to present studies that give us mainly surface impressions of "adjustment."

It is important to note that Smith does *not* believe, as some ethnomethodologists do, that the description and understanding of everyday life are exhausted by the descriptions and understandings people have of their own worlds. On the contrary, to Smith, the descriptions of the everyday world by women would be only the beginning of the development of a theory for women. The final theory about women's place, according to Smith, would be highly technical, not understood necessarily by those who provide the original perspectives on women's worlds. Sociologists may, thus, connect women's experience with the changes in the political economy—as Smith does—starting with biographical and autobiographical descriptions of the life of a woman on a subsistence farm in Canada and comparing it with the experience of a woman on a single-cash-crop wheat farm in a later period.

The implications for theory can be assumed to be a framework that

---

[2]Ronald V. Sampson, *The Psychology of Power* (New York: Vintage Books, 1968).

[3]Betty Friedan, *The Feminine Mystique* (New York: Norton, 1963).

[4]See Pauline Bart, "Depression in Middle-Aged Women," in Vivian Gornick and Barbara K. Moran (eds.), *Woman in Sexist Society* (New York: Signet, 1972), pp. 163–186.

[5]R. Stephen Warner, David T. Wellman, and Lenore J. Weitzman, "The Hero, the Sambo, and the Operator: Three Characterizations of the Oppressed." *Urban Life and Culture* 2(1973):53–84.

mirrors less the rational administrative world constructed by men and more accurately the actual life of women. For example, Oakley's research on housework and Bart's on middle-aged women[6] give some hints of the characteristics of women's world (fragmentation, isolation, ambiguity about outcomes, repetitiveness, dependency, social obsolescence, powerlessness, emotionality) that would be a beginning point for understanding women's social position.

Smith only hints at the procedures that may be followed to develop a sociology *for* women. Technically, how the research moves from these descriptions to the macrolevel awaits development.[7]

In the other selection in this section, Carolyn Shaw Bell describes the neglect of women as independent agents in economic analysis. She focuses her attention on microeconomic analysis of the behavior of people as workers and consumers in the market.

The theoretical framework of traditional microeconomics is based upon neoclassical theory, accepted by most economists but not all.[8] It has its origins in the work of Adam Smith, which has been modified and refined into an internally consistent theoretical framework for analyzing how people in a society choose to use their limited resources in order to satisfy material wants (goods and services). It assumes a voluntary exchange between individuals as producers and as consumers in the market sector of a mixed capitalist economy.[9] Two fundamental propositions of the theory pertinent to Bell's discussion are (1) that economic decisions are based on individual choice, and (2) that people are maximizers. Thus it is assumed that individuals decide how to allocate their limited resources, be it income or time, so as to maximize personal utility or satisfaction.

In the main part of her paper, Bell describes in detail how a woman's decision-making as worker and consumer in the market is affected by her role in the family rather than by her preferences as an independent economic agent. Economists analyzing the participation of married women in the labor force must focus their attention on factors related to a woman's position in the family (such as husband's income and the number and ages of children) rather than just on her individual choice between work and so-called leisure. Furthermore, as long as women's

---

[6]Ann Oakley, *The Sociology of Housework* (New York: Pantheon Books, 1974); Bart, "Depression in Middle-Aged Women."

[7]See Dorothy E. Smith, "Women, the Family and Corporate Capitalism," in Marylee Stephenson (ed.), *Women in Canada* (Toronto: New Press, 1973), pp. 5–35.

[8]For a radical criticism of neoclassical economics, see R. C. Edwards, Michael Reich, and T. E. Weisskopf (eds.), *The Capitalist System* (Englewood Cliffs, N.J.: Prentice-Hall, 1972), and R. C. Edwards, A. MacEwan, et al., "A Radical Approach to Economics," in David M. Gordon (ed.), *Problems in Political Economy* (Lexington, Mass.: D. C. Heath, 1971).

[9]For a discussion of categories of social relationships, see Kenneth Boulding, *Economics as a Science* (New York: McGraw-Hill, 1970), pp. 1–22.

roles in society continue to be defined primarily by their relations to a *household* unit, the analysis of women as *independent* consumers in the market (the model used for men) is inappropriate.

Bell also discusses the current economic analysis of women. Most of this work is concentrated on two aspects of women's market behavior: (1) their participation in the labor force, and (2) the extent to which occupational segregation reflects economic discrimination.

Bell does not consider whether a theory that begins with women's experience would differ from the present theory. This is, of course, the issue raised by Smith in the preceding selection. Is a new theoretical framework needed? That depends upon whether the experience derived from women's activities centered in the home as well as the market differ significantly enough from the experience of men's activities in the market to generate a unique women's perspective of reality and a different ordering of factors that motivate women's choices. Economists have not as yet addressed this difficult question.

Some Implications of a Sociology for Women

Dorothy E. Smith

INTRODUCTION

This paper attempts to explicate a way of thinking sociologically that starts from the perspective of women. The enterprise begins with the simple recognition that, in doing a sociology *of* women, women are made into the objects of its study. The problem arises in attempting to rectify this by making women into the subjects of the sociological act of knowing (Smith 1975a). When we confront how women have been excluded from sociology (indeed from the making of the intellectual world in general), we can recognize how their lack of access to influential positions has prevented their giving themes and subject matters to the sociological discourse.

The problem for women lies in how sociology is established. Sociology is a going concern. The sociological discourse has its place in the world, its relations, its vested interests—the vested interests of those it serves and services as well as its own. It has its systems of professional controls and an organization of training connected to research and education.

As a social organization, the sociological discourse is integrated into the contemporary form of capitalist society in determinate ways and positions. Its themes and relevances take these positions for granted. Criteria and standards of proper professional performance build in these themes and relevances.

This abbreviated statement was prepared for this reader based on a paper presented at the American Sociological Association meetings, San Francisco, 1975. I am indebted to Arlie Hochschild, who chaired the session at which it was presented, for her encouragement.

Knowledge is fundamentally a socially organized relation[1] that constitutes an object among knowers who are related to one another in determinate ways, through their relation to that object. The relation between the knower and the object of her knowledge is a socially organized practice, and knowledge is socially accomplished. Both knower and object of knowledge are constituted as such in the practices that mediate the relation. Thus conceptual practices, methodologies, instrumentalities, and so forth are not merely "tools" that can be picked up and laid down at will. They are together those practices that organize and bring into being the phenomena *as such* of the discipline. They constitute the knower *as such* in her relation to the known, and the known as object of her knowledge. These are integral aspects of the social organization of knowledge (Smith, 1974b).

In the social sciences, the social relations of knowledge take on a second and distinctive property, namely, that *both* knower and known in the "knowledge relation" are human. The methods of inquiry and the methods of thinking thus create not merely a relation among knowers and the object of their knowledge. That the parties to this relation may be rendered specifically anonymous by the procedures used must be viewed as a definite feature of this social relation. Anonymity, impersonality, objectivity itself are accomplished by socially organized practices that bring into being a determinate social form whose character as a social relation disappears (very much as, according to Marx [1954:-71–83], the social relations of labor disappear in the commodity-form). It is still a social relation, but it does not appear as such. In this way, sociologists have been able to take for granted that their knowledge of society can somehow be treated as extra social.

Ordinarily, as sociologists, we function in and operate this social relation in the absence of an "other" who, by looking back on us, makes us aware that the relation is a social relation. Occasionally, when we are in the actual situation of doing fieldwork or interviewing, we experience this relation in actual social interaction. By insisting that women participate in sociology as knowers, and finding that we cannot escape how the relation transforms us into objects, we can "look back" as subjects upon that relation and disclose its essential contradiction.

So long as *men* and the pronouns *he, his,* etc. appeared as general and impersonal terms, there was no visible problem. Once women are in-

---

[1] In exploring the relation of women to sociology, I've learned to think of sociological methods of inquiry and conceptualization as a social relation. In using this term, I am not referring to issues of women's representation on sociology faculties, in professional organizations, and so forth. Though clearly these are important, I want rather to draw attention to how knowing and knowledge in the social sciences are themselves a form of social relation.

serted into sociological sentences as their subjects, however, the appearance of impersonality goes. The knower turns out not to be "abstract knower" after all, but a member of a definite social category occupying definite positions in the society. This is the contradiction that comes to light in considering the implications of how women (though not only women) are constituted as objects in the sociological relation.[2]

THE SOCIOLOGICAL DISCOURSE AND ITS SETTING

The concepts, methods, relevances, and topics of sociology are organized and maintained in the social organization of the discourse. Certain journals and occasions (such as conventions) are legitimatized places for the appearance of sociological work. By virtue of publication or appropriately situated public reading, this work becomes part of the body of literature that *is* sociology. This literature is exemplary in the sense that sociologists look to it as displaying the forms of what is recognizable as sociology, including the questions and problems that define the contemporary relevances of the discourse. The discourse is maintained by practices that determine *who* may participate in it as fully competent members and by an *organization* and *re-organization* of relations among participants through the medium of their work. To be recognized as a proper participant, one must produce work that conforms to appropriate styles and terminologies, that makes the appropriate deferences and is locatable by these and other devices in the traditions, factions, schools, etc., whose themes it elaborates, whose interpretive procedures it intends, and by whose criteria it is to be evaluated. This system of controls regulates the topics, themes, and the problematic and conceptual practices of sociology and ensures that the relevances of the sociological work are the relevances of the discourse. It is in this relation that people's lives and experience become the objects of work that aims at making a contribution to the discourse on and in its terms.

The relevances and perspectives that have become built into sociolo-

---

[2]In this discovery, we learn that the established practices of inquiry and thinking in sociology transform people, generally, into its objects or make use of them as resources for the construction of abstracted social objects (social systems, for example) in which they disappear. The problem of how women cannot escape the status of object in the sociological relation enlivens and brings into focus a more general problem. Sociology attempts to explain behavior. The methods of thinking, the empirical inquiry and practices that accomplish the objectivity, and the recognizably sociological features of entries to the discourse organize an object world from the perspective of a determinate position in society, and thereby organize a determinate relation between those who occupy the positions from which society is known and those who become the objects of the sociological methods of knowing.

Thus in questioning the sociological relation from the perspective of women, we find that we are questioning the organization of the sociological discourse in general, its location in the world, and the social relations built into its method of inquiry and thought.

gy are not, however, developed within the discourse as a social process in isolation. There is also a social and material substructure that determines the relation of the sociologist to those she or he studies in ways that are not attended to in her or his working practices.

With the emergence of the corporate form of capitalism, a differentiated and technical system of management and administration develops. At the same time, there is a corresponding development of the state apparatus that provides the legal, administrative, material, and social environment upon which corporate capitalism depends. As the organizational work of this social form becomes increasingly extensive and intensive in its scope, the work of social scientists has been of increasing importance in providing the necessary conceptual apparatus, methods of inquiry, informational bases, etc.[3]

These are ways in which the sociological discourse is located in the structure of corporate capitalism. This same social form has progressively excluded women from the positions where they may be heard. It is with the development of capitalism in the nineteenth, and increasingly in the twentieth, century that women's scope of action has been narrowed to the domestic.

WOMEN ARE OUTSIDE THE FRAME

Women are outside, subservient to, and silent in the social organization that subtends the sociological discourse and structures its concerns and concepts. The various actualities of women's existence in contemporary society cannot be described or analyzed adequately by a discipline whose themes and domains are largely organized around what goes on in the working contexts and relations of those who organize and control the society and who are men. The accepted fields of sociology—organizational theory, political sociology, the sociology of work, the sociology of mental illness, deviance, and the like—have been defined from the perspective of the professional, managerial, and other administrative structures and in terms of *their* concerns. The determination of what is sociological can be seen as occurring fundamentally from within the professional and managerial structures of the society. Indeed, the universe of sociological phenomena, *the world sociology knows,* is to a large

---

[3]Sociologists share their position and work with other members of a technical and cultural intelligentsia that has emerged with state or corporate capitalism. This intelligentsia is organized as a "discourse" through nonspecialist journals and magazines, such as the *New York Review of Books*, and informal and highly elaborated styles of talk aimed at consensual attitudes towards movies, books, the issues of the day, and the like. Sociology has an active relation to this media-based discourse both in drawing upon it for themes and new notions of relevance and also in feeding back "insights," "perspectives," as well as information.

extent constructed in the working relations of this ruling apparatus with the people whose lives it organizes and controls.

The distinctively male "agentic" approach in research would appear to have its base in this social mode (Bernard, 1973). It is an approach that "operates by way of mastery and control." Similar assumptions are built into models of the social actor, such as that of Talcott Parsons (1937), which represent the actor as a maker of choices among means in relation to ends; or Harré and Secord's (1972) more recent model, which assumes that "a human being has the power to initiate change." These are grounded in a mode of action in which the power to act and coordinate in a planned and rational manner and to exercise control over conditions and means is taken for granted.

This is not the typical experience of women under corporate capitalism. Characteristically for women (as undoubtedly for all those excluded from the ruling apparatus), the organization of their daily experience, their work routines, and indeed their lives is determined and ordered externally to them. The organization of women's lives and everyday worlds of work do not conform to the organization assumed in the "voluntaristic" or "agentic" model. The "consciousness" of a contemporary middle-class housewife with children is necessarily diffuse and open. She may become highly skilled at holding the threads and shreds of a number of lines of action simultaneously while pursuing none continuously and consistently, in large part because she is holding the parts of someone else's action. If we think of how the lives of women are structured by the organization of actions and events that originate externally to the domestic or in the hierarchic structures to which they are subject at workplaces outside the house, we see, for example, that rather than a continuously organized project or a career, their lives have a loose episodic structure, lacking continuity, and being singularly exposed to contingencies. This would yield a different structuring of consciousness and experience and hence different symbolic and conceptual expressions.[4]

The lack of sociological interest in the social structuring of emotions to which Hochschild (1975) has drawn attention may well be based upon the way in which sociological frameworks are isomorphic with the rational modes of action characteristic of the forms of "governing." The rational actor who chooses and calculates is the abstracted model of the organizational man—or the man performing organizationally—whose

---

[4]Recently, a series of plays written and directed by women was performed in Vancouver, Canada. Although their themes were quite different, the plays shared a distinctively episodic structure. The reviewers (all male) consistently failed to understand how the plays were organized and complained of their lack of "plot." The male reviewers could not find, as the women in the audience had no difficulty in finding, the expression of the structure of their own experience in the structure of the plays. Joan Didion's novel, Play It as It Lays (1971) also makes brilliant use of this structuring device.

feelings have no place in his work. Rationality is a normative practice that organizes and prescribes a distinct mode of action. In doing so, it constructs emotion and feeling, in opposition and residually, as distinct modes merely by defining them out.

These assumptions will not do when we begin from the experience and actualities of women's situation, for then we are locating our enterprise with knowers whose perspective is organized on the basis of how they are excluded from participation (other than as underlings and subordinates) in the ruling apparatus. Women's existence is largely determined externally to them; and perhaps even more importantly in this content, the determinations of their existence do not even appear to them to be in direct subordination to a managerial process. Even though women work outside the home, their work lives are still organized to a large extent in relation to household and family.

The work life of women escapes the scope of the bureaucratic professional and administrative princedoms of "the active society" (see, e.g., Etzioni, 1968). The phenomena of women's situation and experience fall between or outside the institutional spheres. Making women as they are placed in this form of society the sociological subject creates a different set of requirements for sociological inquiry in terms of its conceptual frameworks and organization. The established methods of thinking sociologically do not provide us with means to explicate the social organization of experience external to the managerial and professional forms.

Traditionally, the problem of subordinating extramanagerial forms to the conceptual hegemony of rational administrative forms of organization has been worked out in sociology by applying functionalist theory. Functionalism makes possible the application of a model of rational action to social phenomena that could not be assimilated to that model empirically. Unfortunately, much contemporary Marxist thinking on women and the household follows an essentially functionalist procedure by "reducing" women's characteristic work and social relations in the household and family to concepts that analyze them in terms of their relation to capitalist *economic* processes.

The same difficulty dogs the discussion of women and social class. Women sociologists have raised serious critical issues about concepts of class that omit women from analyses and descriptions as well as from the theoretical accounts of class or status structures in society. Concepts of social class appear, however, not merely to have excluded women, but to be based on models derived from a male-dominated universe of action. Models of stratification (including Marxist models of class) are based largely on how men are located in the work organization. The framework of analysis is derived from this. Attempting in various ways to tie women and women's occupational and familial positions to this type of framework will undoubtedly produce important information. In the long run, however, it cannot be satisfactory because the conceptual structures build in assumptions based on the model of male occupational experience and situation.

To develop an account of stratification from the position of women, or one, rather, that "counts that position in" as a fundamental basis of any model, means examining how the work of women in the home as well as in the occupational scheme is hooked into and determined by the economic organization of capitalist society. The household is in fact organized in the context of actual conditions and of social relations created for the family by how it is articulated to the economic structure. That includes a lot more than just the position of the "head of the household" in the occupational structure. Other dimensions of class don't become visible until we examine the work of women in the home as it is in fact organized, rather than treat it selectively so that it reproduces the model we already have. Housework, for example, has a managerial or organizational aspect that articulates the family unit to the bureaucratic, educational, professional, and retailing organizations (e.g., welfare, school, dentist, supermarket, etc.) so as to complete the cycle from production to subsistence. Even a cursory examination of the social organization of what women do in the domestic or private sphere suggests wide differences that point to differences in the actual social organization of classes at different levels. Thus work in the home or private sphere may be concerned with the maintenance and operation of social circles that have become key aspects of the social organization of class relations at levels no longer integrated into and based on a local neighborhood. The wife of the journalist is not necessarily doing the same "work" as the factory worker who is also the wife of a garbage collector. The exploration of class via a serious investigation of women's work and its varieties in the context of actual conditions is capable of restoring some degree of descriptive adequacy to the Marxist analysis of class as generated by the mode of production.

RELOCATING THE SOCIOLOGICAL ENTERPRISE:
THE EVERYDAY WORLD AS PROBLEMATIC

The critique of established sociological frameworks from the perspective of women's positions in society does not, as such, deal with the problem of the structure of the sociological relation as it has been described above. Suppose we began to think about a sociological enterprise that would be capable of providing for women analyses, descriptions, and understandings of their situation, of their everyday world and its determinations in the larger socioeconomic organization. Then, indeed, we would be thinking about how to do a sociology that relocated the sociological subject. Such a sociological enterprise raises the fundamental question of the nature of a sociology addressed not to a knower located in the ruling apparatus of corporate capitalist society, but to knowers who are members of the society and have positions in it outside that ruling apparatus.

This shift in the location of the knower discloses the everyday world as a problem (Smith, 1974). The determinations of the everyday world are not fully available within its own scope. They lie outside and beyond, in the social relations that are analyzed and described at the macrosociological level or as economic processes. The effect of locating the knower in the everyday world of experience is to pull the microsociological level of study of the everyday world and the macrosociological studies of power elites, formal organization, stratification, the state, educational systems, etc., into a relation of interdependence.

The everyday world—the world in which people are located as they live and which organizes their experience—is one that can be viewed as being generated in its varieties by an organization of social relations that originate "elsewhere." That the everyday world is not fully understandable within its own scope but is structured by externally organized and specialized forms of social relations provides a sociological problem (Smith, 1975b). Indeed, it is this feature that provides the central problem of Marx's work, for in the capitalist mode of production, the socially organized forms in and through which individuals depend upon one another are externalized, made abstract, and appear, as Marx says, as relations between things.

An alternative method of inquiry must thus necessarily aim to grasp the actualities of the "autonomous social relations" that generate the different positions in the world and, hence, the conditions of our experience.

Making the everyday world the problem instructs us to look for the organization generating its ordinary features, its order, its contingencies or conditions. Our inquiry can begin from the position of women, explicating the feminine experience as a sociological problem:

> The incomprehensibility of the determinations of our immediate local world is for women a particularly striking metaphor. It recovers an inner organization in common with their typical relation to the world. For women's activities and existence are determined outside them and beyond the world which is their "place." They are oriented by their training, and by the daily practices which confirm it, toward the demands and initiations and authority of others. But

more than that, the very organization of the world which has been assigned to them as the primary locus of their being is determined by and subordinate to the corporate organization of society. Thus as I have expressed her relations to sociology, its logic lies elsewhere. She lacks the inner principle of her own activity. She does not grasp how it is put together because it is determined elsewhere than where she is (Smith, 1974).

THE EVERYDAY WORLD AS THE BEGINNING OF INQUIRY

To do this kind of work means, of course, that we must begin with a knowledge of women's everyday worlds and of their experience. This means, in the first place, learning from them. Much of our work in the field now begins from the framework, concepts and, perhaps even more importantly, the organization of the subject matter that sets up description as an objective account. Observational work in sociology appears indeed to allow the sociologist to incorporate sociological interpretations into the primary descriptive level. The experience we must begin from, however, is that of those who live it rather than those who merely observe for the purposes of entering into the sociological discourse. I am suggesting that the world within the experience of actual individuals should become the place where inquiry begins.

The determinations and social organization of the experienced world are not fully available within its scope. In using individuals' accounts of experience and the teller of the story's own interpretation and description of what is or was happening, we are not aiming at an authoritative and objective version of what was really going on, nor are we trying to develop a picture of the situation of women that is in any way typical of women, or of any subclass thereof. That again returns us to the sociological relation we are remaking. Experience locates only the beginning of inquiry. Let me give a highly simplified example.

Some of the autobiographies and autobiographical novels about Canadian women identify an experience that can be fitted to the traditional and rather romanticized typification of the farm and the farmer's wife in preindustrial North America. Women's worth is held to be recognized within this social form because they make a direct contribution to the productive enterprise.[5] In fact, there is a wide variation in this form of farm family organization, which is brought into focus when we address seriously differences in women's experience in it and make that the basis of our inquiry.

[5]This view is a standard one in the sociology of the family and has been incorporated uncritically into some of the Marxian accounts, such as Eli Zaretsky's in "Capitalism, the family and personal life" (1973), which is reprinted in Part One of this reader.—The Editors

In her autobiography Canadian suffragist Nellie McClung (1964, 1965) describes the farm on which she spent her childhood thus:

> An Ontario farm, in the early eighties, was a busy place, and everyone on our farm moved briskly. My father often said of my mother that she could keep forty people busy. She certainly could think of things for people to do. Maybe that was one reason for my enjoying the farmyard so much. I loved to sit on the top rail of the fence, and luxuriantly do nothing, when I was well out of the range of her vision. Mother herself worked harder than anyone. She was the first up in the morning and the last one to go to bed at night. Our teams were on the land, and the Monday morning washing on the line well ahead of the neighbours (McClung, 1964: 27).

The farmwife in this farm organization played a role having an important managerial aspect. Her organization of the production of subsistence and maintenance for those engaged in work in the fields provided the working schedule of the farm. She appropriated the output of their labor in garden, dairy, and hen house, and other like products. When there was a surplus above what was needed to provide for the members of the farm household, then a local organization of markets allowed her independent sources of money from the sale of this surplus.

There is, however, another experience that is superficially similar but very different in its actualities, both as experience and in underlying structure. In *Wild Geese,* a Canadian novel based on her own experience as a schoolteacher boarding with a farm family, Martha Ostenso (1967) tells the story of the tyranny of a farmer over his wife and daughters and of the special drudgery of the farmwife's existence.

How are we to begin to inquire into the basis of this difference? What is the meaning of *drudgery* in this context? Do drudges work harder than Nellie McClung's mother, or is the difference of another kind?

We can follow one partial chain by examining changes in the economic organization of the family unit in its relation to differences in the later agricultural economy. The change is in the political economy of Canadian farming: primarily, the change from farming in which production for the subsistence of those laboring on the farm was integral to its economy. Political and economic policies in Canada during the late nineteenth and early twentieth centuries combined railroad expansion with land settlement through the promotion of extensive immigration. Land settlement was both a political imperative to counter the threat of incorporation of western Canada into the United States, and an economic move to develop a commodity (wheat) on which the railroad could depend for freight. As a bonus, the railroad created and, to a large extent, dominated a highly speculative real estate market. The immigrants who built up the wheat economy of the Canadian prairies were in many instances financed by mortgages on their land and by bank loans for tools, seed, and other necessities for which their crop stood collateral. Immigrant wheat farmers did not begin, as homesteaders characteristically did, by producing their own subsistence, which left them largely outside the market economy (the family organization of the homesteader is of yet another kind than either of those described so far.)

Ostenso's novel turns on the fact that survival for the immigrant farmer in this squeeze depended on the production of a single cash crop. Everything must be subordinated to that. In this context, then, women's labor is substituted for hired labor, both in working the land and in producing subsistence for the family. Furthermore, her labor is substituted as far as possible for labor in the form of manufactured commodities for which money must be found. Increased inputs of her labor eke out the lack of money at every possible point in the enterprise. Her time and energy, indeed her life, are treated as indefinitely exhaustible. In addition, she must bear children because their labor is also essential. Women were virtually *imported* into Canada at this period to serve these functions.

Further, in this relation the wife is totally subordinate to her husband. She has no independent economic status or independent source of money. There are no local sources of employment for women. The system of matrimonial property in Canada was (and still is to a large extent) organized around the man as sole owner of the small business; his wife's labor makes a contribution to it but gives her no rights in it. Furthermore, while laws of property, debt, credit, etc. endow him with full economic status, they do not do the same for her. Her labor contributes to his capacity to act in the economic sphere but does not further hers. These forms of matrimonial property law establish title in land in such a way as to provide for its standing as collateral for loans or for its being mortgaged. This form of land title is integral to the constitution of that type of economic organization in which the family functions as a small business in a fully developed capitalist economy. Moreover, the functioning of a highly speculative real estate market was facilitated by single and unencumbered title to real property.

The texts that describe women's experience and work do not refer to these aspects of the social organization of family relations. They are not identified for us in the accounts directly. Nevertheless, once we begin to look for them, we can explicate and make observable the underlying structures that determine the actual organization of the everyday world, its social relations and conditions of experience.

Clearly, if we are to offer those who live in our society (including ourselves) a means to understand how our social world comes about, then we must have a method of arriving at adequate description and analysis of *how it actually works*. Our methods cannot rest in problems of validating theories, which to a large extent have become procedures for deciding among different formalized "opinions" about the world. When we approach the problem of experience, we are and must be looking for answers in terms of actual socially organized practices. Situations, types, forms of social organization are then seen to recur because there is an underlying organization of social relations which generates them as "the same."

The problems of establishing relations between the social organization of an actual everyday world and the structures that determine it are those of tracing through the actual practices of social relations rather than of developing formal methods of relating them as conceptually constituted entities in an abstract space. In the example used, we can see that, since we do not make general statements across a class of family organization defined by legal and economic contexts of action as small business units, we recognize that apparently inverse types of role organization and family practices may arise in the same social form.

I am supposing that there is something to be inquired into, that there is indeed a social reality that is organized prior to the sociologist's work. I am not, of course, denying the significance of the sociologist's active participation in the social process of constructing knowledge; however, the very conception of an inquiry presupposes that there is something there from which the sociologist must learn and to which her inquiry must subordinate itself. The substance of the world she addresses as her puzzle is essentially a human accomplishment. It is brought about in the actual practices, work, and practical reasoning of those who live it; and it does not exist apart from that daily ordinary achievement.

Social phenomena do not exist merely as abstract entities, nor do they exist independently of the social practices and activities that constitute them as they become observable. Things, acts, events, etc. are not what they are as a matter intrinsic to their nature but become what they are as they take social form in the process of socially organized activity. Mead's conception of the social act, in which more than one actor participates to complete the whole, provides an account of how social forms come into being in a social practice (Mead, 1934). In his analysis of the commodity form, in which relations between persons are transformed into relations between things, Marx (1967) shows how "commodity" arises as a social form in the social relations of production for exchange on a market. Thus commodities are constituted in a determinate process of social relation and are indeed an integral component of its organization. In general, objects, acts, work, etc. take on their determinate social form from the socially organized processes or relations in which they are embedded. Engels' (1972) analysis of how women's work in the home is transformed by the change from communal to private property, so that her labor ceases to contribute to the general wealth and becomes a personal service to her husband, analyzes a social relation in just this way. This analysis may not be accurate in terms of our later knowledge of anthropology, but the method is important. The change in the social relations of property in which a particular form of labor is embedded changes in fundamental ways the organization of the individual's personal relations, her work and experience, and indeed the very structure of her world.

These relations must be investigated empirically. This is possible only if we are not hampered by the social organization of the discourse among social scientists. In organizing this discourse, social scientists have set up various jurisdictions so that the phenomenal world accords with the social relations among social scientists and with the "ruling" apparatus they service rather than with the world's actual mode of organization. Relations between jurisdictions are transposed into interactions between variables of one class and those of another. Social factors interact with economic factors. Personality factors interact with social systems. The phenomena are disconnected irrevocably, so that the economic processes that provide the developmental context of the cash crop farm are a separate topic from the legal processes that constitute the farm family as an economic unit.

To view forms of knowledge as essentially social suggests that the categories and concepts of the social sciences must be built up by analyzing the actual socially organized practices that bring them into being as phenomena. Marx begins with the categories of the classical political economists and treats them as reflections of functions brought about by the social relations that organize the actual activities of individuals under a given mode of production. Thus the concept of commodity fetishism, through all the strange and metaphoric uses it has been put to, survives as a key to how we can grasp the ways in which the structuring of the everyday world by economic processes does not have to be conceived as casually determining what we do, but rather is an actual social organization that appears to us in the social form of things. The implications of a sociology *for* women in contemporary corporate capitalist society poses again the problem of social science that Marx and Engels originally formulated.

Individuals started, and always start, from themselves. Their relations are the relations of their real life. How does it happen that their relations assume an independent existence over against them? And that the forces of their own life overpower them? (Marx & Engels, 1973:90.)

REFERENCES

Bernard, Jessie.
  1974 "My four revolutions: An autobiographical history of the ASA," in Joan Huber (ed.), Changing Women in a Changing Society. Chicago: University of Chicago Press.
Engels, Frederick.
  1972 Origins of the Family, Private Property, and the State. Eleanor R. Leacock (ed.). New York: International Publishers.
Etzioni, Amitai.
  1968 The Active Society: A Theory of Societal and Political Processes. New York: Free Press.
Harré, Romano, and Paul F. Secord.
  1972 Explanation of Social Behavior. Totowa, N.J.: Rowman and Littlefield.
Hochschild, Arlie Russell.
  1974 "The sociology of feeling and emotion: Selected possibilities," in Marcia Millman and Rosabeth M. Kanter (eds.), Another Voice: Feminist Perspectives on Social Life and Social Science. Garden City, N.Y.: Doubleday Anchor Book.
Marx, Karl.
  1954 Capital. Volume 1. Process of Capitalist Production. Moscow: Foreign Languages Publishing House.
Marx, Karl, and Friedrich Engels.
  1973 Feuerbach: Opposition of the Materialist and the Idealist Outlooks. London: Lawrence and Wishart.
McClung, Nellie L.
  1964 Clearing in the West: My Own Story. Toronto: Thomas Allen.
  1965 The Stream Runs Fast: My Own Story. Toronto: Thomas Allen.
Mead, George Herbert.
  1934 Mind, Self and Society. Chicago: University of Chicago Press.
Ostenso, Martha.
  1967 Wild Geese. Toronto: McClelland and Stewart.
Parsons, Talcott.
  1937 Structure of Social Action. New York: McGraw Hill.
Smith, Dorothy E.
  1974 "Women's perspective as a radical critique of sociology." Sociological Inquiry 4(no. 1): 7–13.
  1975a "An analysis of ideological structures and how women are ex-

cluded." Canadian Review of Sociology and Anthropology 12(no. 4. pt. 1): 353–369.

1975b "What it might mean to do a Canadian Sociology: The everyday world as problematic." Canadian Journal of Sociology 1(no. 3): 363–376.

ADDITIONAL READINGS

Daniels, Arlene Kaplan.
  1975 "Feminist perspectives in sociological research," in Marcia Millman and Rosabeth Kanter (eds.), Another Voice: Feminist Perspectives on Social Life and Social Science. Garden City, N.Y.: Doubleday Anchor Book.

Douglas, Jack D. (ed.)
  1970 Understanding Everyday Life: Toward the Reconstruction of Sociological Knowledge. Chicago: Aldine.

Hamilton, Peter.
  1974 Knowledge and Social Structure: An Introduction to the Classical Argument in the Sociology of Knowledge. London: Routledge and Kegan Paul.

Economics, Sex and Gender

Carolyn Shaw Bell

Who speaks for economics? Men do. Economics deals with questions of choice, decisions about how to use resources that are limited by the nature of things. Without scarcity there would be no economics, and our notions of scarcity have recently become much more powerful. . . . Economics, or the decisions imposed by scarcity, lie at the very foundation of our existence. Economic choices deal with human life itself, to say nothing of how it is lived. Who *makes* these choices and where they are made depends upon the loci of power. . . . Who *advises the powerful* depends on who are the economists, and who among them gravitate to the seats of power.

Economists contribute to the decision-making process by posing alternatives and outlining the implications of choices. Economists teach, that is to say they help others learn concepts and methods useful for analyzing choice-decisions, and some of their students become powerful decision makers. Economists advise governments: they serve as staff to executives, legislative committees, and operating agencies. Economists advise business enterprise; they serve on corporate and legal staffs or they provide consulting services, sometimes within the firm, sometimes as a member of an expert team from outside. Economists also staff those organizations that specialize in economic information: non-profit research institutions include the National Bureau of Economic Research, the Brookings Institution, the Survey Research Center at the University of Michigan. . . . What economists do in all these spheres

Excerpted from Carolyn Shaw Bell, "Economics, Sex, and Gender." *Social Science Quarterly* 55(December 1974):615–631 (Austin: University of Texas Press), by permission of the author and publisher. Copyright © 1974 by the Southwestern Social Science Association.

probably reflects much more of what economists want to do than of the critical questions posed either by society or by special interests within the social system. But the reader will be correct to identify each of these operations as predominately male-dominated. . . .

It does not necessarily follow, of course, that women as a subject for economic inquiry or of economic decisions have been neglected or even treated differently from men. One must first inquire how human beings, people themselves and women among them, enter into the economic calculus. It turns out that they don't, for the most part. Aside from the obvious fact that economic decisions represent human thought and human action, little attention has been given to the economics of human beings. Instead, economics as a field of inquiry deals with people's *roles* in economic activities, specifically their roles as producers and consumers. Neither of these roles is wholly masculine or wholly feminine. Nevertheless, women in their roles as producers and consumers have been differentiated from men. The particular roles assigned to women by society in fact impinge on their economic functions, although this has not been explicitly recognized until very recently. In order to review the distinction between men and women in their economic roles, a simple and well known model of economic activity will be useful.

Figure 1 represents, schematically, the production resulting from the use of scarce resources. This production, or total output, consists of the goods and services turned out by mines, fields, industrial plants, financial institutions, hospitals, shopping centers, utilities, and other enterprises using the available resources. These scarce factors, or the services yielded by them during a given time-period, also appear on the diagram as the inputs of labor and property, the latter including land, mineral and air rights, patents, tangible and intangible capital of all kinds. By setting households apart from producers, the diagram emphasizes that the two economic roles of producing and consuming occur in two different settings. Most production in this country takes place in business firms, although other types of organizations exist and account for a larger share of output elsewhere in the world. Most consumption in this country goes on at home, in what economists title "households" and then subdivide into the two major categories of families and individuals.

But the terms *producer* and *household* carry two types of economic significance. In the model, the abstract units of firm and household represent two economic roles, producing and consuming. In reality, most adults combine these two roles in themselves, and merely choose to organize their activities, of producing and consuming, in two separate *locations*, at work and at home. In both theory and reality, the two processes interact, as the diagram makes clear. Production uses the

FIGURE 1. CIRCULAR FLOW OF ECONOMIC ACTIVITY

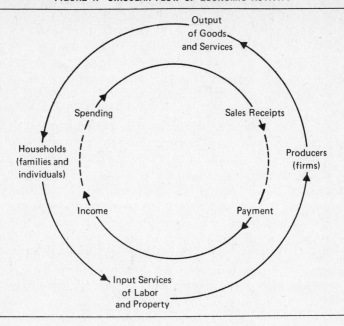

services provided by human beings: it is people who (reading the diagram counterclockwise) we see supplying their labor and property to the productive process. But production also depends on consumption by human beings: it is people who buy the final output. Reading the diagram clockwise, we see that what people spend on their purchases comes from their income, and this in turn reflects producers' payments for the inputs provided.

WOMEN AS PRODUCERS

To analyze the economic role of producer for any human being means analyzing personal choice, the process of deciding how to use the scarce resources belonging to that individual. For most people, this involves a decision about working. We all own our bodies and hence the useful labor we can turn out is at our disposal. But each of us has a finite amount of time, and the physical and mental resources we command are also limited. The real cost of working, therefore, consists of time lost to other pursuits, time that cannot be spent doing all the other things of which the individual is capable. Most elementary discussions of this economic decision suggest leisure as the classic alternative to work: the person chooses how much time to spend working and how much at leisure, dependent on the appeals of each. But work, of course, cannot be seen as an end in itself, because it yields income. And income can be spent on present consumption or it can be saved for future consumption. So the dichotomy is not one of work versus leisure, but of leisure now versus the goods and services (including the right to future consumption) that can be bought with the wages earned. . . .

Much less attention has been paid to the multitude of activities covered by the term *leisure*. In fact, most employed people engage in a great deal of productive activity during their leisure hours, like do-it-yourself repair and maintenance, home gardening, and nonpaid community work as volunteers. . . . Some part of leisure must also be counted as the labor or work effort required to use the consumer goods one has purchased; thus a pair of season tickets to the Symphony may yield two and a half hours a week of leisure and pleasure for the music-lover, but it may require X number of hours of "leisure" spent driving an automobile, or using other forms of transportation to the concert. . . . Some leisure activities, again dependent upon the individual concerned, should be categorized as educational and in that sense an investment in the human being that will yield future return in the form of greater skills, either at producing or consuming.

Within this larger framework of all the alternatives to work, the woman's choice differs significantly from that of the man, because society has assigned her quite different roles as a producer. Although all human beings exercise their functions as producers by working, every society has divided specific tasks between men and women: This is true for the United States today, where work usually means gainful employment outside the home (in the firms, or in other producer units), as it is for less developed countries and in previous centuries where home production dominated. . . . In all these systems, as cultural anthropologists have pointed out, it is society and not sex that determines men's work and women's work. Accepting these chores as natural or appropriate is essential to defining one's gender, only partially indicated by one's sex. . . . That culture determines gender-appropriate characteristics, even in work tasks, must be clear. In nineteenth-century United States, for example, the farmer's wife frequently kept a flock of hens and the egg-money was her responsibility. In Hungary at the same time, tending poultry was men's business and the country wife was responsible for the sheep or goat.

Every society, however, defines women's work to include household care and child tending. In the developed countries, the woman's primary role assignment is that of wife and mother, as the man's is to have a job and support the family. Even the change in the economic status of women, with larger and larger numbers entering the labor force for work outside the home, has not yet altered this role significantly. It follows that the model of economic analysis outlined above is inappropriate for women. Posing a choice-decision between work and leisure simply does not describe the alternatives open to a women. One needs little economic sophistication to recognize that the alternatives, for a women who is or is expected to be a wife and mother, consist not of work and leisure but of paid work outside the home and unpaid work at home. Although men also contribute significantly to household upkeep, the difference in responsibilities shows up most clearly in the parenting function. Women bear children and they are still expected to rear them. Day care centers or child care arrangements constitute *women's* issues, in politics, economics, and action groups. Men procreate children but are not expected to be involved in their growth and development following birth.

That the woman's choice about her economic role as producer has been shaped by the social model that portrays the nuclear family as the dominant mode means that the woman does not exercise any independent choice. Rarely can the woman lead an independent existence without being defined in relation to her family or to a man. Even as more women seek gainful employment, move into unconventional occupations, and press for fuller participation in social and economic life, their economic activities are still being analyzed in terms of this social model. The economics of women, or the study of women's status in the economy, . . . consists overwhelmingly of the analysis of women's participation in the labor force. Most of this work reinforces the role of women in the family, by examining participation rates in terms of family obligations, husband's income and employment opportunities, number of children at various ages. . . .

The economic role of women as producers can perhaps be summed up in a small illustration. Common parlance uses the term *independent income* quite differently for men than for women. We describe a man's profession or job, and if we refer to his independent income we always mean inherited wealth or property income of some kind. "John Jones can pursue his hobby of collecting eighteenth-century snuff boxes because he enjoys an independent income from his holding of oil stocks." But if we speak about Mrs. John Jones and her independent income we mean that she has money of her own, aside from her husband's support. . . . To be economically independent, for a man, means not to have to work for a living; for a woman, not to need a husband for support.

WOMEN AS CONSUMERS

The other important economic role of human beings consists of acting as consumers, using the final output turned out by producers. In a market economy like our own, and like that of most developed countries, we frequently interchange the words *consumer* and *buyer*, emphasizing that people *purchase* most of what they use in their daily living. These purchase transactions correspond to the sales of producers and command a good deal of attention from economists, who have evolved quite sophisticated analyses of the process of market exchange. Like most other subjects in economics, consumption calls for decision-making by the person, in this case as a consumer....

These consumer choices ultimately concern how much income to use in buying: the basic consumer decision is sometimes posed as spending versus saving..... Clearly the consumer's income is finite: borrowing to extend it has limits. Consequently, the real cost of buying anything consists of the alternatives one does not buy—including savings. These alternative costs will be greater or less depending on how much one wants things, the intensity of one's tastes and preference, and the pressure of other needs. The process of decision has been completed when the consumer has disposed of total income between spending and saving, and then divided each total among all the myriad items available, so as to derive equal satisfaction from each dollar of income spent or saved.

This analysis of consumer choice fits precisely into the model already used to explain people's economic roles as producers. There, we found that a person sells labor in order to earn income to buy things, and that the availability (and price) of these things can affect one's willingness to work and to accept a given wage.... As before, this model is sexually neutral: it describes a process of *individual* choice. The decisions made represent individual preferences: freedom to spend one's income (which, after all, the model presumes one has earned by supplying services) as one likes plays an essential part....

... The model may be ... criticised as being totally irrelevant to women, most of whom lack the income to make consumer choices like this.... The income women spend ... accrues chiefly because of their dependence, partial or total, on income earned in the first instance by men, who share it with women in their families, or pay taxes to provide transfer income to women receiving benefits under Social Security, Veterans' payments, or public assistance programs. It might be noted that eligibility for most women under these programs requires their definition as dependent on a man, whether veteran's widow, the elderly wife of a retired worker, or a mother of small children without a father present in the home.

... Consumer decisions have generally been analysed as matters to be decided independently, despite the fact that very few individuals of either sex act in a completely isolated fashion, or make decisions without any consideration of others. ... What, in reality or in theory, is the economic link between the receipt of income by any "consuming unit" and its buying decisions? Who decides? The question has not even been posed in economic theory: the family is somehow assumed to make decisions jointly, or the locus of authority is deemed irrelevant. ...

What remains unexplored is the extent to which the old adage, "He who pays the piper calls the tune," holds true. How, exactly does the income recipient allot control over his income? Do families whose income derives from a husband and father have a different way of deciding about spending and saving than families where two parents provide income?

That these questions about the economic role of human beings as consumers go unanswered implies much for men, of course, as well as for women. But that the questions have been consistently neglected probably reflects the development of economics in a male-oriented milieu where the husband as breadwinner, the man as family mainstay, has been the accepted mode. At the same time a very important share of the consumer's role has been just as unthinkingly accepted as female. In economic literature, in policy statements from business and government, and in advertising "the consumer" nearly always means a woman. ...

The economic role of producer and consumer combine, for a woman, in unpaid labor at home. Society assigns her to the role of wife and mother and in so doing decrees the feminine productive function as that of providing services to the household itself. As consumer, the woman acts as purchasing agent for the family and in effect buys the raw materials that she uses in household production. Neither as producer nor as consumer does she have the freedom of choice allotted to a man. ...

CURRENT ECONOMIC ANALYSIS

As an economic phenomenon demanding attention, the continuing growth in the number of working women ranks first. Research concentrates on two aspects: the determinants of female labor force participation and the extent to which occupational segregation reflects discrimination.

In earlier generations, investigations of women's work focused on the conditions of employment: the threats to health and safety of sweatshop surroundings, long hours, and injuries brought about by unshielded machines or sheer fatigue. . . . Rarely was there protest because the situation [was] inhuman, unfit for any human being. Rather, the conditions of employment constituted an offense to woman, to her feminine nature, her higher sensibilities, and her natural proclivities as a wife and to motherhood. Because of these responsibilities at home, women needed protection on the job. . . .

Although some improvements benefited all (if ventilation had to be increased where women worked, it was probably cheaper to provide light and air to all job-stations), restrictions on hours, night-time work, weight-lifting, and the like meant that men's jobs and women's job were legislated into existence.

This occupational segregation, like the primacy of the homemaker role for women, has been taken for granted for many years. Only recently has it become apparent that women's jobs differ from those of men in being low paid and dead end, in offering irregular employment and a higher probability of lay-offs. . . .

The question then becomes, How much of the occupational segregation represents economic discrimination, and how much does discrimination account for the differential between women's earning-power and that of men? . . .

Most analysts have concluded . . . that discrimination does not account either for the total differential in earnings or for the extent to which occupations are differentiated. . . . The persistent differential in earnings has been attributed to a number of causes: turnover and absenteeism (weaker female labor force "attachment"), specialised training and motivation, age, residence, job preference, part-time work, experience, and occupation. . . .

The other structural characteristic strongly influencing both occupation and earnings consists of work experience, and here most analysts recognize, implicitly or explicitly, that women's job histories involve their marital life histories much more than do those of men. To put it in terms of active decision-making, a woman's job opportunity may be more carefully and deliberately analysed for its potential for fulfilling home responsibilities (in terms of hours of work, commuting time, availability of child care, convenience to shopping facilties, etc.) than a man's.

A model of household production, maximizing total output from home labor and work in the marketplace by both partners in a marriage can be used to analyse the impact of these circumstances, with some new interpretations of the division of labor as a result. Of course, using concepts like a household production function or joint maximization means that men's decisions, too, become intertwined with those of other family members.

Neither empirical nor theoretical research, however, has come to grips with these questions of decision-making and individual freedom.... How much "free" choice or "individual" preference exists, when one's gender dictates so much in life, must be an open question. But that such roles allow less economic freedom to women, as individual producers or consumers, than to men is irrefutable.

Women do exist separately from men in many millions of households that attract current economic attention because of their poverty....

Poverty ... as a topic ... refers generally to questions of how society can be better off.... Such questions deal with choices about ... some redistribution of the income earned by people in the system.... The term *welfare* ... refers to one such form of redistribution: generally people with higher incomes pay taxes that provide benefits to people without incomes, or with low incomes. The rationale for such public assistance has usually been that welfare recipients cannot support themselves: they are too old, too young, or not well enough to earn their living. To this rationale has always been added, for women, the proviso that duties in child care at home may prevent their outside employment. Both the "protective" state legislation around the turn of the century, and the first federal laws providing social security and public assistance in the thirties explicitly opted for providing economic support to mothers caring for their dependent children.

In what represents a major shift in public policy, mothers who are potential welfare recipients may now be required to work, or to register for work, and the transfer income they receive merely supplements, instead of replacing, their earnings outside the home. For a growing group of women, therefore, the economic choice between work at home and work in the marketplace is not free because government authority decides the question.

Both economic analysis and economic policy dealing with individuals, either in their roles as producers or consumers, have been evolved primarily by men. Insofar as economic analysis has developed policy solutions, it has, to quote Representative Martha Griffiths, "met the social concerns of the Nation as defined by men. It has not met the social concerns of the Nation as defined by women, or as defined by men and women. It has met them as defined by men." We have, then, a sexually neutral economics: its gender is indubitably male.

Historical
Perspectives

Introduction   The Editors

*I thank thee, O Lord, that thou has not created me a
woman.*

Orthodox Hebrew Prayer

The long thread of cultural ethos that weaves through our current beliefs and behaviors can be unravelled back to Biblical teachings. Not
only was Eve created from a mere rib of Adam, but also the Old Testament woman functioned only as a vessel for the chosen seed or a chattel
of the prospering husbandman. Virtually excluded from religious ritual,
she became the negative symbol in this prayer, uttered by devout
Jewish men. Thousands of years have elapsed since God spoke to Abra-
ham; oppression has been reduced as more and more people have believed in and gained individual freedoms. Yet, as man advances, woman
lags behind. Along with other minority groups such as blacks, homosex-
uals, political dissidents, and children, American women remain in a
subordinate position. Why? Literature, religious doctrine, social
science, and folk sayings refer to her biological inferiority, her intellectual incompetence, her destructive sexuality, her moral pettiness and—
the final indignity—her enjoyment of subordination and childish
dependency.

A HISTORICAL OVERVIEW

Since the social condition of women has its roots in the past, an accurate
analysis requires some knowledge of that past. This introduction surveys
the changing position of women since the beginning of the industrial
revolution in the seventeenth century, with particular emphasis on the

Anglo-Saxon experience. The survey interrelates women's work and family life with ideology, with industrialization, and with social crises.

Ideology refers to "systems of ideas, opinions, perceptions, and interpretations" as influenced particularly by social class position and contemporary social organization rather than as these derive from objective analysis.[1] It provides people with a rationale for their behavior regardless of the conflict or contradictions in their actions. Although *technology* and *type of economy* are partly related, the latter means a system within which a society decides what goods and services should be produced and how these should be produced and distributed; *technology* means both the machines and the ensemble of practices used to attain narrowly defined ends.[2]

The following discussion considers the early effects of those changes in ideology, technology, and economy that decreased the already low status of women; the second section considers subsequent changes in these factors as well as the social crises that accompanied their improving status.

Declining Social Status. The fate of women has always been especially tied to the organization of the family, while the fate of the family has been interwoven with the organization of the rest of society. The family is the unit of social organization through which men and women experience much of society. This is particularly true of women. It is true whether or not the family is a large extended one with a combination of productive political, educational, and religious activities, or a nuclear family with restricted activities. Traditionally, in the Western world women are subordinate in the family: in childhood, to the father; in adulthood, to the husband, although legally single adult women are often just about the equal of single adult men. In the English-speaking world, married women are subject to laws that derive from the legal fiction that a man and woman become one upon marriage, that "one" being the husband.[3]

The origins of women's social and legal subordination are much debated, and it is difficult to reach well-supported conclusions. Some factors most often discussed are (1) the lesser physical strength of women; (2) the physical limitations of frequent pregnancy; (3) the traditional responsibility of women for early child care. The physical advantages of men over women are incorporated into social structure, most importantly in the economic, familial, and government institutions; women and men, through the process of socialization, learn to accept such institutions as "natural" while religious and/or secular ideology

---

[1] Karl Mannheim, *Ideology and Utopia* (New York: Harcourt Brace Jovanovich, 1955).
[2] Jacques Ellul, *The Technological Society* (New York: Vintage Books, 1967).
[3] Leo Kanowitz, *Women and the Law* (Albuquerque: University of New Mexico Press, 1965).

provides the rationale. A monopoly by men of the technology of coercion (skills in fighting, guns, knives) further supports the inequality, even long after the initial physical advantage has lost its importance.

Woman's place had not always been in the home. That doctrine was a creation of the period when men were being displaced from their homes as their workplace.[4] In spite of woman's supposed physical disadvantage, she has always played a vital and necessary role in the production of goods and services, not only for family use but also for exchange in the market. Before the seventeenth century and the beginnings of the industrial revolution, she was usually a co-worker with her husband in farm work, or home-centered crafts. (All family members worked together, and quite hard at that, to meet the needs of the family.) Women were frequently members of guilds, along with their husbands, and earned income as traders, domestic workers, tavern-keepers; they ran farm estates, breweries, and even an occasional newspaper and blacksmith shop.[5] With the introduction of machinery, single women[6] as well as married and single men, and youngsters of both sexes left the household for factory wage work. Married women, except among the very poor, remained in the household since their labor was needed there. The incomes that married women once could have earned within the household were lost as the guilds dissolved and most such work was transferred to the factory.[7]

Religious doctrine as well as necessity may have supported the concept of women's inferiority. Judaism and Catholicism were both quite anti-woman—the Bible, the Talmud, and canon law are saturated with allusions to the disgraceful state of being a woman, and she remains excluded from complete participation in religious life to the present. No women have been priests.[8] Though nuns were common enough in Roman Catholicism, Judaism did not offer its woman even second-rank position among the clergy. The Mary cult of medieval Europe may have softened the life of women, but this is hardly reflected in either civil or canonical law. On the contrary, with the breakdown of feudalism, women lost many of the rights they had acquired. The courtly love and chivalry of the period may have helped the lady of the castle to pass her

---

[4]Henry Hamilton, *History of Homeland* (London: George Allen and Unwin, 1917).

[5]Elisabeth A. Dexter, *Colonial Women of Affairs* (Boston: Houghton Mifflin, 1924); Alice Clark, *Working Life of Women in the Seventeenth Century* (New York: E. P. Dutton, 1919); Hamilton, *History of Homeland*.

[6]In 1850, the first complete industrial census showed that 24 percent of the total number of persons employed were women. See Edith Abbott, *Women in Industry* (1909; reprint ed., New York: Arno Press, 1969) for an excellent study of the employment of women in eighteenth- and nineteenth-century United States.

[7]Clark, *Working Life of Women.*

[8]Hebrew Union College-Jewish Institute of Religion, Cincinnati, Ohio, began to ordain women in 1972.

leisure hours with the comforts of verse and song, but neither she nor her lowly sisters ever seem to have benefited.[9] This is not to deny that the court lady sometimes had the advantage over her husband of being able to read and to run his estates while he was on a Crusade.

Protestantism radically rewrote the Catholic version of a person's relation to God, and redefined the relation of the devout to economic activity. The Reformation theoretically made women and men equal before God; however, the leading heretics did not have favorable attitudes toward women: "weak, frail, impatient, feeble, inconstant, variable, cruel" described the feminine sex while the abolishment of monastic orders made marriage the only possible means of survival for most women, depriving them of their only profession—and of their only place of learning.[10] Heightened economic activity, which was already beginning to be acceptable to the faithful Catholic without the onus that success would endanger his soul, under Protestantism became, first, an obligation to God, and then was interpreted as a possible sign of grace. Woman's calling was as wife and mother. Man's "calling" was gradually transformed from an initial broadness that included all varieties of statuses into the narrowness of vocation. The remnant of that transformation is visible in the notion that a few special occupations with a religious or humanitarian aspect—minister, nurse, family doctor—were "callings" well into the twentieth century.

As economic gain became a sign of God's possible grace, where were women? When the European and American world shifted from a household to a market economy, women usually remained in the household, partly because their labor was needed. But, perhaps this staying in the household was reinforced by the traditional exclusion of women from full participation in religious life—in this case, economic activity that could be taken as a sign of grace.

During the late eighteenth and nineteenth centuries, secular ideology, too, may have contributed to women's remaining in the home. Just as menial work gradually came to be considered degrading to the man of rising affluence, by extension it was also considered degrading to his wife, who, while his inferior, was also his intimate, the mother of his children, and herself the offspring of a high-status father. Work outside of the home was seen as a threat to womanly virtue, bad for a woman's physical well-being and emotional health, and, even more important, possible evidence of her husband's failure to earn sufficiently to support a family.[11] Idle wives and idle daughters rarely meant idle men.

The Industrial Revolution had other important and long-lasting

---

[9]Emily James Putney, *The Lady* (London: G. P. Putnam's Sons, 1910).
[10]Hamilton, *History of Homeland.*
[11]Robert W. Smuts, *Women and Work in America* (New York: Schocken Books, 1971)

effects. Migration from the farm to the factory encouraged the development of the conjugal family system; except for some earnings from work that married women did in the home, they were economically dependent on their husbands. A woman's work became so restricted to meeting the everyday needs of her family that some historians have suggested she came close to being a high-status family servant.

The movement away from women's status as household drudge and near chattel under Anglo-Saxon law has been exceedingly slow. By the end of the eighteenth century, the American woman had made some gains in property rights, although she, along with her English sisters, was still considered the virtual property of her husband. Her body, her services, her domicile, her children, and her earnings belonged to her husband. In contrast, the unmarried woman at least had a chance to earn a living and the right to her earnings.

While in many ways, the Industrial Revolution eventually improved the standard of living of both women and men, its initial effect was to decrease the social status of women. Women were stripped of a degree of economic independence and prestige that had resulted from working with their husbands and other family members. From being surrounded and supported by an extended family system, woman found herself in the conjugal family. And what legal rights she had gained under feudalism were eroded by juridical opinion originating in England, from where it was brought to the United States.

Toward Improving Social Status. Women do not willingly accept their subordination to men. Legend has Lilith as the first woman and the first feminist, banished from earth, and replaced by Eve, for her presumptive refusal to submit herself to Adam.[12] While religious liberal Anne Hutchinson was no Lilith, American women since colonial days have been involved in social movements for human and women's rights. The seventeenth- and eighteenth-century rationalist movements for the rights of man raised the aspirations of women. Such prominent men as Daniel Defoe, Benjamin Franklin, and Dr. Benjamin Rush advocated the education of women. But, it was really in the fight to abolish slavery that women learned the depths of their inferiority and how to organize to expand their own social rights. Women were also prominent in the social reform movement in the late 1890s and the years before World War I—the movements for the rights of workingmen and women, the immigrant, and the poor. During the Great Depression, women were actively involved in unionization and in government welfare programs

---

[12]According to rabbinical literature, Lilith is Adam's first wife, who refuses to submit to him and flies away to become a demon. God creates a second woman, Eve, who is more pliant and appropriately submissive than his first error. Ancient cultures list no fewer than seventeen versions of this legend. See Robert Graves and Raphael Patai, *Hebrew Myths: The Book of Genesis* (New York: McGraw-Hill, 1966).

to alleviate the sufferings of the unemployed, and they participated in radical politics just as they had done in the nineteenth century, and would do after the Second World War. Their experiences in these movements frequently showed them their own relegation to an inferior position. For example—and this is the most famous example of all, for it led to the founding of the women's suffrage movement—leading abolitionists were refused seating at a World Anti-Slavery convention in London in 1840. Over 120 years later, women in the civil rights and antiwar movements saw that men were interested in them as bed partners, domestic servants, mother surrogates, and economic producers, but not as policymakers.[13]

Experiences during wartime also led women to reassess themselves. Sexuality, political power, and economic capabilities all become salient issues when women are expected to forego a sex life and, at the same time, to assume political and economic responsibilities that have been the usual province of men. At such times, women are needed as a labor force—pulled into the factory and office during wartime, and pushed out when men can replace them, although the movement of married women into the labor force appears to be a long-term gradual trend that is only magnified by war.[14] By these labor force activities, women learn they are capable of doing "man's work," while employers recognized a source of labor far cheaper than men.[15] During the Civil War, for example, women became nurses, seamstresses, teachers, clerks in government offices, and farm laborers. They also developed political skills when they worked for passage of the Thirteenth Amendment.

After the Civil War, many women remained in the labor force, particularly as teachers and clerical workers. Their education made them a valuable labor pool when the need for clerical record-keeping expanded with the growth, in the last decades of the century, of modern industrial capitalism.[16] Middle-class women fought to be admitted to colleges and universities and to enter the professions. Working-class women tried to unionize, or at least, to improve working conditions. But, while women had shown some political successes during the war, they experienced a bitter defeat afterwards when the issue of the vote for women was dropped from the fight to enfranchise the newly emancipated black man. The denial of the vote to women led to a split

---

[13]See, for example, Marge Piercy, "The Grand Coolie Damn," in Robin Morgan (ed.), *Sisterhood is Powerful* (New York: Vintage, 1970), pp. 421–438.

[14]Joan W. Scott and Louise A. Tilly, "Women's Work and the Family in Nineteenth-Century Europe." *Comparative Studies in History and Society* 17(January 1975):36–64.

[15]See Harry Braverman, *Labor and Monopoly Capital: The Degradation of Work in the Twentieth Century* (New York: Monthly Review Press, 1974); J. E. Trey, "Women in the War Economy—World War II." *The Review of Radical Political Economics* 4(July 1972):41–57.

[16]Margery Davies, "Women's Place Is at the Typewriter: The Feminization of the Clerical Labor Force." *Radical America* 8(July-August 1974):1–28.

in the women's rights movement. One faction began a state-by-state fight for suffrage over the next forty years. They conducted 480 campaigns in thirty-three states—just to get the issue on the ballot seventeen times, and to gain suffrage for women in *two* states! The other faction argued, much more in accord with the thinking of contemporary women's movements, that women were social outcasts along with others in the society and that broad social changes—as well as the vote—were necessary for any fundamental change in woman's position. More than fifty years later, in the aftermath of the liberalism that followed World War I, the suffrage movement gained the right to vote for women. This was the last major organized effort to expand women's rights for—dismally—nearly half a century.[17]

World War I had other effects on women than enfranchisement. Participation in the work force, as substitutes for absent men, gave them further confidence in their productive abilities. Also, in the context of a newly developing recognition of the sexual needs of women, the absence of men during the war made middle-class women in particular aware of the frustration of their own needs, while an improvement in contraceptive devices allowed them the freedom of extramarital sex. There was an increase in the proportion of women college graduates, an increase in the proportion of married women in the labor force, and an increase in the sexual freedom demanded by and granted to women. But, the "New Woman" was quickly submerged in the hardships of the Great Depression. Women became acutely aware that formal political equality—the vote—did not mean actual political or economic equality: they were excluded from participation in "the inner circles of the most important men's civic and political clubs, which are the real centers of power in modern political life,"[18] and virtually excluded from political office and government policy making. Once again, hundreds of thousands of women were left unemployed only to find that government relief and public works projects almost always gave jobs to men. (This experience emphasizes, too, the vital importance to women of full employment, for full employment means women can easily enter and stay in the work force.)

One remnant of the pre-Depression "New Woman" remained. Severe economic conditions meant the postponement of marriage but not the postponement of sexual intercourse. The idea of sexual freedom, made possible by new birth control techniques and supported by Freudian theory, continued. The postponement of marriage and the

---

[17]Eleanor Flexner, *A Century of Struggle* (Cambridge, Mass.: The Belknap Press, 1959), pp. 142–155.

[18]Elizabeth K. Nottingham, "Toward an Analysis of the Effects of Two World Wars on the Role and Status of Middle Class Women." *American Sociological Review* 12(December 1947):666–675.

possibility of never marrying made sexual relations outside of marriage an attractive alternative to abstinence, with considerably less social disapproval than earlier.

Women were again pulled into the work force during the Second World War, and again pushed out when the veterans returned to the labor force. Immediately after the war, both young women and men became more family conscious, and the birth rate rose to pre-1930 levels. The feminine mystique, so beautifully documented by Betty Friedan,[19] dominated novels, movies, plays, and social science analysis. The "New Woman"—except for some of her sexual freedoms—now became submerged in the latest version of "Kinder, Kirche and Küche" in the period of political quietism and " love America" that followed the end of the war.

Technological improvements, too, continued to be important in giving women the time and energy to develop an active interest in their position in society.[20] By the second half of the nineteenth century, tremendous technical improvements and the influx of immigrant girls decreased the amount of time and energy women—especially among the middle class—had to give to housework. Such improvement continued to decrease gradually the physical burden of housework, and market goods continued to replace home-produced goods. Both private and public social services further supplanted the wife in the performance of such duties as care for the elderly, the poor, and the sick. However, to meet the rising standards of housekeeping, which were encouraged by advertising, built-in obsolescence, and the drive for profits, housewives spent more than fifty hours per week on housework in the 1960s, just as they did in the 1920s.[21] The expansion of the economy during the 1960s, especially in the service sector (e.g., food service workers, cleaners, nurses, typists, etc.), made available both part-time and full-time jobs that had come to be seen as "women's work." Married women, responding to the availability of jobs and to rising wages, increased their labor force participation by almost 80 percent between 1950 and 1974. Motherhood no longer keeps married women from paid work, for married women with school-age children more than tripled their participation in the labor force and now have a higher labor force participation rate than that for all married women.[22]

Technical control over childbearing released women from their most dangerous burden—frequent, physically debilitating pregnancies and the threat of death from childbirth. Maternal deaths dropped from an

[19]Betty Friedan, *The Feminine Mystique* (New York: Norton, 1963).
[20]Flexner, *A Century of Struggle*, p. 178.
[21]Joann Vanek, "Time Spent in Housework." *Scientific American* 231(November 1974):116–120.
[22]Women's Bureau, *1975 Handbook on Women Workers*, Bulletin no. 297 (Washington D.C.: Department of Labor), pp. 23, 26–27.

estimated 60.1 per 1,000 live births in 1915, to 2.9 by 1956. Contraceptive techniques were so improved by the 1960s that women now have almost complete control over reproduction. Many devices, however, have come to be viewed with suspicion; the "Pill," especially, has been cited as a cause of major health problems and IUD may not be satisfactory. Since the 1973 Supreme Court decision permitting legal abortion, most women now have access—formally, although not necessarily financially—to this method of birth control. Today women have more years without the responsibilities of childbearing and childcare than with them. Women marry earlier, have fewer children (or are more likely to marry and never have children), and complete the years of childbearing earlier than ever before. Also, women increasingly may be deciding not to marry, although not necessarily to forgo motherhood: the proportion of single women under twenty-four years of age has increased while the overall rate of children born outside marriage continues to rise.[23] While childbearing activities have become less time consuming, women have also increased their available time simply by an increase in life expectancy from forty years in 1850 to over seventy years a century later.

Women's sexual rights have altered considerably from the nineteenth century, when criticisms were directed at women who achieved sexual satisfaction,[24] through Sigmund Freud's recognition of female sexuality and his subsequently disproven theory of the infantile clitoral and mature vaginal orgasm,[25] to the recognition of women's enormous potential for sexual pleasure. Contraceptive devices, the acceptance of childbearing and of childrearing outside of marriage, women's "right" to sexual satisfaction and expression—in and out of marriage—along with women's earning ability give women the social context for enjoying new sexual freedom. No doubt there are still problems: sometimes it appears that women have traded the requirements of premarital virginity and marital faithfulness for mandatory participation in sexual activities.[26] To some women, the Masters and Johnson[27] documentation of the multiorgasmic potential of women may appear as "new work" at which they must demonstrate their abilities.

---

[23]Paul C. Glick and Arthur J. Norton, "Frequency, Duration and Probability of Marriage and Divorce," *Journal of Marriage and the Family* 33(May 1971):307–317.

[24]Robert R. Bell, "Some Emerging Sexual Expectations Among Women," in Robert R. Bell and Michael Gordon (eds.), *The Social Dimension of Human Sexuality* (Boston: Little, Brown, 1972); p. 158.

[25]Susan Lyndon, "The Politics of Orgasm," in Bell and Gordon, *Social Dimension of Human Sexuality,* pp. 166–171.

[26]This is commented on by students in the Sociology of Women classes at Portland State University and by antifeminist Midge Decter in *New Chastity and Other Arguments Against Women's Liberation* (New York: Putnam, 1974), but we have been unable to find any social science research on the topic.

[27]William H. Masters and Virginia E. Johnson, *Human Sexual Response* (Boston: Little, Brown, 1966), p. 131.

The double standard of aging still sees older men as desirable and attractive, while older women are seen as having lost their sex appeal—and their sexuality.[28] Finally, the concept of women as sex objects continues to complicate the problem of women's sexual and personal identity.

This brief examination of the impact of the economy, technology, ideology, and social crises on women's position shows initial losses and, later, gains. However, women's social position shows no simple relation in industrial societies to any ideology or economic system. Women are second-class citizens in the mixed economies[29] of the United States and Great Britain, in the welfare economies of Sweden and Denmark, and in the Socialist economies of the Soviet Union and East Germany. While women in the latter two systems have broad job opportunities and earn as much as men in comparable positions—unlike the United States and Great Britain—they still carry the double burden of housewife and worker just as their sisters in the two English-speaking countries do. Some greater accommodations (such as day care centers, and maternity leaves) are made to the childbearing and child care responsibilities of women under the welfare and socialist systems. As in the United States and Great Britain, it is still usually taken for granted that these are women's responsibilities. Socialism has not automatically brought sexual equality, although socialism may be a necessary condition for the liberation of women.

In the developing country of the People's Republic of China, the drive to develop socialism—while also industrializing the country—has proceeded along with a movement to change the social position of women.[30] Although women in China have not become the equal of men in employment, political activity, or administration, since 1948 their social position has altered drastically. Arranged marriages have been eliminated. Women are encouraged to enter the labor force, to train for a wide variety of jobs, and to participate in political life. In the first years after the establishment of the People's Republic of China, and, especially since the Cultural Revolution (1966–1968), the government has been committed explicitly to equality of the sexes. Intensive nationwide education campaigns have been conducted lauding nontraditional activities by women. Study groups (composed of persons who work together in factories, or who live in the rural communes or in the same urban neighborhoods) have been given the task of "studying

---

[28]Susan Sontag, "The Double Standard of Aging," *Saturday Review* 55(September 23, 1972):29–38; Zoe Moss, "It Hurts to be Alive and Obsolete," in Morgan, *Sisterhood is Powerful,* pp. 170–175.

[29]*Mixed economy* means an economy with a significantly large public sector. The government provides jobs, invests, builds, etc., and government policy regulates the rate of activity in the private sector.

[30]See the selection by Stacey in Part Five.

and criticizing Lin Piao and Confucius," two representatives of traditional doctrines about women. Peer group pressure is exerted on men who are reluctant to share household and child care jobs and on women to enter the labor force or do some work for persons outside the family. While we cannot yet judge whether an attack on patriarchy, side by side with the development of socialism, will succeed in creating sex equality, we do know for certain that neither has succeeded separately anywhere in the modern world.

READINGS

Many social scientists see the contemporary Euro-American family as separated from major social institutions—i.e., from the political economy, schools, religious organizations, medical facilities, etc.—and tend to study family life accordingly.[31] First, over the last several centuries, starting with the breakup of the household economy, "work" (income producing activity) has changed from a family activity to the participation of individuals (usually men) in the labor force. This change was accompanied by the development of specialized institutions that took over from the family responsibilities for schooling, religious instruction, the care of the elderly and sick, providing financial credit, etc.[32] Second, the American family has been seen as having become increasingly privatized over the last one hundred years.[33] Reduced in size, narrowed in membership to the conjugal family (wife, husband, their offspring), retreating physically into the confines of the small apartment or single-family house, the family now enacts its roles hidden from public scrutiny and public control, and individuals are freed to enact new family roles.[34]

Eli Zaretsky, in the first selection, challenges the thesis of the separation of the family from society. He argues that the disjunction is an illusion that comes from the preoccupation of the bourgeoisie during the emergence of capitalism with (a) the market economy and (b) attempts to moderate the effects of capitalism on personal life. The devel-

[31]Nona Glazer-Malbin, "The Captive Couple: The Burden of Gender Roles in Marriage," in Don H. Zimmerman et al., *Understanding Social Problems* (New York: Praeger, 1976). pp. 264–268.

[32]Ernest W. Burgess and Harvey J. Locke, *The Family, from Institution to Companionship,* 2d ed. (New York: American Book, 1953).

[33]Barbara Laslett, "The Family as a Public and Private Institution: An Historical Perspective." *Journal of Marriage and the Family* 35(August 1973):480–492.

[34]Family sociologists connect the emergence of the conjugal family as an *ideal* to industrialization and urbanization for, although the conjugal family predominated in feudal Europe, it was apparently from necessity rather than preference. During feudalism, the extended family was infrequent and limited to the upper classes because its existence depended on holdings of considerable wealth, maintained over several generations. William J. Goode, "Family Patterns and Human Rights." *International Social Science Journal* 18, no. 1(1966):41–54.

opment of a market economy certainly changed family life, drawing husbands, wives, and other family members from productive work in the home into wage labor. But, to believe that a change in the organization of productive labor means the isolation of the family from the political economy (and other major social institutions) is to overlook the multiple functions of the contemporary family and the effects of the political economy on family life. It is to ignore both the economic and noneconomic activities of people that result from their being family members, activities that integrate the family into society. First, the family maintains workers for the economy by replenishing the energy of jobholders with food, shelter, and psychological support. Family members depend directly—and, therefore, society depends indirectly —on the work of housewives who carry out the relevant jobs of cooking, shopping, cleaning, etc. Second, families provide new workers for the economy by reproducing and then socializing children to have the proper ideology and habits that will make them suitable workers. For example, the hierarchical organization of the contemporary family accustoms children to the hierarchical organization of work in capitalist enterprises. Hence, in Zaretsky's view, the family is well integrated into the economy, even though work that has "exchange-value" (earns income) occurs outside the home. Thus women make an important contribution to *society,* not just to their families, by their work in the home.[35]

The ideology that the family is and ought to be an "enclave" in society has several important effects. First, it reduces the social position of women by maintaining the fiction that women do not contribute to the well-being of society (by ignoring their housework, child care, and husband care) but only contribute to the well-being of their own families. Second, the ideology supports minimal direct public control over the family by implying that social policy to support families is unnecessary. The ideology legitimatizes the belief that the family is the unit primarily responsible for meeting the social and economic needs of people, while corporations and government are seen as having little or no responsibilities for their effects on family life. These effects include the organization of family life around the time schedules, hiring and firing practices, pensions, safety conditions, wage levels, etc. of firms. Innovations in the enactment of family roles (e.g., single-parent families, married women's labor force activity, gender role reversals, etc.) occur without causing major social friction or invoking pressures from agencies of social control (e.g., pressures from corporations, the courts, etc.) because these new roles continue to include activities compatible with the family being the main unit responsible for people. New innova-

[35]See Margaret Benston's selection in Part Two for a fuller explanation of use-value and exchange-value.

tive demands are not made on the organizations in the political economy or government. Third, the ideology shifts the attention of social scientists from the effects of social institutions on family and family members to the effects of family members on each other, and to the effects of the life cycle, role conflicts, etc. Social scientists thus can ignore easily the social and political consequences of the social context in which families are located.

The recognition that housewives make some economic contribution has been seen by some as a "radical" step forward for women. However, the sharply contrasting interpretations of this recognition illustrate the relevance of whether or not the family is seen as isolated from other social institutions. To those who see the family as isolated, women's labor in the home appears as a contribution to their *families:* economic analyses examine the economic costs and benefits that individual women or their families experience from women's housework or from women's participation in the labor force. Estimates of the monetary value of housewives are seen as a contribution to the well-being of families.[36] Social policy compatible with this perspective includes proposals that women should be paid by their mates for housework; that housewives should automatically be entitled to one-half of their husband's earnings; that divorce insurance should be made available, especially to women; and that, after divorce, women who spent substantial parts of their married years being housewives should receive financial compensation from their former husbands.[37]

In contrast, seeing the family as an integral part of the society suggests a different set of questions about the family roles women enact: How do family roles integrate the group into society? What contributions do women make to the well-being of *society* by taking the dual roles of housewife and paid worker? What is the connection between mental life in families and the structure of the political economy?[38] Social policy consistent with this perspective would include low-cost child care; maternity and paternity leave; children's allowances; and, in general, the assumption by society of the responsibility for insuring that children have adequate food, shelter, education, leisure activities, etc. Thus "family problems" would become just as legitimate a social concern and matter for the expenditure of public monies as the present governmental preoccupation with providing the conditions that encourage capital investment, benefit the development of new industries, support industries in financial difficulties, etc. The

[36]See selection by Nona Glazer in Part Four.
[37]Wendy Edmond and Suzie Fleming (eds.), *All Work and No Pay* (London: Falling Wall Press, 1975).
[38]Nona Glazer, "The New Class Crisis for Women," Paper presented at the Pacific Sociological Association meetings, San Diego, April 27, 1976.

well-being of families would take its place alongside government concern for the well-being of private investors in the corporate economy.

The second selection in this part considers one of the most striking manifestations of women's inferior economic status in the labor force, occupational segregation by sex whereby women are limited to a narrow range of occupations. In 1973, women made up 90 percent of all workers in seventeen occupations.[39] In recent years, labor economists have begun to devote their attention to both the causes and effects of this segmentation in the labor force.

Economist Heidi Hartmann, using a historical approach, investigates patriarchy as one source of occupation segregation in modern capitalist economy. She poses two separate questions: (1) What are the origins of patriarchy? (2) How did this patriarchy system extend itself into the labor market in a capitalist economy? Hartmann briefly considers the first question by reviewing cross-cultural studies of the sex division of labor. Although anthropologists may differ about the origins of patriarchy, they agree that patriarchy emerged before the appearance of capitalism.

Hartmann expands the classical Marxian interpretation, which emphasizes the organization of capitalism and the activities of capitalists, by locating one cause of women's occupational segregation in patriarchy. Hartmann's analysis is a modification of explanations of women's occupational segregation, explanations that consider women's condition to be a result of the existence of private property—maintained today by capitalism (in the radical approach)[40]—or a result of sexist attitudes (in the neoclassical approach).[41]

Hartmann argues that the techniques of hierarchical organization and control are the province of men because of their position in the patriarchal family. With the development of capitalism, knowledge of these techniques allowed men to extend the sex division of labor from the home into the marketplace. Focusing on the activities of male workers, she details the exclusionary policies toward women of, first, the guilds and then the craft and trade union organizations from the sixteenth to the nineteenth century.

Hartmann believes that capitalists have played an important role in maintaining patriarchy in order to retain their power over workers. However, in this article she emphasizes the advantage of occupational segregation by sex to male workers because the topic has been neglected by radical economists. She maintains that capitalism and patriarchy

---

[39]Women's Bureau, *1975 Handbook on Women Workers*, pp. 91–92

[40]See the selection by Michael Reich et al. in Part Two.

[41]See the selection by Francine Blau and Carol Jusenius in Part Two.

interact to their mutual advantage, resulting in the maintenance of women's continued subordinate economic position.

In conclusion, Hartmann suggests that the relative importance of capitalism and unionization in the maintenance of women's job segregation by sex has varied over time. Men workers are more important in maintaining job segregation during times of relative economic stability, while at other times capitalists have had more influence.

The economic role of married women has undergone drastic change since World War II. By 1974, 46 percent of all women 16 years and older were in the labor force,[42] more than double the proportion of women working in 1940. Most of this change is due to the increase of married women in the job market. In 1890, the typical working woman was in her early twenties, single, and the daughter of immigrant parents; upon marriage, she left the labor market permanently.[43] Today, the life-cycle work pattern of women has changed considerably. It now displays two distinct stages: A woman will enter the labor market after completing school and will remain until the birth of her first child. She will then leave for a period of between five and ten years and will tend to return to work only intermittently until her youngest child reaches school age. After this, some women will return permanently to the labor force while others will continue their intermittent pattern.[44]

In the last article in this section, the Manpower Report of the President for 1975 documents the changing characteristics of women's activity in the labor force from 1960 to the present. In addition to a profile of women workers, the report includes information on earnings, occupational structure, and women's educational attainment, attitudes, and life-styles.

Because so many women workers are married today, the problems facing working women are greater than in the past. In addition to the problems associated with low pay and low-status work, many women now must also bear the burden of two jobs (one outside and one inside the home), as well as find cheap and dependable care for their children.[45] Poverty is also becoming an increasingly serious problem for women who head families and work at low-paying jobs. In 1973, 45 percent of families headed by women received income below the poverty level.[46]

Information on women's economic condition, such as reported in the

---

[42]Women's Bureau, *1975 Handbook on Women Workers*, p. 11.

[43]Smuts, *Women and Work in America*.

[44]Women's Bureau, *1975 Handbook on Women Workers*, pp. 59–60.

[45]Myra H. Strober, "Formal Extrafamily Child Care—Some Economic Observations," in Cynthia B. Lloyd (ed.), *Sex, Discrimination, and the Division of Labor* (New York: Columbia University Press, 1975), pp. 364–369.

[46]Women's Bureau, *1975 Handbook on Women Workers*, p. 141.

Manpower Report of the President, provides some of the data necessary to analyze problems facing working women as well as to recommend public policy.

Capitalism,
The Family and
Personal Life

Eli Zaretsky

THE FAMILY AND THE ECONOMY

According to Firestone (1970), both the oppression of women and the split in society between intimate personal experience and anonymous social relations are consequences of the sexual division of labor within the family. Firestone terms the family the base and the political economy the superstructure, but links the two realms only vaguely through "power psychology." While Mitchell (1966) stresses the complexity of their interaction, she retains the conception of the family as a separate realm (socially defined as "natural") outside the economy—indeed she explains the oppression of women, as Firestone does, by their exclusion from social production. In this way, Mitchell and Firestone share with recent socialist movements the idea of a split between the family and the economy. Given this idea, one cannot understand the relation between family life and the rest of society.

The understanding of the family and the economy as separate realms is specific to capitalist society. By the "economy," Firestone and Mitchell mean the sphere in which commodity production and exchange take place, the production of goods and services to be sold, and their sale and purchase. Within this framework of thought, a housewife cooking a meal is not performing economic activity, whereas if she were hired to cook a similar meal in a restaurant she would be. This conception of "economic" excludes activity within the family, and a political struggle waged by "economic classes" would exclude women, except in their role as wage earners. Socialist and communist movements in the developed capitalist countries have also understood the "economy" in this way. And when they have talked of a political struggle between "economic classes," they have essentially excluded both the family and housewives from revolutionary politics.

The historic socialist understanding is based upon an important truth about capitalist society. The capitalist class has organized much of material production as a system of commodity production and exchange, and has organized most forms of labor as wage labor—i.e., as a commodity. By paying the laborer less than the value that the laborer produces, the capitalist is able to appropriate surplus value, unpaid labor time. Surplus value is the social basis for the existence of the capitalist class. The sphere in which surplus value is produced and realized (the "economy") determines the imperatives of society as a whole. The family has changed in capitalist society as the needs generated within the sphere of surplus value production—the needs of the capitalist class—have changed. And since this sphere is organized through wage labor, the destruction of the wage labor system is a central, defining task of a revolutionary movement in a capitalist country. But this task cannot be accomplished by wage labor alone, nor does it exhaust the purposes of a revolutionary movement.

The organization of production in capitalist society is predicated upon the existence of a certain form of family life. The wage labor system (socialized production under capitalism) is sustained by the socially necessary but private labor of housewives and mothers. Child rearing, cleaning, laundry, the maintenance of property, the preparation of food, daily health care, reproduction, etc. constitute a perpetual cycle of labor necessary to maintain life in this society. In this sense the family is an integral part of the economy under capitalism. Furthermore, the functions currently performed by housewives and mothers will be as indispensable to a socialist society as will be many of the forms of material production currently performed by wage labor. A socialist movement that anticipates its own role in organizing society must give weight to all forms of socially necessary labor, rather than only to the form (wage labor) that is dominant under capitalism.

Marx probably intended the larger conception of the economy when, in the preface to the *Critique of Political Economy*, he defined the "economic structure" as the "real foundation" of society. The "economic structure," he wrote, was "the total ensemble of social relations entered into in the social production of existence." That this conception of economic structure must include the family would have been perfectly clear in any analysis of a precapitalist society. In precapitalist society, the family performed such present functions as reproduction, care of the sick and aged, shelter, the maintenance of personal property, and regulation of sexuality, as well as the basic forms of material production necessary to sustain life. There were forms of economic activity that were not based upon family units—such as the building of public works, and labor in state-owned mines or industries. But they do not compare in extent or importance to peasant agriculture, labor based upon some form of the family, or upon the village, an extension of one or several families. In the most "primitive" societies—those in which production is least developed socially—the material necessity of the family, its role in sustaining life, was overwhelming. Even putting aside the dependence of children, adults in "primitive" society had no option but to rely upon the cooperative work of the household and particularly on the sexual division of labor, which by restricting tasks to one sex or the other insured their reciprocal dependence. . . .

It is only under capitalism that material production organized as wage labor, and the forms of production taking place within the family have been separated so that the "economic" function of the family is obscured. . . . Only with the emergence of capitalism has "economic" production come to be understood as a "human" realm outside of "nature." Before capitalism, material production was understood, like sexuality and reproduction, to be "natural"—precisely what human beings shared with animals. From the viewpoint of the dominant culture in previous societies, what distinguished humanity was not production but rather culture, religion, politics, or some other "higher" ideal made possible by the surplus appropriated from material production. . . . Before capitalism, the family was associated with the "natural" processes of eating, sleeping, sexuality, and cleaning oneself, with the agonies of birth, sickness, and death, *and* with the unremitting necessity of toil. It is this association of the family with the most primary and impelling material processes that has given it its connotation of backwardness as society advanced. Historically, the family has appeared to be in conflict with culture, freedom, and everything that raises humanity above the level of animal life. Certainly it is the association of women with this realm that has been among the earliest and most persistent sources of male supremacy and of the hatred of women. . . .

. . . Early capitalism developed a high degree of consciousness concerning the internal life of the family and a rather elaborate set of rules and expectations that governed family life. This led to a simultaneous advance and retrogression in the status of women. On the one hand, women were fixed more firmly than ever within the family unit; on the other hand, the family had a higher status than ever before. But the feminist idea that women in the family were outside the economy did not yet have any basis. As in precapitalist society, throughout most of capitalist history the family has been the basic unit of "economic" production—not the "wage-earning" father but the household as a whole.... Certainly women were excluded from the few "public" activities that existed—for example, military affairs. But their sense of themselves as "outside" the larger society was fundamentally limited by the fact that "society" was overwhelmingly composed of family units based upon widely dispersed, individually owned productive property....

[The] "split" between the socialized labor of the capitalist enterprise and the private labor of women in the home is closely related to a second "split"—between our "personal" lives and our place within the social division of labor. So long as the family was a productive unit based upon private property, its members understood their domestic life and "personal" relations to be rooted in their mutual labor. Since the rise of industry, however, proletarianization separated most people (or families) from the ownership of productive property. As a result, "work" and "life" were separated; proletarianization split off the outer world of alienated labor from an inner world of personal feeling. Just as capitalist development gave rise to the idea of the family as a separate realm from the economy, so it created a "separate" sphere of personal life, seemingly divorced from the mode of production.

This development was a major social advance. It is the result of the socialization of production achieved by capitalism and the consequent decline in socially necessary labor time and rise in time spent outside production.... Under capitalism an ethic of personal fulfillment has become the property of the masses of people, though it has very different meanings for men and for women, and for different strata of the proletariat. Much of this search for personal meaning takes place within the family and is one reason for the persistence of the family in spite of the decline of many of its earlier functions.

The distinguishing characteristic of this search is its subjectivity—the sense of an individual, alone, outside society with no firm sense of his or her own place in a rationally ordered scheme. It takes place on a vast new social terrain known as "personal" life, whose connection to the rest of society is as veiled and obscure as is the family's connection. While in the nineteenth century the family was still being studied through such disciplines as political economy and ethics, in the twentieth century it spawned its own "sciences," most notably psychoanalysis and psychology. But psychology and psychoanalysis distort our understanding of personal life by assuming that it is governed by its own internal laws (for example, the psychosexual dynamics of the family, the "laws" of the mind or of "interpersonal relations") rather than by the "laws" that govern society as a whole. And they encourage the idea that emotional life is formed only through the family and that the search for happiness should be limited to our "personal" relations, outside our "job" or "role" within the division of labor.

Thus, the dichotomies that women's liberation first confronted—between the "personal" and the "political," and between the "family" and the "economy"—are rooted in the structure of capitalist society. . . . The means of overcoming it is through a conception of the family as a historically formed part of the mode of production.

The rise of capitalism isolated the family from socialized production as it created a historically new sphere of personal life among the masses of people. The family now became the major space in society in which the individual self could be valued "for itself." This process, the "private" accompaniment of industrial development, cut women off from men in a drastic way and gave a new meaning to male supremacy. While housewives and mothers continued their traditional tasks of production —housework, reproduction, etc.—this labor was devalued through its isolation from the socialized production of surplus value. In addition, housewives and mothers were given new responsibility for maintaining the emotional and psychological realm of personal relations. For women within the family "work" and "life" were not separated but were collapsed into one another. The combination of these forms of labor has created the specific character of women's labor within the family in modern capitalist society. . . .

Historians of the family in Europe and the United States have focused on its internal institutions—the laws of marriage, inheritance and divorce, the social relations of age and sex. Their emphasis has been formal and legalistic. Their major theories have stressed the slow, almost imperceptible evolution in the internal constitution of the household from the "extended" to the "nuclear" family. Viewed in this way, the seeming inertia of the family has been in marked contrast to the continuous upheaval of political and economic history, a contrast that lends plausibility to the view that "history" is the realm of politics and economics while the family is confined to "nature."

In contrast, I have tried to understand the family as an integral part of a society that changes continuously and as a whole. I have focused on the continually changing social basis of the family as part of the organization of production. . . . With the beginnings of capitalism, the bourgeoisie, in defending private productive property against feudal ties and restrictions, put forth a new conception of the family as an independent economic unit within a market economy (Aires, 1962).

. . . Based upon private productive property, the ideology of the family as an "independent" or "private" institution is the counterpart to the idea of the "economy" as a separate realm, one that capitalism over centuries wrested "free" of feudal restrictions, customary law, and state and clerical intervention. Protestantism reinforced this conception of the family by making it a center of religious observance.... By the nineteenth century, the factory system had eliminated many of the production functions of the family. The bourgeois family was now reduced to the preservation and transmission of capitalist property, while the productive function of the proletarian family lay in the reproduction of the labor force. Hence, through the family each class reproduced its own class function. How did the proletarian family understand itself once it was stripped of private productive property?

To answer this question I have tried to describe the expansion of personal life among the masses of people in the nineteenth and twentieth centuries. Some of the origins of this process lie in the history of the family. The development of the bourgeois family encouraged individualism, self-consciousness, and a new attention to domestic relations. But bourgeois individualism is inseparably linked to private productive property and economic competition. With the rise of industry, individualism begins to turn against capitalism itself in such movements as romanticism and utopian socialism....

By the twentieth century, a sphere of "personal" life emerged among the proletariat itself. In the absence of a political movement that sought to transform both personal life and production, personal life was characterized by subjectivity—the search for personal identity outside the social division of labor. Having no private property to uphold, contemporary individualism upholds the self as an "autonomous" realm outside society. This new emphasis on one's personal feelings and inner needs, one's "head" or "life style," to use contemporary formulations, gives a continued meaning to family life and at the same time threatens to blow it apart.

If we can understand the family as part of the development of capitalism this can help establish the specific historical formation of male supremacy. This, in turn, would help focus the attack upon it. The establishment of private productive property as the basis of the bourgeois household meant that society was organized into separate households each of which was ruled by the father (and grandfather). In the democratic proclamations of the bourgeois revolutions every defense of natural rights or individual freedom assumes that the (male) head of the household represents the women, children, and servants within. Similarly, women are invisible in the bourgeois exaltation of "private property" or the "yeoman"; the real "yeoman" is the collective labor of the household. The emergence of personal life encouraged a sense of self-assertion and individual uniqueness among men while assigning women to the newly discovered worlds of childhood, emotional sensibility, and compassion, all contained within women's "sphere," the family.

Personal life appears to take place in some private, psychological realm outside society. By its critique of male supremacy and of the family women's liberation has demonstrated its systematic and social character. The family is an important material basis for subjectivity in this society, and for psychological life generally. If we can simultaneously view it as part of the "economy" a step would be taken toward understanding the connection between our inner emotional lives and capitalist development. The social terrain of personal life is the contemporary family within which men and women share so much, and in which their antagonism is so deeply rooted.

CAPITALISM AND THE FAMILY

Introduction. An overall tendency toward dissolution has characterized formal kinship relations in Europe and the United States in modern times [Karl Marx in *Neue Rheinische Zeitung*, Dec. 15, 1848; quoted in George (1971:385)]. . . . With the rise of industrial capitalism in the nineteenth and twentieth centuries, the male-dominated bourgeois family began to break up; the family began to be reduced to its individual members, including women and children. Each phase of dissolution has been accompanied by a new attempt at synthesis—for the bourgeoisie, the "patriarchal" or "nuclear" family; for the proletariat, "personal life." . . .

The Early Bourgeois Family in England. The prevalent form of family life in England before the rise of industry in the eighteenth and nineteenth centuries was that of an economically independent, commodity-producing unit. Often referred to as the "patriarchal" family, it survives today only among the petit bourgeoisie. It originated between the disintegration of feudalism in the fourteenth century and the rise of capitalism in the sixteenth. During this period, peasant families extricated themselves from feudal ties to become tenants or (far less often) landowners. In feudal society, separate households were a subordinate part of a larger enterprise, generally the manor. . . . Slowly, the family replaced the . . . manor as the lowest social unit, the head of which was an active citizen, able to buy and sell in the marketplace.

On the basis of small-scale commodity production, a new form of the family developed in the early bourgeois period. The household of a property-owning family in seventeenth-century England was a complicated economic enterprise that included not only children and relatives but servants, apprentices, and journeymen from different social classes. . . . While family life differed vastly among different strata and classes, the early bourgeois family—the family as a self-contained productive unit—furnished the basis for a new ideology of the family linked with the newly emerging ideas of private property and individualism. . . .

The bourgeoisie's acceptance of economic life helped encourage a new acceptance of sexuality, eating, and other noneconomic material processes of the family. The family had been scorned in medieval society as the realm of both production and sexuality. The Catholic Church, antisexual and savagely antifemale, had sanctioned family life only reluctantly, as the alternative to damnation, and had forbidden it to the clergy. The right of the clergy to marry had been a basic issue during the Reformation. In seventeenth-century England, Puritanism, with its acceptance of the life of material necessity, embraced the married state and exalted the family as part of the natural (i.e., God-given) order of productive and spiritual activity. Sexuality and emotional expression were encouraged, so long as they occurred within marriage. . . .

In contrast to the precapitalist divorce of spiritual and economic life, human meaning and purpose was now to be sought in the mundane world of production and the family. Throughout the Reformation, an ever-increasing proportion of religious instruction and prayer was removed from the church to the home. More important, Protestantism blessed the material labor performed by the family as sacred. . . .

Underlying these changes was a new conception of human nature, that of possessive individualism. The bourgeoisie condemned the fixed stratification of medieval society as "artificial" and viewed competitiveness based upon economic self-interest as the natural basis of society. As market relations developed, the identification of the individual with a fixed social position began to give way to a commitment to the "individual" (i.e., the individual family) who would rise or fall on the basis of independent efforts. The family came to be seen as a competitive economic unit apart from, and later even opposed to, the rest of society. . . .

The bourgeois acceptance of a certain degree of selfishness and aggression as part of human nature gave rise to a search for new principles of social order. . . .

The new social and religious functions of the family led to a deepening consciousness concerning domestic life and to public debate over its form. . . .

Taken together, these developments shaped a new ideal of family life. Marriage was coming to be understood as a partnership based upon common love and labor; one's wife was a companion or "helpmeet." The early bourgeois family gave rise to a new set of expectations based upon the couple's common destiny—not only love but mutual affection and respect, trust, fidelity, and premarital chastity....

The bourgeois familial ideal obscured two contradictions that emerged in the course of capitalist development: the oppression of women and the family's subordination to class relations. The rise of the bourgeoisie entailed a simultaneous advance and retrogression in the position of women. In the economic life of medieval England, women were closer to equality with men than they later were under capitalism. For example, women participated as equals in many guilds in the fourteenth century (Beard, 1971). With the rise of capitalism they were excluded and, in general, economic opportunities for women not in families—such as spinsters or widows—declined. On the other hand, women were given a much higher status within the family. For the Puritans, women's domestic labor was a "calling," a special vocation comparable to the crafts or trades of their husbands. Like their husbands, women did God's work. As the lesser partner in a common enterprise, a women was to be treated with respect....

Hence, women were encouraged to think of themselves almost as independent persons at the same time that they were imprisoned within the family. During the English Revolution the question of female equality was debated politically for the first time.... These stirrings of women's equality reached a level in the seventeenth century sufficient to call forth a counter-movement among preachers and others that stressed female subordination within the family. One argument made was that the family was the economic property of the husband, and that married women owned nothing in their own right.

So long as the family was considered the "natural" or God-given basis of society, the issue of women's equality could not emerge on a large scale. The bourgeois view that the family (rather than individuals or classes) was the basic unit of society reinforced the deeply rooted traditions of male supremacy. And this view persisted as long as the family was a basic unit of social production. The issue of women's equality was largely muted until the late eighteenth and nineteenth centuries, when the rise of industry finally destroyed the bourgeois ideal of the family as an independent productive unit....

Decline of the Bourgeois Family. The rise of the factory system made manifest the subjection of the family to the class relations of its members. Until then, the bourgeoisie had accommodated itself to domestic industry, since this was the most expedient and profitable way of organizing production. Once families were brought together in a common workshop, however, they were no longer supervised by the father but by the master. They no longer worked at their own rhythm, but according to the systematic labor discipline required by a coordinated division of labor. The master-manufacturer of the eighteenth century was obsessed with the necessity of instructing the workers in " 'methodical' habits, punctilious attention to instructions, fulfillment of contracts to time, and in the sinfulness of embezzling materials."

The introduction of machinery was the culmination of this process, requiring human beings to "identify themselves with the unvarying regularity of the complex automaton." Industrial capitalism required a rationalized, coordinated and synchronized labor process undisturbed by community sentiment, family responsibilities, personal relations or feelings. These changes in the organization of production led to the formation of a new ideology of the family. Earlier the bourgeoisie had portrayed the family as the progressive center of individualism, but as industrial production destroyed the basis of the early bourgeois family, the family came to be either scorned as a backward institution or nostalgically romanticized. . . .

The family, to the Victorian bourgeoisie, was a "tent pitch'd in a world not right." "This is the true nature of home," wrote John Ruskin; "It is the place of peace; the shelter, not only from all injury, but from all terror, doubt, and division. . . . So far as the anxieties of the outer life penetrate into it . . . it ceases to be a home; it is then only a part of the outer world which you have roofed over and lighted fire in" (Millett, 1970). It stood in opposition to the terrible anonymous world of commerce and industry: "a world alien, not your world . . . without father, without child, without brother." The Victorian family was distinguished by its spiritual aspect: it is remote, ethereal and unreal—"a sacred place, a vestal temple." . . .

Reflecting this separation, the belief in separate "spheres" for men and women came to dominate the ideology of the family in the epoch of industrial capitalism. As the family was now idealized, so was the familial role of women. According to one of the domestic manuals that began to flourish in the 1830s and '40s, "that fierce conflict of worldly interests, by which men are so deeply occupied, [compels them] to stifle their best feelings." Men, according to Ruskin, are "feeble in sympathy." But women, by contrast, whose "everyday duties are most divine because they are most human," nurture within the family the "human" values crushed by "modern life." . . . Now the dominant image of women was that of the mother who, freed from domestic labor by the abundance of servants could devote herself wholly to her child. "A woman when she becomes a mother should withdraw herself from the world," instructed an 1869 domestic manual. In the nineteenth century, childhood was first assigned a separate identity and exalted as the time of life untainted by the roughness of material necessity. To a large extent sexual interest was removed from the bourgeois family and assigned to prostitutes, an important group among working-class women. Filial relations were intensified and charged with unsuspected emotions by the sexual repression and prudery characteristic of the period of capital accumulation. . . .

The Victorian opposition to female equality was bitter and furious, reflecting the idea that the family had become the last refuge from the demands of capitalist society. The emancipation of women threatened to degrade all society to a common level of cynical manipulation (i.e., economic competition in the marketplace). Within the same bourgeois view, feminists argued that bringing women into society would humanize it. Nineteenth-century feminism was closely involved with movements of moral reform such as temperance and the abolition of prostitution. Their participation in these movements supported the idea that women were the guardians of society's morals. Similarly, on the basis of their special capacity for service, certain occupations, for example schoolteaching and nursing, were largely restricted to women, and downgraded.

To the feminist attack on the Victorian ideal the socialists' voice was added. The rise of industrial capitalism had created a new form of the family among the bourgeoisie, but it had eliminated the economic basis of the family—private productive property—among the working class. . . . Marx and Engels rejected the nineteenth-century idealization of the bourgeois family, which they viewed as the retrograde preserve of private wealth. In contrast to Hegel and Mill, they insisted that "civil society" or "political economy"—capitalism—directly infected family life. "On what foundation is the present family, the bourgeois family, based?" they wrote in the *Communist Manifesto.* "On capital. On private gain. . . . The bourgeois sees in his wife a mere instrument of production" whereas, among the proletariat, "all family ties . . . are torn asunder." According to Marx and Engels, the early bourgeois ideals of the family—love, equality, and common work—could not be realized so long as society was organized around private property. The family under capitalism, ostensibly private, was in fact continually transformed by the needs of the dominant class. . . .

The Proletarian Family. With the rise of industrial capitalism, wages replaced productive property as the economic basis of the family. "Private property" was redefined among the proletariat to refer to objects of consumption: food, clothing, domestic articles, and later, for some, a home. The traditional division of labor within the family was threatened as women and children joined men in the factories. Meanwhile, capital was accumulated by restricting domestic consumption and diverting any surplus into industry. The bourgeois ethic of repression and abstinence was extended to the proletariat through the force of material circumstances. The family's internal life was dominated by the struggle of its members for their basic material needs.

This understanding underlay the politics of nineteenth-century socialists and reformers. Many feared that by turning women and children into wage-earners, industrial capitalism was destroying the family. The goal of "saving" the family underlay such nineteenth-century reforms as protective legislation and child labor laws. Over time a series of private and public institutions arose—schools, savings banks, insurance companies, welfare agencies—whose function was to mediate between capitalist production and the fragmented realm of private life. The great trade union struggles through which the nineteenth-century working class both resisted and accommodated itself to industrial capitalism were also intended to establish a new basis for the proletarian family. Women were commonly excluded from trade unions and male trade unionists demanded a wage that could support the entire family.

... Reflecting the struggle for survival that characterized the nineteenth-century proletarian family, Marx and Engels saw no need for a separate program for "personal" life, including the oppression of women by men within the family. Instead they believed that if individuals were freed from economic exploitation they would arrange their private lives according to earlier ideals of domestic and personal fulfillment, unrealizable under conditions of industrial capitalism.

The development of capitalism destroyed this hope and to a great extent "separated" the socialist movement from the subsequent development of the family and of personal life among the proletariat. The reduction of the economically "independent" family to a houseworker and a factory worker was part of a process that led to greatly expanded productivity of labor. . . .

By the middle of the nineteenth century in England and America, bourgeois economists had begun to argue that the development of leisure time among the workers coupled with a rise in wages would benefit capital by greatly expanding the domestic market for consumer goods. This argument was also adopted by the labor movement. . . . In the second half of the nineteenth century, the great industries of domestic consumption arose in England: clothing, food, furniture, housing. By the end of the century, bourgeois spokesmen were proclaiming that workers were becoming "capitalists," since a frugal and fortunate working family could in some cases eventually purchase its own home. Along with this, the bourgeoisie encouraged the belief that human meaning could be found primarily within the sphere of consumption.

... A separate sphere of personal life began to develop among the proletariat. This development can be seen most clearly in the twentieth-century United States.

Personal Life and Subjectivity in the Twentieth-Century United States. As capitalism developed, the productive functions performed by the family were gradually socialized (Davis, 1971). The family lost its core identity as a productive unit based upon private property. Material production within the family—the work of housewives and mothers—was devalued since it was no longer seen as integral to the production of commodities. The expansion of education as well as welfare, social work, hospitals, old age homes, and other "public" institutions further eroded the productive functions of the family. At the same time the family acquired new functions as the realm of personal life—as the primary institution in which the search for personal happiness, love, and fulfillment takes place. Reflecting the family's "separation" from commodity production, this search was understood as a "personal" matter, having little relation to the capitalist organization of society.

The development of this kind of personal life among the masses of people was a concomitant of the creation of a working class in capitalist society. Peasants and other precapitalist laborers were governed by the same social relations "inside" and "outside" work; the proletarian, by contrast, was a "free" man or woman outside work. By splitting society between "work" and "life," proletarianization created the conditions under which men and women looked to themselves, outside the division of labor, for meaning and purpose. Introspection intensified and deepened as people sought in themselves the only coherence, consistency, and unity capable of reconciling the fragmentation of social life. The romantic stress on the unique value of the individual began to converge with the actual conditions of proletarian life, and a new form of personal identity developed among men and women, who no longer defined themselves through their jobs. Proletarianization generated new needs —for trust, intimacy, and self-knowledge, for example—which intensified the weight of meaning attached to the personal relations of the family. The organization of production around alienated labor encouraged the creation of a separate sphere of life in which personal relations were pursued as an end in themselves.

But the creation of a separate sphere of personal life was also shaped by the special problems of the capitalist class in the early twentieth century. Increasing proletarianization, along with deepening economic crises, created increasing labor unrest and class conflict, as well as the growth of the socialist movement. Beginning in the early twentieth century, a significant minority of American capitalists saw the possibility of integrating labor within a capitalist consensus through raising its level of consumption. Besides expanding the market for consumer goods, such a strategy would divert the working class from socialism and from a direct assault on capitalist relations of production.... The emphasis on consumption was an important means through which the newly proletarianized, and still resisting, industrial working class was reconciled to the rise of corporate capitalism, and through which the enormous immigrant influx of the late nineteenth and early twentieth centuries was integrated with the industrial working class. . . .

The family, no longer a commodity-producing unit, received a new importance as a market for industrial commodities. Mass production forced the capitalist class to cultivate and extend that market, just as it forced it to look abroad for other new markets. As a result, American domestic and personal life in the twentieth century has been governed by an ethic of pleasure and self-gratification previously unknown to a laboring class. Working people now see consumption as an end in itself, rather than as an adjunct to production, and as a primary source of both personal and social (i.e., "status") identity. This is symbolized within the "middle class" as "life-style," a word that is used to defend one's prerogatives regardless of the demands of "society."

The rise of "mass consumption" has vastly extended the range of "personal" experience available to men and women while retaining it within an abstract and passive mode: the purchase and consumption of commodities. Taste, sensibility, and the pursuit of subjective experience—historically reserved for leisure classes and artists—have been generalized throughout the population in predetermined and standardized forms by advertising and other means. This is reflected in the modern department store in which the wealth, culture, and treasures of previous ruling classes now appear in the form of cheap jewelry, fashions, and housewares.

On one hand, there has been a profound democratization of the idea that it is good to live well, consume pleasurably, and enjoy the fruits of one's labor. On the other hand, "mass consumption"—within the context of capitalism—has meant the routinization of experience and the deepening of divisions within the proletariat. The deep material deprivation that still characterizes the lives of most Americans—bitter inadequacies of housing, food, transportation, health care, etc.—has taken on added emotional meanings. The "poor" feel personally inadequate and ashamed, while the more highly educated and better-paid sectors of the working class experience guilt toward the "less fortunate." . . .

Increasingly cut off from production, the contemporary family threatens to become a well of subjectivity divorced from any social meaning. Within it a world of vast psychological complexity has developed as the counterpart to the extraordinary degree of rationalization and impersonality achieved by capital in the sphere of commodity production. The individualist values generated by centuries of bourgeois development—self-consciousness, perfectionism, independence—have taken new shape through the insatiability of personal life in developed capitalist society. The internal life of the family is dominated by a search for personal fulfillment for which there seem to be no rules. Much of this search has been at the expense of women.

Already in the late nineteenth century, American women were consumed with a sense of their own diminished role and stature when compared with their mothers and grandmothers (Parker, 1972), women who labored within the productive unity of the family defined by private property. In a letter to Jane Addams in the early twentieth century, Charlotte Gilman described the married woman's sense of living second hand, of getting life in translation, of finding oneself unready and afraid in the "face of experience." By 1970 this fear had become a desperate sense of loss. Meredith Tax (1970:7) describes the "limbo of private time and space" of the housewife: "When I am by myself, I am nothing. I only know that I exist because I am needed by someone who is real, my husband, and by my children. My husband goes out into the real world. . . . I stay in the imaginary world in this house, doing jobs that I largely invent, and that no one cares about but myself. . . . I seem to be involved in some sort of mysterious process" (Tax, 1970:17).

Just as the rise of industry in the eighteenth and nineteenth centuries cut women off from men and gave a new meaning to male supremacy, so the rise of mass education has created the contemporary form of youth and adolescence. The "generation gap" is the result of the family lagging behind the dominant tendencies of the culture and of the transformation of productive skills which children learn in school and through the media. Parents now appear "stupid" and "backward" to their children, representing, as they do, an earlier stage of capitalist development. Beginning in the early twentieth century, the family began to appear to young people as a prison cut off from reality.

At the same time, in the form of "public opinion," the imperatives of capitalist production have been recreated within the family particularly in the "expectations" through which parents bludgeon themselves and their children into submission. Fathers, like schoolteachers or policemen, appear to stand for the whole bourgeois order. Hence, the split between the public and the private is recreated within the family. As in the "outside world," people feel they are not known for themselves, not valued for who they really are.

While serving as a refuge, personal life has also become depersonalized; subjective relations tend to become disengaged, impersonal, and mechanically determined. Introspection has promised to open a new world to men and women, but increasingly the inner life reverberates with the voices of others, the imperatives of social production.

REFERENCES

Aries, Philippe.
  1962   Centuries of Childhood: A Social History of Family Life. Translated
         by Robert Baldick. New York: Knopf.
Beard, Mary.
  1971   Woman as Force in History. New York: Macmillan.
Davis, Angela.
  1971   "Reflections on the black woman's role in the community of slaves."
         Black Scholar 3(December):2–15.
Firestone, Shulamith.
  1970   The Dialectic of Sex. New York: Morrow.
George, C. H.
  1971   "The making of the English bourgeoisie, 1500–1750." Science and
         Society 35(Winter):385–414.
Lukács, Georg.
  1971   History and Class Consciousness. Translated by Rodney Living-
         stone. Cambridge, Mass.: MIT Press.
Millett, Kate.
  1970   Sexual Politics. New York: Doubleday.
Mitchell, Juliet.
  1966   "Women: The longest revolution." New Left Review 40(November/
         December):11–37.
O'Connor, James.
  1970   "The fiscal crisis of the state." Socialist Revolution no. 1(January-
         February); no. 2(March-April).
Parker, Gail (ed.).
  1972   The Oven Birds: American Women on Womanhood, 1820–1920. New
         York: Doubleday Anchor Books.
Tax, Meredith.
  1970   Woman and Her Mind: The Story of Daily Life. Cambridge, Mass.:
         New England Free Press.

Capitalism, Patriarchy, and Job Segregation by Sex

Heidi Hartmann

The division of labor by sex appears to have been universal throughout human history. In our society the sexual division of labor is hierarchical, with men on top and women on the bottom. Anthropology and history suggest, however, that this division was not always a hierarchical one. The development and importance of a sex-ordered division of labor is the subject of this paper. It is my contention that the roots of women's present social status lie in this sex-ordered division of labor. . . .

The primary questions for investigation would seem to be, then, first, how a more sexually egalitarian division became a less egalitarian one, and, second, how this hierarchical division of labor became extended to wage labor in the modern period. . . .

I want to argue that, before capitalism, a patriarchal[1] system was established in which men controlled the labor of women and children in the family, and that in so doing men learned the techniques of hierarchical organization and control. With the advent of public-private separations such as those created by the emergence of state apparatus and economic systems based on wider exchange and larger production units, the problem for men became one of maintaining their control over

Excerpted from Heidi Hartmann, "Capitalism, Patriarchy, and Job Segregation." *Signs: Journal of Women in Culture and Society* 1, no. 3, pt. 2 (Spring 1976):137–169, by permission of the author and the University of Chicago Press. © 1976 by The University of Chicago.

[1]I define patriarchy as a set of social relations that has a material base and in which there are hierarchical relations between men, and solidarity among them, that enable them to control women. Patriarchy is thus the system of male oppression of women. Rubin argues that we should use the term *sex-gender system* to refer to that realm outside the economic system (and not always coordinate with it) where gender stratification based on sex differences is produced and reproduced. Patriarchy is thus only one form, a male dominant one, of a sex-gender system (see Gayle Rubin, "The Traffic in Women," in *Toward an Anthropology of Women,* ed. Rayna Reiter [New York: Monthly Review Press, 1975]).

the labor power of women. In other words, a direct personal system of control was translated into an indirect, impersonal system of control, mediated by society-wide institutions. The mechanisms available to men were (1) the traditional division of labor between the sexes, and (2) techniques of hierarchical organization and control. These mechanisms were crucial in the second process, the extension of a sex-ordered division of labor to the wage-labor system, during the period of the emergence of capitalism in Western Europe and the United States.

The emergence of capitalism in the fifteenth to eighteenth centuries threatened patriarchal control based on institutional authority as it destroyed many old institutions and created new ones, such as a "free" market in labor. It threatened to bring all women and children into the labor force and hence to destroy the family and the basis of the power of men over women (i.e., the control over their labor power in the family). If the theoretical tendency of pure capitalism would have been to eradicate all arbitrary differences of status among laborers, to make all laborers equal in the marketplace, why are women still in an inferior position to men in the labor market? The possible answers are legion; they range from neoclassical views that the process is not complete or is hampered by market imperfections to the radical view that production requires hierarchy even if the market nominally requires "equality." All of these explanations, it seems to me, ignore the role of men—ordinary men, men as men, men as workers—in maintaining women's inferiority in the labor market. The radical view, in particular, emphasizes the role of men as capitalists in creating hierarchies in the production process in order to maintain their power. Capitalists do this by segmenting the labor market (along race, sex, and ethnic lines among others) and playing workers off against each other. In this paper I argue that male workers have played and continue to play a crucial role in maintaining sexual divisions in the labor process.

Job segregation by sex, I will argue, is the primary mechanism in capitalist society that maintains the superiority of men over women, because it enforces lower wages for women in the labor market. Low wages keep women dependent on men because they encourage women to marry. Married women must perform domestic chores for their husbands. Men benefit, then, from both higher wages and the domestic division of labor. This domestic division of labor, in turn, acts to weaken women's position in the labor market. Thus, the hierarchical domestic division of labor is perpetuated by the labor market, and vice versa. This process is the present outcome of the continuing interaction of two interlocking systems, capitalism and patriarchy. Patriarchy, far from being vanquished by capitalism, is still very virile; it shapes the form modern capitalism takes, just as the development of capitalism has transformed patriarchal institutions. The resulting mutual accommodation between patriarchy and capitalism has created a vicious circle for women.

ANTHROPOLOGICAL PERSPECTIVES ON THE DIVISION OF LABOR BY SEX

Some anthropologists explain male dominance by arguing that it existed from the very beginning of human society. Sherry Ortner suggests that indeed "female is to male as nature is to culture."[2] According to Ortner, culture devalues nature; females are associated with nature, are considered closer to nature in all cultures, and are thus devalued. Her view is compatible with that of ... Lévi-Strauss, who assumes the subordination of women during the process of the creation of society.

According to Lévi-Strauss, culture began with the exchange of women by men to cement bonds between families—thereby creating *society*.[3] ... By analogy, Lévi-Strauss suggests that the division of labor between the sexes is the mechanism that enforces "a reciprocal state of dependency between the sexes."[4] ... Thus the existence of a sexual division of labor is a universal of human society, though the exact division of the tasks by sex varies enormously.

Two other major schools of thought on the origins of the sexual division of labor ... reject the universality, at least in theory if not in practice, of the sex-ordered division of labor.[5] One is the "feminist-revisionist" school, which argues that we cannot be certain that the division of labor is male supremacist; it may be separate but equal (as Lévi-Strauss occasionally seems to indicate), but we will never know because of the bias of the observers, which makes comparisons impossible.

The [other] school, the "variationist," also rejects the universality of sex-ordered division of labor but, unlike relativists, seeks to compare societies to isolate the variables that coincide with greater or lesser autonomy of women.... They suggest that increased sexual stratification occurs along with a general process of social stratification (which at least in some versions seems to depend on and foster an increase in social surplus—to support the higher groups in the hierarchy). As a result, a decrease in the social status of woman occurs when (1) she loses

[2]Sherry B. Ortner, "Is Female to Male as Nature Is to Culture?" *Feminist Studies* 1, no. 2 (Fall 1972):5–31.
[3]Claude Lévi-Strauss, "The Family," in *Man, Culture and Society*, ed. by Harry L. Shapiro (New York: Oxford University Press, 1971).
[4]Lévi-Strauss, "The Family," p. 348.
[5]For the first school, see particularly Collier and Stack, *Culture and Society*, ed. Michelle Z. Rosaldo and Louise Lamphere (Stanford, Calif.: Stanford University Press, 1974). For the second school, see particularly Draper, in *Toward an Anthropology of Women*.

control of subsistence through a change in production methods and devaluation of her share of the division of labor; (2) her work becomes private and family centered rather than social and kin focused; and/or (3) some men assert their power over other men through the state mechanism by elevating these subordinate men in their families, using the nuclear family against the kin group. In this way the division of labor between men and women becomes a more hierarchical one. Control over women is maintained directly in the family by the man, but it is sustained by social institutions, such as the state and religion.

The work in this school of anthropology suggests that patriarchy did not always exist, but rather that it emerged as social conditions changed. Moreover, men participated in this transformation. Because it benefited men relative to women, men have had a stake in reproducing patriarchy. Although there is a great deal of controversy among anthropologists about the origins of patriarchy, and more work needs to be done to establish the validity of this interpretation, I believe the weight of the evidence supports it. In any case, most anthropologists agree that patriarchy emerged long before capitalism, even if they disagree about its origins.

In England, ... the formation of the state marks the end of Anglo-Saxon tribal society and the beginning of feudal society. Throughout feudal society the tendencies toward the privatization of family life and the increase of male power within the family appear to be strengthened, as does their institutional support from church and state. By the time of the emergence of capitalism in the fifteenth through eighteenth centuries, the nuclear, patriarchal peasant family had become the basic production unit in society.

THE EMERGENCE OF CAPITALISM AND THE INDUSTRIAL REVOLUTION IN ENGLAND AND THE UNITED STATES

The key process in the emergence of capitalism was primitive accumulation, the prior accumulation that was necessary for capitalism to establish itself.[6] Primitive accumulation was a twofold process that set the preconditions for the expansion of the scale of production: first, free laborers had to be accumulated; second, large amounts of capital had to be accumulated. The first was achieved through enclosures and the removal of people from the land, their subsistence base, so that they were forced to work for wages. The second was achieved through both

---

[6]See Karl Marx, "The So-called Primitive Accumulation," in *Capital*, 3 vols. (New York: International Publishers, 1967), vol. 1, pt. 8; Stephen Hymer, "Robinson Crusoe and the Secret of Primitive Accumulation," *Monthly Review* 23, no. 4 (September 1971):11–36.

the growth of smaller capitals in farms and shops amassed through banking facilities, and vast increases in merchant capital, the profits from the slave trade, and colonial exploitation.

The creation of a wage-labor force and the increase in the scale of production that occurred with the emergence of capitalism had in some ways a more severe impact on women than on men. To understand this impact let us look at the work of women before this transition occurred and the changes that took place as it occurred.[7] In the 1500s and 1600s, agriculture, woolen textiles (carried on as a by-industry of agriculture), and the various crafts and trades in the towns were the major sources of livelihood for the English population. In the rural areas men worked in the fields on small farms they owned or rented and women tended the household plots, small gardens and orchards, animals, and dairies. The women also spun and wove. A portion of these products was sold in small markets to supply the villages, towns, and cities, and in this way women supplied a considerable proportion of their families' cash income, as well as their subsistence in kind. In addition to the tenants and farmers, there was a small wage-earning class of men and women who worked on the larger farms. Occasionally tenants and their wives worked for wages as well, the men more often than the women. As small farmers and cottagers were displaced by larger farmers in the seventeenth and eighteenth centuries, their wives lost their main sources of support, while the men were able to continue as wage laborers to some extent. Thus women, deprived of these essential household plots, suffered relatively greater unemployment, and the families as a whole were deprived of a large part of their subsistence.

In the 1700s, the demand for cotton textiles grew, and English merchants found they could utilize the labor of the English agricultural population, who were already familiar with the arts of spinning and weaving. The merchants distributed materials to be spun and woven, creating a domestic industrial system that occupied many displaced farm families. This putting-out system, however, proved inadequate. The complexities of distribution and collection and, perhaps more important, the control the workers had over the production process (they could take time off, work intermittently, steal materials) prevented an increase in the supply of textiles sufficient to meet the merchants' needs. To solve these problems, first spinning, in the late 1700s, and

---

[7]This account relies primarily on that of Alice Clark, *The Working Life of Women in the Seventeenth Century* (New York: Harcourt, Brace & Howe, 1920). Her account is supported by many others, such as B. L. Hutchins, *Women in Modern Industry* (London: G. Bell & Sons, 1915); Georgiana Hill, *Women in English Life from Medieval to Modern Times*, 2 vols. (London: Richard Bentley & Son, 1896); F. W. Tickner, *Women in English Economic History* (New York: E. P. Dutton & Co., 1923); Ivy Pinchbeck, *Women Workers and the Industrial Revolution, 1750–1850* (London: Frank Cass & Co., 1930; reprinted 1969).

then weaving, in the early 1800s, were organized into factories....

In this way, domestic industry, created by emerging capitalism, was later superseded and destroyed by the progress of capitalist industrialization. In the process, women, children, and men in the rural areas all suffered dislocation and disruption, but they experienced this in different ways. Women, forced into unemployment by the capitalization of agriculture more frequently than men, were more available to labor, both in the domestic putting-out system and in the early factories....

We may never know the facts of the authority structure within the preindustrial family, since much of what we know is from prescriptive literature or otherwise class biased, and little is known about the point of view of the people themselves. Nevertheless, the evidence on family life and on relative wages and levels of living suggests that women were subordinate within the family.

... The history of the early factories suggests that capitalists took advantage of this authority structure, finding women and children more vulnerable, both because of familial relations and because they were simply more desperate economically....

The transition to capitalism in the cities and towns was experienced somewhat differently than in the rural areas.... In the towns and cities before the transition to capitalism, a system of family industry prevailed: a family of artisans worked together at home to produce goods for exchange. Adults were organized in guilds, which had social and religious functions as well as industrial ones. Within trades carried on as family industries, women and men generally performed different tasks: in general, the men worked at what were considered more skilled tasks, the women at processing the raw materials or finishing the end product. Men, usually the heads of the production units, had the status of master artisans. For though women usually belonged to their husbands' guilds, they did so as appendages; girls were rarely apprenticed to a trade and thus rarely became journeymen or masters. Married women participated in the production process and probably acquired important skills, but they usually controlled the production process only if they were widowed, when guilds often gave them the right to hire apprentices and journeymen....

In the seventeenth and eighteenth centuries, the family industry system and the guilds began to break down in the face of the demand for larger output. Capitalists began to organize production on a larger scale, and production became separated from the home as the size of establishments grew. Women were excluded from participation in the industries in which they had assisted men as they no longer took place at home, where married women apparently tended to remain to carry on their domestic work. Yet many women out of necessity sought work in capitalistically organized industry as wage laborers. When women entered wage labor, they appear to have been at a disadvantage relative to men. First, as in agriculture, there was already a tradition of lower wages for women (in the previously limited area of wage work). Second, women appear to have been less well trained than men and obtained less desirable jobs. And third, they appear to have been less well organized than men.

Because I think the ability of men to organize themselves played a crucial role in limiting women's participation in the wage-labor market, I want to offer, first, some evidence to support the assertion that men were better organized and, second, some plausible reasons for their superiority in this area.

As evidence of their superiority, we have the guilds themselves, which were better organized among men's trades than women's, and in which, in joint trades, men had superior positions—women were seldom admitted to the hierarchical ladder of progression. Second, we have the evidence of the rise of male professions and the elimination of female ones during the sixteenth and seventeenth centuries. The medical profession, male from its inception, established itself through hierarchical organization, the monopolization of new, "scientific" skills, and the assistance of the state. Midwifery was virtually wiped out by the men.[8] ... Third, throughout the formative period of industrial capitalism, men appear to have been better able to organize themselves as wage workers. And as we shall see below, as factory production became established, men used their labor organizations to limit women's place in the labor market.

As to why men might have had superior organizational ability during this transitional period, I think we must consider the development of patriarchal social relations in the nuclear family, as reinforced by the state and religion. In Anglo-Saxon England, for example, men's superior position was reinforced by the state, and men acted in the political arena as heads of households and in the households as heads of production units;[9] it seems likely that men would develop more organizational structures beyond their households. Women, in an inferior position at home and without the support of the state, would be less likely to be able to do this. Men's organizational knowledge, then, grew out of their position in the family and in the division of labor.

When women participated in the wage-labor market, they did so in a position as clearly limited by patriarchy as it was by capitalism. Men's

---

[8]See Clark, *Working Life of Women in the Seventeenth Century*, pp. 242–284, for more on the medical profession.

[9]See Viana Muller, "The Formation of the State and the Oppression of Women: A Case Study in England and Wales," mimeographed (New York: New School for Social Research, 1975), for a detailed description of this process.

control over women's labor was altered by the wage-labor system, but it was not eliminated. In the labor market the dominant position of men was maintained by sex-ordered job segregation. Women's jobs were lower paid, considered less skilled, and often involved less exercise of authority or control. Men acted to enforce job segregation in the labor market; they utilized trade-union associations and strengthened the domestic division of labor, which required women to do housework, child care, and related chores. Women's subordinate position in the labor market reinforced their subordinate position in the family, and that in turn reinforced their labor-market position.

The process of industrialization and the establishment of the factory system, particularly in the textile industry, illustrate the role played by men's trade-union associations. Textile factories employed children at first, but as they expanded they began to utilize the labor of adult women and of whole families. While the number of married women working has been greatly exaggerated, apparently enough married women had followed their work into the factories to cause both their husbands and the upper classes concern about home life and the care of children. Smelser has argued that in the early factories the family industry system and male control could often be maintained. For example, adult male spinners often hired their own or related children as helpers, and whole families were often employed by the same factory for the same length of working day. Technological change, however, increasingly made this difficult, and factory legislation which limited the hours of children.[10]

The demands of the factory laborers in the 1820s and 1830s had been designed to maintain the family factory system, but by 1840 male factory operatives were calling for limitations on the hours of work of children between nine and thirteen to eight a day, and forbidding the employment of younger children. . . . This caused parents difficulty in training and supervising their children, and to remedy it male workers and the middle and upper classes began to recommend that women, too, be removed from the factories.

The upper classes of the Victorian Age, the age that elevated women to their pedestals, seem to have been motivated by moral outrage and concern for the future of the English race (and for the reproduction of the working class): "In the male," said Lord Shaftesbury, "the moral effects of the system are very sad, but in the female they are infinitely worse, not alone upon themselves, but upon their families, upon society, and, I may add, upon the country itself. It is bad enough if you corrupt

---

[10]See Neil Smelser, *Social Change and the Industrial Revolution* (Chicago: University of Chicago Press, 1959, chaps. 9–11.

the man, but if you corrupt the woman, you poison the waters of life at the very fountain."[11]

That male workers viewed the employment of women as a threat to their jobs is not surprising, given an economic system where competition among workers was characteristic. That women were paid lower wages exacerbated the threat. But why their response was to attempt to exclude women rather than to organize them is explained, not by capitalism, but by patriarchal relations between men and women: men wanted to assure that women would continue to perform the appropriate tasks at home.

In 1846 the *Ten Hours' Advocate* stated clearly that they hoped for the day when such threats would be removed altogether: "... It is needless for us to say, that all attempts to improve the morals and physical condition of female factory workers will be abortive, unless their hours are materially reduced. Indeed we may go so far as to say, that married females would be much better occupied in performing the domestic duties of the household, than following the never-tiring motion of machinery. We therefore hope the day is not distant, when the husband will be able to provide for his wife and family, without sending the former to endure the drudgery of a cotton mill."[12] Eventually, male trade unionists realized that women could not be removed altogether, but their attitude was still ambivalent. One local wrote to the Women's Trade Union League, organized in 1889 to encourage unionization among women workers: "Please send an organizer to this town as we have decided that if the women here cannot be organized they must be exterminated."[13]

Turning to the United States' experience provides an opportunity, first, to explore shifts in the sex composition of jobs, and, second, to consider further the role of unions, particularly in establishing protective legislation.[14] ...

Conditions in the United States differed from those in England. First, the division of labor within colonial farm families was probably more rigid, with men in the fields and women producing manufactured articles at home. Second, the early textile factories employed young single women from the farms of New England; a conscious effort was made, probably out of necessity, to avoid the creation of a family labor system and to preserve the labor of men for agriculture. This changed, how-

[11]From Mary Merryweather, *Factory Life*, cited in Hill, *Women in English Life from Medieval to Modern Times*, vol. 2, p. 200.

[12]Smelser, *Social Change and the Industrial Revolution*, p. 301.

[13]Quoted in G. D. H. Cole and Raymond Postgate, *The Common People, 1746–1946*, 4th ed. (London: Methuen, 1949), p. 432.

[14]This account is based primarily on Edith Abbott, *Women in Industry* (New York: Arno Press, 1969); Elizabeth F. Baker, *Technology and Woman's Work* (New York: Columbia University Press, 1964).

ever, with the eventual dominance of manufacture over agriculture as the leading sector in the economy and with immigration. Third, the shortage of labor and dire necessity in colonial and frontier America perhaps created more opportunities for women in nontraditional pursuits outside the family; colonial women were engaged in a wide variety of occupations. Fourth, shortages of labor continued to operate in women's favor at various points throughout the nineteenth and twentieth centuries. Fifth, the constant arrival of new groups of immigrants created an extremely heterogeneous labor force, with varying skill levels and organizational development and rampant antagonisms.

Major shifts in the sex composition of employment occurred in boot and shoe manufacture, textile manufacture, teaching, cigar making, and clerical work. In all of these, except textiles, the shift was toward more women. New occupations opened up for both men and women, but men seemed to dominate in most of them, even though there were exceptions. Telephone operating and typing, e.g., became women's jobs.

In all of the cases of increase in female employment, the women were partially stimulated by a sharp rise in the demand for the service or product.... For example, the upward shift in the numbers of clerical workers came between 1890 and 1930, when businesses grew larger and became more centralized, requiring more administration, distribution, transportation, marketing, and communication.

In several cases the shift to women was accompanied by technical innovations, which allowed increased output and sometimes reduced the skill required of the worker. By 1800, boot- and shoemakers had devised a division of labor that allowed women to work on sewing the uppers at home. In the 1850s, sewing machines were applied to boots and shoes in factories. In the 1870s, the use of wooden molds, rather than hand bunching, simplified cigar making, and in the 1880s, machinery was brought in. And in clerical work, the typewriter, of course, greatly increased the productivity of clerical labor. The machinery introduced in textiles, mule spinners, was traditionally operated by males. In printing, where male unions were successful in excluding women, the unions insisted on staffing the new linotypes.

The central purposes of subdividing the labor process, simplifying tasks, and introducing machines were to raise production, to cheapen it, and to increase management's control over the labor process. Subdivision of the labor process ordinarily allowed the use of less skilled labor in one or more subportions of the task. Cheapening of labor power and more control over labor were the motive forces behind scientific management and earlier efforts to reorganize labor.[15] Machinery was an

---

[15]See Harry Braverman, *Labor and Monopoly Capital* (New York: Monthly Review Press, 1974), esp. chaps. 3–5.

aid in the process, not a motive force. Machinery, unskilled labor, and women workers often went together. . . .

Cigar making offers ample opportunity to illustrate both the opposition of male unionists to impending sex changes in labor-force composition in their industries and the form that opposition took: protective legislation. Cigar making was a home industry before 1800, when women on farms in Connecticut and elsewhere made rather rough cigars and traded them at village stores. Early factories employed women, but they were soon replaced by skilled male immigrants whose products could compete with fancy European cigars. By 1860, women were only 9 percent of the employed in cigar making. This switch to men was followed by one to women, but not without opposition from the men. In 1869, the wooden mold was introduced, and so were Bohemian immigrant women (who had been skilled workers in cigar factories in Austria-Hungary). The Bohemian women, established by tobacco companies in tenements, perfected a division of labor in which young girls (and later their husbands) could use the molds. Beginning in 1873, the Cigarmakers International Union agitated vociferously against home work, which was eventually restricted (for example, in New York in 1894). In the late 1880s, machinery was introduced into the factories, and women were used as strikebreakers. The union turned to protective legislation.

The attitude of the Cigarmakers International Union toward women was ambivalent at best. The union excluded women in 1864, but admitted them in 1867. In 1875 it prohibited locals from excluding women, but apparently never imposed sanctions on offending locals. In 1878, a Baltimore local wrote Adolph Strasser, the union president: "We have combatted from its incipiency the movement of the introduction of female labor in any capacity whatever, be it bunch maker, roller, or what not."[16] . . . And let Strasser speak for himself (1879): "We cannot drive the females out of the trade, but we can restrict their daily quota of labor through factory laws. No girl under 18 should be employed more than eight hours per day; all overwork shoud be prohibited. . . ."[17]

Unions excluded women in many ways, not the least among them protective legislation. In this the unions were aided by the prevailing social sentiment about work for women, especially married women, which was seen as a social evil that ideally should be wiped out, and by a strong concern on the part of "social feminists" and others that women workers were severely exploited because they were unorganized. The

---

[16]Baker, *Technology and Woman's Work*, p. 34.
[17]John B. Andrews and W. D. P. Bliss, eds., *History of Women in Trade Unions*, in *Report on Condition of Woman and Child Wage-Earners in the United States*, vol. 10; 61st Cong., 2d sess., Senate Document no. 645 (1911; reprint ed., New York: Arno Press, 1974).

social feminists did not intend to exclude women from desirable occupations but their strategy paved the way for this exclusion, because, to get protection for working women—which they felt was so desperately needed—they argued that women, as a sex, were weaker than men and more in need of protection. Their strategy was successful in 1908 in *Muller* v. *Oregon*, when the Supreme Court upheld maximum hours laws for women, saying: "The two sexes differ in structure of body, in the capacity for long-continued labor particularly when done standing, the influence of vigorous health upon the future well-being of the race, the self-reliance which enables one to assert full rights, and in the capacity to maintain the struggle for subsistence. This difference justifies a difference in legislation and upholds that which is designed to compensate for some of the burdens which rest upon her."[18]

In 1916 in *Bunting* v. *Oregon*, Brandeis used virtually the same data on the ill effects of long hours of work to argue successfully for maximum-hours laws for men as well as women. *Bunting* was not, however, followed by a spate of maximum-hours law for men, the way *Muller* had been followed by laws for women. In general, unions did not support protective legislation for men, although they continued to do so for women. Protective legislation, rather than organization, was the preferred strategy only for women.

The effect of the laws was limited by their narrow coverage and inadequate enforcement, but despite their limitations, in those few occupations where night work or long hours were essential, such as printing, women were effectively excluded. While the laws may have protected women in the "sweated" trades, women who were beginning to get established in "men's jobs" were turned back. Some of these women fought back successfully, but the struggle is still being waged today along many of the same battle lines. As Ann C. Hill argued, the effect of these laws, psychically and socially, has been devastating. They confirmed woman's "alien" status as a worker.[19]

Throughout the above discussion of the development of the wage-labor force in England and the United States, I have emphasized the role of male workers in restricting women's sphere in the labor market. Although I have emphasized the role of men, I do not think that of employers was unimportant. Recent work on labor-market segmentation theory provides a framework for looking at the role of employers.[20]

---

[18]Barbara A. Babcok, Ann E. Freedman, Eleanor H. Norton, and Susan C. Ross, *Sex Discrimination and the Law: Causes and Remedies* (Boston: Little, Brown and Co., 1975), p. 32.

[19]Ann C. Hill, "Protective Labor Legislation for Women: Its Origins and Effect," mimeographed (New Haven, Conn.: Yale Law School, 1970).

[20]Reich, Edwards, and Gordon use labor-market segmentation to refer to a process in which the labor market becomes divided into different submarkets, with each having its own characteristic behaviors; these segments can be different layers of a hierarchy or different groups within one layer. (See their article in Part Two of this volume.)

According to this model, one mechanism that creates segmentation is the conscious, though not necessarily conspiratorial, action of capitalists; they act to exacerbate existing divisions among workers in order to further divide them, thus weakening their class unity and reducing their bargaining power. The creation of complex internal job structures is itself part of this attempt. In fact, the whole range of different levels of jobs serves to obfuscate the basic two-class nature of capitalist society. This model suggests, first, that sex segregation is one aspect of the labor-market segmentation inherent in advanced capitalism, and, second, capitalists have consciously attempted to exacerbate sex divisions. Thus, if the foregoing analysis has emphasized the continuous nature of job segregation by sex—present in all stages of capitalism and before—and the conscious actions of male workers, it is important to note that the actions of capitalists may have been crucial in calling forth those responses from male workers.

But even though capitalists' actions are important in explaining the current virility of sex segregation, labor-market-segmentation theory overemphasizes the role of capitalists and ignores the actions of workers themselves in perpetuating segmentation. Those workers in the more desirable jobs act to hang onto them, their material rewards, and their subjective benefits. Workers, through unions, have been parties to the creation and maintenance of hierarchical and parallel (i.e., separate but unequal) job structures. Perhaps the relative importance of capitalists and male workers in instituting and maintaining job segregation by sex has varied in different periods. Capitalists during the transition to capitalism, for example, seemed quite able to change the sex composition of jobs—when weaving was shifted to factories equipped with power looms women wove, even though most handloom weavers had been men, and mule spinning was introduced with male operators even though women had used the earlier spinning jennies and water frames. As industrialization progressed and conditions stabilized somewhat, male unions gained in strength and were often able to preserve or extend male arenas. Nevertheless, in times of overwhelming social or economic necessity, occasioned by vast increases in the demand for labor, such as in teaching or clerical work, male capitalists were capable of overpowering male workers. Thus, in periods of economic change, capitalists' actions may be more instrumental in instituting or changing a sex-segregated labor force—while workers fight a defensive battle. In other periods male workers may be more important in maintaining sex-segregated jobs; they may be able to prevent the encroachment of, or even to drive out, cheaper female labor, thus increasing the benefits to their sex.[21]

[21]David Gordon suggested to me this "cyclical model" of the relative strength of employer and workers.

CONCLUSION

The present status of women in the labor market and the current arrangement of sex-segregated jobs is the result of a long process of interaction between patriarchy and capitalism. I have emphasized the actions of male workers throughout this process because I believe that emphasis to be correct. Men will have to be forced to give up their favored positions in the division of labor—in the labor market and at home—both if women's subordination is to end and if men are to begin to escape class oppression and exploitation. Capitalists have indeed used women as unskilled, underpaid labor to undercut male workers, yet this is only a case of the chickens coming home to roost—a case of men's co-optation by and support for patriarchal society, with its hierarchy among men, being turned back on themselves with a vengeance. Capitalism grew on top of patriarchy; patriarchal capitalism is stratified society par excellence. If non-ruling-class men are to be free they will have to recognize their co-optation by patriarchal capitalism and relinquish their patriarchal benefits. If women are to be free, they must fight against both patriarchal power and capitalist organization of society.

The Changing Economic Role of Women

Manpower Report

Clear indications that women workers account for significantly larger proportions of the unemployed during the present recession than they did in earlier downturns have underscored the change in the economic role assumed by women in the last decade or more. The same phenomenon raises important issues concerning the situation of women workers in a slackening labor market, where those facing layoffs may become the subject of conflicting pressures between seniority systems and traditional attitudes, on the one hand, and equal employment obligations, on the other.... This chapter explores American women's rapidly changing work profiles, focusing, in turn, on current trends in labor force activity in the United States.

LABOR FORCE PARTICIPATION

The proportion of women of working age in the labor market, which was 33.9 percent in 1950, rose by one-third to 44.7 percent in 1973. This rapid rise in women's labor force participation rates during the past quarter century has had a marked effect on the size and the composition of the work force, on the growth in national product, and on the life-styles of both men and women. Among the many factors promoting or discouraging labor force entry, several—including marital status, presence and age of children, educational level, husband's income,

Excerpted from *Manpower Report of the President, Including Reports of the U.S. Department of Labor and the U.S. Department of Health, Education and Welfare* (Washington, D.C.: Government Printing Office, April 1975).

race, general economic conditions, and potential earnings—can play a determining role in the decision of a woman to seek paid work.

The Age Factor. Although the effects of age on women's labor force activity resemble those prevailing 25 years ago, important changes have occurred in participation rates at all ages (see Figure 1). During the 1950s and early 1960s, the proportion of older women in the work force rose dramatically (partly because many women who had worked during World War II were eager to seek employment again, once their children had entered or completed school). . . . Both the earlier rise in participation by older women and the later rise by younger women were accompanied by a steady growth in participation by the intermediate 35- to 44-year age group during the two and a half decades (see Table 1).

FIGURE 1. CHANGING PATTERNS OF WOMEN'S WORK LIFE

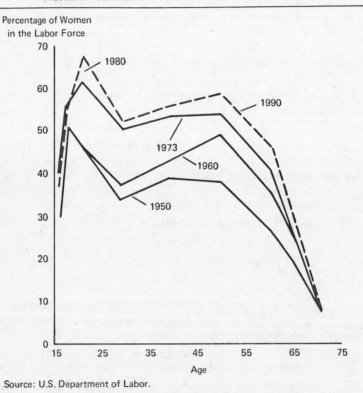

Source: U.S. Department of Labor.

Increases in labor force participation rates are expected to continue for all but the youngest and oldest groups, but a remarkable shift has already occurred. While age still has the same relative effect on partici-

TABLE 1. LABOR FORCE PARTICIPATION RATES OF WOMEN, BY AGE GROUP, SELECTED YEARS 1950 TO 1973 AND PROJECTED 1980 AND 1990

Age	1950	1960	1970	1973	1980	1990
Total	33.9%	37.8%	43.4%	44.7%	45.6%	46.5%
16 and 17 years	30.1	29.1	34.9	39.1	36.1	37.4
18 and 19 years	51.3	51.1	53.7	56.9	55.0	56.3
20 to 24 years	46.1	46.2	57.8	61.1	63.6	66.4
25 to 34 years	34.0	36.0	45.0	50.1	50.4	51.6
35 to 44 years	39.1	43.5	51.1	53.3	53.5	55.4
45 to 54 years	38.0	49.8	54.4	53.7	56.6	58.3
55 to 64 years	27.0	37.2	43.0	41.1	45.1	46.1
65 years and over	9.7	10.8	9.7	8.9	9.1	8.8

Source: *Handbook of Labor Statistics* (Washington: U.S. Department of Labor, Bureau of Labor Statistics, 1974), table 2, p. 31.

pation rates as it did in 1950, the growth in participation rates for all women has been so rapid that the proportion of women aged 25 to 34 who are in the work force today has reached the rate of the most active age groups of 1950. And mothers with school-age children are just as likely to work today as were unmarried young women of the 1950s.

Marital Status and Children. Women who have never married have much higher rates of labor force activity than do women who have (see Table 2). Still, the participation rates of married women have risen sharply since 1950, when they were 14 percentage points below the rate for widowed, divorced, or separated women and nearly 27 percentage points below that for single women.... While marriage still reduces the labor market activity of women, its impact has been greatly lessened. Participation rates for married women are expected to continue to rise, as marital status becomes a less significant factor in determining work force activity.

TABLE 2. LABOR FORCE PARTICIPATION RATES OF WOMEN, BY MARITAL STATUS, SELECTED YEARS, 1950 TO 1974

Year	Never Married	Married, Husband Present	Widowed, Divorced, or Separated
1950	50.5%	23.8%	37.8%
1955	46.4	27.7	39.6
1960	44.1	30.5	40.0
1965	40.5	34.7	38.9
1970	53.0	40.8	39.1
1973	55.8	42.2	39.6
1974	57.2	43.0	40.9

Married women, however, still have significantly different participation rates when they have preschool-age children (Figure 2).

Although the presence of preschool-age children therefore remains

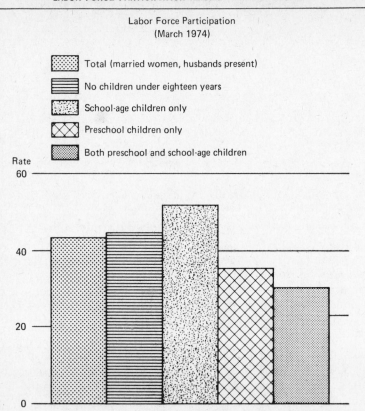

FIGURE 2. IMPORTANCE OF PRESCHOOL CHILDREN IN REDUCING
LABOR FORCE PARTICIPATION AMONG MARRIED WOMEN

Labor Force Participation
(March 1974)

Total (married women, husbands present)

No children under eighteen years

School-age children only

Preschool children only

Both preschool and school-age children

Rate

Married Women

Source: U.S. Department of Labor.

a significant factor in reducing the participation rates of married women, it is important to note a considerable growth in work force participation of this group. In fact, married women with preschool-age children are now in the work force as often as were married women who either had no children under 18 or who had only school-age children in 1950. This development is certain to have important consequences in terms of the cumulative labor force experience and employment continuity of working wives.

However, just as the impact of household duties on women's market work has lessened, so too the constraints imposed by having young children seem to be less severe than in earlier years (or, conversely, the financial and psychological constraints of not working may have become more crucial). Whereas 1950 participation rates for 25- to 34-year-old women were about one-fourth lower than the rates for women aged 20 to 24, by 1974 the participation rate of the 25-to-34 group was less than a fifth below that of the younger women. If this trend continues, traditional female worklife patterns will gradually be replaced by something closer to the patterns of their male coworkers.

Educational Attainment and Husbands' Earnings. Another important factor in female participation rates is the level of education attained. Work force activity rises with educational attainment in a consistent pattern, except for the slightly lower rates for women with 1 to 3 years of college, whose earnings differ only moderately from those of high school graduates. The association of earnings with educational attainment provides a partial explanation of this positive correlation; earnings rise with increased educational attainment, the higher wages providing an added incentive to many women to undertake paid work, even when it is combined with household obligations. In 1952, the average level of educational attainment for working women in the United States was 12.0 years, rising to 12.2 years in 1962 and 12.4 years in 1972—a steady growth that has attracted some women into a widening range of jobs.

It should be noted, however, that higher earnings provide only a portion of the explanation for higher labor force participation rates among college-educated women. Other causal elements may include, for example, the fact that commitment to a particular vocation is likely to be more intense among women who have been willing to pursue supplementary years of education. Exposure in college to an emphasis on lifetime careers may well be another factor of considerable importance in influencing decisions to work.

Although improved educational levels and earnings have been accompanied by higher work force rates for women, higher earnings by husbands have been associated with lower participation rates by their wives. While this still appears to be true to some extent, two important changes have occurred in the last 20 years. First, there has been a continuing upward shift in participation rates by wives with husbands at all income levels, reflecting women's improved earnings and employment opportunities as well as the continuing pressure of family budgetary needs. The positive effect of increases in women's own earnings has more than offset the negative impact of higher earnings of husbands, resulting in increases in both family income and the participation rate of wives over time.

Second, the inverse relationship between husbands' earnings and wives' participation rates has become less consistent. While 1951 participation rates of wives were highest for those whose husbands earned less than $3,000 (in 1973 dollars), wives whose husbands' earnings were in the $5,000-to-$6,999 bracket (in 1973 dollars) were the most likely to be in the labor market by 1960; by 1973, the highest participation rates had shifted to wives with husbands earning between $7,000 and $9,999 (in 1973 dollars). The increased earnings and employment opportunities available to wives with higher levels of educational attainment thus may be changing the earlier inverse relationship between husbands' earnings and wives' participation rates.

Racial Factors. It is important to consider the effect of race, along with age, education, and husbands' earnings, on female labor force participation rates. Except among those who are single or aged 16 to 24 years, the proportion of black women of working age who are in the labor market is significantly higher than that of white women, irrespective of the other factors considered. At each age level, except in the 16- to 24-year-old groups, black women had higher participation rates in 1973, as shown below:

LABOR FORCE PARTICIPATION RATES OF
WOMEN, 1973

Age	Black	White
16 to 17 years	24.3%	41.7%
18 to 19 years	45.1	58.9
20 to 24 years	57.5	61.6
25 to 34 years	61.0	48.5
35 to 44 years	60.7	52.2
45 to 54 years	56.4	53.4
55 to 64 years	44.7	40.8

Source: *Handbook of Labor Statistics,* 1974, table 4, pp. 38-39.

. . . Among married women, blacks display higher participation rates than whites, regardless of husband's earnings. Indeed, 54 percent of black married women with husbands present were in the labor force in 1973, in contrast to 41 percent of white women of similar marital status; and 44 percent of black women who were widowed, divorced, or separated were working or seeking work, in contrast to 39 percent of their white counterparts. The presence of children, especially young children, is also less of a constraint to black married women that it is to white ones. While 54 percent of black women with children under 6 years of age were labor force members in 1973, this was true of only 31 percent of white women with pre-school-age children.

Education, particularly college education, raises participation rates more for black than for white women. However, while black women . . . have traditionally shown a much greater attachment to the labor force than white women, the recent rise in white women's participation rates has been much faster, as the following tabulation shows. Consequently, the long standing difference between participation rates of black and white women is narrowing, as the general rise in these rates continues.

LABOR FORCE PARTICIPATION RATES OF WOMEN

Selected Years	Black	White
1950	46.9%	32.6%
1955	46.1	34.5
1960	48.2	36.5
1965	48.6	38.1
1970	49.5	42.6
1973	49.1	44.1
1974	49.1	45.2

Source: U.S. Department of Labor, Bureau of Labor Statistics

Occupations and Pay. Differences in the occupational distribution of men and women workers remain substantial, both among industry groups and between white- and blue-collar categories. For example, women account for 49 percent of white-collar workers, but only 17 percent of those in blue-collar jobs; similarly, in the service sector, 63 percent of jobholders are women. These differences require further breakdown, however, since significant variations occur within occupational groups. For example, approximately equal proportions of women and men are professional or technical workers, but women are heavily concentrated in the lower paying teaching and nursing fields, while more men are found in such higher paying professions as law, medicine, and engineering.

The service sector remains the most important employer of women. . . . Nearly one-fourth of all women workers are employed in the industry, where they make up over one-half of all employees.

Within the service industry category, nearly two-thirds of the workers in education, and three-fourths of those in medical-health and personal services (including work performed in hotels and private homes), are female. The predominance of women in these areas has been attributed to the similarity of the work to the activities traditionally carried out by women in the home. Teaching children and young adults, nursing the sick, and preparing food are seen as extensions of what women do as homemakers. In addition, the availability of part-time or shift work in this sector is attractive to women who have young children.

The growing number of services available in recent years has provided more and more jobs in the types of work that were familiar to women. Conversely, the rapid growth in the American economy during that period was made possible because the fastest growing sector had access to a large supply of women workers who were able to perform a wide range of services. Tradition notwithstanding, women are also heavily represented in government, retail trade, and manufacturing. Indeed, in 1973, these three groups, along with the service category, accounted for nearly 90 percent of female employment.

Women workers have also entered other industrial sectors in significant numbers, however. Women's share of employment in finance, for example, now exceeds half of all jobs; and in transportation, women have more than one-fifth of the total employment. These apparent gains are tempered, however, by the continued poor representation of women in senior positions within each industry category. There has been a significant decline within the service sector in the proportion of women in professional and technical positions over the last quarter century, offsetting the increase in the numbers of professional and technical women in the trade and manufacturing groups.

Still, some penetration of the industrial sectors traditionally closed to women is occurring. Associated with this is an increase in the proportion of women seeking the necessary training required to undertake new career opportunities. However, much greater progress is needed in this regard if an oversupply of women in the traditional areas of employment is to be avoided in the future, and if women are to attain the level of responsibility within the labor force that their proportional representation in the labor market warrants.

Certain issues—the scheduling of work, the level of unemployment suffered, and wages earned—are of particular importance in this context:

FULL-TIME AND PART-TIME WORK.   About 7 out of 10 women workers have full-time jobs at some time during the year, but only about 4 out of 10 maintain full-time jobs throughout the year. Students, women with family responsibilities, and women over 65 years of age often prefer part-time employment, which is most frequently available in the service and trade industry categories.

UNEMPLOYMENT.   Teenage black women suffer the highest unemployment rates of any group classified by age, race, or sex. About 1 out of every 3 young minority women was unemployed in 1974. White women of all ages and minority women aged 20 and over suffered less joblessness than black female teenagers—but, for all classifications, the unemployment rates for women are significantly higher than those for men (often because of the difficulties experienced by many women in finding reentry jobs after a period of absence from the labor force). Recent job market trends show a worsening of female unemployment as the labor market continues to slacken, particularly as layoffs first affect those with the least seniority. Recently hired workers, including many women and minority group members, have become the early casualties of the economic downturn. In some cases, such layoffs have highlighted the potential legal conflict between affirmative action plans and seniority rules within individual firms, but litigation on this issue is still in process.

EARNINGS. Nearly two-thirds of all full-time, year-round female workers earned less than $7,000 in 1972. In the same year, over three-fourths of full-time, year-round male workers earned over $7,000. Moreover, the large earnings differential between male and female workers has persisted over the past two decades, even when adjusted for hours of work and level of education. . . .

Furthermore, a classification of occupations by earnings reveals a marked similarity to a classification of jobs by sex. In fact, overall average earnings in private industry were $4.06 per hour in March 1974, but average rates in occupations with high proportions of women were often nearer to $3 than to $4. By contrast, the areas of extensive unionization and the lowest female participation, construction (where only 6 percent of the workers were women) and mining (with 8 percent women), had average earnings of $6.75 and $4.99, respectively.

Women are not only concentrated in the lower paying industries but they are also found in relatively large numbers in non-unionized business enterprises and in the lower paying occupational groups, including clerical workers and service workers. In addition, even when both sexes are well represented in an occupational group, women's earnings are substantially lower than those of men (see Table 3).

TABLE 3. MEDIAN INCOMES OF FULL-TIME
WOMEN WORKERS BY OCCUPATION, 1972

Major Occupation Group	Median Income	Percent of Men's Income
Professional and technical workers	$8,796	68
Nonfarm managers and administrators	7,306	53
Clerical workers	6,039	63
Sales workers	4,575	40
Operatives, including transportation	5,021	58
Service workers (except private household)	4,606	59
Private household	2,365	(1)
Nonfarm laborers	4,755	63

1 Percent not shown where median income of men is based on fewer than 75,000 individuals.

Source: Revised tables for the "Fact Sheet on the Earnings Gap" (Washington: U.S. Department of Labor, Women's Bureau, March 1974).

Various studies have found the overall discrepancy between male and female earnings to be around 40 percent....

Although recent action to strengthen equal pay laws may eventually overcome discrimination in earnings for the same job assignments, it will be much more difficult to remove discrimination in the making of job assignments. However, recent evidence suggests that pressures for change may be building. While the average annual discrepancy between the mean incomes of men and women working full time, year round remained substantially unchanged over the 1969–73 period, reports of occupational discrimination doubled.

Changes in Life-Style and Life Expectancy. Traditionally, child-bearing has brought with it not merely a temporary absence from paid employment but a complete withdrawal from the work force for a period of years (the time being extended by the birth of each successive child). Of crucial importance to the woman worker's career development is the fact that this withdrawal generally occurs during those years in which job advancement would be most rapid. Thus, women lose the opportunity to establish their careers or to gain seniority or experience prior to withdrawal. The longer the absence, the less meaningful is previous work in providing credentials for reentry.

The greater the number of children, the more profoundly marked are these effects. It is of major significance, therefore, that recent years have brought a drastic decline in average family size. From 1965 to 1973, the average number of children per husband-wife family with children dropped from 2.44 to 2.18. This decline is not just a postponement of births; the average total number of births expected by women (aged 18 to 24) during their lifetime was 3.2 in 1965, but only 2.3 by 1972. The Nation's birth rate in 1974 was down to 14.8 per thousand of population—lower even than the level reached in the depression of the 1930s. Whereas wives 18 to 24 in 1950 most often expected to have four or more children, in 1972 the commonly expected number was two.

Acceptance of childless marriages is also increasingly widespread. Indeed, as women find paid employment more appealing, the trend toward smaller family size is accentuated. Public concern over the implications of unlimited population growth, along with the greater availability and sophistication of contraceptive devices which enable the spacing and timing of births to conform more nearly to the mother's work preferences, should continue to reduce the average length of time women are out of the work force in the years ahead.

Along with these changes in fertility, other significant family-related factors are encouraging female labor force participation. For example, divorced or separated women with children have had consistently higher participation rates than married women with children, as shown below. Hence, some of the recent increases in female labor force participation must be attributed to rises in the divorce rate.

PARTICIPATION RATES OF WOMEN BY PRESENCE OF HUSBAND AND PRESENCE AND AGE OF CHILDREN, 1973

	Married, Husband Present	Widowed, Divorced, or Separated
Children under 18 years old	41.7	59.7
Children 6 to 17 years old	50.1	68.3
Children 3 to 5 years old	38.3	54.8
Children under 3 years old	29.4	38.5

Source: U.S. Department of Labor, Special Labor Force Report, No. 164, table F, p. 19.

In addition to work-inducing changes in family life-styles, there has been a dramatic rise in female life expectancy during the past half century. The life expectancy of a girl born in 1971 was 74.8 years, nearly 7½ years longer than that of a boy born in the same year. (In 1920, the gap was only 1 year.) The improvement in women's chances for survival after childbirth is illustrated by the increase in life expectancy at age 20. While it rose 2.5 years for white and 4.2 years for black men between 1940 and 1970, it increased 5.7 and 9.5 years for white and black women, respectively, over the same period. A longer lifespan affords an increase as well in the potential worklife of women. In effect, employment for older women has come to fill years that women in earlier eras did not have, since many did not survive far beyond the childbearing age.

Changes in Attitudes and Expectations. Mature women are now in the labor force far more frequently than they expected to be in their earlier years. A longitudinal study of young women aged 14 to 24 in 1968 over the 1968–70 period indicated that about two-fifths of those surveyed altered their plans for age 35. And, overwhelmingly, they moved in the direction of labor force entry:

PROPORTION OF WOMEN (14 TO 24) PLANNING TO WORK AT AGE 35

Race	1968	1970
Black	47%	59%
White	27	42

Source: "Years for Decision," vol. 3 (Columbus: The Ohio State University, Center for Human Resource Research, December 1973), p. 15.

Moreover, these revisions in plans are consistent with those currently exhibited by women in the 35- to 44-year age group, whose present participation rates are 61 percent and 51 percent for black and white women, respectively.

The study attributes women's plans for increased work to their reduced childbearing expectations and their own changing concept of the role of women. Since the young women who were attending school during the period of the survey exhibited the greatest change in plans concerning work, educational influences seem to have played a significant role in forming family and work goals.

Occupational aspirations of this same group of women are even more indicative of an increasing commitment to market careers. About three-fourths of the white and two-thirds of the black women indicated preferences for white-collar occupations, with fully half of the white-collar aspirants looking forward to work in professional, technical, or managerial jobs. These goals appear overly optimistic when compared with the performance of women in the 30- to 44-year age group who were surveyed in a similar longitudinal study. In 1967, only 23 percent of the white and less than 14 percent of the black women who were then 35 to 39 years of age and were employed as wage and salary workers were in professional or managerial positions. . . .

Some of the strongest evidence of the commitment of women to market work has emerged from the survey of women aged 30 to 44. Among the women in this age group, 60 percent of the white and 67 percent of the black workers reported that they would continue to work even if they could live comfortably without their earnings. The survey's findings are reinforced by the fact that the same women displayed considerable attachment to their current jobs; 40 percent of the white and 25 percent of the black respondents indicated that they would not change jobs even for a considerable wage increase. While this may reflect the women's perceptions of the limited jobs available to them, the results nevertheless illustrate the extent to which women have made permanent job commitments. And although most women are found in the lower paying, lower status jobs, they nevertheless express a surprising degree of satisfaction in the jobs held. Over two-thirds of white women and nearly three-fifths of black women reported that they liked their jobs "very much." Whether younger women entering the work force with higher levels of education and aspirations will be similarly content with lower level jobs is uncertain, however.

A married woman's perception of her husband's attitude toward her working is also an important determinant of her labor market decision. White women who reported their husbands' attitudes as favorable were in the labor force nearly four times as long, according to the 1967 survey, as those who reported unfavorable attitudes. For black women, the work period was over one and one-half times as long. It is not clear whether husbands' attitudes are becoming more supportive of female work force participation, but it is clear that wives' commitment to work is becoming more and more like that of their spouses.

One recent study of job satisfaction reports that no significant sex-related difference in overall job satisfaction was found in national surveys conducted during the 1962–73 period. Furthermore, even though women were found to be more concerned with the social and psychological aspects of their jobs, men and women were equally dissatisfied with intellectually undemanding jobs. Finally, just as men work for a living, women, too, work for much more than "pin money." Two out of five working women are economically independent, and in many poorer families, women provided the bulk of the family income.

Educational Changes. In the past, the relatively small proportion of women continuing through college and graduate training was predictable, given the existence of social mores that downgraded feminine education and the lack of suitable job opportunities for educated women. Perception of this lower likely return on investment in human capital discouraged investments in higher education by women and thereby helped to create a chain of factors that maintained the stereotyped occupational distribution of women workers. Enlarged career opportunities and changing attitudes show that this chain may be weakening, however. In recent years, about 70 percent of the girls aged 14 to 17 years expected postsecondary education, while only 29 percent of those aged 20 to 24 and 26 percent of those aged 25 to 29 actually had one or more years of such education. Again, the aspirations of today's 14- to 17-year-olds may be unrealistically high. But they demonstrate an attitude that brings a new perspective to women's future work force participation.

More women than men workers have completed high school, but only three-fourths as many women as men have gone on to college. Furthermore, in 1971, while women earned 42 percent of all bachelor's degrees and 40 percent of all master's degrees, they gained only 14 percent of the doctorates. But, while graduate enrollments are currently falling (for a total decline of 9 percent since 1969), the proportion of women in graduate school is rising. By 1974, the distribution of the female work force in the United States by educational attainment was approaching that of the male, with more women continuing past high school [see table on page 98].

Despite these trends in the education of women, many educational traditions reinforce the stereotyping of male-female job roles. In vocational and technical secondary school courses, for example, girls are

EDUCATIONAL ATTAINMENT OF THE LABOR FORCE, 1974

Level of Education	Percent Distribution	
	Women	Men
Total	100.0	100.0
College: 4 or more years	12.8	16.4
1 to 3 years	15.2	14.9
High school: 4 years	44.2	36.0
1 to 3 years	18.1	18.0
Elementary: 8 years or less	9.7	14.7

Source: B. J. McEaddy, "Educational Attainment of Workers, March 1974," *Monthly Labor Review*, February 1975, p. 66.

concentrated in business and comercial courses (which are 79 percent female), and in health courses (95 percent female), while boys form a vast majority (98 percent) of those taking technical, industrial, and trade subjects.

One of the most significant changes in recent years has been the narrowing of the gap between the educational attainment of white and black women. In just two decades, the median number of school years completed by black women rose from 8.1 in 1952 to 12.3 in 1974, cutting the difference in educational attainment levels of white and black women from 4.0 years to 0.2 year.

PART TWO

The Subjection of Women

That the principle which regulates the existing social relations between the two sexes—the legal subordination of one sex to the other—is wrong in itself, and
now one of the chief hindrances to human improvement; and that it ought to be replaced by a principle
of perfect equality, admitting no power or privilege
on the one side, nor disability on the other.

John Stuart Mill

The first division of labour is that between man and
woman for child-breeding ... the first class antagonism which appears in history coincides with the development of the antagonism between man and
woman in individual marriage, and the first class oppression with that of the female sex by the male. [In-
dividual marriage] is the cell of civilized society, in
which we can already study the nature of the antagonisms and contradictions which develop fully in the
latter.

Frederick Engels

"Why can't a woman be more like a man. . . ?"

Professor Henry Higgins

Even women and men who think that *man* is not the appropriate model
for *woman* seriously ask: "Why are women and men so different?" The

differences between the lives of each sex seem obvious and numerous. Cliches about the differences abound. Women are passive and dependent, while men are assertive and independent. Women stay home to do husband care, child care, and house care, while men leave the household to earn income. Women who do hold jobs consider these secondary to their main work as wives and mothers. Women's activities outside the home are in "cultural" and, therefore, relatively less important activities, while men attend to the "serious" activities of running the society. Men become great poets, painters, writers, statesmen, inventors, and warriors. Few women are among the "greats" noted by historians, although recently more women of excellence have been recognized. Men are considered attractive and interesting late into life, so a man with a much younger wife is admired and envied. Women, as they grow older, are considered decreasingly attractive and interesting as sexual partners and companions, so a woman with a much younger man is an object of ridicule.

A Sociological Perspective

Introduction   Nona Glazer

Much of the serious sociological discussion of the differences between the sexes revolves around (1) *sex differences;* (2) *gender roles;* (3) *the minority status of women;* and (4) *the caste and class statuses of women.*[1] The different focuses can be summarized as follows: (1) *sex differences* research, which has been done mainly by psychologists, compares women and men on emotive and cognitive traits; (2) *gender role* research, which derives its concepts from the perspectives of social scientists such as Mead, Znaniecki, Parsons, and Merton, focuses on roles, role models, and role conflict; (3) *minority group* perspective, which follows the pioneer work of Wirth and others as developed by Myrdal and Hacker, examines discrimination, prejudice, and marginality; and (4) the *politics of caste and class,* which starts from a minority group perspective but also is rooted intellectually in the works of Engels (1884), Mill (1869), Gilman (1898),[2] de Beauvoir (1951), and the more recent work of Rossi (1964), Millett (1970), Firestone (1970), and Mitchell (1971).[3] Hochschild contrasts these approaches:

[1] Arlie Russell Hochschild, "A Review of Sex Role Research." *American Journal of Sociology* 78(January 1973):1011–1029. Other reviews of the sex role literature include Joan Huber, "Sociology." *Signs: Journal of Women in Culture and Society* 1(Spring 1976):685–698, which considers research published from September 1973 to September 1975 in English-language journals. Huber considers the new trends in research rather than concentrating on diverse conceptual approaches. Jean Lipman-Blumen and Ann R. Tickamyer, "Sex Roles in Transition: A Ten-Year Review." *Annual Review of Sociology* 1(1975):296–337, follows in broad terms Hochschild's classification and adds an examination of and suggestions for strategies for research. See also Helena Znaniecki Lopata, "Sociology." *Signs: Journal of Women in Culture and Society* 2(Autumn 1976):165–176.

[2] The title of this reader is an homage to Charlotte Perkins Gilman's *The Man-Made World: Or, Our Androcentric Culture* (1911; reprint ed., New York: Johnson Reprint, 1971).

[3] Frederick Engels, *Origin of the Family, Private Property, and the State,* edited by Eleanor B. Leacock (New York: International Publishers, 1972; first published in 1884); John Stuart Mill, *The*

Each puts a different construction on the behavior of the two sexes; what to type 1 is a feminine trait such as passivity is to type 2 a role element, to type 3 is a minority group characteristic, and to type 4 is a response to powerlessness. Social change might also look somewhat different to each perspective; differences disappear, deviance becomes normal, the minority group assimilates, or power is equalized.[4]

In addition to the distinctions Hochschild notes, there is another important difference that cuts across the types. What is considered to be the major (though not sole) source of sex inequality differs: the *sex differences* and *gender roles* approaches share an emphasis on understanding factors that characterize individuals. These factors may be inherent to each sex or acquired by individuals in the course of socialization. The *minority group* and *caste/class* approaches share an emphasis on factors that are external to individuals, a concern with the structure of social institutions and with the impact of historical events.

For the *sex differences* and *gender roles* approaches, the main concern is to understand the processes of socialization, the content of roles, and closely related phenomena. Hence, theory and research efforts are directed to:

1. Discerning the emotional and cognitive traits of each sex (e.g., female passivity, male assertiveness, sex-linked spatial abilities, etc.)
2. Discovering the main sources (e.g., parents, peers, etc.) and secondary sources (e.g., advertisements, employers, teachers, textbooks, etc.) of socialization
3. Describing how the content of gender roles restricts the capabilities of individual women[5] so that females appear to lack the characteristics necessary for achieving sex equality (e.g., being "dumb" about math means exclusion from training for many high-status and well-paid jobs; learning that being a wife-mother is more "feminine" than being a writer or lawyer discourages women from working hard in these jobs)
4. Exposing the ideology supporting the sexual hierarchy (e.g., exploding such beliefs as "women think with their ovaries," "a wife

Subjection of Women (Boston: M.I.T. Press, 1970; first published in 1869); Gilman, *Man-Made World* (first published in 1898); Simon de Beauvoir, *The Second Sex* (New York: Knopf, 1953); Alice Rossi, "Equality Between the Sexes: An Immodest Proposal." *Daedalus* 93(Spring 1964):607–652; Kate Millett, *Sexual Politics* (Garden City, N.Y.: Doubleday, 1970); Juliet Mitchell, *Women's Estate* (New York: Pantheon Books, 1972). The Rossi article is the basis for the introductory comments to Part Five. Excerpts from Frederick Engels, Helen Mayer Hacker, and Juliet Mitchell are among the selections following these introductory comments.

[4]Hochschild, "Review of Sex Role Research," p. 1013.

[5]Men's capabilities, too, are restricted by socialization; e.g., men may refrain from expressing emotions, seeing this as "unmasculine" behavior.

with a career—not just a job—threatens family solidarity," "children need round-the-clock mothering"—but not fathering—etc.) Socialization, as well as inherent differences, has been used to explain the persistence of sex inequality. It is argued that women do not have the skills, self-concepts, symbol systems, etc. that would enable them to carry out roles that have been, until recently, the prerogative of men. And, men have been so socialized that they, too, have enormous difficulty behaving in "nontraditional" ways. In this view, the persistence of beliefs and behaviors, learned in the early years of childhood and reinforced by socialization in the schools, by peers and the mass media, etc., make it difficult if not impossible to change the behavior of adults easily and drastically.

That the basic (though by no means only) avenue of social change is to alter the socialization experiences of people, especially those of children, would seem to follow. Certainly social policy concerned with eliminating sexism from children's textbooks and storybooks, from advertising, and from gynecological textbooks, and with changing language to include women in descriptions of the people are compatible with a belief in the importance of social learning. Legislation supporting women's access to higher education, to equal pay for equal work, to reproductive control, and similar goals may also be supported but viewed as effective only when people's attitudes and beliefs can be changed. However, those who believe that social changes can only be slow because people's attitudes must change *before* legislation can be enacted (or, if enacted, can be effective) have accepted, far more than appears to be reasonable, a belief in the tenacity of socialization and in the relative importance of characteristics of individuals compared with the organization of society.[6] Beliefs, attitudes, and feelings are seen as taking precedence over structural factors, so that women's lack of participation in areas of our society or their low rewards (e.g., wages) are interpreted as being a result, mainly, of women's own internal characteristics (even though the origins of these characteristics may lie in early childhood experiences, schooling, etc.).

In the *minority group* and *caste/class* approaches, the main concern is to understand the organization of social institutions, including the concentration of power, the legal system, organizational barriers, and other factors external to individuals that generate and maintain the hierarchical relationship between the sexes.[7] Socialization, while given attention, is considered secondary to these organizational factors.

---

[6]See Dennis A. Wrong, "The Oversocialized Conception of Man (sic) in Modern Sociology." *American Sociological Review* 26(April 1961):183–199.

[7]Ernestine Friedl, *Women and Men: An Anthropologist's View* (New York: Holt, Rinehart and Winston, 1975).

Theory and research efforts are thus directed to:

1. Finding the sources of power (e.g., the importance of participation in subsistence; the legal basis for the power of women compared with the manipulative base;[8] etc.)
2. Locating the structural barriers to women's full participation in the economy and in political activities (e.g., women's use as a cheap reserve labor pool;[9] the impact of contraceptive control and the right to abortion; etc.)
3. Seeing the uses of ideology to legitimatize the subordination of women and prevent their developing an awareness of their oppression
4. Exposing the monopoly over what is taken seriously and what is conveyed to the public (e.g., the presentation and dissemination through science, literature, art, song, the electronic media, etc. of portraits of women that treat them as inadequate in the world outside the home, as sex objects for men, as responsible for children, etc.)

Social policy guided by this perspective is directed toward reorganizing structures that are seen as barriers to sex equality. Hence, establishing the legal equality of the sexes would be a beginning, after which structures must be changed to make formal equality into actual equality. For example, low-cost or free twenty-four-hour-a-day child care is a prerequisite to women's access to jobs, training, and equal pay with men. Full employment would also appear to be mandatory, since unemployment affects women more than men in both capitalist and socialist systems.

READINGS

The first set of articles in Part Two of this reader has been chosen for their relevance to the four approaches noted by Hochschild. Many of the articles in other parts of the book have been selected, in contrast, because they explore structural rather than social psychological factors; such a selection is intended to draw the reader's attention to the comparatively neglected sociological concern with structural factors. This seems important as a complement to the social psychological analyses that have dominated sociological thinking (as well as American political and social ideologies). But, certainly, both social psychological and structural analyses are necessary for a complete picture of society. Un-

[8]Carolyn J. Matthiasson (ed.), *Many Sisters: Women in Cross-Cultural Perspective* (New York: Free Press, 1974).
[9]See Betty MacMorran Gray's article in Part Three.

fortunately, sociologists have not connected successfully the different factors; thus it is not possible to present in this reader a theory that integrates them. (Dorothy Smith, whose selection is presented in Part One, demonstrates how one would make such a blending, moving from biographies and autobiographies of women to highly technical questions about the political economy. However, other such synthetic work *for* women still must be done.)

Sex Differences. A recurring debate in social science is the nature vs. nurture controversy. As applied to women's social position, this debate raises two questions: One, in what ways are the sexes different from each other? Two, how much of the difference—and the apparent resulting social inequalities—can be explained by biological differences? Today, few social scientists would consider the issue to be a question of nature vs. nurture, preferring to ask about the relative impact of inherent factors and social factors, and the interaction between the two. Reasoning about these factors moves in two directions. First, some social scientists reason from data collected about individuals (by sex) to social behavior. After observing these individual sex differences, they then raise the question of how these differences can explain women's social position, beliefs, social roles, etc., compared with men's. For example, Matina Horner's widely quoted (though now suspect) findings about sex differences in the "motive to avoid success" have been used to explain why women do not succeed in challenging situations.[10] Second, some social scientists reason in the other direction, from data collected about sex differences in social behavior to supposed inherent biological differences. These social scientists argue that the sex differences in social roles, beliefs, attitudes, etc., are due to basic biological differences between women and men. Hence, Tiger and Shepher explain the change from communal child rearing to family-centered child rearing on some Israeli kibbutzim as a response by women to a biological pull to children and child-care jobs and away from men's work and the civic responsibilities of running the kibbutz. Presumably the same biological character then keeps women away from such activities long after the years of rearing their own children are past.[11]

---

[10]Matina S. Horner, "Toward an Understanding of Achievement-Related Conflicts in Women," and Lois Wladis Hoffman, "Fear of Success in Males and Females: 1965 and 1971," in Martha T. Shuch Mednick, Sandra Schwartz Tangri, and Lois Wladis Hoffman (eds.), *Women and Achievement* (New York: Wiley, 1975), pp. 206–220 and pp. 221–230, respectively.

[11]Lionel Tiger and Joseph Shepher, *Women in the Kibbutz* (New York: Harcourt Brace Jovanovich, 1975), pp. 272–273. Tiger and Shepher's work is an example of what I would call "biologizing and psychologizing" social structure out of existence: e.g., social change must be understood in terms of individual characteristics such as motivation rather than also being a product of processes of change in social structural factors themselves. See the discussion of women "who made their own decisions" on page 275.

Before it is possible to argue from studies of sex differences to an explanation of societal differences, it is necessary to know what the differences are. The most exhaustive examination of the literature on sex differences is the work of Eleanor Maccoby and Carol Jacklin who review some fourteen hundred research studies published between 1967 and the spring of 1973, including studies on animals other than humans. They find no evidence to support beliefs about sex differences in sociability and suggestibility, self-esteem levels, rote learning and simple repetitive task performance, higher level cognitive processing, the inhibition of learned responses, analytic ability, achievement motivation, and auditory and visual abilities.[12] Among the beliefs about sex differences that the authors found to be "fairly well established" were: girls have greater verbal ability than boys; boys have greater visual-spatial ability than girls; after the age of twelve or thirteen, boys have greater math ability than girls; and boys are more physically and verbally aggressive than girls.[13] Finally, Maccoby and Jacklin conclude that certain supposed sex differences are still open questions: tactile sensitivity; fear, timidity, and anxiety; activity level; competitiveness; dominance, compliance; and nurturance and "maternal" behavior.[14]

The selection by David Tresemer considers the methodology of studies of sex differences directly, pointing out the importance of the assumptions that social scientists make about the nature of gender roles for how they go about constructing measuring devices and analyzing their results. He considers the implications of decisions that researchers make about key concepts, and the implications of the scope of study on the probability of finding a difference. He notes a difference between a social as distinct from a statistical meaning of a sex difference and urges cautiousness in cumulating measures when searching for sex differences. Tresemer then turns to the problem of the internalization of norms, values, beliefs, etc., distinguishing between public behavior and private acceptance, and suggesting that behavioral conformity does not necessarily indicate psychological commitment. Tresemer concludes by discussing alternative modes of gender-role changes, noting the problems to be found in men's as well as women's traditional roles compared with the strengths in androgynous roles.

Tresemer's article can be read as a critique both of those who have reported widespread and frequently observed differences between the sexes (based on social science research) and of those who argue that observed differences result from some profound biological differences

---

[12]Eleanor E. Maccoby and Carol N. Jacklin, *The Psychology of Sex Differences* (Stanford, Calif.: Stanford University Press, 1974), pp. 349–350.

[13]Maccoby and Jacklin, *Psychology of Sex Differences*, pp. 351–352.

[14]Maccoby and Jacklin, *Psychology of Sex Differences*, pp. 352–355.

between sexes. If Tresemer's methodological criticisms are reasonable, then we must examine studies of sex differences carefully for biases— e.g., ignoring the continuous nature of social and psychological as well as biological characteristics; and overstating the social meaning of small statistical differences while disregarding the greater variations within as compared with between the sexes. Furthermore, the attempt to seek biological roots for observed social differences seems tenuous if the variability of biology is accepted. Tresemer's criticisms should not lead, as the author himself notes, to rejecting the existence of *any* biological differences between the sexes, for such do exist. However, the social significance of these differences, which are yet to be documented, must be carefully considered.

Gender Roles. Considerable efforts by theorists and researchers have been directed to the socialization of gender roles, the sources of socialization, and the content and impact of gender roles on women.[15] First, a caution: while there is an abundance of materials on socialization, most studies have been of white, middle-class, urban children, and conclusions cannot be generalized to black Americans, Chicanos, rural children, etc. Aware of this limitation, Maccoby and Jacklin conclude after their survey of hundreds of recent studies that there is a remarkable uniformity in the socialization of the sexes: parents treat both boys and girls similarly. For example, parents do not appear to be more permissive toward boys' aggressive behavior than toward girls' according to available evidence; however, parents more strongly discourage their sons from doing girls' activities than they do their daughters from doing boys' activities. Also, adults appear to treat boys as if they were more interesting than girls—and Maccoby and Jacklin suggest boys may *be* more interesting because they are more active. Parents do not, however, treat sexuality, autonomy, and dependency differently in each sex.[16]

In addition to content, social scientists have examined the many

---

[15]Probably the majority of sociological efforts have been directed to theory and research within a role approach. For examples among recent publications, see the new journals *Sex Roles; Signs: A Journal of Women in Culture and Society;* and *Feminist Studies.* See also many of the fine articles that appear in Marcia Millman and Rosabeth Moss Kanter (eds.), *Another Voice* (Garden City, N.Y.: Doubleday, 1975); and in Jo Freeman (ed.), *Women: A Feminist Perspective* (Palo Alto, Calif.: Mayfield Publishing, 1975). Ann Oakley *The Sociology of Housework* (New York: Pantheon Books, 1974), applies a role perspective to this specific topic. See also the reviews of the sex role literature referred to in Part One; and recent bibliographies, such as Naomi Lynn, Ann Matasar, Marie Rosenberg, *Research Guide in Women's Studies* (Morristown, N.J.: General Learning Press, 1974); Helen S. Astin, Allison Parelman, Ann Fisher, *Sex Roles: A Research Bibliography* (Washington, D.C.: U.S. Government Printing Office, DHEW Publication no. (ADM) 75–166); Marie Barovic Rosenberg and Len V. Bergstron, *Women and Society: A Critical Review of the Literature with a Selected Annotated Bibliography* (Beverly Hills, Calif.: Sage Publications, 1975). While these are not concerned exclusively with gender role research, since this approach is the major one these are excellent source materials.

[16]Maccoby and Jacklin, *Psychology of Sex Differences,* pp. 338–342.

sources of gender role socialization. Children's textbooks, the mass media, advertising, as well as school teachers, parents, and peers have been recognized as agents of socialization that portray males as assertive, active, adventurous, etc., and females as passive, submissive, fearful, nurturing, etc. Also there are, of course, agents of socialization that affect people throughout their lives: employers, new spouses, friends and relatives as well as secondary contacts who play such a role,[17] often by expecting each sex to conform to stereotyped models.

What is the content of social roles assigned to females? Girls are taught to expect to grow up to be wives and mothers and, in the course of growing up, are taught some of the skills associated with these roles. Girls are discouraged from thinking of themselves as having a career (although they may expect to have a job) when they are adults. Furthermore, girls are expected to be courteous, submissive, gentle, kind, adaptable, etc. They are socialized to expect to find their main satisfaction in helping others, in supporting their husbands' and children's search for personal fulfillment while sacrificing their own needs for those of their families.[18]

Research on the *impact* of gender roles on women considers a wide array of topics. The findings are distressing: marriage appears to be better for men than women (while singleness appears to be better for women than men);[19] depression in middle-aged women has been connected to role loss after confinement to traditional roles;[20] the "maternal role" may be ideal for neither mothers nor children.[21] The traditional model of female sexuality contradicts the source of female sexual responsiveness and female orgasmic potential,[22] and may carry

---

[17]See Lenore J. Weitzman, Deborah Eifler, Elizabeth Hokado, and Catherine Ross, "Sex Role Socialization in Picture Books for Pre-school Children," mimeographed (Davis, Calif.: Lenore J. Weitzman, University of California at Davis, 1971); *Women and Film* 1, nos. 5, 6 (1974); Textbook Study Group, "Sex Role Stereotyping in Ontario Primary Readers," (York, Ont.: Regional Municipality of York, 1972); Alleen Pace Nilsen, "Women in Children's Literature," *College English*, 32(May 1971):918–926. For adult socialization experiences, see eight articles on professions in Chapter 5 in Athena Theodore (ed.), *The Professional Woman* (Cambridge, Mass.: Schenkman, 1971); see also Helena Z. Lopata, *Occupation: Housewife* (New York: Oxford University Press, 1971), pp. 77–88, 138–165, 187–192; Ann Oakley, *The Sociology of Housework* (New York: Random House, 1974), pp. 113–134.

[18]See Wendy Edmond and Suzie Fleming, *All Work and No Pay, Women, Housework and the Wages Due* (London: Falling Wall Press, 1975).

[19]Jessie Bernard, *The Future of Marriage* (New York: World Publishing, 1972), pp. 15–20, 28–33; Jessie Bernard , "The Paradox of the Happy Marriage," in Vivian Gornick and Barbara K. Moran (eds.), *Woman in Sexist Society* (New York: Basic Books, 1971), pp. 145–162.

[20]Pauline B. Bart, "Depression in Middle-Aged Women," in Gornick and Moran, *Women in Sexist Society*, pp. 163–186.

[21]Rochelle Paul Wortis, "The Acceptance of the Concept of the Maternal Role by Behavioral Scientists: Its Effects on Women," *The American Journal of Orthopsychiatry* 41, no. 5(1971):733–746; reprinted in Arlene Skolnick and Jerome H. Skolnick (eds.), *Intimacy, Family and Society* (Boston: Little, Brown, 1974), pp. 360–376.

[22]See William H. Masters and Virginia E. Johnson, *Human Sexual Response* (Boston: Little, Brown, 1966).

demeaning responsibilities that are unrelated to love between two equals.[23]

The selection by Judith K. Brown considers the issue of the *content* of gender roles. A basic issue about the assignment of roles by sex has to do with the origins of the division of labor and role differentiation in general (a topic that will be examined in more detail in Part Three).[24] The smaller average size of women compared with men, women's frequent pregnancies (before adequate contraceptive practices), their tendency to be anemic because of menstrual bleeding, the nursing of children, and the fatigue associated with all of these biological functions have been cited as responsible for women's exclusion from the economy (and their subordination in society).[25] Brown argues, however, that women's participation in the economy does not depend on various physiological and biological factors but on the social assignment to women of the responsibilities for child care. (Why women are inevitably assigned to child care, although not necessarily having exclusive responsibility for it, is another question.) It then follows that women's participation in the economy is related to how compatible child care is with the main economic activity of the society. In societies where it is possible to take children "to work," where children are not put in danger by the work tasks, and where the tasks do not require steady attention so that children's demands would interrupt the flow of work, women participate in the economy in important ways. Obviously, in contemporary industrial societies, women with children can participate in the economy only to the extent that alternative child caretakers are available.

Brown's analysis also has implications for other aspects of gender roles. Women's skills at repetitive tasks, their ability to do a series of tasks and yet cope with interruptions, their lack of involvement in large-scale long-term projects—these characteristics of women, if accurate, may be explained by the child-care tasks assigned to women, tasks that are conducive to such models of working. We need not look for innate feminine lacks in intellect and character; rather we should look to the effects of child care.

Minority Group Status. In *An American Dilemma,* Gunnar Myrdal suggests that the position of women in American society is in many ways

---

[23]Robert Seidenberg, "Is Sex Without Sexism Possible?" in Leonard Gross (ed.), *Sexual Behavior* (New York: Spectrum, 1974), pp. 59–68; includes commentary by Judith M. Bardwick, David G. Rice, Constantina Safilios-Rothschild, and Jessie Bernard.

[24]See especially the section in Part Three on gender role differences, which includes selections by Talcott Parsons, Alan Craddock, and William D. Crano and Joel Aronoff, and the selection by economist Robert Gubbels in the section on the job market.

[25]Clarice Stasz Stoll, *Female and Male* (Dubuque, Ia.: Wm. C. Brown, 1974), pp. 32–36 discusses myths about female physiology and biology.

comparable to that of black Americans. A minority group, to Myrdal, is not a proportion but a condition: it is composed of people who are considered inferior because of their membership in a social category, so that they are denied rights accorded to others and are held in low esteem. A minority group may be any proportion of a population—5 percent, as the Jews are in the United States, or 70 percent, as the Bantus are in the Union of South Africa. Since *minority group* is a concept, not an empirical entity, the question is not whether women are "really" a minority group but whether the concept can be applied to women without violating the definition, and whether by so doing we gain some understanding of women's condition.

The definition as developed by Louis Wirth (as Helen Hacker notes in her selection that follows these comments) includes self-perception: minority group members "regard themselves as objects of collective discrimination." Yet we know that awareness and objective condition need not go together. People may have certain objective characteristics for a considerable period of time before they become aware of their position. Furthermore, such awareness may fluctuate over time, as in the case of women and the poor, workers and peasants, Jews and Catholics, all of whom may intermittently form organizations to change their status only to find their problems pushed into obscurity as other issues become critical. Given this fluctuation, we would have to say that women were a minority group in the 1840s, again in the 1890s, again in the years before and briefly after World War I, and then again in the mid-1960s. Hence, awareness seems most adequately considered as a question: *When*, and under *what* conditions, do members of a minority group become aware of their plight, a plight that has objective characteristics?

Helen Hacker applies parts of minority group theory to the condition of women in the United States. She contrasts *sexism* (though that term antedates her essay) with *racism* to clarify the meaning of the treatment of women, and the social, psychological, and economic experiences they have. She is particularly careful to consider the husband-wife relationship, whose social intimacy might, at first glance, contradict the usual taboo against familial intimacy between minority and majority group persons. Her application of the theory to women explains some apparent contradictions in the behaviors of women and men as well as accounts for woman's inability to use her "opportunities," her position in the economy and her low earnings, her lack of self-esteem, and her apparent lack of resentment against men for her social condition, whether she remains in "woman's place" or passes over into a "man's world."

The application of minority group theories to women suggests other questions that might be asked. Many characteristics of the recent civil rights movement and society's reactions could also be usefully analyzed by using other theories of minority group relations. In addition, the question of what might happen to the women's movement (both the rights and liberation sections) if, for example, the United States continues its severe economic crisis or experiences further political repression or a war, might be suggested by studying similar problems encountered by minority groups, including minorities other than blacks.

The minority group approach has limits. It starts with the notion of persons experiencing a particular status because of a perceived individual characteristic (e.g., race, sex, religion). It then investigates how that status influences the social experience—life chances, self-concept, language and gestures, patterns of social interactions, etc. However, it neglects, relatively, issues related to how discrimination fits into the patterns of societal organization. The emphasis is on the "victim" members of a minority group, and little attention goes to the "victimizers." Hence, women's reactions to being "put down" by men—and by other women—because of their sex are considerably more understood than men's beliefs in women's inferiority, their motivations for putting women down, and their psychological and social reactions when discrimination is challenged, and their covert and overt attempts to maintain the subordinate position of women.

Caste/Class Status. The caste and class approaches are the broadest in the study of the social condition of women. They consider women's situation at the macrosociological level and draw together descriptions of a wide variety of social institutions—the family, the political economy, sexuality, production—in order to develop an integrated theory. The *caste* approach shares with the minority group approach the assumption that as a social type women occupy a peculiar position in society (much like black Americans). It departs from minority group theory by elaborating dimensions of women's status and relating these to power in its various forms, especially political and economic power.[26] A wide variety of attributes have been considered to indicate that women are a caste: the general psychological power of patriarchy over women,[27] a shared "women's language" (special kinds of grammars, words, inflections),[28] a legal status different from men's, and close to that of dependent children,[29] women's consignment to housework and child care, with attendant restrictions of their participation in the political economy.[30]

The *class* approach differs from the caste approach by conceptualiz-

[26]Carol Andreas, *Sex and Caste in America* (Englewood Cliffs, N.J.: Prentice-Hall, 1971).

[27]Shulamith Firestone, *The Dialectic of Sex* (New York: Morrow, 1970).

[28]Robin Lakoff, *Language and Woman's Place* (New York: Harper & Row, 1975).

[29]Jo Freeman, "The Legal Basis of the Sexual Caste System," *Valparaiso University Law Review*, 5, no. 2, symposium issue (1971):203–236.

[30]Nona Glazer, "Housewifery and the Caste Status of American Women." Paper presented at the annual meeting of the American Sociological Association, Sept. 1, 1976, New York City.

ing the problems of women to be rooted in the organization of the political economy. It considers women's social position to be not only a function of her sex status but also the result of the general economic exploitation in society to which women (especially black women in American society) fall victim. Capitalism is an economic system organized for the maximization of profit by those who control capital, a maximization that eliminates the possibility of meeting many other human needs. Hence women are a reserve labor force, moving in and out of jobs to suit the demands of employers. Women's work in the home is invisible, unpaid, and unrewarded by financial support provided by pensions, medical care, vacations, etc. Furthermore, exclusion from well-paid work keeps women locked into patriarchal dependency, and may make men accept conditions of work—meaningless work, low wages, lack of participation in planning, concentration of wealth, etc.— rather than seek alternatives because they realize how much the economic well-being of their families depends on them.

The three articles in this section are concerned with women in a class system, although the last also draws upon ideas of women as a caste, placing them in a special location within the class system. The first selection is an excerpt from Frederick Engels' *The Origins of the Family, Private Property and the State*, probably the single most influential theory about the origin of women's subordination to men. His theory serves as a base both for many contemporary analyses and for demands for social changes. In these excerpts, Engels considers the relationship between the development of private property, changes in the structure of the family, and the social position of women. He develops a structural and materialist interpretation to explain the condition of women, in contrast to the ideas of his day that explained her subordination as a natural phenomenon (she *was* inferior), or as the will of God, or as one part of an evolutionary process that placed the bourgeois family at the pinnacle. To Engels, the final stage of evolution—for he, like many of his contemporaries, was an evolutionist—is the establishment of socialism, with its subsequent disappearance of the family and the consequential freeing of women. Obviously, his conclusions about the future have not been widely supported, for the disappearance of private ownership of the means of production in certain societies has not eliminated the subordination of women; however, it indeed alleviates many aspects of their condition and narrows some of the gaps between the general social conditions of women and men.

Engels' influence makes it important to assess the accuracy of his analysis, especially in relation to the findings and theories of contemporary anthropology. In the next reading, Kathleen Gough presents a detailed critique of Engels on the evolution of the family. Gough is critical of many of Engels' conclusions and indicates some of the limitations of his data, as well as areas of importance that he neglects in his study. Nevertheless, she concludes that the general trend of his argument is correct, and she stresses that economic changes appear to be critical to any improvement in the status of women.

The final reading is a brief excerpt from a much longer and detailed analysis by Juliet Mitchell. Mitchell criticizes socialist theory for its failure to analyze women apart from other oppressed peoples; the theory has been limited by its consideration of the problems of women within a social class framework. The position of women is considered a derivative of the existing economic system and automatically is presumed to cease being a problem with the eventual and inevitable establishment of socialism: specifically, women's social condition is analyzed as if the economy and the family were the only two structures in which women are located. Mitchell proposes a more complex differentiation of structures into production, reproduction, sexuality, and socialization. Her argument has several special merits. First, she discards the usually unexamined assumption that the family is a natural unit and, moreover, the only natural unit in which women must be analyzed, and she replaces it with a direct analysis of the functions of women. (Analytically, it would be as if slavery, as a natural context for the analysis of pre-Civil-War blacks, were discarded and replaced by a consideration of immediate structures—such as production, politics, etc.—in which blacks were located at that point in history.) Second, by freeing the interpretation of the condition of women from a simple economic determinism, Mitchell is able, without any difficulty, to incorporate some of the many recent findings of psychology, child development, and anthropology into her analysis. Finally, her views of these four interrelated structures suggest that many further studies, cross-cultural and interdisciplinary, should be conducted within nonfamilial as well as familial settings. Studies are needed of women living outside of marriage, in women's communes, in mixed sex communes, in group marriages, and in settings apart from any of these. Studies of varieties of sexuality—of men as well as women, of children as well as adults—are needed. The use of a theoretical framework that does not view the conjugal family system as a necessary basic social unit might encourage investigations of existing life-styles within American society, and in other countries. Such studies might find that some social innovations could be considered bona fide alternative social systems, in the process of emerging, rather than aberrant offshoots incorporating those women—and men, too—who presumably have "failed" at marriage and family living. Such forms might also incorporate those women who, given the excess of females in the society, would never have had a chance at conventional marriage.

Assumptions
About Gender Role

David E. Tresemer

The major misleading assumptions about gender roles are that observed differences between the sexes are reflected in biological sex differences, that differences between the sexes are more important than similarities, that the trait of masculinity-femininity is a bipolar, unidimensional, continuous, normally distributed variable that is highly important and consistently viewed, and that observed differentiation between the sexes at a societal level reflects deep personality differences in the expression of male and female principles. . . .

SEX AND GENDER

Classification by "sex" refers to the dichotomous distinction between male and female based on physiological characteristics; classification by "gender" refers to the psychological and cultural definitions of the dimensions "masculine" and "feminine," and only tends to a strictly dichotomous distinction between groups. When speaking of learned roles, the proper term is *gender role* (Stoller, 1968; Oakley, 1972; also, Holter, 1968; Sears, 1965; and Bernard, 1971). Despite the wealth of literature assuming that "sex" and "gender" are interchangeable, the primatologists persist in using the term *sex role* correctly to describe positions in intercourse. Thus there is every reason to regard most *sociological* uses of male-female differences as involving *gender role*.

Excerpted from "Assumptions Made About Gender Roles," by David E. Tresemer from the book *Another Voice*, edited by Marcia Millman and Rosabeth Moss Kanter. Copyright © 1975 by Sociological Inquiry. Reprinted by permission of Doubleday & Company, Inc.

The old argument between nature ("anatomy is destiny") and nurture (socialization) interpretations of sex differences at the root of this confusion is bypassed here by the suggestion of a *continuum* of sex differences as a heuristic device. At one end of this continuum are *biological sex characteristics,* which we shall call, in accord with developmental biology, primary and secondary. Primary sex characteristics include a penis for the male, a vagina and a womb for the female; secondary sex characteristics include certain differences in muscular and skeletal development, fat distribution, shape of pelvis, etc.

Then we begin to encounter tertiary, quartic, quintic, etc., effects of being a biological male or female. At the far end of the continuum, we encounter gender role, purely culturally determined. Examples of, say, quintic differences are use of facial cosmetics, preference for mathematics vs. literature, etc....

It is clear that neither nature nor nurture influences are alone responsible for differences between the sexes. The standard integration of the two lines of argument first affirms that all these views are right, and next suggests that genetic differences are *predispositions* for behavioral differences. Differences are expressed only if socialization and the social setting allow or encourage what is already there.

An interactionist view adds a new factor to biological and cultural influences: different experiences of different biological equipment. Thus differences in the perceptual predispositions of the two sexes—females showing hypersensitivity, responsiveness to whole configurations, and nonanalytic and nonrestructuring responsiveness to stimulus patterns, with males showing the reverse (Silverman, 1970)—lead to different experiences of the world and ultimately to different personalities. Similarly, some psychoanalytic writing suggests that the experience of having a penis, or a vagina, or a menstrual period, leads, dependent on relevant social factors, to different experiences of the world. This emphasis on the complexity of interaction between one's biological predispositions and one's experience, given focus and meaning in a field of social interaction, is preferable to a single explanation....

MODELS OF GENDER ROLES

Folk or common-sense models of the sexes have them as utterly dichotomous. Qualities of behavior that are found or thought to be found "on the average" for men or women—i.e., aspects of gender roles—become dichotomized by association. In terms of the previous section, this is an exaggeration of the basic dichotomy assumed to be God-given into all social and psychic areas. It is a profound confusion of the symbolic use of metaphor as an aid in describing the "active" and "passive" elements in all of us and the literal facts of real differences between biological males and females.

For simplicity in the description of personality, social scientists accept and perpetuate these folk models: biological males are described as aggressive, independent, and so on, females as nonaggressive, dependent, etc....

Extent of Differences. Just how great are these differences? Though there are many summaries of sex differences (e.g. Terman & Tyler, 1954; Garai & Schenfield, 1968; Bardwick, 1971; Sherman, 1971), it is necessary to go back to the original sources of data to find out how exaggerated the picture is.

Most rare are studies of actual behavior (excluding behavior on a paper-and-pencil test) that report enough data to assess the extent of differences between the sexes. Sutton-Smith and Rosenberg (1973) report a reanalysis of the Berkeley Guidance Study, examining the yearly ratings of 35 categories of behavior for each of 57 females and 58 males from the ages of 4 through 16. Of 442 tests of male-female differences, 31 (or 7 percent) achieved the 5 percent level of significance. This is hardly greater than the number of findings that would be expected by chance. For the Fels Institute longitudinal study, Kagan and Moss (1962) found minimal differences between means and variances for many behavioral observations made from ages 0 to 24; this was also true for observations of young infants (Kagan, 1971).[1] ...

Differences between the sexes—in behavior or belief—do not either exist or not exist. There is a whole range of effect sizes, some of crucial and some of minor importance. By including such information, future investigators could show the relative size of a sex difference in relationship to other sorts of differences between the sexes. Secondary analysis of the actual data from oft-cited studies that purport to show significant sex differences would put these differences into perspective....

Further, using methods for combining results from several studies, we may begin to create a continuum of lesser to greater effect sizes for primary, secondary, tertiary, and so on effects of biological sex differences and cultural gender differentiation, as alluded to earlier....

Measuring Masculinity and Femininity. Despite considerable overlap between the sexes, beliefs are pervasive among social scientists

---

[1]A large number of variables increases the possibility of Type I error, or the chance that we could accept as an important difference a variable that is "really" not important. A study employing 200 variables and using the 5 percent level of statistical significance should produce ten significant findings by chance alone. Only replication can give support for a "real" vs. an accidental finding. For this reason, the findings of studies using hundreds or even thousands of variables (as in Terman & Miles, 1936) should be treated with caution.

that sex differences are strong and do exist. A great deal of effort has gone toward developing measures of the psychological *traits* of masculinity and femininity, using biological sex as the discriminating criterion. Thus a questionnaire item that is endorsed by males significantly more than by females is thought to characterize "masculinity." . . . Confusion about what empirical differentiation between biological males and females means, as well as highly unique methods for deriving a scale for a general trait, seem not to have slowed down usage of these scales. For example, the well-known MMPI MF scale was based on an intensive study of 17 young men seeking therapy for homosexual problems, and who showed evidence, such as mannerisms and voice pattern, of a tendency to "sexual inversion." Test items were retained that differentiated the inverts and 108 female airline workers from 117 servicemen during World War II (cf. Sanford, 1966). . . . The underlying assumptions of the models, as well as the scales devised to measure them, are that *masculinity-femininity is a bipolar, unidimensional, continuous, normally distributed variable that is highly important and consistently viewed within the sampled population.*

Let us review the evidence of these assumptions:

1. Bipolarity: This is the assumption of dichotomy, and of logical reversal—that characteristics of one endpoint of the continuum are *opposite* to those of the other endpoint. This is evident in the prevalent use of the term *the opposite sex.*

But bipolarity of gender needs to be discussed, not assumed. Even in the area of primary sex differences, nearly half a percent of the population (a "conservative" estimate, Overzier, 1963) is markedly intersexual (biologically hermaphrodite). Other cultures treat these challenges to a bipolar system quite differently: the Navaho revered them as possessed of some special power (Hill, 1935); the Potok of Kenya were somewhat indifferent to them because they did not fit into their bride-price system of exchange (Edgerton, 1964). Interestingly, though Levi-Strauss (1966) and Piaget (1970) consider binary thinking the most primitive, it is our more advanced civilization that treats the intersexual as an unclassifiable monster and tries, through surgical and/or behavioral engineering (Laub & Fisk, 1974; Barlow et al., 1973), to fit the person into one role *or* the other. Thus, bipolarity better describes what we think about sex differences rather than what they necessarily are.

On many characteristics of central importance to human personality, there is great overlap between the sexes. For those characteristics that are statistically significantly different, the bipolarity assumption calls for an exaggeration of these differences. This is the most dangerous use of statistics, and leads to generalizations such as "men are instrumental, women are expressive." MF scales still characterize interest in concrete things and scientific and outdoor activities as masculine, and interest in music, literature, art, and verbal activities and humanitarian concerns as feminine (Diamond, 1973). This view is far too simplified. . . .

Oppositeness implies a negative correlation between endpoints. But Vroegh (1971) found a positive relationship between the correlates of masculinity and femininity in grades 1–3 and 4–6 for the ratings of peers. Jenkin and Vroegh (1969) found a correlation of .42 between ratings of "most masculine person" and "most feminine person"; of the 45 adjectives describing the most masculine person and 32 describing the most feminine person, 17 were used for both.

2. Unidimensionality: Another assumption underlying models of MF as a psychological trait is that there exists only one dimension of masculinity and of femininity. Yet, numerous factor analyses of MF scales (many summarized by Constantinople, 1973) have shown that there is not one MF dimension but several. . . .

Multidimensionality should not really be a surprise. We do not have single scales for other fundamental human differentiations: e.g., scales for childishness and negroidness. The complexity with which maturity (age) and race differences have been treated need also to be applied to sex differentiation.

3. Continuity: From extremely masculine along a graded interval through a zero point to extreme femininity is assumed by folk models and statistical procedures alike. This assumption allows one to say that a certain behavior is just as masculine as another behavior is feminine. Thus Stein (1967; cf. Stein et al., 1971) called the "masculine" task that one that she labeled for her elementary school subjects as measuring "potential skill at building and fixing things"; the "feminine" task was the one that was labeled as measuring "potential skill at taking good care of a baby." In this way, she could manipulate the appropriateness of the task, as labeled, for the child's gender role. Yet it is unclear just how masculine "building and fixing things" is, and if, for any one child, that sample of children, all children that age, or all men and women, "taking good care of a baby" is equal and opposite to this degree of masculinity. . . .

4. Normal distribution: Although a normal distribution is assumed for use of MF scores in most statistical procedures, the simplest folk model (dichotomy) would at best reveal a two-humped platykurtic distribution for both sexes combined.

Several [statistical] assumptions . . . contradicted by any of the profusion of gender-role typologies: e.g., nun, witch, and playmate for women (Richardson, 1971), or warrior, wise old man, and trickster for men (from Jung). There are many stereotypes for each gender that cannot be combined in a smooth, normally distributed curve of MF. . . .

5. Consistency of content: A set of assumptions about the characteristics of the psychological trait MF involves the internal consistency (reliability) and generalizability (validity) of MF scores or statements about men and women. Results are sometimes generalized from a sample of observed subjects to much larger populations. The frequent assumption of consensuality of gender role over ages, races, geographical location, year of collection of data, etc., continues to be ridiculed and continues to be practiced—in the literature, at professional meetings, and in informal conversations with colleagues. But it is easy to see that the ghetto man's view of the male gender role, perhaps including a sense of the streetbound territory to be protected, and the middle-class prep school male's view of masculine poolside heterosexual style are utterly different. . . .

Consistency is also expected from situation to situation—that is, the feminine woman will be as nonaggressive, empathetic, and so on in one situation as in another. In this way, a general measurement of character traits is expected to predict her behavior to some extent in *all* settings.

Finally, a kind of assumption of consistency operates in the granting of coequal status to the different traits used in MF scales and in the description of male and female personality. . . . This practice ignores the different effect sizes, and also the uneven social significances of these differences, as discussed below (cf. Tresemer, 1975).

6. Importance: We have reviewed some of the issues concerning importance of gender-role differences above. The low percentage of variance explained by MF scales is the characteristic finding for masculinity-femininity measurement. . . . For example, women's buttocks are reliably larger than men's (National Center of Health Statistics, 1965:37). Are larger buttocks indicative of greater femininity? Might we read too much significance into this?

. . . Differentiation between gender roles has been grossly exaggerated. A focus of the criticism has been very much on the narrow conception of gender role prevalent in current sociology. The demand on social science is to integrate the complex diversity of the individual interpretation and enactment of standards for gender-role behavior that differ from one social context to another.

THE USES OF GENDER ROLES

The global qualities or capabilities of being, feeling, and social-emotional orientation are associated with the feminine *principle;* of doing, thinking, and task-orientation with the masculine *principle.* To many psychologists and sociologists, it is clear that the healthiest, most effective personality (as well as social system) requires an integration of both of these conceptual poles: "feminine" warmth and interpersonal sensitivity, and "masculine" leadership and goal-oriented striving.

Too often the metaphorical identification of the first set of traits with the female sex and the second set with the male sex is taken too literally, implying the mutual exclusion that these principles seldom show in actual persons.

Yet the temptation to say that males are "greater than" or "less than" females on some dimension of interest, often confusing the symbolic and the literal, is great; generalizations for large audiences founded on slim evidence are frequently made.... The task is not to get a more significant finding than someone else, but rather, through a series of investigations in similar and different settings, using methods of cross-validation and double cross-validation (Mosteller & Tukey, 1968), to *estimate the relative size of an effect.* ...

PLAYING DUMB ON DATES. An excellent example is one of the most widely cited essays in the sociological literature on sex roles, Mirra Komarovsky's (1946) paper "Cultural Contradictions and Sex Roles." Based on interviews with 153 Barnard College women, Komarovsky strongly suggested that these intelligent women "play dumb" on social dates, presenting themselves as less than they actually are in order not to challenge the culturally expected inferiority of the female gender role and thus become less desirable to their male dates....

A recent replication (Powers et al., 1972; also Dean et al., 1973) used a carefully selected sample of women comparable to those in the earlier studies, and questions identical to Wallin's. Contrary to their expectations, the distribution of responses in our supposedly more liberated era was almost identical to that reported by Wallin. But a closer look at the data revealed a gross overestimation in the earlier studies. Responses had been added from several categories to show inferior-role-playing: "once or twice," "several times," "very often," and "often." But Powers et al. found that the average woman had 9.5 dates each month, making "once or twice" an insignificantly rare event. Since only 10 percent of the women downplayed their own abilities "very often" or "often," Powers et al. (1972) concluded that the original hypothesis was not supported.

The recent study (Dean et al., 1973) also included males, and found that males engaged in inferior-role-playing to the same small extent as the females....

MOTIVE TO AVOID SUCCESS. A second example involves the research on "fear of success." A study by Matina Horner (1968) was embraced as the answer to the problem of observed differences between men and women in enacted career achievement. Horner found that college women responded more frequently than men with negative imagery in stories written to the verbal cue, "At the end of the first-term finals, Anne finds herself at the top of her medical school class." ...

These results also seemed to confirm some notions about gender roles in our culture, and were quickly integrated into the mainstream of sociology (cf. the many references in Huber, 1973) as well as the popular press (e.g., "Most Women Fear Success, Doctor Says," *National Enquirer*, Feb. 4, 1973). Scores of replication studies (summarized in Tresemer, 1974, 1976) revealed that males responded with the negative imagery used as an indicator of "fear of success" about as often as females.[2] ... But from the results that are already available, it seems that there is something about writing these stories involving negative imagery, or about achievement situations, rather than something about discrimination against women, that leads to restriction of performance capabilities. ...

The Nature of Oppression. These two examples share with much sociological research in this area several other assumptions about gender roles. First of all, it is assumed that these differences in gender-role behavior stem from fundamental personality differences, socialized early in life. An integrative paper by Warner et al. (1973) labels this the Sambo characterization of oppression: the victims internalize the maladaptive set of values of the oppressive system. Thus behavior that appears incompetent, deferential, and self-degrading is assumed to reflect the crippled capabilities of the personality. The Sambo stereotype relegates change to future generations, where more equalitarian childhood socialization does not permanently destroy the personalities of the oppressed group.

Warner et al. (1973) convincingly suggest that the Operator characterization of oppression be accepted instead. The Operator may *appear* to be self-demeaning, unable to comprehend the simplest instructions, childlike, and so on, but this is really a "put-on," a sensitive calculated reaction to a difficult situation of structural powerlessness. This change in basic assumption about the nature of oppression related to gender roles grants competence to the oppressed and allows us to consider change of the oppressing aspects of the social structure now.

A second assumption is the seldom explicit greater value placed on achievement and power in the occupational professional world, where the rewards are "deference, power, reputation, and money," as one sociologist put it. But how can we be certain that an individual woman, for example, finds more subjective value in "landing that deal with Acme" than in "making fingers and toes today" (completed in the thir-

---

[2]Current work by Horner et al. (1973) as well as many others may set this area of research in a constructive direction.

teenth week of pregnancy, Rugh and Shettles, 1971)? Feelings of meaningful "success" in life cannot be assumed to be limited to any one domain for everybody.

Based on the second assumption is the frequent assumption that women have it "worse" than men because what is really worthwhile in personal development—namely a career as a meaningful form of work—has been denied to them. But a growing number of references are claiming that gender-role boundaries are narrower and more restrictive for the male, especially in adolescence (cf. Hartley, 1959; Brenton, 1966)....

MODELS OF GENDER-ROLE CHANGE

Three very different patterns can be discerned in the literature proposing and documenting new forms of male and female role behavior: (1) *role reversal*, where increasing numbers of males take over "women's work" (e.g., becoming "househusbands") and females begin to enter the work world, or other forms of realignment of gender roles where polarity is retained; (2) *"unisex,"* or the degradation of differences and the rise of a homogeneous mass of identical persons; and (3), like (2), an increase in similarities, but in this case each person retaining his gender-role-congruent skills and gaining others—the model of the *androgyne*, from the mythic tradition of the masculofeminine warrior lover....

Role Reversal.   The main theme in this perspective is the desire on the part of women for a greater share of the occupational professional cake and a rejection of their previous "feminine" roles. Secondarily, males wish to leave the world of work and develop their previously repressed emotional side. We have ample evidence that people think in these terms....

These ... changes are all based on and perpetuate a sort of dualism thought necessary for gender-role identity. This is a "flip-flop," trading one set of limitations and possibilities for its opposite....

Androgyny and Ego Strength.   Androgyny is currently being widely used to describe a freer society where the more fully developed individual is not inhibited from expressing "masculine" and "feminine" qualities (cf. Bazin & Freeman, 1974). While some original uses of this term were exceedingly negative, there is a strong tradition of reverence and awe before a complete biological hermaphrodite, as a metaphor for a psychological androgyny (Delcourt, 1958; Jung, 1954; also Jones and Scott, 1971). The myths of the Amazons and the Dionysian pederasts also expressed the themes of this integration (Malamud, 1972)....

There are scattered pieces of psychological evidence for [androgyny]. Maccoby (1966) found that greater intellectual development seems to be associated with relatively greater masculinity in females and relatively greater femininity in males. Sanford (1966) suggested that femininity in men, when sublimated, leads to creativity, intellectual or artistic achievement; but, when not sublimated, leads to a kind of compulsive masculinity and rigidity. Gump (1972) found that female subjects with the highest ego-strength test scores were actively pursuing both marriage and a career.

These examples illustrate a crucial point: The combination of masculinity and femininity can be crippling or enabling, depending to a great extent on the strength of the individual to encompass these possibilities. . . .

Developmental Change. Studies show that oversimplifications of divisions between the sexes are characteristic of, and perhaps necessary for, early stages of development in the human life cycle. But it is important to place more emphasis on the potentialities of maturing beyond those models. More comprehensive ways of understanding the complex matters of styles of thinking, patterns of living—the plurality of ways of interacting between self and society—are implicit in the new models of the androgyne.

This would mean a shift of at least some of the focus on neonatal learning and early childhood socialization to the possibilities of adult socialization and change. Though gender roles are perceived clearly in the first few years of life (Kagan, 1972), they are not laid down permanently (another assumption made frequently in the literature).

CONCLUSION

It is clear that differences between the biological sexes exist, but we do not yet have a sense of the relative importance of various differences. In addition, it is unclear how much biological differences are used as the basis for gross exaggerations about members of the classes "male" and "female." Of course, these judgments are often made within the context of an unstated set of values. Rather than only documenting and bewailing the inhibitions of contragender qualities and capabilities imposed early in life, more attention should be directed to the future—to the possibilities of change in adulthood. . . . The indices of decreased gender-based prejudice will not be more women in the work world and more men in the home, but some kinds of assessment of attitudes about life, and feelings that what one is doing has personal meaning and importance. Social scientists must take great care to avoid affirming assumptions about the dualistic stereotypes of mutually exclusive groups. They must also avoid facile, but rigid, solutions to gender-role change.

REFERENCES

Bardwick, Judith.
  1971   Psychology of Women: A Study of Bio-cultural Conflicts. New York: Harper and Row.
Barlow, David H.; Joyce E. Reynolds; and W. Stewart Agras.
  1973   "Gender identity change in a transsexual." Archives of General Psychiatry 28:569–576.
Bazin, Nancy T., and Alma Freeman.
  1974   "The androgynous vision." Women's Studies 2:185–215.
Bernard, Jessie.
  1971   Women and the Public Interest. Chicago: Aldine-Atherton.
Brenton, Myron.
  1966   The American Male. Greenwich, Conn.: Fawcett.
Constantinople, Anne.
  1973   "Masculinity-femininity: An exception to a famous dictum?" Psychological Bulletin 80:389–407.
Dean, Dwight; Rita Braito; Edward Powers; and Brent Bruton.
  1973   "Replication and fallacy: Cultural contradictions and sex roles revisited." Paper presented at the annual meeting of the American Sociological Association, New York City.
Delcourt, Marie.
  1958   Hermaphrodite: Mythes et rites de la bisexualité dans l'antiquité classique. Paris: Presses Universitaires de France.
Diamond, Esther E.
  1973   "Masculinity-femininity scale in interest measurement: An idea whose time has passed." ERIC document no. ED 069 795. Paper presented at the annual meeting of the American Psychological Association, Honolulu.
Edgerton, Robert B.
  1964   "Pokot intersexuality: An East African example of the resolution of sexual incongruity." American Anthropologist 66:1288–1299.
Garai, Josef F., and Amram Scheinfeld.
  1968   "Sex differences in mental and behavioral traits." Genetic Psychology Monographs 77:169–299.
Gump, Janice P.
  1972   "Sex-role attitudes and psychological well-being." Journal of Social Issues 28:79–92.
Hartley, Ruth E.
  1959   "Sex-role pressures and the socialization of the male child." Psychological Reports 5:457–468.

Hill, W. W.

1935 "The status of the hermaphrodite and transvestite in Navaho culture." American Anthropologist 37:273–279.

Holter, Harriet.

1970 Sex Roles and Social Structure. Oslo: Universitetsforlaget.

Horner, Matina S.

1968 "Sex differences in achievement motivation and performance in competitive and non-competitive situations." Doctoral dissertation, University of Michigan. Ann Arbor, Mich.: University Microfilms, no. 69-12, 135.

Horner, Matina S.; David Tresemer; Anne E. Berens; and Robert I. Watson, Jr.

1973 "Scoring manual for an empirically derived scoring system for motive to avoid success." Unpublished manuscript. Cambridge, Mass.: Harvard University.

Huber, Joan (ed.).

1973 "Changing women in a changing society." American Journal of Sociology 78(4).

Jenkin, Noel, and Karen Vroegh.

1969 "Contemporary concepts of masculinity and femininity." Psychological Reports 25:679–697.

Jones, Howard W., Jr., and William W. Scott.

1971 "The origin of the concept of hermaphroditism in Graeco-Roman culture." Pp. 3–15 in Genital Anomalies and Related Endocrine Disorders. Second Edition. Baltimore: Williams and Wilkins.

Jung, Carl G.

1954 Mysterium Coniunctionis: An Inquiry into the Separation and Synthesis of Psychic Opposites in Alchemy. Second Edition. Princeton, N.J.: Princeton University Press (Bollingen series), 1970.

Kagan, Jerome.

1971 Change and Continuity in Infancy. New York: Wiley.

1972 "The emergence of sex differences." School Review 80:217–227.

Kagan, Jerome, and H. Moss.

1962 Birth to Maturity. New York: Wiley.

Komarovsky, Mirra.

1946 "Cultural contradictions and sex roles." American Journal of Sociology 52:184–189.

Laub, Donald R., and Norman Fisk.

1974 "A rehabilitation program for gender dysphoria syndrome by surgical sex change." Plastic and Reconstructive Surgery 53:388–403.

Levi-Strauss, Claude.

1966 The Savage Mind. Chicago: University of Chicago Press.

Maccoby, Eleanor E. (ed.).

1966 "Sex differences in intellectual functioning." Pp. 25–55 in E. E. Maccoby (ed.), The Development of Sex Differences. Stanford, Calif.: Stanford University Press.

Malamud, Rene.
    1971   "The Amazon problem." Spring: An Annual of Archetypal Psychology and Jungian Thought 1–21.
Mosteller, Frederick, and John Tukey.
    1968   "Data analysis including statistics." Pp. 80–203 in G. Lindzey and E. Aronson (eds.), Handbook of Social Psychology. Volume 2. Second Edition. Reading, Mass.: Addison-Wesley.
National Center of Health Statistics.
    1965   Weight, Height, and Selected Body Dimensions of Adults: U.S.: 1960–62. Publication no. 1000, Series 11, no. 8. Washington, D.C.: U.S. Public Health Service.
Oakley, Anne.
    1972   Sex, Gender, and Society. London: Temple Smith.
Overzier, Claus (ed.).
    1963   "True hermaphroditism." Pp. 192–229 in Intersexuality. New York: Academic Press.
Piaget, Jean.
    1970   Structuralism. New York: Basic Books.
Powers, Edward A.; Rita Braito; and Dwight Dean.
    1972   "Cultural contradictions and sex roles: Fact or anti-fact?" Paper presented at the meeting of the National Council of Family Relations, Portland, Ore.
Richardson, Herbert W.
    1971   Nun, Witch, and Playmate. New York: Harper and Row.
Rugh, Roberts and Landrum Shettles.
    1971   From Conception to Birth. New York: Harper and Row.
Sanford, Nevitt.
    1966   "Masculinity and femininity in the structure of the personality." Pp. 191–202 in Self and Society. New York: Atherton.
Sears, Robert R.
    1965   "Development of gender role." Pp. 133–163 in F. Beach (ed.), Sex and Behavior. New York: Wiley.
Sherman, Julia A.
    1971   On the Psychology of Women. Springfield, Ill.: Charles C Thomas.
Silverman, Julian.
    1970   "Attentional styles and the study of sex differences." Pp. 61–98 in D. I. Mostofsky (ed.), Attention: Contemporary Theory and Analysis. New York Appleton-Century-Crofts.
Stein, Aletha H.
    1967   "Children's achievement behavior on sex-typed tasks." Paper presented at the meeting of the Society for Research in Child Development, New York.
Stein, Aletha; S. R. Pohly; and E. Mueller.
    1971   "The influence of masculine, feminine, and neutral tasks on children's achievement behavior, expectancies of success, and attainment values." Child Development 42:195–207.

Stoller, Robert.
   1968   Sex and Gender: On the Development of Masculinity and Feminini-
          ty. New York: Science House.
Sutton-Smith, Brian, and Benjamin G. Rosenberg.
   1973   "Sex differences in the longitudinal prediction of adult personality."
          Paper presented at the meeting of the Society for Research in Child
          Development, Philadelphia.
Terman, Lewis M., and Catherine C. Miles.
   1936   Sex and Personality: Studies in Masculinity and Femininity. New
          York: McGraw-Hill.
Terman, Lewis M., and L. Tyler.
   1954   "Psychological sex differences." Pp. 1064–1114 in L. Carmichael
          (ed.), Manual of Child Psychology. Second Edition. New York: Wiley.
Tresemer, David.
   1974   "Fear of success: Popular but unproven." Psychology Today 7(10):82
          –85.
   1975   "Measuring 'sex differences.' " Sociological Inquiry 45(4).
   1976   "The cumulative record of research on fear of success." Sex Roles:
          A Journal of Research 2.
Vroegh, Karen.
   1971   "Masculinity and femininity in the elementary and junior high
          school years." Developmental Psychology 4:254–261.
Wallin, Paul.
   1950   "Cultural contradictions and sex roles: A repeat study." American
          Sociological Review 15:288–293.
Warner, R. Stephen; David T. Wellman; and Lenore J. Weitzman.
   1973   "The hero, the sambo, and the operator: Three characterizations of
          the oppressed." Urban Life and Culture 2:53–84.

Gender Roles

A Note on the Division
of Labor by Sex   Judith K. Brown

In spite of the current interest in the economic aspect of tribal and
peasant societies, the division of labor by sex continues to elicit only the
most perfunctory consideration. This paper attempts to reassess the
scant theoretical literature dealing with this division of labor and to
suggest a reinterpretation based on some of the available ethnographic
evidence.

I will begin with Durkheim. According to his theory, among the very
primitive (both in the distant past and today), men and women are fairly
similar in strength and intelligence. Under these circumstances the
sexes are economically independent and therefore "sexual relations
[are] preeminently ephemeral" (Durkheim, 1893:61). With the
"progress of morality," women became weaker and their brains became
smaller. Their dependence on men increased, and division of labor by
sex cemented the conjugal bond. Indeed, Durkheim asserts that the
Parisienne of his day probably had the smallest human brain on record.
Presumably she was able to console herself with the stability of her
marriage, which was the direct result of her underendowment and
consequent dependence.

Unlike Durkheim, Murdock does not attempt to reconstruct history,
but his explanatory principle is also naively physiological. He writes:

> By virtue of their primary sex differences, a man and a woman make
> an exceptionally efficient cooperating unit. Man, with his superior
> physical strength, can better undertake the more strenuous

Reproduced by permission of the American Anthropological Association from "A Note on the
Division of Labor by Sex" by Judith K. Brown, *The American Anthropologist* 72(5), 1970.

tasks. . . . Not handicapped, as is woman, by the physiological burdens of pregnancy and nursing, he can range farther afield to hunt,
to fish, to herd, and to trade. Woman is at no disadvantage, however,
in the lighter tasks which can be performed in or near home. . . . All
known human societies have developed specialization and cooperation between the sexes roughly along this biologically determined
line of cleavage (Murdock, 1949:7).

This overly simple explanation is contradicted by numerous ethnographic accounts of heavy physical labor performed by women. The
greater spatial range of male subsistence activities may also not be
based on physiology as Murdock suggests. Recently, Munroe and
Munroe (1967) have reported sex differences in environmental exploration among Logoli children. According to the authors, the greater geographical range of boys' activities in this society may result from
learning, although innate sex-linked factors are suggested as a possible
alternative explanation.

Lévi-Strauss also suggests the economic interdependence of the sexes
as the basis for the conjugal (or nuclear) family. This interdependence
does not so much arise from actual sex differences as from culturally
imposed prohibitions that make it impossible for one sex to do the tasks
assigned to the other. He writes of the division of labor by sex as "a
device to make the sexes mutually dependent on social and economic
grounds, thus establishing clearly that marriage is better than celibacy"
(Lévi-Strauss, 1956:277).

Taking their cue from ethnographic descriptions that suggest that
women often perform the dull and monotonous subsistence activities
(for example, Pospisil, 1963), other authors have offered "psychologizing" theories concerning the division of labor by sex. Malinowski
(1913:287) suggested that women, owing to their docility, are forced to
do such work: "Division of labor is rooted in the brutalization of the
weaker sex by the stronger." Others have suggested that women are
psychologically better fitted for dull work. Mead (1949:164) summarizes
this view, stating "Women have a capacity for continuous monotonous
work that men do not share, while men have a capacity for the mobilization of sudden spurts of energy, followed by a need for rest and reassem-
blage of resources."

What facts have these theories tried to explain? First, division of labor
by sex is a universal. Planned societies such as Israel and Communist
China have attempted to implement an ideology that views men and
women as interchangeable parts within the economy, but have done so
with only mixed success (Spiro, 1956; Huang, 1961, 1963). Second, in
spite of the physiological constants and the possible, but less well-
substantiated, psychological ones, women may contribute nothing to

subsistence—as among the Rajputs (Minturn & Hitchcock, 1963); or they may support the society almost completely—as among the Nsaw (Kaberry, 1952). This variation, briefly noted by Mead (1949), has never been fully explained.

I would like to suggest that the degree to which women contribute to the subsistence of a particular society can be predicted with considerable accuracy from a knowledge of the major subsistence activity. It is determined by the compatibility of this pursuit with the demands of child care. (Female physiology and psychology are only peripheral to this explanation.) This fact has been noted repeatedly by ethnographers, but it has never been articulated in the theoretical literature dealing with the division of labor by sex.

Nowhere in the world is the rearing of children primarily the responsibility of men, and in only a few societies are women exempted from participation in subsistence activities. If the economic role of women is to be maximized, their responsibilities in child care must be reduced or the economic activity must be such that it can be carried out concurrently with child care.

The former is the method familiar to us among industrial or industrializing societies. Whether in the United States or in Communist China, the working mother is separated from her child, who is in the care of specialists in the school or the residential nursery while the mother is in her place of employment. In our society, controversy over the presence of mothers in the labor force inevitably centers on the desirability and quality of this substitute care (Maccoby, 1960).

Tribal societies also resort to substitute care so that mothers may work. Among the Gusii, women are responsible for the cultivation on which the society depends, and young child nurses (usually girls) are in charge of younger children and infants. However, the mother must periodically supervise the young caretakers. Minturn and Lambert (1964:244, 252) write:

> This does not mean that the Nyasongo [Gusii] mothers spend a great deal of time actually interacting with their children. They have domestic and agricultural duties that take up most of their time. . . . Older children are often left with no one to look after them directly, but are kept close to home and within earshot of their mothers. . . . The burden of such supervision is clear, for instance, with respect to infant care. Older children chiefly care for infants but mothers must, in turn, supervise older children.

Among the Yoruba (Marshall, 1964) an intricate system of reciprocity makes possible the trade activities of the women. During the early years of marriage, when her children are very young, a woman carries on only limited commercial activities. At this time she is likely to take into her home an older child as a helper. When her children are older, they in turn are placed in the homes of women who are still in the previous stage, and the mother's market activities increase in scope.

I have greatly oversimplified both examples. They illustrate two contrasts with the substitute care patterns of our own society. First, the women are not freed as completely for their economic pursuits. Second, the ethnographic accounts suggest that such substitute care is viewed not only as desirable but as an absolute necessity. Finally, the two cases are similar to the cases that are the focus of this paper, in that the work the women perform is not incompatible with child watching, even though the supervision of children may be only sporadic.

My main concern is with those societies that, without the intercession of schools, child-care centers, or child nurses, nevertheless depend on the subsistence activities of working mothers. These societies are able to draw on womanpower because their subsistence activities are compatible with simultaneous child watching. Such activities have the following characteristics: they do not require rapt concentration and are relatively dull and repetitive; they are easily interruptible and easily resumed once interrupted; they do not place the child in potential danger; and they do not require the participant to range very far from home.

Anthropologists have long noted the narrow range of subsistence activities in which women make a substantial contribution: gathering, hoe agriculture, and trade (Lippert, 1886/87; Schmidt, 1955; Murdock, 1957; Aberle, 1961). Although men do gather, carry on hoe cultivation, and trade, no society depends on its women for the herding of large animals, the hunting of large game, deep-sea fishing, or plow agriculture. That women can be proficient at these activities [Jenness (1923) reports women seal hunters among the Copper Eskimo; Forde (1934) reports that women herd reindeer for parts of the year among the Tungus] is evidence that the division of labor by sex is not based entirely on immutable physiological facts of greater male strength and endurance. However, it is easy to see that all these activities are incompatible with simultaneous child watching. They require rapt concentration, cannot be interrupted and resumed, are potentially dangerous, and require that the participant range far from home.

Bogoras' report of the summer herding of the reindeer Chukchee provides an especially appropriate illustration of a subsistence activity that is incompatible with child watching. Bogoras suggests that the division of labor is not sexually determined; instead the population is divided according to child-watching and non-child-watching members. He writes:

With the beginning of summer, when sledges become useless and tents cannot be moved around the country, the Chukchee herdsmen usually leave their families in camp, and move with the herd about twenty miles away, to the summer pastures. Boys and girls of more than ten years, and young women having no small children, usually go along for a time. While moving about with the herd, the herdsmen have to carry on their backs all necessaries, such as extra clothing, rifle and ammunition, kettles, and provisions. . . . The burdens are carried by girls and by men who are not very agile; while the best herdsmen must remain unencumbered for moving swiftly around the herd (Bogoras, 1904:83).

The reindeer Chukchee lived by herding and hunting, both very incompatible with simultaneous child care, and the women of the society made a negligible contribution to subsistence. In contrast, the Azande, as described by De Schlippe, are hoe cultivators, and the contribution of women to subsistence is considerable. De Schlippe offers a very detailed description of the division of labor by sex. Only a portion will be cited here because it illustrates the compatibility of the women's activities with simultaneous child watching:

In all those field types which are grouped around the homestead and to which the common name of garden has been applied, as a rule women work alone or with their children. This may be explained by the proximity to the homestead and accordingly by the nature of this work. It consists of a great variety of different small tasks, many of which can be packed into one single day. A woman, trained in household work, is capable of doing a great deal of minor independent tasks without losing the order of her day's work (De Schlippe, 1956:40).

Another account that demonstrates the compatibility of hoe agriculture with simultaneous child watching is offered in the early nineteenth-century biography of the adopted Indian captive Mary Jemison (Seaver, 1823). It is the only description of Iroquois agricultural activity given from the point of view of a participant. It runs as follows:

Our labor was not severe; and that of one year was exactly similar, in almost every respect, to that of the others. . . . Notwithstanding the Indian women have all the fuel and bread to procure . . . their cares certainly are not half as numerous, nor as great [as those of white women]. In the summer season, we planted, tended and harvested our corn, and generally had all our children with us . . . we could work as leisurely as we pleased (Seaver, 1823:55).

The carefree tone of this account is deceptive. The agricultural activities of the Iroquois women were highly productive. Not only was the tribe well provided with food, but the harvested surplus was carefully preserved and constituted a considerable part of the tribe's wealth. Morgan (1851) had high praise for the industry of the Iroquois women. It is all the more remarkable that such high productivity was possible with simultaneous child-care responsibilities.

The relaxed atmosphere that characterized the agricultural-child-watching activities of the Iroquois women also characterized the gathering-child-watching activities of the Lunga women, inhabitants of the Kimberley District of Western Australia. Phyllis Kaberry (1939:18) writes of the Aborigine women, "If livelihood is sometimes precarious, it is belied by the absence of any feverish haste." Children accompanied the small groups of women gatherers on their daily forays into the bush. Kaberry describes one of these forays in great detail, ending her account as follows:

> They lie for a while in the shade, gossip, eat some of the fish and roots, sleep, and about three o'clock move homeward. For all their desultory searching, there is little that they miss, or fail to note for a future occasion.... In actual quantity, the woman probably provides more over a fixed period than the man, since hunting is not always successful. She always manages to bring home something, and hence the family is dependent on her efforts to a greater extent than on those of the husband (Kaberry, 1939:22, 25).

A more recent study, that by Rose of the Angus Downs Aborigines, focuses on the effects of White contact on Aborigine economic activity and kinship structure. Under precontact conditions, according to Rose (1965:99), when women gathered nuts and seeds for grinding, they formed themselves into "collectives of co-wives for the purpose of sharing the burdens of caring for children." With the introduction of white flour, the women's economic role became what Rose considers a passive one, "collectives" were no longer necessary, and polygyny decreased markedly.

The final ethnographic example I will offer is that of the Yahgan as described by Gusinde. This tribe was rated by Murdock (1957) as being supported mostly by the subsistence activities of its women. It was the only tribe that depended on fishing, marine hunting, and marine gathering that was so rated in the world sample of 565 societies. Gusinde (1961:538) writes:

> Far beyond the limited participation of the man in procuring food, she makes a considerable, altogether independent contribution to the support of her family by means of an activity that she alone can carry out. This is gathering, for which she is equipped by nature and

to which she can devote herself without jeopardizing her more important duties as mother and wife.

His description of subsistence activities is extremely detailed. Only a small portion will be cited here:

> Assuming that low tide set in during the day, one woman will make a date with another. . . . Each of them brings along her baby clinging to her back, and little girls run ahead, each with her own little basket. Sometimes a boy or two will run along out of curiosity and sheer pleasure, and they will watch for a while, but it would never occur to them to help because that is not their work. These women are only short distances apart. Walking slowly, they go from one spot to another, for the entire ocean floor is usually densely strewn with mussels. . . . They stop working only when their little baskets are full (Gusinde, 1961: 541–542).

The ethnographers cited here have all addressed themselves to the relationship between women's economic activities and their child-rearing responsibilities. It is obvious that certain subsistence activities are extremely compatible with simultaneous child care and that societies depending on such subsistence bases invite considerable economic contribution by women. In the past, theoretical considerations of the division of labor by sex have suggested that women do only certain kinds of work for physiological and psychological reasons. On the basis of the ethnographic evidence I have presented here, I would like to suggest a further explanation: in tribal and peasant societies that do not have schools and child-care centers, only certain economic pursuits can accommodate women's simultaneous child-care responsibilities. Repetitive, interruptible, nondangerous tasks that do not require extensive excursions are more appropriate for women when the exigencies of child care are taken into account.

REFERENCES

Aberle, David.
    1961   "Matrilineal descent in cross-cultural perspective," in David M. Schneider and Kathleen Gough (eds.), Matrilineal Kinship. Berkeley: University of California Press.
Bogoras, Waldemar.
    1904   "The Chukchee. The Jesup North Pacific expedition." American Museum of Natural History Memoir 7(1). New York: Stechert.
De Schlippe, Pierre.
    1956   Shifting Cultivation in Africa: The Zande System of Agriculture. London: Routledge and Kegan Paul.

Durkheim, Emile.
1893   The Division of Labor in Society. Translated by George Simpson, Glencoe, Ill.: Free Press, 1933.

Forde, C. Daryll.
1963   Habitat, Economy and Society. New York: Dutton.

Gusinde, Martin.
1961   The Yamana: The Life and Thought of the Water Nomads of Cape Horn. Translated by Frieda Schutze. New Haven: Human Relations Area Files.

Huang, Jen Lucy.
1961   "Some changing patterns in the communist Chinese family." Marriage and Family Living 23(May):137–146.
1963   "A re-evaluation of the primary role of the communist Chinese woman: The homemaker or the worker." Marriage and Family Living 25(May):162–166.

Jenness, Diamond.
1923   "The Copper Eskimo." Report of the Canadian Arctic Expedition, 1913–18. Volume 12. Ottawa: Acland.

Kaberry, Phyllis.
1939   Aboriginal Woman: Sacred and Profane. London: Routledge.
1952   "Women of the grass fields: A study of the economic position of women in Bamenda, British Cameroons." Colonial Research Publication, no. 14. London: Her Majesty's Stationery Office.

Lévi-Strauss, Claude.
1956   "The family," in Harry L. Shapiro (ed.), Man, Culture, and Society. New York: Oxford University Press.

Lippert, Julius.
1886– The Evolution of Culture. Translated and edited by G. P. Murdock.
1887   New York: Macmillan, 1931.

Maccoby, Eleanor E.
1960   "Effects upon children of their mothers' outside employment," in Norman W. Bell and Ezra F. Vogel (eds.), A Modern Introduction to the Family. Glencoe, Ill.: Free Press.

Malinowski, Bronislaw.
1913   The Family Among the Australian Aborigines: A Sociological Study. London: University of London Press.

Marshall, Gloria.
1964   "Women, trade and the Yoruba family." Unpublished doctoral dissertation. New York: Columbia University.

Mead, Margaret.
1949   Male and Female: A Study of the Sexes in a Changing World. New York: Morrow.

Minturn, Leigh, and John T. Hitchcock.
1963   "The Rājputs of Khalapur, India," in Beatrice B. Whiting (ed.), Six Cultures: Studies of Child Rearing. New York: Wiley.

Minturn, Leigh, and William Lambert.
 1964 Mothers of Six Cultures: Antecedents of Child Rearing. New York: Wiley

Morgan, Lewis Henry.
 1851 League of the Iroquois. Reprint edition. New York: Corinth Books, 1962.

Munroe, Robert L., and Ruth H. Munroe.
 1967 "Maintenance-system determinants of child development among the Logoli of Kenya." Paper presented at the American Anthropological Association meetings, Washington, D.C.

Murdock, George Peter.
 1949 Social Structure. New York: Macmillan.
 1957 "World ethnographic sample." American Anthropologist 59:664–687.

Pospisil, Leopold.
 1963 "Kapauku Papuan economy." Yale University Publications in Anthropology, no. 67. New Haven, Conn.: Department of Anthropology, Yale University.

Rose, Frederick G. G.
 1965 The Wind of Change in Central Australia: The Aborigines at Angus Downs, 1962. Berlin: Akademic Verlag.

Schmidt, Wilhelm S. V. D.
 1955 "Das Muterrecht." Studia Instituti Anthropos, no. 10. Vienna-Mödlingen: Missions-druckerei St. Gabriel.

Seaver, James E.
 1823 A Narrative of the Life of Mrs. Mary Jemison. Reprint edition. New York: Corinth Books, 1961.

Spiro, M. E.
 1956 Kibbutz: Venture in Utopia. Cambridge, Mass.: Harvard University Press.

Women as a
Minority Group

Helen Mayer Hacker

The purpose of this paper is to apply to women some portion of that
body of sociological theory and methodology customarily used for investigating such minority groups as Negroes, Jews, immigrants, et
cetera.

... In defining the term *minority group*, the presence of discrimination is the identifying factor. According to Louis Wirth (1945:347):

> A minority group is any group of people who because of their physi-
> cal or cultural characteristics, are singled out from the others in the
> society in which they live for differential and unequal treatment,
> and who therefore regard themselves as objects of collective dis-
> crimination.

It is apparent that this definition includes both objective and subjective
characteristics of a minority group: the fact of discrimination and the
awareness of discrimination, with attendant reactions to that awareness. A person who on the basis of his group affiliation is denied full
participation in those opportunities which the value system of his culture extends to all members of the society satisfies the objective criterion, but there are various circumstances which may prevent him from
fulfilling the subjective criterion.

In the first place, a person may be unaware of the extent to which his
group membership influences the way others treat him.

He may have formally dissolved all ties with the group in question and
fondly imagine his identity is different from what others hold it to be.

Consequently, he interprets their behavior toward him solely in terms of his individual characteristics. Or, less likely, he may be conscious of his membership in a certain group but not be aware of the general disesteem with which the group is regarded. A final possibility is that he may belong in a category which he does not realize has group significance. An example here might be a speech peculiarity which has come to have unpleasant connotations in the minds of others. Or a lower-class child with no conception of "class as culture" may not understand how his manners act as cues in eliciting the dislike of his middle-class teacher.

... It is frequently the case that a person knows that because of his group affiliation he receives differential treatment, but feels that his treatment is warranted by the distinctive characteristics of his group. A child may accept the fact that physical differences between him and an adult require his going to bed earlier than they do. A Sudra knows that his lot in life has been cast by divine fiat, and he does not expect the perquisites of a Brahmin. A woman does not wish for the rights and duties of men. In all these situations, clearly, the person does not regard himself as an "object of collective discrimination."

For the two types presented above—(1) those who do not know that they are being discriminated against on a group basis, and (2) those who acknowledge the propriety of differential treatment on a group basis— the subjective attributes of a minority group member are lacking. They feel no minority group consciousness, harbor no resentment, and, hence, cannot properly be said to belong in a minority group. Although the term *minority group* is inapplicable to both types, the term *minority group status* may be substituted.

... Women often manifest many of the psychological characteristics which have been imputed to self-conscious minority groups. Kurt Lewin (1941) has pointed to group self-hatred as a frequent reaction of the minority group member to his group affiliation. This feeling is exhibited in the person's tendency to denigrate other members of the group, to accept the dominant group's stereotyped conception of them, and to indulge in "mea culpa" breast-beating. He may seek to exclude himself from the average of his group, or he may point the finger of scorn at himself. Since a person's conception of himself is based on the defining gestures of others, it is unlikely that members of a minority group can wholly escape personality distortion. Constant reiteration of one's inferiority must often lead to its acceptance as a fact.

Certainly women have not been immune to the formulations of the "female character" throughout the ages. From those, to us, deluded creatures who confessed to witchcraft to modern sophisticates who speak disparagingly of the cattiness and disloyalty of women, women

reveal their introjection of the prevailing attitudes toward them.
... Like those minority groups whose self-castigation outdoes dominant group derision of them, women frequently exceed men in the
violence of their vituperations of their sex. They are more severe in
moral judgments, especially in sexual matters. ... Women express themselves as disliking other women, as preferring to work under men, and
as finding exclusively female gatherings repugnant.

... Militating against a feeling of group identification on the part of
women is a differential factor in their socialization. Members of a
minority group are frequently socialized within their own group.... But
only rarely does a woman experience this type of group belongingness.
Her interactions with members of the opposite sex may be as frequent
as her relationships with members of her own sex. Women's conceptions of themselves, therefore, spring as much from their intimate relationships with men as with women. Although this consideration might
seem to limit the applicability to women of research findings on minority groups, conversely, it may suggest investigation to seek out useful
parallels in the socialization of women, on the one hand, and the socialization of ethnics living in neighborhoods of heterogeneous population,
on the other.

... Women [like] racial and ethnic minorities ... tend to develop a
separate subculture. Women have their own language, comparable to
the argot of the underworld and professional groups. It may not extend
to a completely separate dialect, as has been discovered in some prelit-
erate groups, but there are words and idioms employed chiefly by
women. Only the acculturated male can enter into the conversation of
the beauty parlor, the exclusive shop, the bridge table, or the kitchen.
In contrast to men's interest in physical health, safety, money, and sex,
women attach greater importance to attractiveness, personality, home,
family, and other people. How much of the "women's world" is predicated on their relationship to men is too difficult a question to discuss
here.

... We must return now to the original question of the aptness of the
designation of minority group for women. If we assume that there are
no differences attributable to sex membership as such that would justify
casting men and women in different social roles, it can readily be shown
that women do occupy a minority group status in our society.

MINORITY GROUP STATUS OF WOMEN

... Formal discriminations against women are too well-known for any
but the most summary description. In general they take the form of

being barred from certain activities or ... being treated unequally.

As female, in the economic sphere, women are largely confined to sedentary, monotonous work under the supervision of men, and are treated unequally with regard to pay, promotion, and responsibility.... Women's colleges are frequently inferior to men's. In coeducational schools women's participation in campus activities is limited.... Socially, women have less freedom of movement and are permitted fewer deviations in the properties of dress, speech, manners. In social intercourse they are confined to a narrower range of personality expression.

[Except as affected by the Civil Rights Act of 1964] in the specially ascribed status of wife, a woman—in several states—has no exclusive right to her earnings, is discriminated against in employment, must take the domicile of her husband, and in general must meet the social expectation of subordination to her husband's interests. As a mother, she may not have the guardianship of her children, bears the chief stigma in the case of an illegitimate child, is rarely given leave of absence for pregnancy. As a sister, she frequently suffers unequal distribution of domestic duties between herself and her brother, must yield preference to him in obtaining an education and in such other psychic and material gratifications as cars, trips, and living away from home.

If it is conceded that women have a minority group status, what may be learned from applying to women various theoretical constructs in the field of intergroup relations?

SOCIAL DISTANCE BETWEEN MEN AND WOMEN

One instrument of diagnostic value is the measurement of social distance between dominant and minority group.... One extreme would represent a complete "ghetto" status, the women whose contacts with men were of the most secondary kind. At the other extreme ... we put the woman who has prolonged and repeated associations with men, but only in those situations in which sex-awareness plays a prominent role or the woman who enters into a variety of relationships with men in which her sex identity is to a large extent irrelevant.

... Social distance may be measured from the standpoint of the minority group or the dominant group with different results. In point of fact, tension often arises when one group feels less social distance than the other. A type case here is the persistent suitor who underestimates his desired sweetheart's feeling of social distance toward him.... On all scales marriage represents the minimum social distance, and implies willingness for associations of all levels of lesser intimacy. May the customary scale be applied to men and women?

... In our culture, men who wish to marry must perforce marry women; and even if they accept this relationship, they may still wish to limit their association with women in other situations. The male physician may not care for the addition of female physicians to his hospital staff. The male poker player may be thrown off his game if women participate. A damper may be put upon the hunting expedition if women come along. The average man may not wish to consult a woman lawyer. And so on.

... The question may be raised as to whether marriage in fact represents the point of minimum social distance. It may not imply anything but physical intimacy and work accommodation.

... Part of the explanation may be found in the subordination of wives to husbands in our culture, which is expressed in the separate spheres of activity for men and women.

... The presence of love does not in itself argue for either equality of status nor fullness of communication. We may love those who are either inferior or superior to us, and we may love persons whom we do not understand.

... Since inequalities of status are preserved in marriage, a dominant group member may be willing to marry a member of a group which, in general, he would not wish admitted to his club. The social distance scale which uses marriage as a sign of an extreme degree of acceptance is inadequate for appreciating the position of women, and perhaps for other minority groups as well. The relationships among similarity of status, communication as a measure of intimacy, and love must be clarified before social distance tests can be applied usefully to attitudes between men and women.

CASTE-CLASS CONFLICT

Is the separation between males and females in our society a caste line? Folsom (1943) suggests that it is, and Myrdal (1944), in his well-known Appendix 5, considers the parallel between the position of and feelings toward women and Negroes in our society. The relation between women and Negroes is historical as well as [analogous]. In the seventeenth century, the legal status of Negro servants was borrowed from that of women and children, who were under the patria potestas; and until the Civil War, there was considerable cooperation between the Abolitionist and woman suffrage movements. According to Myrdal, the

TABLE 1. CASTELIKE STATUS OF WOMEN AND NEGROES

Negroes	Women

1. High Social Visibility

Negroes	Women
a. Skin color, other "racial" characteristics.	a. Secondary sex characteristics.
b. (Sometimes) distinctive dress—bandana, flashy clothes.	b. Distinctive dress, skirts, et cetera.

2. Ascribed Attributes

Negroes	Women
a. Inferior intelligence, smaller brain, less convoluted, scarcity of geniuses.	a. Ditto.
b. More free in instinctual gratifications. More emotional, "primitive" and childlike: Imagined sexual prowess envied.	b. Irresponsible, inconsistent, emotionally unstable. Lack strong superego. Women as "temptresses."
c Common stereotype "inferior."	c. "Weaker."

3. Rationalizations of Status

Negroes	Women
a. Thought all right in his place.	a. Woman's place is in the home.
b. Myth of contented Negro.	b. Myth of contented woman—"feminine" woman is happy in subordinate role.

4. Accommodation Attributes

Negroes	Women
a. Supplicatory whining intonation of voice.	a. Rising inflection, smiles, laughs, downward glances.
b. Deferental manner.	b. Flattering manner.
c. Concealment of real feelings.	c. "Feminine wiles."
d. Outwit "white folks."	d. Outwit "menfolk."
e. Careful study of points at which dominant group is susceptible to influence.	e. Ditto.
f. Fake appeals for directives; show of ignorance.	f. Appearance of helplessness.

5. Discriminations

Negroes	Women
a. Limitations on education—should fit "place" in society.	a. Ditto.
b. Confined to traditional jobs—barred from supervisory positions.	b. Ditto.
c. Their competition feared, no family precedents for new aspirations. Deprived of political importance.	c. Ditto.
d. Social and professiona. segregation	d. Ditto.
e. More vulnerable to criticism.	e. For example, conduct in bars.

6. Similar Problems

a. Roles not clearly defined, but in flux as result of social change. Conflict between achieved status and ascribed status

problems of both groups are resultants of the transition from a preindustrial, paternalistic scheme of life to individualistic, industrial capitalism. Obvious similarities in the status of women and Negroes are indicated in Table 1.

While these similarities in the situation of women and Negroes may lead to increased understanding of their social roles, account must also be taken of differences which impose qualifications on the comparison of the two groups. Most importantly, the influence of marriage as a social elevator for women, but not for Negroes, must be considered. Obvious, too, is the greater importance of women to the dominant group, despite the economic, sexual, and prestige gains which Negroes afford the white South. Ambivalence is probably more marked in the attitude of white males toward women than toward Negroes. The "war of the sexes" is only an expression of men's and women's vital need of each other.

... Women's privileges exceed those of Negroes. Protective attitudes toward Negroes have faded into abeyance, even in the South, but most boys are still taught to take care of girls, and many evidences of male chivalry remain.

... Exemplary of the possible usefulness of applying the caste principle to women is viewing some of the confusion surrounding women's roles as reflecting a conflict between class and caste status. Such a conflict is present in the thinking and feeling of both dominant and minority groups toward upper-class Negroes and educated women. Should a woman judge be treated with the respect due a judge or the gallantry accorded a woman? The extent to which the rights and duties of one role permeate other roles so as to cause a role conflict has been treated elsewhere by the writer (Hacker, n.d.). Lower-class Negroes who have acquired dominant group attitudes toward the Negro resent upper-class Negro pretensions to superiority. Similarly, domestic women may feel the career woman is neglecting the duties of her proper station.

Parallels in adjustment of women and Negroes to the class-caste conflict may also be noted. Point 4, "Accommodation Attitudes" [Table 1], indicates the kinds of behavior displayed by members of both groups who accept their caste status. Many "sophisticated" women are retreating from emancipation with the support of psychoanalytic derivations.

... Role segmentation as a mode of adjustment is illustrated by Negroes who indulge in occasional passing and women who vary their behavior according to their definition of the situation.

A third type of reaction is to fight for recognition of class status. Negro race leaders seek greater prerogatives for Negroes. Feminist women, acting either through organizations or as individuals, push for public disavowal of any differential treatment of men and women.

RACE RELATIONS CYCLE

The "race relations cycle," as defined by Robert E. Park (1926), describes the social processes of reeducation in the relations between two or more groups who are living in a common territory under a single political or economic system. The sequence of competition, conflict, accommodation, and assimilation may also occur when social change introduces dissociative forces into an assimilated group or causes accommodated groups to seek new definitions of the situation.

... The sex relations cycle bears important similarities to the race relations cycle. In the wake of the Industrial Revolution, as women acquired industrial, business, and professional skills, they increasingly sought employment in competition with men. Men were quick to perceive them as a rival group and made use of economic, legal, and ideological weapons to eliminate or reduce their competition. They excluded women from the trade unions, made contracts with employers to prevent their hiring women, passed laws restricting the employment of married women, caricatured the working woman, and carried on ceaseless propaganda to return women to the home or keep them there. Since the days of the suffragettes there has been no overt conflict between men and women on a group basis. Rather than conflict, the dissociative process between the sexes is that of contravention, a type of opposition intermediate between competition and conflict. According to Wiese and Becker, it includes rebuffing, repulsing, working against, hindering, protesting, obstructing, restraining, and upsetting another's plans (Becker, 1932:263–268).

The present contravention of the sexes, arising from women's competition with men, is manifested in the discriminations against women, as well as in the doubts and uncertainties expressed concerning women's character, abilities, motives. The processes of competition and contravention are continually giving way to accommodation in the relationships between men and women. Like other minority groups, women have sought a protected position, a niche in the economy which they could occupy, and, like other minority groups, they have found these positions in new occupations in which dominant group members had not yet established themselves and in old occupations which they no longer wanted.

... What would assimilation of men and women mean? Park and Burgess (1924:735) in their classic text define assimilation as "a process of interpenetration and fusion in which persons and groups acquire the memories, sentiments, and attitudes of other persons or groups, and, by sharing their experiences and history, are incorporated with them in a cultural life." If accommodation is characterized by secondary contacts, assimilation holds the promise of primary contacts. If men and women were truly assimilated, we would find no cleavages of interest along sex lines. The special provinces of men and women would be abolished. Women's pages would disappear from the newspaper and women's magazines from the stands. All special women's organizations would pass into limbo. The sports page and racing news would be read indifferently by men and women. Interest in cookery and interior decoration would follow individual rather than sex lines. Women's talk would be no different from men's talk, and frank and full communication would obtain between the sexes.

THE MARGINAL WOMAN

Group relationships are reflected in personal adjustments. Arising out of the present contravention of the sexes is the marginal woman, torn between rejection and acceptance of traditional roles and attributes. Uncertain of the ground on which she stands, subjected to conflicting cultural expectations, the marginal woman suffers the psychological ravages of instability, conflict, self-hate, anxiety, and resentment.

In applying the concept of marginality to women, the term *role* must be substituted for that of *group* (Lewin, 1948:181). Many of the traditional devices for creating role differentiation among boys and girls, such as dress, manners, activities, have been deemphasized in modern urban middle-class homes.

Parental expectations in the matters of scholarship, conduct toward others, duties in the home may have differed little for herself and her brother. But in high school or perhaps not until college she finds herself called upon to play a new role. Benedict (1938) has called attention to discontinuities in the life cycle, and the fact that these continuities in cultural conditioning take a greater toll of girls than of boys is revealed in test scores showing neuroticism and introversion. In adolescence girls find the frank spontaneous behavior toward the neighboring sex no longer rewarding. High grades are more likely to elicit anxiety than praise from parents, especially mothers, who seem more pleased if male callers are frequent. There are subtle indications that to remain home with a good book on a Saturday night is a fate worse than death. But even if the die is successfully cast for popularity, all problems are not solved. Girls are encouraged to heighten their sexual attractiveness, but to abjure sexual expression.

Assuming new roles in adolescence does not mean the complete relinquishing of old ones. Scholarship, while not so vital as for the boy, is still important but must be maintained discreetly and without obvious effort. . . . Even more than to the boy is the "all-round" ideal held up to girls, and it is not always possible to integrate the roles of good date, good daughter, good sorority sister, good student, good friend, and good citizen. The superior achievements of college men over college women bear witness to the crippling division of energies among women. Part of the explanation may lie in women's having interiorized cultural notions of feminine inferiority in certain fields, and even the most self-confident or most defensive women may be filled with doubt as to whether she can do productive work.

... Widening opportunities for women will call forth a growing number of women capable of performing roles formerly reserved for men, but whose acceptance in these new roles may well remain uncertain and problematic.

Other avenues of investigation suggested by the minority group approach can only be mentioned. What social types arise as personal adjustments to sex status? What can be done in the way of experimental modification of the attitudes of men and women toward each other and themselves? What hypotheses of intergroup relations may be tested in regard to men and women? For example, is it true that as women approach the cultural standards of men, they are perceived as a threat and tensions increase?

... This paper is exploratory in suggesting the enhanced possibilities of fruitful analysis, if women are included in the minority group corpus, particularly with reference to such concepts and techniques as group belongingness, socialization of the minority group child, cultural differences, social distance tests, conflict between class and caste status, race relations cycle, and marginality.

REFERENCES

Becker, Howard.
    1932   Systematic Sociology on the Basis of the "Beziehungslehre" and "Gebildelehre" of Leopold von Wiese. New York: Wiley.
Benedict, Ruth.
    1938   "Continuities and discontinuities in cultural conditioning." Psychiatry 1:161–167.
Folsom, Joseph.
    1943   The Family and Democratic Society. New York: Wiley.
Hacker, Helen M.
    n.d.   "Towards a definition of role conflict in modern women." Unpublished manuscript.
Lewin, Kurt.
    1941   "Self-hatred among Jews." Contemporary Jewish Record 4:219–232.
    1948   Resolving Social Conflicts. New York: Harper.
Myrdal, Gunnar.
    1944   "Appendix 5: A parallel to the Negro problem." Pp. 1073–1078 in An American Dilemma. New York: Harper.
Park, Robert E.
    1926   "Our racial frontier on the Pacific." Survey Graphic 56(May 1):192–196.

Park, Robert E., and Ernest W. Burgess.
  1924   Introduction to the Science of Sociology. Reprint Edition. Westport,
         Conn.: Greenwood Press.
Wirth, Louis.
  1945   "The problem of minority groups," in Ralph Linton (ed.), The
         Science of Man in the World Crisis. New York: Columbia University
         Press.

ADDITIONAL READING

Hacker, Helen Mayer.
  1975   "Women as a minority group: Some twenty years later." Pp. 103–115
         in R. K. Unger and F. L. Denmark (eds.), Woman: Dependent or
         Independent Variable. New York: Psychological Dimensions.

The Origins of
the Status
of Women   Frederick Engels

The development of the family ... is founded on the continual contraction of the circle, originally comprising the whole tribe, within which
marital intercourse between both sexes was general. By the continual
exclusion, first of near, then of ever remoter relatives, including finally
even those who were simply related legally, all group marriage becomes
practically impossible. At last only one couple, temporarily and loosely
united, remains; that molecule, the dissolution of which absolutely puts
an end to marriage. Even from this we may infer how little the sexual
love of the individual in the modern sense of the word had to do with
the origin of monogamy. The practice of all nations of that stage still
more proves this. While in the previous form of the family the men were
never embarrassed for women, but rather had more than enough of
them, women now became scarce and were sought after. With the
pairing family, therefore, the abduction and barter of women
began—widespread symptoms, and nothing but that, of a new and
much more profound change.

The pairing family, being too weak and too unstable to make an
independent household necessary or even desirable, in no way dis-
solves the traditional communistic way of housekeeping. But household
communism implies supremacy of women in the house as surely as
exclusive recognition of a natural mother and the consequent impossi-
bility of identifying the natural father signify high esteem for women,
that is, mothers. It is one of the most absurd notions derived from

Excerpted from Frederick Engels, *The Origins of the Family, Private Property, and the State*
(Chicago: Charles H. Kerr and Company, 1902).

eighteenth-century enlightenment, that in the beginning of society woman was the slave of man. Among all savages and barbarians of the lower and middle stages, sometimes even of the higher stage, women not only have freedom, but are held in high esteem. What they were even in the pairing family, let Arthur Wright, for many years a missionary among the Seneca Iroquois, testify: As to their families, at a time when they still lived in their old long houses (communistic households of several families) . . . a certain clan (gens) always reigned, so that the women choose their husbands from other clans (gentes). . . . The female part generally ruled the house; the provisions were held in common; but woe to the luckless husband or lover who was too indolent or too clumsy to contribute his share to the common stock. No matter how many children or how much private property he had in the house, he was liable at any moment to receive a hint to gather up his belongings and get out. And he could not dare to venture any resistance; the house was made too hot for him and he had no other choice, but to return to his own clan (gens) or, as was mostly the case, to look for another wife in some other clan. The women were the dominating power in the clans (gentes) and everywhere else. The communistic household, in which most or all the women belong to one and the same gens, while the husbands come from different gentes, is the cause and foundation of the general and widespread supremacy of women in primeval times.

. . . The division of labor between both sexes is caused by other reasons than the social condition of women. Nations where women have to work much harder than is proper for them in our opinion often respect women more highly than Europeans do. . . . Riches, once they had become the private property of certain families and augumented rapidly, gave a powerful impulse to society founded on the pairing family and the maternal gens. The pairing family had introduced a new element. By the side of the natural mother it had placed the authentic natural father. According to the division of labor in those times, the task of obtaining food and the tools necessary for this purpose fell to the share of the man; hence he owned the latter and kept them in case of a separation, as the women did the household goods. According to the social custom of that time, the man was also the owner of the new source of existence, the cattle, and later on of the new labor power, the slaves. But according to the same custom, his children could not inherit his property, for the following reasons: By maternal law, that is, while descent was traced only along the female line, and by the original custom of inheriting in the gens, the gentile relatives inherited the property of their deceased gentile relative. The wealth had to remain in the gens. In view of the insignificance of the objects, the property may have gone in practice to the closest gentile relatives, this is, the consanguine relatives on the mother's side. The children of the dead man, however, did not belong to his gens, but to that of their mother. They inherited first together with the other consanguine relatives of the mother, later on perhaps in preference to the others. But they could not inherit from their father, because they did not belong to his gens, where his property had to remain. Hence, after the death of a cattle owner, the cattle would fall to his brothers, sisters and the children of his sisters, or to the offspring of the sisters of his mother. His own children were disinherited.

In the measure of the increasing wealth man's position in the family became superior to that of woman, and the desire arose to use this fortified position for the purpose of overthrowing the traditional law of inheritance in favor of his children. But this was not feasible as long as maternal law was valid. The simple resolution was [the abolishment of] ... the tracing of descent by female lineage and the maternal right of inheritance, and instituted descent by male lineage and the paternal right of inheritance. How and when this revolution was accomplished by the nations of the earth, we do not know. . . .

The downfall of maternal law was the historic defeat of the female sex. The men seized the reins also in the house, the women were stripped of their dignity, enslaved, tools of men's lust and mere machines for the generation of children. This degrading position of women, especially conspicuous among the Greeks of heroic and still more of classic times, was gradually glossed over and disguised or even clad in a milder form. But it is by no means obliterated.

The first effect of the established supremacy of men became now visible in the reappearance of the intermediate form of the patriarchal family. Its most significant feature is "the organization of a certain number of free and unfree persons into one family under the paternal authority of the head of the family. In the Semitic form this head of the family lives in polygamy, the unfree members have wife and children, and the purpose of the whole organization is the tending of herds in a limited territory." The essential points are the assimilation of the unfree element and the paternal authority. Hence the ideal type of this form of the family is the Roman family. The word *familia* did not originally signify the composite ideal of sentimentality and domestic strife in the present-day philistine mind. Among the Romans it did not even apply in the beginning to the leading couple and its children, but to the slaves alone. Famulus means domestic slave, and familia is the aggregate number of slaves belonging to one man. At the time of Gajus, the familia, *id est patrimonium* (that is, paternal legacy), was still bequeathed by testament. The expression was invented by the Romans in order to designate a new social organism, the head of which had a wife, children and a number of slaves under his paternal authority and according to Roman law the right of life and death over all of them.

Marx adds: "The modern family contains the germ not only of slavery (*servitus*), but also of serfdom, because it has from the start a relation to agricultural service. It comprises in miniature all those contrasts that later on develop more broadly in society and the state." In order to secure the faithfulness of the wife, and hence the reliability of paternal lineage, the women are delivered absolutely into the power of the men; in killing his wife, the husband simply exercises his right.

Such was the origin of monogamy, as far as we may trace it in the most civilized and most highly developed nation of antiquity. It was by no means a fruit of individual sex-love and had nothing to do with the latter, for the marriages remained as conventional as ever. Monogamy was the first form of the family not founded on natural, but on economic conditions, . . . the victory of private property over primitive and natural collectivism. Supremacy of the man in the family and generation of children that could be his offspring alone and were destined to be the heirs of his wealth—these were openly avowed by the Greeks to be the sole objects of monogamy.

Monogamy, then, does by no means enter history as a reconciliation of man and wife and still less as the highest form of marriage. On the contrary, it enters as the subjugation of one sex by the other, as the proclamation of an antagonism between the sexes unknown in all preceding history. In an old unpublished manuscript written by Marx and myself in 1846, I find the following passage: "The first division of labor is that of man and wife in breeding children." And to-day I may add: The first class antagonism appearing in history coincides with the development of the antagonism of man and wife in monogamy, and the first class oppression with that of the female by the male sex. Monogamy was a great historical progress. But by the side of slavery and private property it marks at the same time that epoch which, reaching down to our days, takes with all progress also a step backwards, relatively speaking, and develops the welfare and advancement of one by the woe and submission of the other. It is the cellular form of civilized society which enables us to study the nature of its now fully developed contrasts and contradictions.

With the rise of different property relations, in the higher stage of barbarism, wage labor appears sporadically by the side of slavery, and at the same time its unavoidable companion, professional prostitution of free women by the side of the forced surrender of female slaves. It is the heirloom bequeathed by group marriage to civilization, a gift as ambiguous as everything else produced by ambiguous, double-faced, schismatic and contradictory civilization. Here monogamy, there hetaerism and its most extreme form, prostitution. Hetaerism is as much a social institution as all others. It continues the old sexual freedom—for the benefit of the men. In reality not only permitted, but also assiduously practiced by the ruling class, it is denounced only nominally. Still in practice this denunciation strikes by no means the men who indulge in it, but only the women. These are ostracized and cast out by society, in order to proclaim once more the fundamental law of unconditional male supremacy over the female sex.

However, a second contradiction is thereby developed within monogamy itself. By the side of the husband, who is making his life pleasant by hetaerism, stands the neglected wife. And you cannot have one side of the contradiction without the other, just as you cannot have the whole apple after eating half of it. Nevertheless this seems to have been the idea of the men, until their wives taught them a lesson. Monogamy introduces two permanent social characters that were formerly unknown: the standing lover of the wife and the cuckold. The men had gained the victory over the women, but the vanquished magnanimously provided the coronation. In addition to monogamy and hetaerism, adultery became an unavoidable social institution—denounced, severely punished, but irrepressible.

Thus we have in the monogamous family, at least in those cases that remain true to historical development and clearly express the conflict between man and wife created by the exclusive supremacy of men, a miniature picture of the contrasts and contradictions of society at large.

The monogamous family, by the way, did not everywhere and always appear in the classic severe form it had among the Greeks. Although monogamy was the only one of all known forms of the family in which modern sex love could develop, this does not imply that it developed exclusively or even principally as mutual love of man and wife. The very nature of strict monogamy under man's rule excluded this. Among all historically active, that is, ruling, classes matrimony remained what it had been since the days of the pairing family—a conventional matter arranged by the parents.

In those countries where a legitimate portion of the parental wealth is assured to children and where these cannot be disinherited—in Germany, in countries with French law, et cetera—the children are bound to secure the consent of their parents for marrying. In countries with English law, where the consent of the parents is by no means a legal qualification of marriage, the parents have full liberty to bequeath their wealth to anyone and may disinherit their children at will. Hence it is clear that among classes having any property to bequeath the freedom to marry is not a particle greater in England and America than in France and Germany.

The legal equality of man and woman in marriage is by no means better founded. Their legal inequality inherited from earlier stages of society is not the cause, but the effect of the economic oppression of women. In the ancient communistic household comprising many married couples and their children, the administration of the household entrusted to women was just as much a public function, a socially necessary industry, as the procuring of food by men. In the patriarchal and still more in the monogamous family this was changed. The administration of the household lost its public character. It was no longer a concern of society. It became a private service. The woman became the first servant of the house, excluded from participation in social production. Only by the great industries of our time the access to social production was again opened for women—for proletarian women alone, however. This is done in such a manner that they remain excluded from public production and cannot earn anything, if they fulfill their duties in the private service of the family; or that they are unable to attend to their family duties, if they wish to participate in public industries and earn a living independently. As in the factory, so women are situated in all business departments up to the medical and legal professions. The modern monogamous family is founded on the open or disguised domestic slavery of women, and modern society is a mass composed of molecules in the form of monogamous families. In the great majority of cases the man has to earn a living and to support his family, at least among the possessing classes. He thereby obtains a superior position that has no need of any legal special privilege. In the family, he is the bourgeois; the woman represents the proletariat.

We are now approaching a social revolution, in which the old economic foundations of monogamy will disappear just as surely as those of its complement, prostitution. Monogamy arose through the concentration of considerable wealth in one hand—a man's hand—and from the endeavor to bequeath this wealth to the children of this man to the exclusion of all others. This necessitated monogamy on the woman's, but not on the man's part. Hence this monogamy of women in no way hindered open or secret polygamy of men. Now, the impending social revolution will reduce this whole care of inheritance to a minimum by changing at least the overwhelming part of permanent and inheritable wealth—the means of production—into social property. Since monogamy was caused by economic conditions, will it disappear when these causes are abolished?

One might reply, not without reason: not only will it not disappear, but it will rather be perfectly realized. For with the transformation of the means of production into collective property, wage labor will also disappear, and with it the proletariat and the necessity for a certain, statistically ascertainable number of women to surrender for money. Prostitution disappears and monogamy, instead of going out of existence, at last becomes a reality—for men also.

With the transformation of the means of production into collective property the monogamous family ceases to be the economic unit of society. The private household changes to a social industry. The care and education of children becomes a public matter. Society cares equally well for all children, legal or illegal. This removes the care about the "consequences" which now forms the essential social factor—moral and economic—hindering a girl to surrender unconditionally to the beloved man. Will not this be sufficient cause for a gradual rise of a more unconventional intercourse of the sexes and a more lenient public opinion regarding virgin honor and female shame? And finally, did we not see that in the modern world monogamy and prostitution, though antitheses, are inseparable and poles of the same social condition? Can prostitution disappear without engulfing at the same time monogamy?

Hence the full freedom of marriage can become general only after all minor economic considerations that still exert such a powerful influence on the choice of a mate for life, have been removed by the abolition of capitalistic production and of the property relations created by it. Then no other motive will remain but mutual fondness.... Those peculiarities that were stamped upon the face of monogamy by its rise through property relations, will decidedly vanish, namely, the supremacy of men and the indissolubility of marriage. The supremacy of man in marriage is simply the consequence of his economic superiority and will fall with the abolition of the latter.

The indissolubility of marriage is partly the consequence of economic conditions, under which monogamy arose, partly tradition from the time where the connection between this economic situation and monogamy, not yet clearly understood, was carried to extremes by religion. Today, it has been perforated a thousand times. If marriage founded on love is alone moral, then it follows that marriage is moral only as long as love lasts.

What we may anticipate about the adjustment of sexual relations after the impending downfall of capitalist production is mainly of a negative nature and mostly confined to elements that will disappear. But what will be added? That will be decided after a new generation has come to maturity: a race of men who never in their lives have had any occasion for buying with money or other economic means of power the surrender of a woman; a race of women who have never had any occasion for surrendering to any man for any other reason but love, or for refusing to surrender to their lover from fear of economic consequences. Once such people are in the world, they will not give a moment's thought to what we today believe should be their course. They will follow their own practice and fashion their own public opinion about the individual practice of every person—only this and nothing more.

An Anthropologist
Looks at Engels
Kathleen Gough

In *The Origin of the Family, Private Property and the State*, Engels, building on Lewis Henry Morgan's *Ancient Society*, tried to set forth the development of humanity with respect to economic, political, and domestic life. As a whole, the attempt has not been surpassed by any subsequent writer. Several have recently outlined parts of the period of human evolution in the light of modern data. But these studies suffer from one of two drawbacks. Those of anthropologists familiar with recent prehistory and ethnography are almost entirely by upper- and middle-class men. They tend to assume universal male dominance, both in power and creativity, and to ignore the changing conflicts of men and women, as well as of social classes. Those by women are chiefly the work of nonanthropologists whose data tend to be outmoded or inaccurate.[1]

SUMMARY

Engels, like Morgan, posits three main stages of cultural evolution, which Engels divides into nine substages: Lower, Middle, and Upper

---

The editors are grateful to Kathleen Gough for kindly preparing this article especially for this anthology.

[1]Among the best of the works of male anthropologists are Leslie A. White, *The Evolution of Culture* (New York: McGraw-Hill, 1959); Elman R. Service, *Primitive Social Organization* (New York: Random House, 1962); and Morton H. Fried, *The Evolution of Political Society* (New York: Random House, 1967). Those by women who are not anthropologists include Simone de Beauvoir's *The Second Sex* (New York: Bantam Books, 1965) and Kate Millett's *Sexual Politics* (Garden City, N.Y.: Doubleday, 1970).

Savagery; Lower, Middle, and Upper Barbarism; and Civilization, divided into centralized states characterized, in developmental order, by slavery, serfdom, and wage labor.

According to Engels, in Lower Savagery, humans, or perhaps prehumans, still lived partly in trees and subsisted on fruits, nuts, and roots. Speech developed in this period. Members of the small local group had promiscuous sexual relations. Toward the end of the period, sex relations were banned between adjacent generations, but within each generation, brothers, sisters, and cousins continued to mate indiscriminately and to form consanguine families.

In Middle Savagery, humans spread over the earth, developed fishing, fire-making, and some hunting, and invented such weapons as clubs and spears. Engels puts the whole of the Paleolithic into Middle Savagery. Mating became outlawed within the local kin-group, but a group of sisters and female cousins in one band received and shared mates from other bands—often, the group of brothers and male cousins of an adjacent band. This kind of group marriage, which Morgan and Engels called punaluan, yielded a large matrilineal, matrilocal communistic household whose members continued to cooperate economically as well as in sex and in child care.

Upper Savagery saw the bow and arrow invented, hunting increased, and polished stone, basketry, timber houses, villages, and dugout canoes come into use. The matrilineal communistic household persisted, but toward the end of the period women effected a change from group marriage to pairing marriage—that is, serial monogamy, or occasional polygyny or polyandry, in which both spouses were free to divorce. Engels saw this happening partly because incest and marriage prohibitions became extended so widely that it was hard to continue with sororal or fraternal group marriage, and partly because feminine powers in the matrilocal household became strong enough to put an end to multiple sex unions, which the women found burdensome. The matrilocal communistic household, ruled largely by women, persisted into the era of Barbarism. As population increased, groups of related matrilineal households formed dispersed, out-marrying *gentes* (today more commonly called clans) within the larger tribe.

Pottery was invented in Lower Barbarism. Middle Barbarism began when plants were domesticated in the New World, and animals in the Old. Engels thought that cultivation came much later than the domestication of animals in the Old World, toward the end of Middle Barbarism. The period is represented by the Mexicans, Peruvians, Pueblo Indians, and Central Americans in the New World and by the early Aryans and Semites in the Old. During this period in the Old World, private property—especially herds—began to be accumulated by men, who thus acquired new powers over women and were able to switch the descent rule from matriliny to patriliny. Matriarchy, or the rule of women in the domestic economy, was thus overthrown and patriarchy was instituted. Engels calls this the "world historic defeat of the female sex."

Patriarchy continued as the dominant mode through Upper Barbarism into Civilization, and persists in modified form in Western society. As men became supreme in the family as well as in society, they changed pairing marriage with its easy divorce and high status for women into monogamy, in which divorce was either prohibited entirely or permitted only to men. Engels, like Bachofen and others, thought that patriliny and patriarchy were made possible by the newly acquired knowledge of the male role in procreation and thus by the ability to determine physiological fatherhood with accuracy. This knowledge, plus the growth of heritable property in male hands, caused men to institute rules of legitimacy and chastity so that they could be sure that only their physiological sons inherited from them. Such rules, of course, greatly restricted the sexual and social freedom of women.

The position of women was further degraded in Middle Barbarism by slavery—a parallel to the subjugation of domesticated animals. Once slavery had arisen, class society was born, and men of the upper, property-owning class were able to exploit slave women both for their labor and as sexual rivals with their wives. From its beginnings, therefore, monogamy, far from being the culmination of equal sex love between men and women (as Victorian society portrayed it) in fact marked the oppression of women both as wives and as concubines, and the "double standard" in sexual morality. Women retaliated, however, by creating the cuckold and the paramour.

Along with monogamy, herding, and slavery came the patriarchal household, composed now not solely of relatives but of a nuclear family or group of patrilineal kinsfolk plus their bondservants. The head patriarch might share government of the group with a council of his adult male kinfolk or might have sole rights of life and death over the women, children, and slaves.

The patriarchal family became consolidated in Upper Barbarism with the smelting of iron, the invention of the plow, wagon, chariot, et cetera, and the growth of large populations in fortified towns. The Homeric Greeks, the pre-Roman Italians, Tacitus' Germanic tribes, and the Viking Age Normans, exemplified Upper Barbarism.

Alphabetic writing ushered in the age of Civilization, and the state arose, as found in early Athens and Rome. Engels thought that these classical European powers plumbed the lowest depths in the degradation of women, Athens even more so than Rome. In some of the smaller or more peripheral states of early civilization, however, tribal vestiges remained, something similar to pairing marriage persisted, and women had a higher status. Among these were Sparta and—more significant—the Germans who overran the declining Roman Empire. Engels erroneously thought that individual sex love arose among the German peoples because of their tendencies to pairing marriage, although he admits somewhat confusingly that it began as courtly or adulterous love, flourishing first in Provence, and only much later superseding the arranged marriages of the Germans.

In spite of the modern European tradition of romantic love and the transition from patriarchal to nuclear family households, marriage in the 1880s showed only a trifling improvement on that in the classical empires. Engels grimly satirizes the French arranged marriage, exhibiting "the fullest unfolding of the contradictions inherent in monogamy—flourishing hetaerism on the part of the husband, and flourishing adultery on the part of the wife." The Catholic church had abolished divorce because "it was convinced that for adultery, as for death, there is no cure whatsoever." Protestant "love" marriage was even worse: "Since the citizens of Protestant countries are mostly Philistines, Protestant monogamy leads merely ... to a wedded life of leaden boredom, which is described as domestic bliss." In both types marriage was in fact determined by class position and the wife "differs from the ordinary courtesan only in that she does not hire out her body, like a wage worker, on piecework, but sells it into slavery once and for all."

Engels romanticized proletarian marriage, believing that women's work outside the home had removed "the last remnants of male domination in the home"—despite traces of "some of that brutality towards women which became firmly rooted with the establishment of monogamy." Among the propertied classes, however, the husband's position as breadwinner makes him the "bourgeois" within the family, while "the wife represents the proletariat" living in disguised domestic enslavement. Just as the sexual division of tasks in Savagery formed the foundation of all subsequent division of labor, and the subordination of women in Barbarism foreshadowed the birth of class society, so the modern bourgeois family contains within it the contradiction between bourgeoisie and proletariat. It can be resolved only by abolishing the sexual division of labor and instituting communal management of property, collective domestic work and child care, and the full entry of women into all forms of public work in a socialist society.

SOURCES

Engels' theories were limited by the knowledge of his time, and perhaps in part by his own predilections. To give salient examples, modern prehistory suggests that speech developed only long *after* prehumans descended to earth, evolved upright posture, separated the functions of hand and foot, and relied much on hunting.[2] Hunting as a male specialty, separate from female gathering and child care, may have been established up to two million years ago, and there is little evidence to date of its being preceded by an era of predominant fishing. The bow lacks the focal significance in hunting that Engels thought it possessed. All of this suggests a sexual division of labor between hunting and gathering coincident with, or even preceding, the development of language, which is the accepted criterion of the transition to humanness.[3]

Engels dismisses as dead-end side developments the societies of non-human primates as evidence of prehuman social life. Yet comparative primatology (greatly developed since Engels' time), combined with human paleontology and archeology, are the sole sources of real data for reconstructions and speculations about prehuman society. Similarly, accounts of the actual social lives of primitive hunters and gatherers in modern times, although imperfect, are better guides to those of early humans than are Morgan's and Engels' speculations about early family life on the basis of present day kinship terminologies or of classical mythology. The former do not in fact require group marriage to account for the "lumping" of relatives into categories reflective of clans, lineages or other types of kinship group.[4] The "evidence" on which Engels erects his theory of early group marriage is thus quite inadequate.

In the later periods, the domestication of plants in the Old World probably preceded or coincided with that of animals, rather than post-dating it. Again, Engels apparently thought that ancient Greece was the first state to have arisen in history, whereas the Greek states were of course preceded by much earlier empires in Egypt, Mesopotamia, India, and China. While he may not have known of the antiquity of Asian civilizations, Engels did know a great deal about their structure and about the types of production relations found in them, for he and Marx had earlier differentiated "Asiatic societies" both from slave states and from feudalism. Surprisingly, Engels makes almost no reference to

---

[2]See, for example, Charles F. Hockett and Robert Ascher, "The Human Evolution," in Yehudi A. Cohen (ed.), *Man in Adaptation: The Biosocial Background* (Chicago: Aldine, 1968).

[3]Speculations about the dating of speech vary greatly, however. Hockett (1968) puts it as early as the Australopithecenes, up to 1,750,000 years ago; Livingstone, as late as the Upper Paleolithic, some 70,000 to 50,000 years ago. [See Frank B. Livingstone, "Genetics, Ecology and the Origin of Incest and Exogamy," *Current Anthropology* 10(February 1969):45–49, 57–61.] A more common view would see language, fire making, and some kind of family with incest prohibitions established sometime between the Pithecanthropines of 500,000 years ago and the Neanderthal people of about 100,000 years ago.

[4]For this and other criticism of Morgan's and (by implication) Engels' theories of group marriage, see Robert H. Lowie, *The History of Ethnological Theory* (New York: Holt, Rinehart & Winston, 1937), p. 65.

Asian societies in this work, and leaves out the "Asiatic mode of production" as an alternative to slavery and to serfdom. This is unfortunate, for the position of women in the ancient Asian and Middle Eastern empires substantiates Engels' theory that women reached their lowest point of subordination and degradation after the rise of "civilization," the state and the alphabet.

EARLY PROMISCUITY

Having mentioned some of the deficiencies of data, let us turn to the theories themselves. First, in spite of the modern increase in knowledge of early society, it must be frankly stated that the earliest forms of human sexual association, and the circumstances surrounding the origin of the family, are unknown. It is not even known whether some kind of family, with restrictions on mating, developed before or after we became human (that is, developed language).

Of mankind's nearer kinsfolk (the great apes), gibbons live in monogamous family groups of a female, her male partner, and her young children. Orangutans live in small clusters of one or two females plus young, with perhaps a nearby male, or in temporary male-female pairs, or in troops of young, unattached males. Gorillas have male-dominant polygynous families of an older male with several mates, sometimes accompanied by young males who may copulate occasionally with a female when the chief is tired or not looking. All of this suggests the possibility of a kind of prehuman family, although without any division of labor or cooperation between the sexes in food provision. (Each adult forages and nests independently; mothers share nests and food with their young.) There *may* have been prehuman restrictions on intercourse between parents and children. Gibbon parents drive off their young of opposite sex at puberty, although no such practice has been noted for orangutans or gorillas.[5]

On the other hand, chimpanzees—our closest primate relatives—do have promiscuous hordes varying in size from three or four to forty individuals. And of the modern great apes, chimpanzees, as well as being genetically closest to man, inhabit ecological settings most similar

[5] Useful studies of primate social life include F. Clark Howell and Francois Bourlière (eds.), *African Ecology and Human Evolution* (Chicago: Aldine, 1964); Sherwood L. Washburn (ed.), *Social Life of Early Man* (New York: Wenner-Gren Foundation for Anthropological Research, 1961) and *Classification and Human Evolution* (Chicago: Aldine, 1963); James N. Spuhler (ed.), *Genetic Diversity and Human Behavior* (Chicago: Aldine, 1968)—all Viking Fund Publications in Anthropology. See also John Buettner-Janusch, *Origins of Man* (New York: Wiley, 1966); Desmond Morris (ed.), *Primate Ethology* (Chicago: Aldine, 1967); and, as an introduction, Thomas W. McKern and Sharon McKern, *Human Origins: An Introduction to Physical Anthropology* (Englewood Cliffs, N.J.: Prentice-Hall, 1969).

to those from which early humans emerged. They live partly in trees but often on the ground, fleeing into trees from danger. Fruits, nuts, worms, grubs, or small or sick animals provide their food. Chimpanzees go mainly on all fours but sometimes on two feet, and can use and make simple tools. Males are dominant, but not very dominant, over females. Hierarchy among males is unstable, and males often move between groups. A mother attends her young until their puberty at about age ten, and the mother-child group is the only stable unit. That humans emerged—as Engels thought—from similar promiscuous bands seems a plausible, and to me the most likely, theory.

GROUP MARRIAGE

Assuming promiscuous prehuman or protohuman bands, through what stages did families develop? Here Engels is on shakier ground. There is no evidence whatever of actual, ongoing group marriage among modern hunters and gatherers, although, as Engels saw, there *is* a group quality to marriage in most hunting and gathering, and also in most horticultural and herding societies. Thus, individual marriages are arranged between groups, group members may substitute for dead spouses, and occasional group orgies may occur at festive seasons. But all of this is readily explicable in terms of existing group solidarity and group cooperation in production, distribution, and defense; it cannot legitimately be attributed to prior group marriage. Similarly, the prevalence of premarital sex relations in hunting societies does not necessarily point to prior group marriage. It can be understood in that—given the sexual division between male hunting and female gathering—marriage and the family are economic necessities for both adults and children. But sex restrictions on women before marriage do not normally develop until male control of the state and of durable property make them the masters over women, imbued with notions of legitimacy and feminine chastity.

Again, the majority of hunting households are not "communistic" extended families at all but nuclear families of father, mother and children, with occasional polygyny. Still less commonly does the whole band constitute a common household, and when it does, the component nuclear families usually persist as separate residential, mating and commensal units. Although some 50 percent of hunting societies do contain some extended families or smaller stem-families,[6] large extended

[6]For exact figures on types of household, marriage, sexual division of labor, band structure, incest and exogamic prohibitions, and other variables among hunters and gatherers compared with other kinds of societies, see George Peter Murdock, "World Ethnographic Sample." *American Anthropolo-*

families as economic cooperative units are far more prevalent in cultivating and herding societies than among the more primitive hunters. And although sororal polygyny occurs in about 77 percent of known hunting societies, the rare institutions that are more suggestive of group marriage (combined polyandry and polygyny within one household, multiple visiting husbands, or what Engels aptly calls the "club" marriages of the Nayars) are found in a small number of specialized, relatively advanced cultivating societies—even in some states—rather than among hunters and gatherers.[7]

MATRIARCHY

Matrilocal residence and the germs of matrilineal descent, although found in some 16 percent of hunting societies today, are far less common than is patrilocal residence (63 percent) with incipient patrilineal descent. Statistically, matriliny and matrilocal residence are most closely related not with hunting but with preplow horticulture in the absence of large domesticated animals—that is, with types of economy that Engels would have placed in Lower Barbarism.[8] This does not mean that the very earliest human settlements, following the establishment of incest prohibitions, were definitely *not* matrilocal. In fact, they may have been, for male primates tend to wander between bands far more than do females, and many primate species exclude young bachelors from sex relations with females of their natal groups, driving them off or causing them to live on the periphery until they are old enough to oust their elders.

The earliest human incest prohibitions may, therefore, have involved the expulsion of pubertal males by their elders and their attachment to females of neighboring groups. We cannot, however, say that this was

gist 59(August 1957):664–687; Allan C. Coult, *Cross-Tabulations of Murdock's World Ethnographic Sample* (Columbia: University of Missouri, 1965); and George Peter Murdock, *Ethnographic Atlas* (Pittsburgh: University of Pittsburgh Press, 1967). In the last mentioned survey, out of 175 hunting societies, 47 percent had only nuclear families, 38 percent had stem-families, and 14 percent had extended families.

[7]Soviet anthropologists continued to believe in Morgan's and Engels' early "stages" longer than did anthropologists in the West, and some still think that a form of group marriage intervened between promiscuity and pairing marriage. Semyonov, for example, argues that in the stage of group marriage, mating was forbidden within the band but the men of one band had multiple visiting sex relations with the women of a paired, adjacent band. The difficulty is that most of the "survivals" from which Semyonov draws his evidence are found not among hunters but among horticulturalists. (See Y. I. Semyonov, "Group Marriage: Its Nature and Role in the Evolution of Marriage and Family Relations." Seventh International Congress of Anthropological and Ethnological Sciences, Moscow, 1967. Vol. 4, pp. 26–31.)

[8]See David F. Aberle, "Matrilineal Descent in Cross-Cultural Perspective," in David M. Schneider and Kathleen Gough (eds.), *Matrilineal Kinship* (Berkeley: University of California Press, 1961), pp. 655–730. The book as a whole is relevant to this discussion of matriliny and "matriarchy." See also Kathleen Gough, "The Origin of the Family." *Up From Under*, January 1971.

definitely so, and we must acknowledge that patrilocal residence must have occurred among a large proportion of hunting societies long before the domestication of plants and animals—and that it predominates among hunters today. It seems likely, in fact, that matrilineal descent and matrilocal residence never characterized a *general* evolutionary stage of cultural development, but only that they occurred as a common alternative among horticultural (but not predominantly herding) societies and even persisted in some few plow agricultural societies (for example, Nayar, Minangkabau), for some time after the rise of the state.

This leads us to two other points in connection with matriliny. One is that matriliny and patriliny are not related to ignorance or knowledge of physiological paternity, as Engels, Bachofen, and others thought they were. All known matrilineal societies—indeed, all known societies—possess a social role of fatherhood, whether or not they understand the male role in procreation. *Social* fatherhood, found in the most primitive known societies, evidently springs not from physiological knowledge but from the sexual division of labor between men and women, especially in relation to the protection and maintenance of children. It is present in embryo among male apes, who protect females and young from predators, but it became crystalized with the human *economic* division of labor between the sexes, found to date in all known human societies.

The other point is that matriliny does not involve "matriarchy" or female dominance, either in the home or in society, as Engels tended to believe. Matriarchy, as the reverse of patriarchy, has in fact almost certainly never existed.[9] It is true that in most matrilineal societies women have greater personal freedom regarding movement, sexuality, divorce, property ownership and household management than in patrilineal societies of corresponding levels of productivity. These freedoms are perhaps most pronounced in matrilocal, horticultural tribes, where durable property is not yet extensive and husbands move to live with their wives. In particular, women in matrilineal societies experience relatively little control from their fathers and husbands, who belong to different kin groups from their own. Nevertheless, men predominate as heads of households, lineages, and communities in matrilineal as in patrilineal societies, and women experience greater or less authority from their mothers' brothers, elder brothers, or even their

---

[9]Morgan himself disproves the idea of female dominance among the Iroquois, one of the prime instances of "matriarchy" cited by Engels and by many later Marxists. Morgan refers to "the absence of equality between the sexes" and notes that women were subordinate to men, ate after men, and the women (but not the men) were publicly whipped as punishment for adultery. War leaders, tribal chiefs, and *sachems* (heads of matrilineal lineages) were men. Women did, however, have a large say in the government of the long house or name of the matrilocal extended family, figured as tribal counsellors and religious officials, and arranged marriages. Lewis H. Morgan, *The League of the Ho-de-no-Sau-nee or Iroquois*, 2 vols. (New Haven, Conn.: Human Relations Area Files, 1954).

grown sons. Some degree of male dominance has, in fact, been universal to date in human society, although matrilineal systems are usually kinder to women.

GENERAL APPROACHES

Like other nineteenth-century evolutionists, Engels placed uncritical reliance on what he thought were "survivals" of customs he wished to posit for the distant past. Temple prostitution, for example, is explicable as a product of class societies dominated by priesthoods, just as modern prostitution is explicable as a product of class societies dominated by private, secular ownership of property and by wage labor. Neither form offers evidence of earlier group marriage, or anything else.

With reference to general theory, also, Engels' analysis contains two major flaws. One is that although he purports to offer a "materialist" interpretation of history—that is, one that traces laws and beliefs to their foundations in modes and relations of production—he does not in fact always do so. This is especially true with reference to group marriage, for Engels does not explain what changes in subsistence patterns underlay the transition from promiscuous to consanguine, consanguine to punaluan, or punaluan to pairing relations. If one considers how a promiscuous, chimpanzeelike group of partly arboreal, largely fructivorous prehunters might have descended to earth in a period of drought, developed a hunting and gathering way of life, and instituted a sexual division of labor and of child protection, it is in fact plausible to argue that they went straight from promiscuity to nuclear families of a kind similar to those among most hunters today. All that would be needed would be for particular male hunters to attach themselves to particular female gatherers and their young, instead of each individual's foraging alone. By such a simple union both sexes would be assured of adequate food, even though (as in most primate societies) they would continue to rely on the combined defense of several males for protection of the band and its young from predators. More durable attachments between male and female might then lead to the expulsion of pubertal males from the family by their mother's ongoing partner, as among gibbons, and perhaps also, of pubertal females by their mothers. This would mean that young males would be likely to mate with young females from other families or even from other bands. Partial "incest prohibitions" may thus have been instituted, which would become extended and regularized with the growth of language, wider economic cooperation, and moral precepts. Although it is not impossible that group marriage intervened between the eras of promiscuity and of family households, it is hard to see how this would come about on the basis of changing material relations, and Engels does not explain it.

The second objection is that when he does rest his argument on changes in material relations, Engels sometimes neglects the secondary impact of political institutions on family structures. Thus, while he traces—correctly, I think—the effect of the growth of private property in increasing male dominance, Engels does not directly refer to the rise of the state as *itself* a powerful factor further subordinating women of both ruling and subject classes. Yet it is clear that men—already the warriors and political leaders in prestate societies—occupied almost all the major governmental roles in early states. This allowed them to vest the male heads of households with previously unknown, despotic powers over women, children, and slaves.

APPRAISAL

Despite these criticisms—and many more that could be made—the general trend of Engels' argument still appears to be sound. It is probable that our prehuman ancestors lived in promiscuous bands. It is improbable, but not disproven, that early humans passed through various types of group marriage before they instituted the forms of "pairing marriage," with occasional polygyny and polyandry, that characterize the hunting bands and the horticultural and fishing tribes of modern times. It is true that *gentes* or clans have developed almost universally out of smaller kin groups in "Upper Savagery" or in "Barbarism." It is true that although it is not group marriage in Engels' sense, marriage has a group character in many hunting bands and in most of the more complex tribal societies that have developed with the domestication of plants and animals. In such societies, each individual belongs to a household, a local kin group, a clan or a lineage, whose members are collectively responsible for one another and marry outside their group. Marriage thus entails the movement of either men or women between groups. It is arranged by group representatives; there may be occasional sexual sharing within the group; second spouses are commonly drawn from the same group as the first one; and a group may be obliged to substitute new spouses if former ones die or fail in their obligations. With the development of privately owned, heritable property, and especially with the rise of the state, this group character gradually disappears. Especially in the greater agrarian and commercial empires, women become the personal wards of their fathers, their husbands, the male heads of the households in which they reside, or, in the case of bondservants, of their masters. In capitalist society the operative kin group becomes still further whittled away to the nuclear family, in which, in Engels' time, fathers and husbands retained virtually despotic *de facto* power over "their" womenfolk.

Although matriarchy is a fantasy, it is true that matrilineal descent and inheritance—arising historically out of matrilocal residence—is found in some hunting societies and is common, and may once have been very widespread, in horticultural tribes, chiefdoms, and even some small, simply organized states. It is true that women's status is usually higher in such societies than in patrilineal societies of comparable productivity. Engels does not do justice to the variety of kinship systems found in prestate societies—the many forms of bilateral, nonunilineal, or even double-unilineal systems. It is true, however, that predominantly herding societies tend to be patrilineal and to encourage polygyny for men wealthy in herds. When such societies are not yet states, women are usually freer than they are in the patriarchal empires. They are often, for example, permitted relative freedom of divorce, remarriage, and even of having their children begotten by lovers, provided that such children are strictly allotted to the woman's legal husbands. Nevertheless, the emergence of male private property in herds does seem to have played a large role in the establishment of early patriarchal households and in the concept of legitimacy.

Again, monogamy is not as universal in "civilized" societies as Engels thought; the Islamic and many of the Far Eastern empires preserved optional polygyny, especially for the wealthy and powerful. But it is true that in the archaic states with their sharply divided ruling and subject classes and their reliance on permanent, often irrigated, landed estates and large-scale heritable property, the patriarchal family flowered almost universally, prostitution became endemic, and women of all classes were subjugated in the varying ways that Engels describes.

Engels' ironic picture of marriage in capitalist society largely applies today. The chief difference is that, as he foresaw, the *legal* rights of men and women have become progressively more equal, but (as in the case of racism) this only reveals more nakedly the social and economic discrimination applied to women in every sphere of public and domestic life. Engels is right, moreover, in asserting that only the abolition of privately owned productive property, the movement of women into public work, *and* the socialization of domestic work and of child care can bring about equality between men and women. Modern socialist societies, whatever their problems, have gone a considerable distance in the first two respects but have tended to fail in the third. They have also failed to grant women control over their own bodily functions through free access to contraception and abortion and through the abolition of legitimacy. It may even yet be left to Western society to usher in the full emancipation of women, along with the abolition both of capitalism and of the state.

Women: The Longest
Revolution
Juliet Mitchell

The situation of women is different from that of any other social group.
This is because they are not one of a number of isolable units, but half
a totality: the human species. Women are essential and irreplaceable;
they cannot therefore be exploited in the same way as other social
groups can. They are fundamental to the human condition; yet in their
economic, social, and political roles, they are not marginal. It is
precisely this combination—fundamental and marginal at one and the
same time—that has been fatal to them. Within the world of men, their
position is comparable to that of an oppressed minority: but they also
exist outside the world of men. The one state justifies the other and
precludes protest. In advanced industrial society, women's work is only
marginal to the total economy. Yet it is through work that man changes
natural conditions and thereby produces society. Until there is a
revolution in production, the labor situation will prescribe women's
situation within the world of men. But women are offered a universe of
their own: the family. Like woman herself, the family appears as a
natural object, but it is actually a cultural creation. There is nothing
inevitable about the form or role of the family any more than there is
about the character or role of women. It is the function of ideology to
present these given social types as aspects of Nature itself. Both can be
exalted, paradoxically, as ideals. The "true" woman and the "true"
family are images of peace and plenty: in actuality, they may both be
sites of violence and despair. The apparently natural condition can be

made to appear more attractive than the arduous advance of human beings towards culture. But what Marx wrote about the bourgeois myths of the Golden Ancient World describes precisely women's realm:

> ... In one way the childlike world of the ancients appears to be superior, and this is so, insofar as we seek for closed shape, form, and established limitation. The ancients provide a narrow satisfaction, whereas the modern world leaves us unsatisfied or where it appears to be satisfied with itself, is vulgar and mean.

WOMEN IN SOCIALIST THEORY

The problem of the subordination of women and the need for their liberation was recognized by all the great socialist thinkers in the nineteenth century. It is part of the classical heritage of the revolutionary movement. Yet today, in the West, the problem has become a subsidiary, if not an invisible element in the preoccupations of socialists. Perhaps no other major issue has been so forgotten. In England, the cultural heritage of Puritanism, always strong on the Left, contributed to a widespread diffusion of essentially conservative beliefs among many who would otherwise count themselves as "progressive." A *locus classicus* of these attitudes is Peter Townsend's remarkable statement:

> Traditional Socialists have ignored the family or they have openly tried to weaken it—alleging nepotism and the restrictions placed upon individual fulfilment by family ties. Extreme attempts to create societies on a basis other than the family have failed dismally. It is significant that a Socialist usually addresses a colleague as "brother" and a Communist uses the term *comrade*. The chief means of fulfilment in life is to be a member of, and reproduce a family. There is nothing to be gained by concealing this truth.[1]

... Part of the explanation for the decline in socialist debate on the subject lies not only in the real historical processes, but in the original weaknesses in the traditional discussion of the subject in the classics. For while the great studies of the last century all stressed the importance of the problem, they did not solve it theoretically. The limitations of their approach have never been subsequently transcended.

Fourier was the most ardent and voluminous advocate of women's liberation and of sexual freedom among the early socialists. ... Fourier's ideas remained at the level of utopian moral injunction.[2] Marx used and

---

[1] Peter Townsend, "A Society for People," in Norman MacKenzie (ed.), *Conviction* (London: MacGibbon & Kee, 1958), pp. 119–120.

[2] Charles Fourier, "Theorie des Quatre Mouvements," in *Oeuvres Completes*, Vol. 1 (1841), p. 195;

transformed them, integrating them into a philosophical critique of human history. But he retained the abstraction of Fourier's conception of the position of women as an index of general social advance. This in effect makes it merely a symbol—it accords the problem a universal importance at the cost of depriving it of its specific substance. Symbols are allusions to or derivations of something else. In Marx's early writings, woman becomes an anthropological entity, an ontological category, of a highly abstract kind. Contrarily, in his later work, where he is concerned with describing the family, Marx differentiates it as a phenomenon according to time and place.... What is striking is that here the problem of women has been submerged in an analysis of the family. The difficulties of this approach can be seen in the somewhat apocalyptic note of Marx's comments on the fate of the bourgeois family.... There was little historical warrant for the idea that it was in effective dissolution, and indeed could no longer be seen in the working class. Marx thus moves from general philosophical formulations about women in the early writings to specific historical comments on the family in the later texts.... There is a serious disjunction between the two. The common framework of both, of course, was his analysis of the economy, and of the evolution of property.

ENGELS

It was left to Engels to systematize these theses in *The Origin of the Family, Private Property and the State*, after Marx's death. Engels declared that the inequality of the sexes was one of the first antagonisms within the human species. The first class antagonism "coincides with the development of the antagonism between man and woman in the monogamous marriage, and the first class oppression with that of the female sex by the male...."[3]

Bebel, Engel's disciple, attempted to provide a programmatic account of woman's oppression as such, not simply as a by-product of the evolution of the family and of private property: "From the beginning of time, oppression was the common lot of woman and the labourer.... Woman was the first human being that tasted bondage, woman was a slave before the slave existed."[4] He acknowledged, with Marx and Engels, the importance of physical inferiority in accounting for women's subordination; but while stressing inheritance, added that a

cited in Karl Marx and Friedrich Engels, *The Holy Family* (1845), tr. by R. Dixon (London: Lawrence & Wishart, 1957), p. 259.

[3]Friedrich Engels, *Origins of the Family, Private Property and the State* (Chicago: Charles H. Kerr, 1902).

[4]August Bebel, *Woman in the Past, Present and Future*, tr. by H. B. Adams Walther (1886; reprint ed., New York: AMS Press), p. 7.

biological element—her maternal function—was one of the fundamental conditions that made her economically dependent on the man. But Bebel, too, was unable to do more than state that sexual equality was impossible without socialism. . . .

The liberation of women remains a normative idea, an adjunct to socialist theory, not structurally integrated into it.

THE SECOND SEX

The contrary is true of de Beauvoir's massive work *The Second Sex*—to this day the greatest single contribution on the subject.[5] Here the focus is the status of women through the ages. But socialism as such emerges as a curiously contingent solution at the end of the work, in a muffled epilogue. De Beauvoir's main theoretical innovation was to fuse the "economic" and "reproductive" explanations of women's subordination by a psychological interpretation of both. . . . Concurrent, however, with the idealist psychological explanation, de Beauvoir uses an orthodox economist approach. This leads to a definite evolutionism in her treatment in Volume 1, which becomes a retrospective narrative of the different forms of the feminine condition in different societies through time—mainly in terms of the property system and its effects on women. To this she adds various suprahistorical themes—myths of the eternal feminine, types of women through the ages, literary treatments of women—which do not modify the fundamental structure of her argument. The prospect for women's liberation at the end is quite divorced from any historical development.

Thus, the classical literature on the problem of woman's condition is predominantly economist in emphasis, stressing her simple subordination to the institutions of private property. Her biological status underpins both her weakness as a producer, in work relations, and her importance as a possession, in reproductive relations. . . .

What is the solution to this impasse? It must lie in differentiating woman's condition, much more radically than in the past, into its separate structures, which together form a complex—not a simple—unity. This will mean rejecting the idea that woman's condition can be deduced derivatively from the economy or equated symbolically with society. Rather, it must be seen as a specific structure, which is a unity of different elements. . . .

The lesson of [my] . . . reflections is that the liberation of women can only be achieved if all four structures in which they are integrated are

---

[5]Simone de Beauvoir, *The Second Sex*, ed. and tr. by H. M. Parshley (New York: Knopf, 1953); see also, Simone de Beauvoir, *Force of Circumstance*, tr. by Richard Howard (New York: Putnam, 1965).

transformed.[6] A modification of any one of them can be offset by a reinforcement of another, so that mere permutation of the form of exploitation is achieved. The history of the last sixty years provides ample evidence of this. In the early twentieth century, militant feminism in England or the U.S.A. surpassed the labor movement in the violence of its assault on bourgeois society, in pursuit of suffrage. This political right was eventually won. Nonetheless, though a simple completion of the formal legal equality of bourgeois society, it left the socioeconomic situation of women virtually unchanged.

The Russian Revolution produced a quite different experience. In the Soviet Union in the 1920s, advanced social legislation aimed at liberating women above all in the field of sexuality: divorce was made free and automatic for either partner, thus effectively liquidating marriage; illegitimacy was abolished, abortion was free, et cetera. The social and demographic effects of these laws in a backward, semiliterate society bent on rapid industrialization (needing, therefore, a high birthrate) were—predictably—catastrophic. Stalinism soon produced a restoration of iron traditional norms. Inheritance was reinstated, divorce inaccessible, abortion illegal, et cetera.

Women still retained the right and obligation to work; but because these gains had not been integrated into the earlier attempts to abolish the family and free sexuality, no general liberation has occurred. In China, still another experience is being played out today. At a comparable stage of the revolution, all the emphasis is being placed on liberating women in production. This has produced an impressive social promotion of women. But it has been accompanied by a tremendous repression of sexuality and a rigorous puritanism (currently rampant in civic life). This corresponds not only to the need to mobilize women massively in economic life, but to a deep cultural reaction against the corruption and prostitution prevalent in Imperial and Kuo Ming Tang China (a phenomenon unlike anything in Czarist Russia). Because the exploitation of women was so great in the ancien regime, women's participation at village level in the Chinese Revolution was uniquely high. As for reproduction, the Russian cult of maternity in the 1930s and 1940s has not been repeated for demographic reasons: indeed, China may be one of the first countries in the world to provide free state-authorized contraception on a universal scale to the population. Again, however, given the low level of industrialization and fear produced by imperialist encirclement, no all-round advance could be expected.

It is only in the highly developed societies of the West that an authentic liberation of women can be envisaged today. But for this to occur,

---

[6]The four structures are (1) production, (2) reproduction, (3) socialization, and (4) sexuality.

there must be a transformation of all the structures into which they are integrated, and an *unité de rupture*. A revolutionary movement must base its analysis on the uneven development of each, and attack the weakest link in the combination. This may then become the point of departure for a general transformation. What is the situation of the different structures today?

Production. The long-term development of the forces of production must command any socialist perspective. The hopes which the advent of machine technology raised as early as the nineteenth century have ... proved illusory. Today, automation promises the technical possibility of abolishing completely the physical differential between man and woman in production; but under capitalist relations of production, the social possibility of this abolition is permanently threatened and can easily be turned into its opposite, the actual diminution of woman's role in production as the labor force contracts. ... Woman's role in production is virtually stationary, and has been so for a long time now. In England in 1911, 30 percent of the work force were women; in the 1960s, 34 percent. The composition of these jobs has not changed decisively either. The jobs are very rarely careers. When they are not in the lowest positions on the factory floor, they are normally white-collar auxiliary positions (such as secretaries)—supportive to masculine roles. They are often jobs with a high expressive content, such as service tasks. Parsons says bluntly: "Within the occupational organization they are analogous to the wife-mother role in the family."[7] The educational system underpins this role structure. Seventy-five percent of eighteen-year-old girls in England are receiving neither training nor education today. The pattern of "instrumental" father and "expressive" mother is not substantially changed when the woman is gainfully employed, as her job tends to be inferior to that of the man's, to which the family then adapts.

Reproduction. Scientific advance in contraception could ... make involuntary reproduction—which accounts for the vast majority of births in the world today, and for a major proportion even in the West—a phenomenon of the past. But oral contraception—which has so far been developed in a form that exactly repeats the sexual inequality of Western society—is only at its beginnings. It is inadequately distributed across classes and countries and awaits further technical improvements. Its main initial impact is, in the advanced countries, likely to be psychological—it will certainly free women's sexual experience from many of the anxieties and inhibitions that have always afflicted it.

The demographic pattern of reproduction in the West may or may not

---

[7]Talcott Parsons and Robert F. Bales, *Family Socialization and Interaction Process* (Glencoe, Ill.: Free Press, 1955), p. 15 n.

be widely affected by oral contraception. One of the most striking phenomena of very recent years in the United States has been the sudden increase in the birthrate.... In fact, this reflects simply the lesser economic burden of a large family in conditions of economic boom in the richest country in the world. But it also reflects the magnification of familial ideology as a social force. This leads to the next structure.

Socialization. The changes in the composition of the work force, the size of the family, the structure of education, et cetera—however limited from an ideal standpoint—have undoubtedly diminished the societal function and importance of the family. As an organization it is not a significant unit in the political power system, it plays little part in economic production, and it is rarely the sole agency of integration into the larger society; thus at the macroscopic level, it serves very little purpose.

The result has been a major displacement of emphasis on to the family's psychosocial function, for the infant and for the couple. Parsons writes: "... the society is dependent more exclusively on it for the performance of certain of its vital functions."[8] The vital nucleus of truth in the emphasis on socialization of the child has been discussed [elsewhere].... It is essential that socialists should acknowledge it and integrate it entirely into any program for the liberation of women.

... There is no doubt that the need for permanent, intelligent care of children in the initial three or four years of their lives can (and has been) exploited ideologically to perpetuate the family as a total unit, when its other functions have been visibly declining. Indeed, the attempt to focus women's existance exclusively on bringing up children is manifestly harmful to children.

An increased awareness of the critical importance of socialization, far from leading to a restitution of classical maternal roles, should lead to a reconsideration of them—of what makes a good socializing agent, who can genuinely provide security and stability for the child.

The beliefs that the family provides an impregnable enclave of intimacy and security in an atomized and chaotic cosmos assumes the absurd—that the family can be isolated from the community, and that its internal relationships will not reproduce in their own terms the external relationships which dominate the society. The family as refuge in a bourgeois society inevitably becomes a reflection of it.

Sexuality. It is difficult not to conclude that the major structure which at present is in rapid evolution is sexuality.

... The dominant sexual ideology is proving less and less successful

---

[8]Parsons and Bales, *Family Socialization and Interaction Process*, pp. 9–10.

in regulating spontaneous behavior. Marriage in its classical form is increasingly threatened by the liberalization of relationships before and after [marriage], which affects all classes today. In this sense, it is evidently the weak link in the chain—the particular structure that is the site of the most contradictions.

In a context of juridical equality, the liberation of sexual experience from relations which are extraneous to it—whether procreation or property—could lead to true intersexual freedom. But it could also lead simply to new forms of neocapitalist ideology and practice. For one of the forces behind the current acceleration of sexual freedom has undoubtedly been the conversion of contemporary capitalism from a production-and-work ethos to a consumption-and-fun ethos.

The gist of [David] Riesman's argument is that in a society bored by work, sex is the only activity, the only reminder of one's energies, the only competitive act; the last defense against *vis inertiae*.[9] This same insight can be found, with greater theoretical depth, in Marcuse's notion of repressive de-sublimation—the freeing of sexuality for its own frustration in the service of a totally coordinated and drugged social machine.[10] Bourgeois society at present can well afford a play area of premarital nonprocreative sexuality. Even marriage can save itself by increasing divorce and remarriage rates, signifying the importance of the institution itself. These considerations make it clear that sexuality, while it presently may contain the greatest potential for liberation—can equally well be organized against any increase of its human possibilities.

This is a reminder that while one structure may be the weak link in a unity like that of woman's condition, there can never be a solution through it alone. The utopianism of Fourier or Reich was precisely to think that sexuality could inaugurate such a general solution. Lenin's remark to Clara Zetkin is a salutary if overstated corrective: However wild and revolutionary [sexual freedom] may be, it is still really quite bourgeois. It is mainly a hobby of the intellectuals and of the sections nearest them. . . .

For a general solution can only be found in a strategy that affects all the structures of women's exploitation. This means a rejection of two beliefs prevalent on the left:

REFORMISM. This now takes the form of limited ameliorative demands: equal pay for women, more nursery schools, better retraining facilities, et cetera. In its contemporary version, it is wholly divorced from any fundamental critique of women's condition or any vision of their real liberation (it was not always so).

VOLUNTARISM. This takes the form of maximalist demands—the

---

[9]David Riesman, *The Lonely Crowd* (New Haven, Conn.: Yale University Press, 1950).
[10]Herbert Marcuse, *Eros and Civilization* (Boston: Beacon Press, 1955).

abolition of the family, abrogation of all sexual restrictions, forceful separation of parents from children—which have no chance of winning any wide support at present, and which merely serve as a substitute for the job of theoretical analysis or practical persuasion. By pitching the whole subject in totally intransigent terms, voluntarism objectively helps to maintain it outside the framework of normal political discussion.

What, then, is the responsible revolutionary attitude? It must include both immediate and fundamental demands, in a single critique of the whole of women's situation, that does not fetishize any dimension of it. Modern industrial development, as has been seen, tends towards the separating out of the originally unified functions of the family—procreation, socialization, sexuality, economic subsistence, et cetera—even if this structural differentiation (to use a term of Parsons') has been checked and disguised by the maintenance of a powerful family ideology. This differentiation provides the real historical basis for the ideal demands which should be posed: structural differentiation is precisely what distinguishes an advanced from a primitive society (in which all social functions are fused en bloc).

In practical terms this means a coherent system of demands. The four elements of women's condition cannot merely be considered each in isolation; they form a structure of specific interrelations. The contemporary bourgeois family can be seen as a triptych of sexual, reproductive, and socializatory functions (the woman's world) embraced by production (the man's world)—precisely a structure which in the final instance is determined by the economy. The exclusion of women from production—social human activity—and their confinement to a monolithic condensation of functions in a unity—the family—which is precisely unified in the natural part of each function, is the root cause of the contemporary social definition of women as natural beings. Hence the main thrust of any emancipation movement must still concentrate on the economic element—the entry of women fully into public industry. The error of the old socialists was to see the other elements as reducible to the economic; hence the call for the entry of women into production was accompanied by the purely abstract slogan of the abolition of the family. Economic demands are still primary, but must be accompanied by coherent policies for the other three elements, policies which at particular junctures may take over the primary role in immediate action.

Economically, the most elementary demand is not the right to work or receive equal pay for work—the two traditional reformist demands—but the right to equal work itself. At present, women perform unskilled, uncreative service jobs that can be regarded as extensions of their expressive familial role. . . . But only two in a hundred women are in administrative or managerial jobs, and less than five in a thousand are in the professions. Women are poorly unionized (25 percent) and receive less money than men for the manual work they do perform: in 1961, the average industrial wage for women was less than half that for men, which, even setting off part-time work, represents a massive increment of exploitation for the employer.

EDUCATION

The whole pyramid of discrimination rests on a solid extraeconomic foundation—education. The demand for equal work, in Britain, should above all take the form of a demand for an equal educational system, since this is at present the main single filter selecting women for inferior work roles. . . .

Until these injustices are ended, there is no chance of equal work for women. It goes without saying that the content of the educational system, which actually instills limitation of aspiration in girls, needs to be changed as much as methods of selection. Education is probably the key area for immediate economic advance at present.

. . . Reproduction, sexuality, and socialization also need to be free from coercive forms of unification. Traditionally, the socialist movement has called for the "abolition of the bourgeois family." This slogan must be rejected as incorrect today. It is maximalist in the bad sense, posing a demand that is merely a negation without any coherent construction subsequent to it.

The reasons for the historic weakness of the [socialist] notion is that the family was never analyzed structurally—in terms of its different functions. It was a hypostatized entity; the abstraction of its abolition corresponds to the abstraction of its conception. The strategic concern for socialists should be for the equality of the sexes, not the abolition of the family. . . .

The family as it exists at present is, in fact, incompatible with the equality of the sexes. But this equality will not come from its administrative abolition, but from the historical differentiation of its functions. The revolutionary demand should be for the liberation of these functions from a monolithic fusion that oppresses each. Thus dissociation of reproduction from sexuality frees sexuality from alienation in unwanted reproduction (and fear of it), and reproduction from subjugation to chance and uncontrollable causality. It is thus an elementary demand to press for free state provision of oral contraception. The legalization of homosexuality—which is one of the forms of nonreproductive sexuality—should be supported for just the same reason, and regressive campaigns against it in Cuba or elsewhere should be unhesitatingly criticized. The straightforward abolition of illegitimacy as a legal notion, as in Sweden and Russia, has a similar implication; it would separate marriage civically from parenthood.

FROM NATURE TO CULTURE

The problem of socialization poses more difficult questions, as has been seen. But the need for intensive maternal care in the early years of a child's life does not mean that the present single sanctioned form of socialization—marriage and family—is inevitable. Far from it. The fundamental characteristic of the present system of marriage and family is in our society its monolithism: there is only one institutionalized form of intersexual or intergenerational relationship possible.

. . . All human experience shows that intersexual and intergenerational relationships are infinitely various—indeed, much of our creative literature is a celebration of the fact—while the institutionalized expression of them in our capitalist society is utterly simple and rigid.

Socialism should properly mean not the abolition of the family, but the diversification of the socially acknowledged relationships that are today forcibly and rigidly compressed into it. This would mean a plural range of institutions—where the family is only one, and its abolition implies none. Couples living together or not living together, long-term unions with children, single parents bringing up children, children socialized by conventional rather than biological parents, extended kin groups, et cetera—all could be encompassed in a range of institutions that match the free invention and variety of men and women. Socialism will be a process of change, of becoming. A fixed image of the future is in the worst sense ahistorical; the form that socialism takes will depend on the prior type of capitalism and the nature of its collapse.

The liberation of women under socialism will not be "rational" but a human achievement in the long passage from Nature to Culture, which is the definition of history and society.

ADDITIONAL READINGS

Mitchell, Juliet.
  1972   Woman's Estate. New York: Pantheon Books.
  1974   Psychoanalysis and Feminism. New York: Pantheon Books.

An Economic Perspective

Introduction   Helen Youngelson Waehrer

Over its two-hundred-year history, modern economics (that is, since Adam Smith) has gradually narrowed its focus from the study of general societal questions to those relating to market activities (e.g., the production and distribution of goods and services). Thus, since women's economic activities have been centered in the home, the problems and responsibilities arising from these nonmarket activities have remained outside the scope of most economic inquiry. Beginning in the late 1950s, however, economists broadened their studies to include women's activities, recognizing the economic role of women both inside and outside the market. This change in perspective was a result not only of the increasing importance of women's participation in the paid labor force, but also a recognition of the economic value of housework.

Much of the new research may be grouped under two broad topics: *labor market activities* and *nonmarket activities* (primarily unpaid work in the home).[1]

LABOR MARKET ACTIVITIES

The research on women's labor market activities is concerned with (1) *labor force participation* (why and how often women enter and leave the work force) and (2) *labor market differences* (differences between

[1]This brief discussion is by no means complete. Areas excluded are education, social policy, and empirical studies. For an extensive nontechnical review of the literature on women in market and nonmarket activities, see Hilda Kahne, "Economic Perspective on the Roles of Women in the American Economy." *Journal of Economic Literature* 13(December 1975):1249–1292.

men's and women's work experiences, e.g., in earnings, occupational distribution, rate of unemployment, etc.)

Studies of women's labor force participation examine a complex set of factors that influence women's decisions to participate in the labor force. These include: (1) women's family situation (e.g., marital status; age, number, and spacing of children; husband's income and occupation —see discussion by Mincer in this part); (2) women's years of education and training (e.g., higher levels of educational attainment have a positive influence on women's participation);[2] (3) growth in job opportunities (e.g., growth in traditional women's occupations create more job opportunities);[3] and (4) the general level of economic activity (e.g., high level of unemployment discourages women's participation).[4]

Studies in labor market differences attempt primarily to analyze the causes of the differences in earnings and occupational distribution. Among those factors studied are, first, the differences in productivity caused by women's traditional role in the family and by past discriminatory practices (affecting the aspirations, extent of education and training, and work experience); second, direct wage discrimination (wage differentials not based on productivity differences) attributed to employer's mistaken belief that women are less productive or have a preference for discrimination; and, third, occupational segregation by sex (which limits women to low-pay, low-status jobs within a relatively limited number of occupations) attributable to gender-role differentiation, exclusionary job classifications within firms, and discriminatory practices of male employees (e.g., trade unions and professional organizations—see discussion by Blau and Jusenius and by Reich et al. in this part).

In addition, studies have examined differences in the rate of unemployment focusing on (1) interlabor force mobility (how often women enter and leave the work force during their work lives), and (2) women as a reserve army, pulled into the work force when there are shortages of workers and pushed out when they are no longer needed (see discussion by Gray in Part Three).

NONMARKET ACTIVITIES

Research on women's *nonmarket activities* includes three general topics: (1) studies of work in the home (these consider work as a nonmarket

[2] James A. Sweet, *Women in the Labor Force* (New York: Seminar Press, 1973).

[3] Valerie K. Oppenheimer, *The Female Labor Force in the United States: Demographic and Economic Factors Governing its Growth and Changing Composition*, Population Monograph Series no. 5 (Berkeley: University of California, 1970).

[4] W. B. Bowen and T. A. Finegan, *The Economics of Labor Force Participation* (Princeton, N.J.: Princeton University Press, 1969), chap. 16.

household production and assume that a scarcity of time influences a women's choice about how she allocates her time among alternative combinations of household tasks);[5] (2) attempts to measure the monetary value of nonmarket work (these focus mainly on housework and child rearing within the family unit—see discussion by Glazer in Part Four); and (3) family-related issues affecting both market and nonmarket activities (see discussion by Benston in this part). This last category includes patterns and choices in marriage,[6] historic changes in the economic functions of the family,[7] and issues relating to child care and fertility.[8]

THEORETICAL APPROACHES

Across these major categories of labor activities, three distinct theoretical approaches can be identified in the analysis of women's economic role.

The *neoclassical* framework (the dominant approach among American economists) focuses on the workings of the market sector. Neoclassical economists, such as Samuelson,[9] Becker,[10] Mincer,[11] and Bergmann,[12] concern themselves primarily with how the market maximizes efficiency in the production of goods and services to the neglect of questions concerning the distribution of income and wealth (e.g., problems concerning poverty, racism, and sexism). Neoclassical theory assumes a voluntary exchange between business firms and households in the market. Prices are determined by the interaction of business firms and households to their mutual advantage. It emphasizes the role of the individual decision maker,[13] with business firms acting so as to maximize

[5]Gary S. Becker, "A Theory of the Allocation of Time." *Economic Journal* 75(September 1965):493 –517; and R. Gronau, "The Intrafamily Allocation of Time: Value of Housewives." *American Economic Review* 63(September 1973):634–651.

[6]For example, see Fredricka P. Santos, "The Economics of Marital Status," in Cynthia B. Lloyd (ed.), *Sex, Discrimination, and the Division of Labor* (New York: Columbia University Press, 1975), pp. 244–268.

[7]Isabel Sawhill, Heather Ross, and Anita MacIntosh, "The Family in Transition," Working Paper no. 776-02 (Washington, D.C.: The Urban Institute, September 14, 1973).

[8]For a review of the literature, see Harvey Leibenstein, "An Interpretation of the Economic Theory of Fertility: Promising Path or Blind Alley?" *Journal of Economic Literature* 12(June 1974):457–479.

[9]Among his works, see Paul Samuelson, *Economics*, 10th ed. (New York: McGraw-Hill, 1976).

[10]Among his works, see Gary S. Becker, *The Economics of Discrimination*, 2nd ed. (Chicago: University of Chicago Press, 1971).

[11]See selection by Jacob Mincer in this section.

[12]Barbara R. Bergmann, "Occupational Segregation, Wages and Profits When Employers Discriminate by Race or Sex." *Eastern Economic Journal* 1(April/July 1974):103–110; and her article coauthored with Irmal Adelman, "The 1973 Report of the President's Council of Economic Advisors: The Economic Role of Women." *American Economic Review* 63(September 1973):509–514.

[13]This approach is similar to the exchange theory in sociology that borrowed its assumptions from neoclassical economics; see Peter Blau, *Exchange and Power in Social Life* (New York: Wiley, 1964)

profits, and households acting so as to maximize personal satisfaction. Entering the market with given "tastes," individuals are influenced in their economic decisions by prices and income. Thus, differences between people are assumed to be because of differences in personal tastes. Social institutions (e.g., government, school, family), although recognized as affecting those tastes, are not variables in the theory and, hence, remain unexplored (see discussion by Bell in Part One).

Neoclassical economists assume that women's economic situation is, thus, a result of "tastes" (of the women themselves, of employers, employees, teachers, etc.) acquired through socialization by individuals.

Public policy following this approach includes programs that effect individual tastes by attempting to change attitudes and beliefs by resocializing people. Such policies would concentrate on eliminating sexism in education (e.g., in textbooks and career counseling) and providing schooling and training programs that would prepare women for the job market on an equal basis with men.

The second theoretical approach focuses on *social institutions*, studying in detail the historic development of specific organizations (e.g., schools, business firms, industries, trade unions, etc.). Economists as diverse as Veblen,[14] Galbraith,[15] and Doeringer and Piore[16] focus their attention on institutional growth and technological change affecting the economy. These institutionalists give prime importance in their theories to the social context in which people function. Institutionalists assume women's economic opportunities and actions are restricted by sexist institutional practices.

Public policy proposals following this approach would be compatible with changing institutional practices that discriminate against women. Thus institutionalists would promote legislation such as antidiscrimination laws and Affirmative Action programs. Such laws would ensure legally that women receive equal pay for equal work and have equal access to credit at lending institutions, and they would prohibit discriminatory practices by employers in recruiting, hiring, training, and promotions.

Radical political economics, the third theoretical approach, draws heavily from Marxian and neo-Marxian analyses (e.g., Baran and Sweezy, and Mandel).[17] Diverse groups of radical political economists,

and John Scanzoni, *Sexual Bargaining: Power Politics in the American Marriage* (Englewood Cliffs, N.J.: Prentice-Hall, 1972).

[14]Thorstein Veblen, *Theory of the Leisure Class*, Modern Library Edition (New York: Random House, 1934).

[15]Among his works, see John Kenneth Galbraith, *Economics and Public Purpose* (Boston: Houghton Mifflin, 1973).

[16]Peter B. Doeringer and Michael J. Piore, *International Labor Markets and Manpower Analysis* (Lexington, Mass.: D. C. Heath, 1971).

[17]Paul A. Baran and Paul M. Sweezy, *Monopoly Capital: An Essay on the American Economic and*

such as Franklin and Tabb, and Reich, Gordon, and Edwards,[18] provide a radical critique of modern capitalism. Combining Marxian theory, which assumes exploitation of one class by another, with the institutional approach, the radical political economists detail how the development of monopoly capitalism and the actions of capitalists in their quest for capital accumulation, profits, and power inevitably create social inequities (e.g., poverty, racism, and sexism). They are concerned with creating a theoretical framework that provides both an understanding of social change and a basis for promoting fundamental changes in the social order. These changes would be to secure more equitable distribution of income and a just society. Radical political economists usually assume that women's condition is a result primarily of capitalism, which requires sexism to maximize the accumulation of capital.

Social policy following this approach would be aimed at transforming the economy from capitalism to socialism, including the ownership of production by workers, humanization of the work process itself, and a more equitable distribution of income and wealth (see the discussions by Feldman and Kohen in Part Three; by Glazer and by Brandwein et al. in Part Four; and by Vajda and Heller in Part Five).

READINGS

The readings presented in this section were chosen to provide the reader with varied economic perspectives on women's differentiated economic role. They are divided into the subject areas described in the introduction: labor force participation, labor market differences, and nonmarket activities.

Labor Force Participation. Recent economic research on women has focused on factors affecting the increase in the labor force participation of married women since World War II (see the Manpower Report of the President in Part One). Glen Cain notes:

> Married women have become so important a segment of the labor force that attention to their patterns is necessary for a full understanding of many important economic problems: economic growth and cyclical behavior of national income, the personal distribution

---

Social Order (New York: Monthly Review Press, 1966); Ernest Mandel, *An Introduction to Marxist Economic Theory* (New York: Merit Publishers, 1967).

[18]Raymond S. Franklin and William E. Tabb, "The Challenge of Radical Political Economics," *Journal of Economic Issues,* 8(March 1974):127–150; and see the selection by Reich, Gordon, and Edwards in this part.

of income, the effects of income taxes on labor supply and birth rates.[19]

This increasing entry of women into the work force does not conform to the expectations derived from traditional economic analysis of labor force participation. Concerned with understanding individual choice between "work" and "leisure," traditional economics sees housework as "leisure" because it is unpaid work in the home. As a result, it ignores how women's decisions are affected by their roles as housewives and caretakers of children (see the discussion by Bell in Part One). Jacob Mincer, in the first reading, pioneers in rectifying this shortcoming by incorporating women's household responsibilities into traditional theory. He adds "work in the home" to "work in the market" and "leisure" as alternative choices facing married women.

Labor Market Differences. A measure of the glaring inequities women face in the labor market is the earnings differential between the sexes. In 1973, women's median income for full-time work was 57 percent of men's.[20] A significant part of this differential (after taking account of individual differences) can be explained by occupational segregation by sex. (See Fuchs article in Part Three). Consequently, economists have devoted increasing attention to the explanation of both wage differentials and occupational segregation by sex.

The two readings in this section examine the three major alternative approaches discussed in the introduction: neoclassical, institutional, and radical.

In the first selection, Francine Blau and Carol Jusenius use the neoclassical and institutional approaches to examine critically the contribution of those theories to an understanding of wage differentials and occupational segregation by sex.

The authors compare three neoclassical theories explaining wage differences between men and women: (1) overcrowding, (2) human capital, and (3) monopsony. Although each theory emphasizes different causal factors and assumes different degrees of market competition (that is, the degree of influence a firm has on the wage rate in the market), they all assume a free exchange market; the relationship between demand for workers and supply of workers is considered to be the major determinant of employment and wages.

In appraising the neoclassical approach, Blau and Jusenius concede that these theories may explain wage differences, but they do not adequately explain occupational segregation. The assumption that wages

[19]Glen G. Cain, *Married Women in the Labor Force: An Economic Analysis* (Chicago: University of Chicago Press, 1966), pp. 120–121.

[20]Women's Bureau, *1975 Handbook on Women Workers* (Washington, D.C.: U.S. Department of Labor, 1975), p. 131.

rates will automatically adjust to small changes in either the demand or supply of workers (e.g., wage rates will rise automatically in response to either an increase in demand for workers or a decrease in their supply; alternatively, wage rates will fall in response to either a decrease in demand for workers or an increase in their supply) does not provide a plausible explanation of occupational segregation. It follows from this assumption that sex (or any other characteristic) can be explained only by assuming extreme differences in tastes or by a preference for segregation by employees.

Blau and Jusenius then turn their attention to the institutional approach, which they assert provides a better understanding of the relation between wage differences and occupational segregation. They consider two institutional frameworks—dual labor theory and internal labor market analysis. These theories assume that wages and the allocation of jobs within a firm are determined by administrative rules governed by custom. These rules divide jobs into different categories. Some job categories are characterized by access to upward mobility by providing the worker with on-the-job training and opportunity for promotion to higher skilled, higher paid jobs. Other job categories mean little or no upward mobility within the firm, so workers holding these jobs remain low skilled and low paid.

The authors find that the internal labor market analysis is especially useful for explaining how sex discrimination leads to occupational segregation. Employers distinguish women from men by assigning women to traditional women's "dead-end" low-pay job categories that offer little opportunity for career advancement.

In the other selection, Michael Reich, David Gordon, and Richard Edwards present a radical explanation of occupational segregation with their theory of labor market segmentation. David Gordon describes the radical approach as drawing

> heavily on a precedent Marxist tradition, but it has molded and recast classical Marxism in response to modern social and historical development; much of the classical Marxist methodology has been retained while some of the substantive generalizations of nineteenth-century Marxism have been revised to fit current realities.[21]

The theory argues that the rise and perpetuation of segmented labor markets result from political and economic forces within American capitalism. Using a Marxian and institutional approach, the authors present four segmentation processes that have developed during the transition from competitive to monopoly capitalism. These are (1) the

---

[21]David M. Gordon (ed.), *Theories of Poverty and Unemployment: Orthodox, Radical, and Dual Labor Market Perspectives* (Lexington, Mass.: Lexington Books, 1972), p. 53.

division of the labor market into primary and secondary markets, the former encouraging stable work habits and the latter usually discouraging those habits; (2) a further subdivision into "subordinate" and "independent" markets, with the former encouraging traits of discipline and dependability and the latter encouraging traits of creativity and decision making; (3) a division by race; and (4) a division by sex.

The authors see this segmentation process resulting from the use of monopoly power by capitalists to divide workers in order to minimize workers' demand for improved working conditions, and to prevent their developing class consciousness and engaging in collective opposition to capitalism. The authors conclude that occupational segregation is part of the dynamic institutional development of capitalism.

Nonmarket Activity. From the neoclassical perspective, the major contribution women make to the economy is as producers for the family in the home (see Zaretsky, Feldberg and Kohen, and Glazer for alternative views on the contribution of housewives as producers for society). Their responsibilities for housework, child rearing, and maintaining the well-being of the family comprise 90 percent of all estimated nonmarket activity.[22] In addition, much of women's volunteer work outside the home is an extension of their traditional activities as wives and mothers (e.g., den mothers, volunteer teacher aides, PTA members, fund raisers for charities, etc.).

There are a number of differences between work done in the home and work done in the market, and these differences provide the key to understanding the inferior status of women in this society.[23] For instance, housework is done individually in each home with little contact between others doing the same work; it is difficult to assess the quality of this work against any realistic objective standard; production in the home is generally small scale and economically inefficient; and women's jobs in the home require the generalist's knowledge to organize and complete many tasks, whereas most jobs in the marketplace require a specialist's knowledge to complete one or a few specific tasks. All of these reinforce the lack of status given to women's work in the home and add to women's sense of frustration and lack of self-esteem.[24] (For a review of the social science literature on housework, see Glazer in Part Four.) The most important difference, however, is that housework is unpaid. Unlike workers in the market, housewives do not receive direct wage payments for their labor.

---

[22]I. A. Sirageldin, *Non-Market Components of National Income* (Ann Arbor: Survey Research Center, Institute for Social Research, University of Michigan, 1969).

[23]For an early analysis of women's role in the home, see Charlotte Perkins Gilman, *Women and Economics,* ed. by Carl Degler (New York: Harper & Row, 1966).

[24]For a discussion of proposals to improve the position of the housewife, see Shirley B. Johnson, "The Impact of Women's Liberation on Marriage, Divorce, and Family Life Style," in Lloyd, *Sex, Discrimination and the Division of Labor,* pp. 417–424.

(Although women do receive economic support in return for their work, the amount received is unrelated to the quantity or quality of that work; a housewife's "indirect wages" are determined by her husband's income.) In a society in which the value of work is defined in terms of money earned, women's unpaid work in the home is not only "valueless," it is not considered work at all.

This lack of money value (exchange value) is the basis of Margaret Benston's article on the economic foundation of women's inferior status. Extending Marxian analysis, Benston distinguishes women from men by their relation to the productive process—a woman produces goods in the household with use value but no exchange value, whereas a man produces goods in the market economy with both use value and exchange value. This lack of exchange value of a woman's household production leaves her outside the main area of economic activity, the market economy, and thus makes her production seem valueless. This is the economic foundation of women's inferior status. In conclusion, Benston further extends Marxian analysis by asserting that socialism alone is not a sufficient precondition for the liberation of women: the additional necessity is the transformation of household production through industrialization into market production (which Benston calls public economy).

Labor Force Participation of Married Women: A Study of Labor Supply

Jacob Mincer

INTRODUCTORY: STATEMENT OF THE PROBLEM

On the assumption that leisure time is a normal good, the standard analysis of work-leisure choices implies a positive substitution effect and a negative income effect on the response of hours of work supplied to variations in the wage rate. An increase in the real wage rate makes leisure time more expensive and tends to elicit an increase in hours of work. However, for a given amount of hours worked, an increase in the wage rate constitutes an increase in income which leads to an increase in purchases of various goods, including leisure time. Thus, on account of the income effect, hours of work tend to decrease. In which direction hours of work change on balance, given a change in the wage rate, cannot be determined a priori. It depends on the relative strengths of the income and substitution effects in the relevant range. The single assumption of a positive income elasticity of demand for leisure time is not sufficient to yield empirical implications on this matter.

An empirical generalization which fills this theoretical void is the "backward-bending" supply curve of labor. This is the notion that, on the average, the income effect is stronger than the substitution effect, so that an increase in the wage rate normally results in a decreased amount (hours) of work offered by suppliers of labor. Extreme examples of such behavior have been repeatedly observed in underdeveloped countries. On the American scene, several kinds of empirical evidence

Excerpts reprinted from Jacob Mincer, "Labor Force Participation of Married Women: A Study of Labor Supply," in a report of the National Bureau of Economic Research, *Aspects of Labor Economics* (Princeton, N.J.: Princeton University Press, 1962), 63–68.

apparently point to the same relationship: the historically declining work week in industry; historically declining labor force participation rates of young and old males; an inverse relation between wages of adult males and labor force participation rates of females by cities in cross sections; an inverse relation between incomes of husbands and labor force participation of wives, by husbands' incomes, in budget studies. Similar phenomena have been reported from the experience of other modern economies.

The secular negative association between the length of the work week, participation rates of males, and rising real incomes is clearly consistent with the backward-bending supply curve. Whether this is also true of cross-sectional data on males is a question which has as yet received little attention. Superficially, the cross-sectional behavior of females seems similarly capable of being rationalized in terms of a backward-bending supply response, or at least in terms of a positive income elasticity of demand for leisure. Such views, however, are immediately challenged by contradictory evidence in time series. One of the most striking phenomena in the history of the American labor force is the continuing secular increase in participation rates of females, particularly of married women, despite the growth in real income. Between 1890 and 1960, labor force rates of all females fourteen years old and over rose from about 18 percent to 36 percent. In the same period, rates of married women rose from 5 percent to 30 percent, while real income per worker tripled.

The apparent contradiction between time series and cross-sections has already stimulated a substantial amount of research. The investigation reported [here] is yet another attempt to uncover the basic economic structure which is, in part, responsible for the observed relations.

The study starts from the recognition that the concepts of work, income, and substitution need clarification and elaboration before they can be applied to labor force choices of particular population groups, in this instance married women. The resulting analytical model, even though restricted to two basic economic factors, seems capable of explaining a variety of apparently diverse cross-sectional behavior patterns. It also, in principle, reconciles time series with cross-section behavior, though further elaboration is needed for a proper explanation of the former. . . .

CONCEPTUAL FRAMEWORK

Work. The analysis of labor supply to the market by way of the theory of demand for leisure time viewed as a consumption good is strictly appropriate whenever leisure time and hours of work in the market in fact constitute an exhaustive dichotomy. This is, of course, never true even in the case of adult males. The logical complement to leisure time is work broadly construed, whether it includes remunerative production in market or work that is currently "not paid for." The latter includes various forms of investment in oneself, and the production of goods and services for the home and the family. Educational activity is an essential and, indeed, the most important element in the productive life of young boys and girls. Work at home is still an activity to which women, on the average, devote the larger part of their married life. It is an exclusive occupation of many women, and of a vast majority when young children are present.

It is, therefore, not sufficient to analyze labor force behavior of married women in terms of the demand for leisure. A predicted change in hours of leisure may imply different changes in hours of work in the market depending on the effects of the causal factors on hours of work at home. Technically speaking, if we are to derive the market supply function in a residual fashion, not only the demand for hours of leisure but also the demand for hours of work at home must be taken into account. The latter is a demand for a productive service derived from the demand by the family for home goods and services. A full application of the theory of demand for a productive service to the home sector has implications for a variety of socioeconomic phenomena beyond the scope of this paper.

Family Context. The analysis of market labor supply in terms of consumption theory carries a strong connotation about the appropriate decision-making unit. We take it as self-evident that in studying consumption behavior the family is the unit of analysis. Income is assumed to be pooled and total family consumption is positively related to it. The distribution of consumption among family members depends on tastes. It is equally important to recognize that the decisions about the production of goods and services at home and about leisure are largely family decisions. The relevant income variable in the demand for home services and for leisure of any family member is total family income. A change in income of some family member will, in general, result in a changed consumption of leisure for the family as a whole. An increase in one individual's income may not result in a decrease in *his* hours of work, but in those of other family members. The total amount of work performed at home is, even more clearly, an outcome of family demand for home goods and for leisure, given the production function at home. However, unlike the general consumption case, the distribution of leisure, market work, and home work for each family member as well as among family members is determined not only by tastes and by biological or cultural specialization of functions, but by relative prices which are specific to individual members of the family. This is so, because earning powers in the market and marginal productivities in alternative pursuits differ among individual family members. Other things equal (including family income), an increase in the market wage rate for some family member makes both the consumption of leisure and the production of home services by that individual more costly to the family, and will as a matter of rational family decision encourage greater market labor input by him (her). Even the assumption of a backward-bending supply curve would not justify a prediction of a decrease in total hours of work *for the particular earner,* if wages of other family members are fixed.

Recognition of the family context of leisure and work choices, and of the home-market dichotomy within the world of work, is essential for any analysis of labor force behavior of married women, and perhaps quite important for the analysis of behavior of other family members, including male family heads. For the purpose of constructing a simple model of labor force behavior of married women, it will be sufficient to utilize these concepts only insofar as they help to select and elucidate a few empirically manageable variables to represent the major forces of income and substitution contained in the market supply function.

Work Choices. Let us consider the relevant choices of married women as between leisure, work at home, and work in the market. Income is assumed to have a positive effect on the demand for leisure, hence a negative effect on total amount of work. With the relevant prices fixed, increased family income will decrease total hours of work. Since the income effect on the demand for home goods and services is not likely to be negative, it might seem that the increased leisure means exclusively a decrease in hours of work in the market. Such a conclusion, however, would require a complete absence of substitutability between the wife and other (mechanical, or human) factors of production at home, as well as an absence of substitution in consumption between home goods and market-produced goods. Domestic servants, laborsaving appliances, and frozen foods contradict such assumption. Substitutability is, of course, a matter of degree. It may be concluded therefore that, given the income elasticity of demand for home goods and for leisure, the extent to which income differentially affects hours of work in the two sectors depends on the ease with which substitution in home production or consumption can be carried out. The lesser the substitutability the weaker the negative income effect on hours of work at home, and the stronger the income effect on hours of work in the market.

Change in this degree of substitutability may have played a part in the historical development. At a given moment of timne, the degree of substitutability is likely to differ depending on the content of home production. Thus substitutes for a mother's care of small children are much more difficult to come by than those for food preparation or for physical maintenance of the household. It is likely, therefore, that the same change in income will affect hours of market work of the mother more strongly when small children are present than at other times in the life cycle.

While family income affects the total amount of work, the market wage rate affects the allocation of hours between leisure, the home, and the market. An increase in the real wage rate, given productivity in the home, is an increase in prices (alternative costs) of home production as well as of leisure in terms of prices of wage goods. To the extent of an existing substitution between home goods and wage goods, such a change will lead to an increase in work supplied to the market. Again, the strength of the effect is a matter of the degree of substitution between wage goods and home production.

TEMPORAL DISTRIBUTION OF WORK

In a broad view, the quantity of labor supplied to the market by a wife is the fraction of her married life during which she participates in the labor force. Abstracting from the temporal distribution of labor force activities over a woman's life, this fraction could be translated into a probability of being in the labor force in a given period of time for an individual, hence into a labor force rate for a large group of women.

If leisure and work preferences, long-run family incomes, and earning power were the same for all women, the total amount of market work would, according to the theory, be the same for all women. Even if that were true, however, the *timing* of market activities during the working life may differ from one individual to another. The life cycle introduces changes in demands for and marginal costs of home work and leisure. Such changes are reflected in the relation between labor force rates and age of woman, presence, number, and ages of children. There are life-cycle variations in family incomes and assets which may affect the timing of labor force participation, given a limited income horizon and a less than perfect capital market. Cyclical and random variations in wage rates, employment opportunities, income and employment of other family members, particularly of the head, are also likely to induce temporal variations in the allocation of time between home, market, and leisure. It is not surprising, therefore, that over short periods of observation, variation in labor force participation, or turnover, is the outstanding characteristic of labor force behavior of married women. ...

An Economic
Perspective

Labor Market Differences

Sex Segregation
in the Labor Market

Francine D. Blau
Carol L. Jusenius

The purpose of this paper is to appraise the contribution of economic theory to an understanding of the causes of sex segregation and pay differentiation between men and women in the labor market. We do not attempt to review the large and growing body of empirical literature in this area, although our assessment of alternative theoretical approaches does rely upon a broad knowledge of the empirical findings. In particular, three points are taken as given:.

1. Sex segregation in the labor market exists, and it is of considerable magnitude.

2. Women are segregated by occupational categories and within occupations by industry and firm. (While we concentrate primarily on occupational segregation, much of the discussion is relevant to an analysis of these other dimensions.)

3. Aggregate pay differentials between men and women in the labor market exist.

Contemporary economic analysis may be divided into several schools of thought. Considerations of time and space have compelled some degree of selectivity, and this paper provides an evaluation of only two main approaches: the neoclassical and institutional schools. An additional school—radical economics—has also contributed important insights into an understanding of labor market segmentation. For the most

Excerpted from Francine D. Blau and Carol L. Jusenius, "Economists' Approaches to Sex Segregation in the Labor Market: An Appraisal," *Signs: Journal of Women in Culture and Society* 1, no. 3, pt. 2(Spring 1976):181–199, by permission of the authors and the University of Chicago Press. © 1976 by The University of Chicago.

part, however, we feel that the radicals' major contribution in this area has been to raise and analyze a number of important questions which are often ignored in traditional economic analyses.

In both their theoretical and empirical work, neoclassical economists have concentrated their attention primarily on the male-female pay differential and only secondarily on sex segregation per se. Their examination of segregation has largely been a by-product of investigations of wage-related issues. Such an emphasis is indeed understandable, since, to the neoclassical economist, the monetary manifestation of possible labor market inequities is an obvious focal point for the analysis. However, the coexistence in the labor market of both pay differentiation by sex and sex segregation along occupational and other dimensions strongly suggests (although it certainly does not prove) a link between the two. This posited linkage may be considered an underlying assumption of this paper and thus a major criterion in our evaluation of the merits of alternative approaches.

NEOCLASSICAL APPROACHES

In their attempts to explain the wage differential between men and women, some neoclassical economists employ models of perfect competition in which wages equal the value of workers' marginal products. Within this school are two particular approaches which are at variance with one another. One approach advocates the "overcrowding" hypothesis, in which the low productivity of women workers is explained by the exclusionary behavior of employers. The other approach is based on human capital theory, which argues that women's productivity is low because women have relatively low stocks of accumulated human capital. Other neoclassical economists reject the assumption of a perfectly competitive labor market. Instead, they focus on the wage implications of monopsony, that is, monopoly power on the buyer's side—in this case, the firm's power in the labor market.

The Competitive Model: The Overcrowding Approach. To begin the analysis we must first define *overcrowding.* Put simply, overcrowding is the interplay of a relatively low demand for a particular type of worker with a relatively large supply of that same type of worker. Thus, overcrowding can result from an excessive number of individuals trained (in a broad sense) for a given occupation or set of occupations and/or it can result from an excessive number of limitations being placed on the total set of occupations open to an identifiable group of workers.

The first mention of what has come to be termed overcrowding is found in Fawcett[1] and Edgeworth.[2] ... It was not until the early 1970s, however, that Bergmann formalized the overcrowding hypotheses in her analyses of occupational segregation.[3] Bergmann argued that women are restricted by demand factors to a limited set of occupations. This restriction results first in women receiving lower wages, and second in the nonrestricted group (men) receiving higher wages than if the constraints to mobility between the male and female sectors did not exist. In other words, Bergmann contrasts two equilibrium positions. In both these positions workers earn the value of their marginal products. Women, however, because they are forced into a relatively small number of occupations and the capital-labor ratio associated with these occupations are thus relatively low, have a lower productivity than men.

Two key elements comprise the Bergmann formulation. The first is that workers are identical with respect to potential productivity; that is, they are perfectly substitutable for one another but they have clearly differentiable ascriptive characteristics. The second important element, already noted, is that demand-side conditions are responsible for the overcrowding. Tastes of employers prevent integration.

It is important to note here that through her inclusion of employer tastes, Bergmann unites Becker's theory of discrimination.[4] with Fawcett's and Edgeworth's. In Becker, employers who have a taste for discrimination against women workers will hire them only when the wage difference between male and female labor is large enough to compensate for the disutility they incur by hiring women. Thus, the Bergmann approach is an extreme case of Becker; only if employer tastes for discrimination against women in male occupations are "very large" will total exclusion, as posited by Bergmann, exist.

This reliance on employer tastes as the causal factor of occupational segregation does not appear to be sufficient. It is not clear why so many employers would have such tastes against women in certain occupations, nor is it clear why employers' aversion should be so "strong" that they are not compensated for their disutility by the prevailing male-female pay differential. ...

... Furthermore, it is not obvious that the case of perfect substitutability between men and women in the production process is general

[1]Millicent G. Fawcett, "Equal Pay for Equal Work." *Economic Journal* 28(March 1918):1–6.

[2]F. Y. Edgeworth, "Equal Pay to Men and Women for Equal Work." *Economic Journal* 32(September 1922):431–457

[3]Barbara R. Bergmann, "The Effect on White Incomes of Discrimination in Employment." *Journal of Political Economy* 79(March/April 1971):294–313, and "Occupational Segregation, Wages and Profits When Employers Discriminate by Race or Sex." *Eastern Economic Journal* 1(April-July 1974):103–110.

[4]Gary S. Becker, *The Economics of Discrimination* (Chicago: University of Chicago Press, 1957).

enough to shed light on the whole pattern of occupational segregation. In sum, we are forced to conclude that Bergmann's contribution lies more in her analysis of the *consequences* of occupational segregation than in her approach to explanations of its *causes*.

The Competitive Model: The Human Capital Approach. The major point of the human capital approach is that men and women are not perfectly substitutable for one another. Although they may be similarly distributed across IQ categories and levels of education, women accumulate less human capital through work experience because they spend proportionately fewer years in the labor force than men.[5] Thus, productivity differentials between men and women will appear. In other words, the quality of labor supplied by the two groups varies because of their different patterns of labor force participation, of which the presumedly higher turnover rates among women are a short-run manifestation. Pay differentials merely reflect the quality differentials between men and women.

Closing the circle of this argument is the human capital school's model of the family and women's role within it. By revising the traditional work-leisure dichotomy in economic theory, they have been able to conceptualize the effects of the family on a woman's supply curve of labor. Arguments in their household utility functions include not only leisure and goods derived from market work, but also goods derived from nonmarket work—work traditionally performed by women. Thus, from the perspective of a utility-maximizing household, a woman's decision not to work continuously, that is, not to accumulate a relatively large stock of human capital, is a rational one.

It should be noted that this theory is one of pay differentials and that occupational segregation is *not* a necessary adjunct. Wage rates sufficiently flexible to allow for quality differences among workers in the same occupation are theoretically possible. Yet the human capital approach can be used to explain the phenomenon of occupational segregation. The theory would predict that women would tend to enter those occupations which provide few opportunities for increases in productivity through labor market experience. Anticipating or reacting to the needs of the family, women would enter occupations which, while they may not reward work experience, also do not penalize their incumbents for discontinuities in employment (such as waitressing). This same line of reasoning suggests that women would tend to exclude themselves

---

[5]The most rigorous formulation of this argument is found in Jacob Mincer and Solomon Polacheck, "Family Investments in Human Capital: Earnings of Women." *Journal of Political Economy* 82(March/ April 1974):76–111. See also Larry E. Suter, "Occupation, Employment, and Lifetime Work Experience of Women" (Paper presented at the meetings of the American Sociological Association, New York, August 27, 1973).

from a second type of occupation, that is, those which embody a lengthy process of general training (such as lawyers)—the costs of which the women themselves must bear—unless they planned to work throughout the greater part of their life span. Also implied is that employers would tend to exclude women from a third type of occupation—that which embodies a lengthy firm-specific training process (such as executive-trainee programs or, more broadly conceived, any "learning by doing" process)—because of actual or perceived high turnover rates (labor quality differences).

However, a major problem exists with this logic; *both* male and female occupations require varying amounts and types of skills. . . .

The point is that men and women are in occupations of each skill type and that within each category certain occupations are "more" acceptable for women to enter than others. The human capital school's reliance on the primacy of the family in a woman's life could only explain a greater tendency of women to be in "low-skill" jobs. With this reasoning, they could not explain the concentration of women in a small number of female occupations within each skill category. To explain this concentration the school would have to rely on women's "tastes."

An elaboration of this point necessitates a brief description of their implicit theory of occupational choice, essentially a slightly modified version of the revealed preference theory of consumer behavior which states: "If their [two respective goods] price tags tell us that A is not cheaper than B, then there is only one plausible explanation of the consumer's choice—he bought A because he *likes* it better (italics added)." We believe that an analogous description of a theory of occupational choice for women within the human capital framework would be: "If their [two respective occupations] wage tags tell us that A does not offer more than B, then there is only one explanation of the worker's choice—she entered A because she *likes* it better."

It is clear from our analogy that the model assumes freedom of choice. There is no acknowledgement or concern expressed over the constraints imposed by society which limit women's freedom to make their own decisions or influence the way in which others, such as employers, make decisions for them. Women's decisions to become secretaries and nurses rather than surveyors and pharmacists are seen as a matter of personal preferences. While human capital theorists do acknowledge that the extant set of tastes may reflect the socialization process of women's youth, they also note that attempts to understand this process are outside the scope of their analyses.

In conclusion, the human capital model is subject to criticism on several grounds. It, too, relies on an elusive factor termed *tastes* to explain why women "choose" to enter a given occupation or to have a given preference for nonmarket work, without providing an underlying theory which would explain that choice. Moreover, it is not clear why *only* women should have such tastes nor is it clear why a large proportion of women should exhibit the same set of tastes—as demonstrated by their occupational distribution. An outcome of occupational segregation again requires an extreme distribution of tastes—only in this case it is the distribution of women's tastes which is relevant. Finally, just as the approach taken by Bergmann neglects supply-side considerations, the human capital school often fails to consider demand-side (employer) factors, despite the elementary principle of economics that prices (wages) are determined by the intersection of both supply and demand curves.

The Monopsony Model. The theories discussed thus far have been based on models of perfect competition. In such a system a worker's wage equals the value of his or her marginal product and wage differentials between men and women reflect differing productivities—due either to women's lower level of accumulated human capital or to overcrowding with its associated implications of a relatively low capital-labor ratio. An important departure from this approach is the monopsony model, first presented by Robinson and more recently developed by Madden.[6]

As is well known in economic theory, a worker who faces a monopsonist receives a wage which is less than the value of his or her marginal product. The degree of divergence between wages and marginal value products depends upon the extent to which monopsony elements are present in a given labor market. Alternatively stated, the divergence is determined by the wage elasticity of the supply of labor to the firm.

A crucial element of the monopsony model as developed by Madden is this relationship between elasticity of supply and wages. To explain, the less elastic the supply curve of labor, the lower will be the wage, assuming (1) a profit-maximizing firm and (2) an upward-sloping supply curve of labor to the firm. Thus, it is argued that women's wages are lower than those of men because the supply curve of women to the firm is less wage-elastic than that of men. In other words, a firm has greater monopsony power over women than over men.

Furthermore, this greater degree of power is caused by women's relative immobility—a lack of mobility which may be caused by the fixity of the woman's place of residence (a supply-side problem) or by

---

[6]Janice Fanning Madden, *The Economics of Sex Discrimination* (Lexington, Mass.: Lexington Books, 1973); and Joan Robinson, *The Economics of Imperfect Competition* (1933; reprint ed., New York: St. Martin's Press, 1965).

a lack of demand for women in alternative occupations. In the first case, this is equivalent to the location of the husband's job, rather than that of the wife's, determining the family's place of residence; one possibility in the second case is occupational segregation.

While this model is intriguing, its general applicability may be limited. In the model, wage differences may be explained by women having a *less* elastic supply curve of labor to the firm; it is quite possible, however, that women's supply curve may, in fact, be more wage-elastic. An examination of the elements which underlie the supply curves of men and women helps to explain this possibility. First, since women have a socially acceptable occupation (housewife) outside the labor force, they have more mobility than men—in one sense at least. Their relative immobility within the labor force could be counterbalanced by their greater ability to move in and out of the labor market altogether. Second, offsetting men's greater possibilities for occupational and geographic mobility are the mobility-reducing factors of firm-specific training and pension rights, which could be postulated to affect men more than women. Given these countervailing forces for both men and women, then, the wage-elasticity of women's supply curve of labor relative to that of men appears to be indeterminate a priori and may reasonably be expected to differ by occupational category.

An Assessment of the Neoclassical Models. In general, the neoclassical approach has generated a number of plausible explanations for the male-female pay differential. However, sex segregation is far from a necessary outcome in these models, and the factors which are identified as causes of pay differentials are not persuasive as causes of sex segregation *within* the neoclassical model.

A major problem is that the smooth marginal adjustments inherent in neoclassical models, particularly with respect to wage rates, make the extreme outcome of segregation highly unlikely. This also implies that segregation would be an unlikely outcome in a world for which the neoclassical models are a reasonably accurate description. This is the case regardless of the location of the postulated forces, that is, either on the demand or the supply side. . . .

On a purely theoretical level, such difficulties can be relatively easily surmounted. One may simply postulate an extreme distribution of tastes or summon the necessary price or other rigidities. However, it is our view that placing the issue within the context of a model which explicitly takes into account the institutions of the labor market is a more useful approach. Such an approach removes the need for an assumption of an *extreme* structure of tastes and enables one to specify more completely the rigidities within the system which provide the impetus toward segregation.

The particular institutional model which is presented here is derived from the internal labor market analysis.[7] The major application of this model to pay differentials and employment distribution differences among groups has been the dual labor market formulation. While the dual labor market analysis is relevant for understanding the causes and consequences of sex segregation, for a variety of reasons, we see it as an inadequate characterization of the total problem. Thus, what follows may be considered a more direct application of the internal labor market analysis to the problem of pay and employment distribution differences by sex, although it incorporates some of the insights of the dual labor market theorists. The intention is not to develop a rigorous formulation but to indicate the potential of this mode of analysis.

The Internal Labor Market Approach. The notion of an internal labor market focuses upon the division of the job structure of the enterprise into two categories of occupations. First are those job categories which are filled from sources external to the firm through the recruitment of new workers. Within clusters of related occupations, such entry jobs are generally restricted to lower-level positions. Second are those job categories which are filled from internal sources through the promotion and upgrading of presently employed workers. For the most part, access to this latter type of position occurs through advancement up well-defined promotion ladders. The process by which workers advance from entry-level positions to higher-level jobs is conceptualized within this approach as one in which they acquire, either formally or informally, added knowledge or skills which, for the most part, are specific or unique to the firm.

Within this framework, the market forces delineated by neoclassical economic analysis are perceived as operating principally in occupations at the entry level. On the other hand, the requirement of enterprise-specific skills for the performance of internally allocated jobs works to prevent the development of a competitive market (in the traditional sense) for these categories of occupations. In the place of the direct operation of market forces, an internal labor market develops, that is,

---

[7]For early expositions of relevant concepts, see, e.g., John T. Dunlop, "The Task of Contemporary Wage Theory," in George W. Taylor and Frank C. Pierson (eds.), *New Concepts in Wage Determination* (New York: McGraw-Hill, 1957), pp. 117–139; E. Robert Livernash, "The Internal Wage Structure," in Taylor and Pierson, pp. 140–172; and Clark Kerr, "The Balkanization of Labor Markets," in *Labor Mobility and Economic Opportunity* (Cambridge, Mass.: M.I.T. Press, 1954), pp. 92–110. We have in this presentation drawn heavily on the synthesis of the human capital and institutional analyses provided by Peter B. Doeringer and Michael J. Piore, *Internal Labor Markets and Manpower Analysis* (Lexington, Mass.: D. C. Heath, 1971), and have also benefited from the recent clarification of a number of important issues by Michael L. Wachter, "Primary and Secondary Labor Markets: A Critique of the Dual Approach," in Arthur M. Okun and George L. Perry (eds.), *Brookings Papers on Economic Activity*, vol. 3 (Washington, D.C.: Brookings Institution, 1975), pp. 637–693.

an administrative apparatus which allocates labor and determines wage rates within the firm.

With respect to the allocation of labor ... the advancement opportunities open to workers within the enterprise are generally determined by the original entry-level job the worker had obtained.

With respect to wage determination, job evaluation plans and other administrative arrangements are frequently used to establish base pay rates for each occupational category and to specify wage relationships among occupations. Custom, as well as administrative arrangements, plays a role in maintaining interoccupational wage relationships. Within occupational categories, pay differentials among workers are generally based on seniority and merit considerations.

Thus, the internal labor market structure is seen as specifying a relatively rigid set of wage relationships and promotional possibilities, both of which are defined primarily in terms of job categories. The wage relationships among individuals and the promotional possibilities for any given individual are for the most part established as a consequence of their job assignment.

Sex Segregation and Male-Female Pay Differentials. Two points in this theoretical framework are particularly relevant for an understanding of occupational segregation and its relationship to pay differentials by sex. First, within the internal labor market, group or categorical treatment of individuals is the norm. Such group treatment will be most efficient (result in the discarding of the least information), the greater the degree of intragroup homogeneity with respect to whatever characteristics are considered important. Clearly, sex is an obvious basis for such differentiation, due to employers' distaste for hiring women in male occupations and/or real or perceived quality differences between male and female labor.

Furthermore, while prejudice and stereotyping may cloud employers' decisions regarding occupational assignments for men and women, this does not prevent considerable differentiation *within* the group of female workers (i.e., on the basis of characteristics such as education, age, and marital status). Thus, we are postulating more than a simple dichotomy between male and female labor markets. This analysis is consistent with the observed range of characteristics of female jobs which was noted earlier.

Second, within the internal labor market framework, the "extreme outcome of segregation is no longer surprising. Indeed, such segregation is the primary way in which employers can differentiate between men and women, *even* with respect to wage rates. Under the constraints imposed by the administered system of the internal labor market, the latitude of the employer to differentiate among individuals (or sex groups) is broadest with respect to the selection of new workers for entry jobs. It is somewhat less broad, but still considerable, with respect to the allocation of workers among job categories filled from internal sources. (Here the employer is constrained to select individuals only from job categories along "appropriate" promotion ladders and may be forced in some cases to give a greater than desired weight to seniority.) It is narrowest with respect to wage differentiation among individuals within the same job category (such differentiation must be within the relatively narrow bounds determined by seniority and merit considerations), and with respect to the alteration of wage relationships among occupational categories.

Indeed, within the internal labor market, wage rates might almost be considered the monetary (or value) dimension of the job structure. Once this conceptual linkage between occupational categories and wage rates has been established, it becomes clear that any factor that would tend to cause male-female pay differences would also tend to cause segregation along sex lines.

Illustrations of the Usefulness of the Internal Labor Market Analysis. The purpose of this section is to provide a few illustrations of the way in which the institutional approach sheds light on the process of sex segregation and pay differentials between men and women. It also demonstrates the way in which this approach differs from the previously discussed neoclassical models.

STATISTICAL DISCRIMINATION. One factor working to restrict the access of women to job categories (or firms) to which the internal labor market analysis calls attention is the possibility of what has [been] termed *statistical discrimination,* a situation in which decisions regarding individuals are based on group-derived probabilities. Thus, if employers perceive women as less stable workers (i.e., as having higher rates of turnover and/or absenteeism than men), then individual women may be excluded from certain types of employment on a probabilistic basis. This is appropriately defined as a form of discrimination even if employers' perceptions of the average sex differential are correct, since it is a manifestation of stereotyping, the treatment of each individual member of a group as if he/she possessed the average characteristics of the group.

In a neoclassical world, such a consideration would be expected to result in pay differentials by sex, since employers would discount female wages in compensation for the higher fixed labor costs associated with the higher anticipated female turnover/absenteeism rates. However, given flexible wage rates, such labor costs differences would not necessarily result in segregation in these models. In the internal labor market model, it becomes clear that segregation is the inevitable result, since higher labor costs are not an institutionally acceptable basis of intraoccupational pay differentiation.

OCCUPATIONAL ASSIGNMENT VERSUS OCCUPATIONAL CHOICE. In the neoclassical world, and particularly within the framework of the human capital analysis, individuals are expected to select an occupation on the basis of taste. ... [However,] the employer may determine the occupation of the worker within the broad limits set by the worker's tastes and alternative employment options.

Many jobs are unique to certain industries and even to certain enterprises. Individuals frequently come to a firm in search of work within a broad and rather vaguely defined category or categories of jobs. Employers (or those performing the personnel function within the firm) determine whether the individual is to be hired and for which entry-level job. If the worker remains with the firm, then this initial decision will determine the promotion opportunities open to him or her in succeeding years. Furthermore, management will decide whether such promotions occur and the speed with which the worker advances up the promotion ladder. Thus, in many cases a concept of occupational assignment may be more reflective of reality than the accepted notion of occupational choice. The occupational distribution differences between men and women may to some extent reflect employer decisions to exclude women from certain entry-level positions and their associated promotion ladders and/or to promote and upgrade women more slowly than men. Indeed, the very structure of the jobs typically open to women is likely to reflect employer perceptions regarding the average characteristics of female workers. Predominantly female occupations may be characterized by fewer possibilities for promotion and more numerous ports of entry than comparable male jobs—the common complaint that "women's jobs" are "dead-end jobs."

EXOGENEITY OF WORKER QUALITY. Proponents of the human capital school often seem to imply that individual productivity is uniquely and exogeneously determined by the characteristics of workers. On the other hand, while advocates of the overcrowding hypothesis do acknowledge productivity variations between men and women due to occupation or establishment of employment, they specify the capital-labor ratio as the underlying cause of productivity differences. An institutional approach calls attention to these and other factors.

Within an internal labor market framework, worker productivity is determined partly on the basis of individual characteristics but more importantly as a function of the attributes of each worker in combination with the characteristics of occupations and firms. The model suggests that a range of equal cost alternatives are open to the firm in terms of hiring practices, work organization, and wage policies. For example, the amount of labor turnover (and thus the average years of experience obtained by workers) in specific occupational categories or firms may be seen as the outcome of the personal characteristics of workers, the wage rate paid, the opportunities offered for advancement, working conditions, and the quality of management. Similarly, the skill levels of employees may reasonably be related to the existence and quality of training programs. Furthermore, the diligence and effort expended by workers in job-related tasks may be related to the wage standing of the firm and other personnel practices. Thus, denial of access to certain job categories or firms may mean not only that certain workers—for example, some women—receive lower wages but also that they are less productive. This further implies that reallocating individuals from one work environment to another could change their productivity, as well as their wage rate.

The Dual Labor Market Analysis.   As noted earlier, the dual labor market analysis has been the major application of the internal labor market approach to the set of wage and employment questions under consideration in this paper. The dual labor market analysis postulates that a dichotomy between "primary" and "secondary" employment characterizes the labor market position of disadvantaged groups like blacks.[8] It has been suggested that the analysis may also be applied to women.

The primary market has the characteristics of a highly developed internal labor market. As noted earlier, entry is restricted to relatively few lower-level jobs; promotion ladders are long; worker stability is encouraged by high wages, opportunities for advancement, good working conditions, and provisions for job security. The administration of work rules is characterized by adherence to the principles of equity and due process.

At the other extreme, the secondary market more closely approximates a set of "unstructured markets." The occupational distribution is characterized by numerous ports of entry; promotion ladders are short or nonexistent; worker stability tends to be discouraged by low wages, little opportunity for advancement, poor working conditions, and little provision for job security. The administration of work rules may be characterized by arbitrary and even harsh discipline.

The desired long-term attachment between workers and firms in primary sector jobs leads employers to select new workers who have good future performance prospects, particularly with respect to job

---

[8]For elucidations of the dual labor market analysis, see, e.g., Doeringer and Piore, *Internal Labor Markets and Manpower Analysis*; Michael J. Piore, "The Dual Labor Market: Theory and Implications," in David M. Gordon (ed.), *Problems in Political Economy* (Lexington, Mass.: D. C. Heath, 1971), pp. 90–94; and David M. Gordon, *Theories of Poverty and Underemployment* (Lexington, Mass.: D. C. Heath, 1973).

stability. Thus, statistical discrimination (as well as pure discrimination à la Becker) is seen to be a factor governing the access of workers to primary employment.

According to this theory, many job candidates who are excluded on such grounds do in fact possess the requisite behavioral characteristics for primary sector employment. While productivity (and/or labor cost) differences may account for a significant portion of the wage difference between these erroneously excluded individuals and those employed in the primary sector, such differences would be due to the way in which the work is structured in the secondary sector rather than to particular characteristics of these individuals.

It is likely that a higher proportion of women than men are in secondary jobs, and the dual labor market analysis is useful in understanding the causes and consequences of this distinction. However, this approach does not explain the further sex segregation which certainly exists in each sector. Nor does it do justice to the range of characteristics of predominantly female jobs, that is, the differentiation which occurs *within* the female sector. Further, in contrast to our formulation, it is not helpful in elucidating the differential treatment accorded to women and men *within* the primary sector, that is, within reasonably highly developed internal labor markets. Additional empirical research would be necessary to determine the relative importance of the primary-secondary distinction for women's labor market status.

An Assessment of the Internal Labor Market Model. Some controversy among economists surrounds the question of whether the allocative and wage outcomes of the internal labor market do, in fact, diverge from those of a competitive market system, or whether the institutional arrangements emphasized by the internal labor market analysis are merely trappings which overlie, but do not alter, the outcomes predicted by neoclassical models. Such a question is clearly of great importance to economists, since the necessity and usefulness of an institutional approach hinges upon its resolution. Although this paper has not fully examined this question, it has demonstrated that an institutional approach can help to explain why sex segregation and wage differentiation occur.

In a situation in which the market simply is not available, recourse must be had to other arrangements. Thus, while the institutional arrangements of the internal labor market do introduce a certain degree of rigidity and inflexibility into the processes of labor allocation and wage determination, they also serve to remove uncertainties which would hamper both the day-to-day operations and long-range planning needs of the individual firm. For example, where the firm-specific component of the skills necessary to perform internally allocated jobs is substantial, a situation of "bilateral monopoly" is created. On one side, the employer acquires a degree of monopsony power, since the worker's firm-specific skills are not transferable or valuable to other firms. On the other side, the worker acquires a degree of monopoly power over his or her job, since a supply of similarly qualified individuals is not available from outside the firm (and perhaps even from other sources within the firm) without considerable cost.

The wage outcome of such a situation is indeterminate within certain boundaries. Therefore, an administered system, despite its rigidities, may be preferable to both employers and workers than the alternative frequent haggling over wages and other working conditions—a constant test of the relative bargaining strength of each side. Similarly, where workers are not easily replaceable, employers may be more concerned about such factors as morale and are therefore more willing to adhere to the customs and traditions of the workplace.

While the internal labor market may be relatively efficient with respect to many aspects of its operation, it is not necessarily rational in its treatment of women and minorities—and it does not appear to produce socially satisfactory outcomes for these groups.

A Theory of Labor Market Segmentation

Michael Reich
David M. Gordon
Richard C. Edwards

... Orthodox theory assumes that profit-maximizing employers evaluate workers in terms of their *individual* characteristics and predicts that labor market differences among groups will decline over time because of competitive mechanisms (Arrow, 1971). But by most measures, the labor market differences among groups have not been disappearing.... The continuing importance of *groups* in the labor market thus is neither explained nor predicted by orthodox theory.

Why is the labor force in general still so fragmented? Why are group characteristics repeatedly so important in the labor market? In this paper, we summarize an emerging radical theory of labor market segmentation; we develop the full arguments in Reich, Gordon, and Edwards (1973). The theory argues that political and economic forces within American capitalism have given rise to and perpetuated segmented labor markets, and that it is incorrect to view the sources of segmented markets as exogenous to the economic system.

PRESENT LABOR MARKET SEGMENTATION

We define labor market segmentation as the historical process whereby political-economic forces encourage the division of the labor market into separate submarkets, or segments, distinguished by different labor market characteristics and behavioral rules. Segmented labor markets

Reprinted from Michael Reich, David M. Gordon, and Richard C. Edwards, "A Theory of Labor Market Segmentation." *American Economic Review* 63(May 1973):359–365, by permission of the authors.

are thus the outcome of a segmentation process. Segments may cut horizontally across the occupational hierarchy as well as vertically. We suggest that present labor market conditions can most usefully be understood as the outcome of four segmentation processes.

Segmentation into Primary and Secondary Markets. The primary and secondary segments, to use the terminology of dual labor market theory, are differentiated mainly by stability characteristics. Primary jobs require and develop stable working habits; skills are often acquired on the job; wages are relatively high; and job ladders exist. Secondary jobs do not require and often discourage stable working habits; wages are low; turnover is high; and job ladders are few. Secondary jobs are mainly (though not exclusively) filled by minority workers, women, and youth.

Segmentation Within the Primary Sector. Within the primary sector we see a segmentation between what we call "surbordinate" and "independent" primary jobs. Subordinate primary jobs are routinized and encourage personality characteristics of dependability, discipline, responsiveness to rules and authority, and acceptance of a firm's goals. Both factory and office jobs are present in this segment. In contrast, independent primary jobs encourage and require creative, problem-solving, self-initiating characteristics and often have professional standards for work. Voluntary turnover is high and individual motivation and achievement are highly rewarded.

Segmentation by Race. While minority workers are present in secondary, subordinate primary, and independent primary segments, they often face distinct segments within those submarkets. Certain jobs are "race typed," segregated by prejudice and by labor market institutions. Geographic separation plays an important role in maintaining divisions between race segments.

Segmentation by Sex. Certain jobs have generally been restricted to men; others to women. Wages in the female segment are usually lower than in comparable male jobs; female jobs often require and encourage a "serving mentality"—an orientation toward providing services to other people and particularly to men. These characteristics are encouraged by family and schooling institutions.

HISTORICAL ORIGINS OF SEGMENTATION

The present divisions of the labor market are best understood from a historical analysis of their origins. We argue that segmentation arose during the transition from competitive to monopoly capitalism. Our historical analysis focuses on the era of monopoly capitalism, from roughly 1890 to the present, with special emphasis on the earlier transitional years.

During the preceding period of competitive capitalism, labor market developments pointed toward the progressive *homogenization* of the labor force, not toward segmentation. The factory system eliminated many skilled craft occupations, creating large pools of semiskilled jobs (Ware, 1964). Production for a mass market and increased mechanization forged standardized work requirements. Large establishments drew greater numbers of workers into common working environments.

The increasingly homogeneous and proletarian character of the work force generated tensions that were manifest in the tremendous upsurge in labor conflict that accompanied the emergence of monopoly capitalism: in railroads dating back to 1877, in steel before 1901 and again in 1919, in coal mining during and after the First World War, in textile mills throughout this period, and in countless other plants and industries around the country. The success of the Industrial Workers of the World (IWW), the emergence of a strong Socialist party, the general (as opposed to industry-specific) strikes in Seattle and New Orleans, the mass labor revolts in 1919 and 1920, and the increasingly national character of the labor movement throughout this period indicated a widespread and growing opposition to capitalist hegemony in general. More and more, strikes begun "simply" over wage issues often escalated to much more general issues (Commons et al., 1935; Brecher, 1974).

At the same time that the work force was becoming more homogeneous, those oligopolistic corporations that still dominate the economy today began to emerge and to consolidate their power. The captains of the new monopoly capitalist era, now released from short-run competitive pressures and in search of long-run stability, turned to the capture of strategic *control* over product and factor markets. Their new concerns were the creation and exploitation of monopolistic control, rather than the allocational calculus of short-run profit-maximization. . . .

The new needs of monopoly capitalism for control were threatened by the consequences of homogenization and proletarianization of the work force. Evidence abounds that large corporations were painfully aware of the potentially revolutionary character of these movements. As Commons notes, the employers' "mass offensive" on unions between 1903 and 1908 was more of an ideological crusade than a matter of specific demands. The simultaneous formation of the National Civic Federation (NCF), a group dominated by large "progressive" capitalists, was another explicit manifestation of the fundamental crises facing the capitalist class (Weinstein, 1968). The historical analysis that follows suggests that to meet this threat employers actively and consciously fostered labor market segmentation in order to "divide and conquer" the labor force. Moreover, the efforts of monopolistic corporations to gain greater control of their product markets led to a dichotomization of the industrial structure, which had the indirect and unintended, though not undesired, effect of reinforcing their conscious strategies. Thus labor market segmentation arose both from conscious strategies and systemic forces.

Conscious Efforts. Monopoly capitalist corporations devised deliberate strategies to resolve the contradictions between the increased proletarianization of the work force and the growth and consolidation of concentrated corporate power. The central thrust of the new strategies was to break down the increasingly unified worker interests that grew out of the proletarianization of work and the concentration of workers in urban areas. As exhibited in several aspects of these large firms' operations, this effort aimed to divide the labor force into various segments so that the actual experiences of workers were different and the basis of their common opposition to capitalists undermined.

The first element in the new strategy involved the internal relations of the firm. The tremendous growth in the size of monopoly capitalist work forces, along with the demise of craft-governed production, necessitated a change in the authority relations upon which control in the firm rested. . . . Efforts toward change in this area included Taylorism and Scientific Management, the establishment of personnel departments, experimentation with different organizational structures, the use of industrial psychologists, "human relations experts" and others to devise appropriate "motivating" incentives, and so forth. . . . From this effort emerged the intensification of hierarchical control, particularly the "bureaucratic form" of modern corporations. In the steel industry, for example, a whole new system of stratified jobs was introduced shortly after the formation of U.S. Steel. . . . The effect of bureaucratization was to establish a rigidly graded hierarchy of jobs and power by which "top-down" authority could be exercised.

The restructuring of the internal relations of the firm furthered labor market segmentation through the creation of segmented "internal labor markets." Job ladders were created, with definite "entry-level" jobs and patterns of promotion. White-collar workers entered the firm's work force and were promoted within it in different ways from the blue-collar production force. Workers not having the qualifications for particular entry-level jobs were excluded from access to that entire job ladder. In response, unions often sought to gain freedom from the arbitrary discretionary power of supervisors by demanding a seniority criterion for promotion. In such cases, the union essentially took over the management of the internal labor markets: they agreed to allocate workers and discipline recalcitrants, helping legitimize the internal market in return for a degree of control over its operation (Doeringer & Piore, 1972).

One such effort at internal control eventually resulted in segmentation by industry. Firms had initially attempted to raise the cost to workers of leaving individual companies (but not the cost of entering) by restricting certain benefits to continued employment in that company. Part of this strategy was "welfare capitalism," which emerged from the NCF in particular, and achieved most pronounced form in the advanced industries. At Ford, for example, education for the workers' children, credit, and other benefits were dependent on the workers' continued employment by the firm and therefore tied the worker more securely to the firm. For these workers, the loss of one's job meant a complete disruption in all aspects of the family's life. Likewise, seniority benefits were lost when workers switched companies (Weinstein, 1968). As industrial unions gained power, they transformed some of these firm-specific benefits to industry-wide privileges. The net effect was an intensification not only of internal segmentation, but also of segmentation by industry, which, as we discuss in the next section, had other origins as well.

At the same time that firms were segmenting their internal labor markets, similar efforts were under way with respect to the firm's external relations. Employers quite consciously exploited race, ethnic, and sex antagonisms in order to undercut unionism and break strikes. In numerous instances during the consolidation of monopoly capitalism, employers manipulated the mechanisms of labor supply in order to import blacks as strikebreakers, and racial hostility was stirred up to deflect class conflicts into race conflicts. For example, during the steel strike of 1919, one of the critical points in U.S. history, some 30,000 to 40,000 blacks were imported as strikebreakers in a matter of a few weeks. Employers also often transformed jobs into "female jobs" in order to render those jobs less susceptible to unionization. . . .

Employers also consciously manipulated ethnic antagonisms to achieve segmentation. Employers often hired groups from rival nationalities in the same plant or in different plants. During labor unrest the companies sent spies and rumormongers to each camp, stirring up fears, hatred, and antagonisms of other groups. The strategy was most successful when many immigrant groups had little command of English. . . .

The manipulation of ethnic differences was, however, subject to two grave limitations as a tool in the strategy of "divide and conquer." First, increasing English literacy among immigrants allowed them to communicate more directly with each other; second, mass immigration ended in 1924. Corporations then looked to other segmentations of more lasting significance.

Employers also tried to weaken the union movement by favoring the conservative "business-oriented" craft unions against the newer "social-oriented" industrial unions. An ideology of corporate liberalism toward labor was articulated around the turn of the century in the NCF. Corporate liberalism recognized the potential gains of legitimizing some unions but not others; the NCF worked jointly with the craft-dominated American Federation of Labor to undermine the more militant industrial unions, the Socialist party, and IWW (Weinstein, 1968).

As the period progressed, employers also turned to a relatively new divisive means, the use of educational "credentials." For the first time, educational credentials were used to *regularize* skill requirements for jobs. Employers played an active role in molding educational institutions to serve these channeling functions. The new requirements helped maintain the somewhat artificial distinctions between factory workers and those in routinized office jobs and helped generate some strong divisions within the office between semiskilled white-collar workers and their more highly skilled office mates....

SYSTEMIC FORCES

The rise of giant corporations and the emergence of a monopolistic core in the economy sharply accentuated some systemic market forces that stimulated and reinforced segmentation. As different firms and industries grew at different rates, a dichotomization of industrial structure developed.... The larger, more capital-intensive firms were generally sheltered by barriers to entry, enjoyed technological, market power, and financial economies of scale and generated higher rates of profit and growth than their smaller, labor-intensive competitive counterparts. However, it did not turn out that the monopolistic core firms were wholly to swallow up the competitive periphery firms.

Given their large capital investments, the large monopolistic corporations required stable market demand and stable planning horizons in order to insure that their investments would not go unutilized (Galbraith, 1967). Where demand was cyclical, seasonal, or otherwise unstable, production within the monopolistic environment became increasingly unsuitable. More and more, production of certain products was subcontracted or "exported" to small, more competitive and less capital-intensive firms on the industrial periphery.

Along with the dualism in the industrial structure, there developed a corresponding dualism of working environments, wages, and mobility patterns. Monopoly corporations, with more stable production and sales, developed job structures and internal relations reflecting that stability. For example, the bureaucratization of work rewarded and elicited stable work habits in employees. In peripheral firms, where product demand was unstable, jobs and workers tended to be marked also by instability. The result was the dichotomization of the urban labor market into "primary" and "secondary" sectors, as the dual labor market theory has proposed. . . .

In addition, certain systemic forces intensified segmentation within corporations in the primary sector. As Piore (1972) has argued, the evolution of technology within primary work places tended to promote distinctions between jobs requiring general and specific skills. As new technologies emerged that replicated these differential skill requirements, employers found that they could most easily train for particular jobs those workers who had already developed those different kinds of skills. As highly technical jobs evolved in which the application of generalized, problem-solving techniques were required, for instance, employers found that they could get the most out of those who had already developed those traits. Initial differences in productive capacities were inevitably reinforced.

SOCIAL FUNCTIONS OF SEGMENTATION

As the preceding historical analysis has argued, labor market segmentation is intimately related to the dynamics of monopoly capitalism. Understanding its origins, we are now in a position to assess its social importance.

Labor market segmentation arose and is perpetuated because it is *functional*—that is, it facilitates the operation of capitalist institutions. Segmentation is functional primarily because it helps reproduce capitalist hegemony. First, as the historical analysis makes quite clear, segmentation divides workers and forestalls potential movements uniting all workers against employers. . . . Second, segmentation establishes "fire trails" across vertical job ladders and, to the extent that workers perceive separate segments with different criterial for access, workers limit their own aspirations for mobility. Less pressure is then placed on other social institutions—the schools and the family, for example—that reproduce the class structure. Third, division of workers into segments legitimizes inequalities in authority and control between superiors and subordinates. For example, institutional sexism and racism reinforce the industrial authority of white male foremen.

Political Implications.   One of the principal barriers to united anticapitalist opposition among workers has been the evolution and persistence of labor market segmentation. This segmentation underlies the current state of variegation in class consciousness among different groups of workers. A better understanding of the endogenous sources of uneven levels of consciousness helps to explain the difficulties involved in overcoming divisions among workers. Nonetheless, if we more clearly understand the sources of our divisions, we may be able to see more clearly how to overcome them.

REFERENCES

Arrow, Kenneth J.
    1972   "Some models of racial discrimination in the labor force," in Anthony H. Pascal (ed.), The American Economy in Black and White. Lexington, Mass.: Lexington Books.
Brecher, Jeremy.
    1974   Strike. New York: Fawcett World Library.
Commons, John R., et al.
    1935   History of Labor in the United States. New York: Macmillan.
Doeringer, Peter, and Michael J. Piore.
    1972   Internal Labor Markets and Manpower Analysis. Lexington, Mass.: Lexington Books.
Edwards, Richard C.
    1972   "Alienation and inequality: Capitalist relations of production in bureaucratic enterprises." Unpublished Ph.D. dissertation. Cambridge, Mass.: Harvard University.
Edwards, Richard C., Michael Reich, and T. E. Weisskopf.
    1972   The Capitalist System. Englewood Cliffs, N.J.: Prentice-Hall.
Galbraith, John Kenneth.
    1967   The New Industrial State. Boston: Houghton Mifflin.
Piore, Michael J.
    1972   "Notes for theory of labor market stratification. Working Paper no. 95. Cambridge, Mass.: Department of Economics, Massachusetts Institute of Technology, October.
Reich, Michael, and David M. Gordon, and Richard C. Edwards.
    1973   "Labor market segmentation in American capitalism," forthcoming.
Ware, Norman J.
    1964   The Industrial Worker, 1840–1860. Chicago: Quadrangle Books.
Weinstein, James.
    1968   The Corporate Ideal in the Liberal State: 1910–1918. Boston: Beacon Press.

The Political Economy
of Women's Liberation
Margaret Benston

The "woman question" is generally ignored in analyses of the class structure of society. This is so because, on the one hand, classes are generally defined by their relation to the means of production and, on the other hand, women are not supposed to have any unique relation to the means of production. The category seems instead to cut across all classes; one speaks of working-class women, middle-class women, et cetera. The status of women is clearly inferior to that of men, but analysis of this condition usually falls into discussing socialization, psychology, interpersonal relations, or the role of marriage as a social institution. Are these, however, the primary factors? In arguing that the roots of the secondary status of women are in fact economic, it can be shown that women as a group do indeed have a definite relation to the means of production and that this is different from that of men. The personal and psychological factors then follow from this special relation to production, and a change in the latter will be a necessary (but not sufficient) condition for changing the former. If this special relation of women to production is accepted, the analysis of the situation of women fits naturally into a class analysis of society.

The starting point for discussion of classes in a capitalist society is the distinction between those who own the means of production and those who sell their labor power for a wage. As Ernest Mandel says:

> The proletarian condition is, in a nutshell, the lack of access to the
> means of production or means of subsistence which, in a society of

Excerpted from Margaret Benston, "The Political Economy of Women's Liberation," *Monthly Review*, vol. 21, no. 4 (New York: Monthly Review Press, 1969), pp. 13–27.

generalized commodity production, forces the proletarian to sell his labor power. In exchange for this labor power he receives a wage which then enables him to acquire the means of consumption necessary for satisfying his own needs and those of his family.

This is the structural definition of wage earner, the proletarian. From it necessarily flows a certain relationship to his work, to the products of his work, and to his overall situation in society, which can be summarized by the catchword alienation. But there does not follow from this structural definition any necessary conclusions as to the level of his consumption ... the extent of his needs, or the degree to which he can satisfy them.[1]

We lack a corresponding structural definition of women. What is needed first is not a complete examination of the symptoms of the secondary status of women, but instead a statement of the material conditions in capitalist (and other) societies which define the group "women." Upon these conditions are built the specific superstructures which we know. An interesting passage from Mandel points the way to such a definition:

The commodity ... is a product created to be exchanged on the market, as opposed to one which has been made for direct consumption. *Every commodity must have both a use-value and an exchange-value.*

It must have a use-value or else nobody would buy it. ... A commodity without a use-value to anyone would consequently be unsalable, would constitute useless production, would have no exchange-value precisely because it had no use-value.

On the other hand, every product which has use-value does not necessarily have exchange-value. It has an exchange-value only to the extent that the society itself, in which the commodity is produced, is founded on exchange, is a society where exchange is a common practice. ...

In capitalist society, commodity production, the production of exchange-values, has reached its greatest development. It is the first society in human history where the major part of production consists of commodities. It is not true, however, that all production under capitalism is commodity production. Two classes of products still remain simple use-value.

The first group consists of all things produced by the peasantry for its own consumption, everything directly consumed on the farms where it is produced. ...

The second group of products in capitalist society which are not commodities but remain simple use-value consists of all things pro-

---

[1]Ernest Mandel, "Workers Under Neocapitalism." Paper delivered at Simon Fraser University. (Available through the Department of Political Science, Sociology and Anthropology, Simon Fraser University, Burnaby, B.C., Canada.)

duced in the home. Despite the fact that considerable human labor goes into this type of household production, it still remains a production of use-values and not of commodities. Every time a soup is made or a button sewn on a garment, it constitutes production, but it is not production for the market.

The appearance of commodity production and its subsequent regularization and generalization have radically transformed the way men labor and how they organize society.[2]

What Mandel may not have noticed is that his last paragraph is precisely correct. The appearance of commodity production has indeed transformed the way that *men* labor. As he points out, most household labor in capitalist society (and in the existing socialist societies, for that matter) remains in the premarket stage. This is the work which is reserved for women and it is in this fact that we can find the basis for a definition of women.

In sheer quantity, household labor, including child care, constitutes a huge amount of socially necessary production. Nevertheless, in a society based on commodity production, it is not usually considered "real work" since it is outside of trade and the marketplace. It is precapitalist in a very real sense. This assignment of household work as the function of a special category "women" means that this group *does* stand in a different relation to production than the group "men." We will tentatively define women, then, as that group of people who are responsible for the production of simple use-values in those activities associated with the home and family.

Since men carry no responsibility for such production, the difference between the two groups lies here. Notice that women are not excluded from commodity production. Their participation in wage labor occurs but, as a group, they have no structural responsibility in this area and such participation is ordinarily regarded as transient. Men, on the other hand, are responsible for commodity production; they are not, in principle, given any role in household labor. For example, when they do participate in household production, it is regarded as more than simply exceptional; it is demoralizing, emasculating, even harmful to health. (A story on the front page of the *Vancouver Sun* in January 1969 reported that men in Britain were having their health endangered because they had to do too much housework!)

The material basis for the inferior status of women is to be found in just this definition of women. In a society in which money determines value, women are a group who work outside the money economy. Their work is not worth money, is therefore valueless, is therefore not even

[2]Ernest Mandel, *An Introduction to Marxist Economic Theory* (New York: Merit Publishers, 1967), pp. 10–11.

real work. And women themselves, who do this valueless work, can hardly be expected to be worth as much as men, who work for money. In structural terms, the closest thing to the condition of women is the condition of others who are or were also outside of commodity production, that is, serfs and peasants.

In her recent paper on women, Juliet Mitchell introduces the subject as follows:

> In advanced industrial society, women's work is only marginal to the total economy. Yet it is through work that man changes natural conditions and thereby produces society. Until there is a revolution in production, the labor situation will prescribe women's situation within the world of men.[3]

The statement of the marginality of women's work is an unanalyzed recognition that the work women do is *different* from the work that men do. Such work is not marginal, however; it is just not wage labor and so is not counted. She even says later in the same article, "Domestic labor, even today, is enormous if quantified in terms of productive labor." She gives some figures to illustrate: in Sweden, 2,340 million hours a year are spent by women in housework compared with 1,290 million hours spent by women in industry. And the Chase Manhattan Bank estimates a woman's overall work week at 99.6 hours.

However, Mitchell gives little emphasis to the basic economic factors (in fact she condemns most Marxists for being "overly economist") and moves on hastily to superstructural factors, because she notices that "the advent of industrialization has not so far freed women." What she fails to see is that no society has thus far industrialized housework. Engels points out that the

> first premise for the emancipation of women is the reintroduction of the entire female sex into public industry.... And this has become possible not only as a result of modern large-scale industry, which not only permits the participation of women in production in large numbers, but actually calls for it and, moreover, strives to convert private domestic work also into a public industry.[4]

And later in the same passage:

> Here we see already that the emancipation of women and their equality with men are impossible and must remain so as long as

---

[3] Juliet Mitchell, "Women: The Longest Revolution," *New Left Review,* December 1966.

[4] Friedrich Engels, *Origin of the Family, Private Property and the State* (Moscow: Progress Publishers, 1968), chap. 9, p. 158. The anthropological evidence known to Engels indicated primitive woman's dominance over man. Modern anthropology disputes this dominance but provides evidence for a more nearly equal position of women in the matrilineal societies used by Engels as examples. The arguments in this work of Engels do not require the former dominance of women but merely their former equality, and so the conclusions remain unchanged.

women are excluded from socially productive work and restricted to housework, which is private.

What Mitchell has not taken into account is that the problem is not simply one of getting women into *existing* industrial production but the more complex one of converting private production of household work into public production.

For most North Americans, domestic work as "public production" brings immediate images of Brave New World or of a vast institution—a cross between a home for orphans and an army barracks—where we would all be forced to live. For this reason, it is probably just as well to outline here, schematically and simplistically, the nature of industrialization.

A preindustrial production unit is one in which production is small-scale and reduplicative; that is, there is a great number of little units, each complete and just like all the others. Ordinarily such production units are in some way kin-based and they are multipurpose, fulfilling religious, recreational, educational, and sexual functions along with the economic function. In such a situation, desirable attributes of an individual, those which give prestige, are judged by more than purely economic criteria: for example, among approved character traits are proper behavior to kin or readiness to fulfill obligations.

Such production is originally not for exchange. But if exchange of commodities becomes important enough, then increased efficiency of production becomes necessary. Such efficiency is provided by the transition to industrialized production, which involves the elimination of the kin-based production unit. A large-scale, nonreduplicative production unit is substituted which has only one function, the economic one, and where prestige or status is attained by economic skills. Production is rationalized, made vastly more efficient, and becomes more and more public—part of an integrated social network. An enormous expansion of man's productive potential takes place. Under capitalism such social productive forces are utilized almost exclusively for private profit. These can be thought of as *capitalized* forms of production.

If we apply the above to housework and child rearing, it is evident that each family, each household, constitutes an individual production unit, a preindustrial entity, in the same way that peasant farmers or cottage weavers constitute preindustrial production units. The main features are clear, with the reduplicative, kin-based, private nature of the work being the most important. (It is interesting to notice the other features: the multipurpose functions of the family, the fact that desirable attributes for women do not center on economic prowess, et cetera.) The rationalization of production effected by a transition to large-scale production has not taken place in this area.

Industrialization is, in itself, a great force for human good; exploitation and dehumanization go with capitalism and not necessarily with industrialization. To advocate the conversion of private domestic labor into a public industry under capitalism is quite a different thing from advocating such conversion in a socialist society. In the latter case the forces of production would operate for human welfare, not private profit, and the result should be liberation, not dehumanization, In this case we can speak of *socialized* forms of production.

These definitions are not meant to be technical but rather to differentiate between two important aspects of industrialization. Thus the fear of the barrackslike result of introducing housekeeping into the public economy is most realistic under capitalism. With socialized production and the removal of the profit motive and its attendant alienated labor, there is no reason why, *in an industrialized society,* industrialization of housework should not result in better production, that is, better food, more comfortable surroundings, more intelligent and loving child care, et cetera, than in the present nuclear family.

The argument is often advanced that, under neocapitalism, the work in the home has been much reduced. Even if this is true, it is not structurally relevant. Except for the very rich, who can hire someone to do it, there is for most women, an irreducible minimum of necessary labor involved in caring for home, husband, and children. For a married woman without children, this irreducible minimum of work probably takes fifteen to twenty hours a week; for a woman with small children, the minimum is probably seventy or eighty hours a week. (There is some resistance to regarding child rearing as a job. That labor is involved, that is, the production of use-value, can be clearly seen when exchange-value is also involved—when the work is done by babysitters, nurses, child care centers, or teachers. An economist has already pointed out the paradox that if a man marries his housekeeper, he reduces the national income, since the money he gives her is no longer counted as wages.) The reduction of housework to the minimums given is also expensive; for low-income families more labor is required. In any case, household work remains structurally the same—a matter of private production.

One function of the family, the one taught to us in school and the one which is popularly accepted, is the satisfaction of emotional needs: the needs for closeness, community, and warm secure relationships. This society provides few other ways of satisfying such needs; for example, work relationships or friendships are not expected to be nearly as important as a man-woman-with-children relationship. Even other ties of kinship are increasingly secondary. This function of the family is important in stabilizing it so that it can fulfill the second, purely economic, function discussed above. The wage earner, the husband-father, whose earnings support himself, also "pays for" the labor done by the mother-wife and supports the children. The wages of a man buy the labor of two people. The crucial importance of this second function of the family can be seen when the family unit breaks down in divorce. The continuation of the economic function is the major concern where children are involved; the man must continue to pay for the labor of the woman. His wage is very often insufficient to enable him to support a second family. In this case his emotional needs are sacrificed to the necessity to support his ex-wife and children. That is, when there is a conflict, the economic function of the family very often takes precedence over the emotional one. And this in a society which teaches that the major function of the family is the satisfaction of emotional needs.

As an economic unit, the nuclear family is a valuable stabilizing force in capitalist society. Since the production which is done in the home is paid for by the husband-father's earnings, his ability to withhold his labor from the market is much reduced. Even his flexibility in changing jobs is limited. The woman, denied an active place in the market, has little control over the conditions that govern her life. Her economic dependence is reflected in emotional dependence, passivity, and other "typical" female personality traits. She is conservative, fearful, supportive of the status quo.

Furthermore, the structure of this family is such that it is an ideal consumption unit. But this fact, which is widely noted in Women's Liberation literature, should not be taken to mean that this is its primary function. If the above analysis is correct, the family should be seen primarily as a production unit for housework and child rearing. *Everyone* in capitalist society is a consumer; the structure of the family simply means that it is particularly well suited to encourage consumption. Women in particular *are* good consumers; this follows naturally from their responsibility for matters in the home. Also, the inferior status of women, their general lack of a strong sense of worth and identity, make them more exploitable than men and hence better consumers.

The history of women in the industrialized sector of the economy has depended simply on the labor needs of that sector. Women function as a massive reserve army of labor. When labor is scarce (early industrialization, the two world wars, et cetera) then women form an important part of the labor force. When there is less demand for labor (as now under neocapitalism) women become a surplus labor force—but one for which their husbands and not society are economically responsible. The "cult of the home" makes its reappearance during times of labor surplus and is used to channel women out of the market economy. This is relatively easy since the pervading ideology ensures that no one, man or woman, takes women's participation in the labor force very seriously. Women's real work, we are taught, is in the home; this holds whether or not they are married, single, or the heads of households.

At all times household work is the responsibility of women. When they are working outside the home they must somehow manage to get both outside job and housework done (or they supervise a substitute for the housework). Women, particularly married women with children, who work outside the home simply do two jobs; their participation in the labor force is only allowed if they continue to fulfill their first responsibility in the home. This is particularly evident in countries like Russia and those in Eastern Europe where expanded opportunities for women in the labor force have not brought about a corresponding expansion in their liberty. Equal access to jobs outside the home, while one of the preconditions for women's liberation, will not in itself be sufficient to give equality for women; as long as work in the home remains a matter of private production and is the responsibility of women, they will simply carry a double work load.

A second prerequisite for women's liberation which follows from the above analysis is the conversion of the work now done in the home as private production into work to be done in the public economy. To be more specific, this means that child rearing should no longer be the responsibility solely of the parents. Society must begin to take responsibility for children; the economic dependence of women and children on the husband-father must be ended. The other work that goes on in the home must also be changed—communal eating places and laundries for example. When such work is moved into the public sector, then the material basis for discrimination against women will be gone.

These are only preconditions. The idea of the inferior status of women is deeply rooted in the society and will take a great deal of effort to eradicate. But once the structures which produce and support that idea are changed, then, and only then, can we hope to make progress. It is possible, for example, that a change to communal eating places would simply mean that women are moved from a home kitchen to a communal one. This *would* be an advance, to be sure, particularly in a socialist society where work would not have the inherently exploitative nature it does now. Once women are freed from private production in the home, it will probably be very difficult to maintain for any long period of time a rigid definition of jobs by sex. This illustrates the interrelation between the two preconditions given above: true equality in job opportunity is probably impossible without freedom from housework, and the industrialization of housework is unlikely unless women are leaving the home for jobs.

The changes in production necessary to get women out of the home might seem to be, in theory, possible under capitalism. One of the sources of women's liberation movements may be the fact that alternative capitalized forms of home production now exist. Day care is available, even if inadequate and perhaps expensive; convenience foods, home delivery of meals, and takeout meals are widespread; laundries and cleaners offer bulk rates. However, cost usually prohibits a complete dependence on such facilities, and they are not available everywhere, even in North America. These should probably then be regarded as embryonic forms rather than completed structures. However, they clearly stand as alternatives to the present system of getting such work done. Particularly in North America, where the growth of "service industries" is important in maintaining the growth of the economy, the contradictions between these alternatives and the need to keep women in the home will grow.

The need to keep women in the home arises from two major aspects of the present system. First, the amount of unpaid labor performed by women is very large and very profitable to those who own the means of production. To pay women for their work, even at minimum wage scales, would imply a massive redistribution of wealth. At present, the support of a family is a hidden tax on the wage earner—his wage buys the labor power of two people. And second, there is the problem of whether the economy can expand enough to put all women to work as a part of the normally employed labor force. The war economy has been adequate to draw women partially into the economy but not adequate to establish a need for all or most of them. If it is argued that the jobs created by the industrialization of housework will create this need, then one can counter by pointing to (1) the strong economic forces operating for the status quo and against capitalization discussed above, and (2) the fact that the present service industries, which somewhat counter these forces, have not been able to keep up with the growth of the labor force as presently constituted. The present trends in the service industries simply create "underemployment" in the home; they do not create new jobs for women. So long as this situation exists, women remain a very convenient and elastic part of the industrial reserve army. Their incorporation into the labor force on terms of equality—which would create pressure for capitalization of housework—is possible only with an economic expansion so far achieved by neocapitalism only under conditions of full-scale war mobilization.

In addition, such structural changes imply the complete breakdown of the present nuclear family. The stabilizing consuming functions of the family, plus the ability of the cult of the home to keep women out of the labor market, serve neocapitalism too well to be easily dispensed with. And, on a less fundamental level, even if these necessary changes in the nature of household production were achieved under capitalism it would have the unpleasant consequence of including *all* human relations in the cash nexus. The atomization and isolation of people in Western society is already sufficiently advanced to make it doubtful if such complete psychic isolation could be tolerated. It is likely in fact that one of the major negative emotional responses to women's liberation movements may be exactly such a fear. If this is the case, then possible alternatives—cooperatives, the kibbutz, et cetera—can be cited to show that psychic needs for community and warmth can in fact be better satisfied if other structures are substituted for the nuclear family.

At best the change to capitalization of housework would only give women the same limited freedom given most men in capitalist society. This does not mean, however, that women should wait to demand freedom from discrimination. There *is* a material basis for women's status; we are not merely discriminated against, we are exploited. At present, our unpaid labor in the home is necessary if the entire system is to function. Pressure created by women who challenge their role will reduce the effectiveness of this exploitation. In addition, such challenges will impede the functioning of the family and may make the channeling of women out of the labor force less effective. All of these will hopefully make quicker the transition to a society in which the necessary structural changes in production can actually be made. That such a transition will require a revolution I have no doubt; our task is to make sure that revolutionary changes in the society do in fact end women's oppression.

PART THREE

Sex and Social Roles

Who am I? What am I? Early socialization, in the family and in other primary groups, gives women such a deep sense of inferiority, reinforced later by further socialization, low-status roles, and political and economic powerlessness, that they have not yet been able to develop a sustained movement to change their social condition. However, social movements in the 1960s that supported civil rights for blacks and opposed the war in Indochina, and expanding employment opportunities reawakened woman's concern about her customary low status. She has begun to probe her conflicting and ambiguous social roles. Women who have generally accepted their mixed feelings, frustrations, and lack of satisfaction with their lives as being due to some inner fault—a failure to be a "good woman" according to Biblical injunction, or Freudian precepts, or the latest findings of child psychologists—are now seeking new explanations.

THE PROBLEM

The essentials of woman's problem in the United States can be reduced to this: *Can I be both a successful woman and a successful person?* The dilemma has its contradictions in feelings and actions, in opportunities and rewards, and in rights and responsibilities. Every woman feels some of the effects of the ambiguous demands, of the low prestige, of the lesser power of *woman* as compared with *person* (which, in its common usage, often means *man*). Some effects are very evident: the desire for children and the inability to afford them or, conversely, unwanted children; the lack of child-care facilities, low pay, unequal job opportunities and training; the sharp drop in income after being widowed or divorced; the two jobs of the working wife. Other effects are more subtle, but no less important: the stigma attached to being an intellectual woman; the cult of youthfulness and of woman as sex object; a woman's vague feelings of worthlessness if she accepts only the traditional roles of wife and mother, and her feelings of being unfeminine if she does not; her frequent lack of self-confidence; and her self-contempt, which makes her prefer the company of men to that of women, perpetuating the myth of feminine duplicity.

What Is the Sign of a Successful Woman? Marriage. This is the cultural definition of the setting within which a woman is supposed to make a success of her life. The failure to marry or failure in marriage is total failure for many women, while for men it is only a partial failure. Marriage defines a woman's responsibilities and her appropriate social character. She does housework and cares for her children, while her husband leaves home to earn a living for the family. If she holds a job outside the home, she must not take it seriously. In her role as wife, she is expected to be dependent and acquiescent; in her role as mother, she is expected to be independent and assertive. She must be more concerned with meeting the emotional needs of her husband and her children than with growing through an understanding of her own needs; this proves she has the so-called "giving ability" of the mature woman. She must cope with a technical, bureaucratic society without having been encouraged, usually, to develop the necessary logic and assertiveness to do so. Furthermore, she must somehow manage to remain an interesting person in her own right, sexually and emotionally attractive to her husband and to other men (though disinterested in other men!).

What Is the Sign of a Successful Person? Occupational achievement. A person's worth in American society is generally thought to be indicated by occupation (which is closely related to income) so that physicians, architects, businessmen, and college professors are considered of greater worth than upholsterers, taxi drivers, or salesmen. Men are usually expected to demonstrate their manhood by providing an income for their families. Physical attractiveness, the ability to attract and hold the affection of a member of the other sex, and performance as a spouse and parent are the criteria by which women are usually judged. None of these comes anywhere near to being as important in judging a man. To a minority of men, the argument that child-rearing and homemaking are very creative may carry a good deal of weight.

Even to them, however, it is likely that homemaker and mother are not considered to be genuine equivalents of activities men do outside the home.

The primary occupation of most married women is that of housewife (known as "just a housewife" to television interviewers of many American women). She is treated as an unanalyzed, residual statistical unit in many social science analyses. Housewives are lumped together in most studies or, at most, categorized in terms of the occupation of the husband. The work women do in the household is considered less valuable than that performed in the marketplace. Thus, cooking, cleaning, sewing, home decorating, child care, and home entertaining carry relatively little prestige while large-scale food preparation, industrial cleaning, tailoring, interior decorating, teaching, and catering services are respected market activities. This low evaluation is partly perpetuated by the exclusion of household work from the calculation of Gross National Product—the most important measure of a nation's wealth.

There are occupations that are considered to be compatible with being an ideal woman; nursing, secretarial work, public school teaching, writing, and painting, for example, are acceptable. Women frequently find it difficult to get the necessary training for "less womanly" work. If she has the training, she may face other problems: she frequently finds it difficult to get a job, to be promoted, and to be paid the same as a comparably capable man. On the job, she may find herself excluded from colleagueship and sponsorship—each of which is important in the furthering of careers. Moreover, a woman's full-time commitment to a job or a career is considered a stumbling block in the fulfillment of her duties as a woman. If she pursues a career, she supposedly lessens her likelihood of marrying; if she does marry, the career woman presumably will neglect her husband and children. When convenient, the norms can be changed. Thus, low-income mothers are urged to leave their children while they enter the labor force to increase their self-respect.

In contrast, a man's commitment to a career or to community activity is not considered to reduce his willingness to marry nor is it considered to interfere with his duties to his wife and children; in fact these enhance his worth in the eyes of both society, and his marriageable women friends.

Being a woman and a person is further complicated for married women who are in the labor force. While working wives make an important contribution to family income (44.4 percent worked full time in 1975), they continue to have the major responsibility for homemaking and child care. A wife's job may even be seen by her husband as a threat to his own sense of success. It may even be a major source of tension between them, although this may exist more as a potential in the view of nonworking wives and their spouses than it does among couples where the wife works.

Some younger women may be rejecting "wife" as a defining social status. Demographic studies show a noticeable increase in "singles" among those between twenty and twenty-four years of age, as well as a continued rise in the overall rate of divorce and separation.[1] (The change in rates for men is less than for women.) Whether the increase in singles means that people are postponing or rejecting marriage will only really be known after another decade or so has passed.

We will now examine the problems outlined in this discussion in more detail. The articles fall into three categories: (1) role differentiation by sex, (2) the marriage relationship, and (3) the job market.

___

[1]Paul C. Glick, "A Demographer Looks at American Families." *Journal of Marriage and the Family* 37(February 1975):15–27.

Gender Role Differentiation

Introduction   Nona Glazer

In American society, as in all others, some tasks are considered to be appropriately performed by women, others to be appropriately performed by men, and some to be appropriately performed by either sex. There seems to be little relationship between the task that is assigned and the biological capabilities of the two sexes. In Western societies, as far as the day-by-day work tasks are concerned, the woman traditionally carries out home duties, while practically everything else is man's work. Within the institutions outside the family, there is a similar division of labor by sex. Charlotte Perkins Gilman, a leading feminist, summarized the distribution of social roles, which still pertains today in spite of many changes, when she wrote in 1911:

> From her first faint struggles toward freedom and justice, to her present valiant efforts toward full economic and political equality, each step has been termed *unfeminine,* and resented as an intrusion upon man's place and power. Woman's natural work as a female is that of the mother; man's natural work as a male is that of the father—but human work covers all our life outside of these specialties. That one sex should have monopolized all human activities, called them "man's work," and managed them as such, is what is meant by the phrase "Androcentric Culture." [1]

What accounts for the division of labor by sex? The sociological explanation of the division of labor (without considering gender) can be traced to Adam Smith, who saw the division as necessary for an efficient

[1]Charlotte Perkins Gilman, *Man-Made World: Our Androcentric Culture* (1911; reprint ed., New York: Johnson Reprint, 1971).

productive process.[2] Sociological explanations of the sex division of labor derive from the theory of Emile Durkheim, who saw the differences in the roles of women and men as resulting from physical evolution and as providing the basis for marital solidarity. According to Durkheim, each sex performs complementary and (for each other) indispensable functions.[3] The sex division of labor means that

> ... woman leads a completely different existence from that of man. One might say that the two great functions of psychic life are thus dissociated, that one of the sexes takes care of the affective functions and the other of intellectual functions.[4]

Today, when sociologists regard the wife/mother as the socioemotional leader and the husband/father as the instrumental leader, they are restating Durkheim's view in contemporary language without changing the nineteenth-century view of the differences between the sexes.

Talcott Parsons, whose article is the first in this section, has written the most well-thought-out theory about the different roles taken by wives and husbands in middle-class twentieth-century United States. Parsons argues that the gender roles in middle-class marriage arise from two circumstances. First, Parsons believes, the two roles—affective functions (Durkheim's words) or expressive leader (Parsons' words), and intellectual functions (Durkheim's words) or instrumental leader (Parsons' words)—cannot be filled by the same person. His reasoning is based on studies of male undergraduates who appeared unable to like best those in their experimental groups who were the main problem-solvers.[5] Second, according to Parsons, the socialization functions of the family—especially the care and training of the young—automatically and universally are assigned to women because of their lactation ability.[6] Hence, and almost by default, the breadwinner role (a basic instrumental role) is assigned to men. Parsons certainly never thought that the family role assigned to women in the United States was without frustrations. Indeed, he attributes the neuroticism of women to the limitations of the wife/mother roles. These roles are all the more frustrating since women, as children and

---

[2]Adam Smith, *The Wealth of Nations*, Modern Library Edition (New York: Random House, 1937).
[3]Emile Durkheim, *The Division of Labor in Society* (New York: Free Press, 1964), pp. 58–59, 270.
[4]Durkheim, *Division of Labor*, p. 60.
[5]Robert F. Bales and Philip E. Slater, "Role Differentiation in Small Decision-Making Groups," in Talcott Parsons and Robert F. Bales, *Family Socialization and Interaction Process* (Glencoe, Ill.: Free Press, 1955), pp. 259–306. One thing seems to be ignored when this study is used as a basis for asserting the need for differentiation in groups and, hence, in families: only one-half of the groups of undergraduates ever reached consensus on which individual played which role. Thus, while it is true that, overall, an individual was not seen as playing both roles, different group members saw the same person as playing quite different roles (see, especially, pp. 274–278).

[6]Talcott Parsons in Parsons and Bales, *Family Socialization and Interaction Process*, pp. 27–28 and pp. vii–viii. See also Morris Zelditch, Jr., "Role Differentiation in the Nuclear Family: A Comparative Study," in Parsons and Bales, pp. 307–352.

adolescents, were trained for more varied roles than those of wife and mother. Thus, it is inaccurate to dismiss Parsons as a simple "male chauvinist" (as many have, inaccurately, simply dismissed Freud), although it is reasonable to dispute Parsons' argument about the nature of groups and the inevitability of specialization of roles by sex.

The second article, by Alan Craddock, describes an empirical test of Parsons' theory about the nuclear family in industrial society. Craddock analyzes which activities women and men undertake in marriage and which partner suggests that a job or activity be done. According to Parsons' theory of role specialization, women do "expressive" activities (e.g., nurturing, being supportive, expressing love and affection, and performing tasks related to being the person responsible for the housework), while men do "instrumental" activities (e.g., managing affairs that relate the family to organizations outside itself). Conversely, wives usually would not perform typical "husband's tasks" and husbands would not do "wife's work." Craddock's data dispute this.

The third selection, by Joel Aronoff and William Crano, considers Parsons' theory of role differentiation in the family by looking at how jobs are distributed to women and men in 862 societies. The sociologists found that women are not excluded from the "instrumental role" outside the home (obviously women do instrumental jobs, such as meal preparation, cleaning, etc., *within* the household). On the contrary, they found that the women in their cross-cultural sample contribute about 44 percent of the subsistence production, and in some societies women contribute more than one-half of all subsistence production. While there are no data that can tell us whether the sexes are happier or better adjusted or whether children are more emotionally secure, etc., when women are excluded rather than included in productive activities, the cross-cultural evidence is clear: women are not excluded from productive activities because of their child-rearing responsibilities. Judith Brown's article (in Part Two) complements the Aronoff and Crano selection by showing how women's participation in subsistence activities varies with the degree of compatibility between child-care and economic activities. Thus, women are shown not to be automatically excluded from so-called instrumental activities outside the home but are excluded only when the two conflict and when child care by the mother—rather than by other women, men, or older children—is preferred by the society.

Sex Roles and Family Structure

Talcott Parsons

It has been noted that the primary source of family income lies in occupational earnings. It is above all the presence of the modern occupational system and its mode of articulation with the family which accounts for the difference between the modern, especially American, kinship system and *any* found in nonliterate or even peasant societies. . . .

In this type of society the basic mode of articulation between family and the occupational world lies in the fact that the *same* adults are both members of nuclear families and incumbents of occupational roles, the holders of "jobs." The individual's job and not the products of the cooperative activities of the family as a unit is of course the primary source of income for the family.

Next it is important to remember that the *primary* responsibility for this support rests on the one adult male member of the nuclear family. It is clearly the exceptional "normal" adult male who can occupy a respected place in our society without having a regular "job," though he may of course be "independent" as a professional practitioner or some kind of a "free lance" and not be employed by an organization, or he may be the proprietor of one. . . .

The occupational role is . . . both a role in the occupational system, *and* in the family; it is a "boundary-role" between them. The husband-father, in holding an acceptable job and earning an income from it is performing an essential function or set of functions for his family (which

Reprinted with permission of Macmillan Publishing Company, Inc., from "Sex Role and Family Structure," in *Family Socialization and Interaction Process* by Talcott Parsons and Robert F. Bales. Copyright by The Free Press, a Corporation, 1955.

of course includes himself in one set of roles) as a system. The status of the family in the community is determined probably more by the "level" of job he holds than by any other single factor, and the income he earns is usually the most important basis of the family's standard of living and hence "style of life." Of course, as we shall see, he has other very important functions in relation both to wife and to children, but it is fundamentally by virtue of the importance of his occupational role *as a component of his familial role* that in our society we can unequivocally designate the husband-father as the "instrumental leader" of the family as a system.

The membership of large numbers of women in the American labor force must not be overlooked. Nevertheless there can be no question of symmetry between the sexes in this respect, and, we argue, there is no serious tendency in this direction. . . . The role of "housewife" is still the overwhelmingly predominant one for the married woman with small children.

But even where this type does have a job, as is also true of those who are married but do not have dependent children, above the lowest occupational levels it is quite clear that in general the woman's job tends to be of a qualitatively different type and not of a status which seriously competes with that of her husband as the primary status-giver or income-earner.

It seems quite safe in general to say that the adult feminine role has not ceased to be anchored primarily in the internal affairs of the family, as wife, mother and manager of the household, while the role of the adult male is primarily anchored in the occupational world, in his job and through it by his status-giving and income-earning functions for the family. Even if, as seems possible, it should come about that the average married woman had some kind of job, it seems most unlikely that this relative balance would be upset; that either the roles would be reversed, or their qualitative differentiation in these respects completely erased.

PRINCIPAL FUNCTIONS OF THE NUCLEAR FAMILY

A primary function and characteristic of the family is that it should be a social group in which in the earliest stages the child can "invest" *all* of his emotional resources, to which he can become overwhelmingly "committed" or on which he can become fully "dependent." . . .

The second primary function of the family, along with socialization of children, concerns regulation of balances in the personalities of the adult members of both sexes. It is clear that this function is concentrated on the marriage relation as such. From this point of view a particularly significant aspect of the isolation of the nuclear family in our society is again the sharp discrimination in status which it emphasizes between family members and nonmembers. In particular, then, spouses are thrown upon each other, and their ties with members of their own families of orientation, notably parents and adult siblings, are correspondingly weakened. In its negative aspect as a source of strain, the consequence of this may be stated as the fact that the family of procreation, and in particular the marriage pair, are in a "structurally unsupported" situation. . . .

SEX ROLE AND FAMILY STRUCTURE

It goes without saying that the differentiation of the sex roles within the family constitutes not merely a major axis of its structure, but is deeply involved in both of these two central function-complexes of the family and in their articulation with each other. Indeed we argue that probably the importance of the family and its functions for society constitutes the primary set of reasons why there is a *social* as distinguished from purely reproductive, differentiation of sex roles. . . . We will argue that the differentiation of sex role in the family is, in its sociological character and significance, primarily an example of a basic qualitative mode of differentiation which tends to appear in *all* systems of social interaction regardless of their composition. In particular, this type of differentiation, that on "instrumental-expressive" lines, is conspicuous in small groups of about the same membership-size as the nuclear family.

We suggest that this order of differentiation is generic to the "leadership element" of small groups everywhere and that the problem with respect to the family is not *why* it appears there, given the fact that families as groups exist, but why the man takes the more instrumental role, the woman the more expressive, and why in detailed ways these roles take particular forms. In our opinion the fundamental explanation of the allocation of the roles between the biological sexes lies in the fact that the bearing and early nursing of children establish a strong presumptive primacy of the relation of mother to the small child and this in turn establishes a presumption that the man, who is exempted from these biological functions, should specialize in the alternative instrumental direction.

However the allocation may have come about in the course of biosocial evolution, there can be little doubt about the ways in which differentiation plays into the structure and functioning of the family as we know it. It is our suggestioin that the recent change in the American family itself and in its relation to the rest of the society which we have taken as our point of departure, is far from implying an erasure of the differentiation of sex roles; in many respects it reinforces and clarifies it. In the first place, the articulation between family and occupational system in our society focuses the instrumental responsibility for a family very sharply on its one adult male member, and prevents its diffusion through the ramifications of an extended kinship system. Secondly, the isolation of the nuclear family in a complementary way focuses the responsibility of the mother role more sharply on the one adult woman, to a relatively high degree cutting her off from the help of adult sisters and other kinswomen; furthermore, the fact of the absence of the husband-father from the home premises so much of the time means that she has to take primary responsibility for the children. This responsibility is partly mitigated by reduction in the number of children and by aids to household management, but by no means to the point of emancipating the mother from it. Along with this goes, from the child's point of view, a probable intensification of the emotional significance of his parents as individuals, particularly and in the early stages, his mother, which, there is reason to believe, is important for our type of socialization.

Hence, it is suggested that, if anything, in certain respects the *differentiation* between the roles of the parents becomes more rather than less significant for the socialization process under modern American conditions. It may also be suggested that in subtle ways the same is true of the roles of spouses vis-à-vis each other. The enhanced significance of the marriage relationship, both for the structure of the family itself and for the personalities of the spouses, means that the *complementarity* of roles within it tends to be accentuated. The romantic love complex and our current strong preoccupation with the emotional importance of the "significant person" of opposite sex strongly suggests this. Indeed there has been, we think, a greatly increased emphasis on the importance of good heterosexual relations, which overwhelmingly means *within* marriage. Such disorganization within this field as there is, apart from premarital experimenting, takes primarily the form of difficulties with the current marriage relationship and, if its dissolution is sought, the establishment of a *new* one. It does not mainly take the form of centering erotic interests outside the marriage relation.

All of this seems to us to indicate that the increased emphasis, manifested in all sorts of ways, on overt, specifically feminine attractiveness, with strong erotic overtones, is related to this situation within the family. The content of the conceptions of masculinity and femininity has undoubtedly changed. But it seems clear that the accent of their differentiation has not lessened.

... [Two] conspicuous and related features of our modern society, which are closely related to marriage and the family, may be called to mind. The first of these is the enormous vogue of treating "human" problems from the point of view of "mental health" and in various respects of psychology....

The second, and related, phenomenon is what is sometimes called, with reference to child training, the "professionalization" of the mother role. It is, starting with the elementary matters of early feeding and other aspects of physical care, the attempt to rationalize, on the basis of scientific—though often pseudo-scientific—authority, the technical aspects of the care of children....

This involvement of applied science in so many aspects of the intimate life of personalities, as in the mother's care of her children and in the marriage relationship, suggests an important aspect of the developing American feminine role that should not be overlooked. This is that, though the tendency in certain respects is probably increasing, to specialize in the expressive direction, the American woman is not thereby sacrificing the values of rationality. On the contrary, she is heavily involved in the attempt to rationalize these areas of human relations themselves. Women do not act only in the role of patient of the psychiatrist, but often the psychiatrist also is a woman. The mother not only "loves" her children, but she attempts to understand rationally the nature, conditions and limitations of that love, and the ways in which its deviant forms can injure rather than benefit her child. In this, as in other respects, the development we have been outlining is an integral part of the more general development of American society.

SELECTED REFERENCES

Bales, Robert F.
    1953   "The equilibrium problem in small groups." Chapter 4 in Talcott
            Parsons, R. F. Bales, and E. A. Shils, Working Papers in Theory of
            Action. Glencoe, Ill.: Free Press.
Bales, Robert F., and Philip E. Slater.
    1955   "Role differentiation in small decision-making groups," in Talcott
            Parsons and Robert F. Bales, Family Socialization and Interaction
            Processes. Glencoe, Ill.: Free Press.

Task and Emotional Behavior in the Marital Dyad

Alan E. Craddock

Bales and Parsons (1955) reported finding leadership role differentiation along an instrumental-expressive axis in small experimental groups. Generalizing from these findings to the nuclear family, Bales and Parsons maintained that the husband-father was the instrumental leader and the wife-mother the expressive or emotional leader in the nuclear family. These generalizations were formalized and given empirical support by Zelditch (1955). The impact of the Bales-Parsons' hypothesis has been great in sociology and social psychology but doubt has been expressed concerning its validity by a number of authors of recent articles reviewing marital research. For example, Rossi (1968:36) referred to the "Parsonian distinction between instrumental and expressive ... that is unfortunately applied in an indiscriminate way to all manner of social phenomena ... and the primary roles or personality tendencies of men compared to women." Mowrer (1969) demonstrated a shift in actual marital behaviors from the Bales-Parsons "traditional" conceptualization of role differentiation. Barry (1970:49) noted in relation to the Bales-Parsons' view that one can "raise serious questions as to whether the sex role differentiation postulated by Parsons and Bales actually typifies interaction between spouses."

Levinger (1964) questioned the validity of generalizations from small-group studies to the nuclear family, and in terms of dyadic interaction between husbands and wives Levinger predicted role differentiation

Reprinted from Alan E. Craddock, "Task and Emotional Behavior in the Marital Dyad." *Australian Journal of Psychology* 26(1974):15–23, by permission of the author and the courtesy of the Australian Psychological Society.

for instrumental activities but not for emotional or expressive activities. Levinger qualified the Bales-Parsons' view and considered that it appeared "largely correct for describing the roles of father and mother in the childbearing nuclear family ... [but] it does not apply as readily to the roles of husband and wife considered purely in the context of the marriage relationship." ... Thus a group's task orientation encourages specialization in division of labor but expressive or emotional behavior cannot be delegated in the same manner. Levinger proposed that emotional specialization could not occur in the marital dyad since task activity refers to a subject-object relation (and thus specialization can occur in a dyadic system) but emotional activity represents a subject-subject relation, is thus reciprocal and not able to be delegated when only two people are involved.

[According to] Levinger's reported ... study, which provided an empirical test of these hypotheses, ... activity task specialization was evident for eight out of ten activities under scrutiny. It was not evident in the analysis whether the specialization was stratified according to sex (i.e., male specialization) as hypothesized by Bales and Parsons. In the case of expressive activity, role specialization was not evident in four out of five activities studied. ...

There are three important problems associated with Levinger's study.

1. The analysis of task behaviors indicates that specialization occurs but the sex of the specialist is not evident in the data as reported by Levinger. ... An analysis that identifies the sex of the specialist is desirable in order to test the Bales-Parsons' view that task specialization is always in terms of male specialization. The present writer maintains that the style of specialization is related to the efficiency of task performance, that is, that role differentiation in task behaviors occurs when the nature of the activity would lead to a more efficient performance by one member of the marital dyad than the other. In the Bales-Parsons' view, most task activity is more efficiently performed by males since they are physically better equipped for certain manual activities and/or are more readily available than the female (in the marital dyad) because of the demands of child-rearing and home maintenance upon the female. It is clear, however, that some task activities could be more efficiently performed by females (because of training, irrelevancy of some physical factors to specific tasks, and availability of the wife at critical times) or by either the male or female (because of the irrelevance of the previous factors). ... [A] general research hypothesis can be stated:

Hypothesis (1): Task role performance in the marital dyad will be marked by male specialization provided that the specific task activity under consideration can be most efficiently performed by a male and is traditionally considered (by the society relevant to the study) to be a male task. When these qualifiers do not apply, female task specialization is predicted if the qualifiers point toward a more efficient performance by a female. When the situation is ambiguous, task specialization independent of the sex of the specialist would be predicted.

Hypothesis (1) was not tested in Levinger's study and is in opposition to the universality of the Bales-Parsons' view of male task specialization.

2. The second problem in Levinger's study relates to the fact that his analysis does not unequivocally demonstrate the tenability of his hypothesis since only one of the five activities studies showed significantly that the activity was performed equally by both partners as distinct from performance to a different degree. Levinger (1964:438) stated that for these activities "there was as much or more mutuality in the spouses' reported behavior as there was specialization." . . . The study to be detailed shortly was concerned with testing Levinger's hypothesis as it related to emotional activity and this is stated below:

Hypothesis (2): Emotional or expressive role performance in the marital dyad will be marked by mutuality rather than role specialization. That is, neither spouse will be a specialist since emotionality encourages and requires reciprocity.

3. The third problem in Levinger's study relates to the distinction drawn by many researchers between the performer of an activity (the "doer") and the initiator of that activity (the "decider"). Levinger (1964:447) suggested that his findings (nonspecialization in emotional behaviors) do not conflict "with the probability that the average wife initiates more than half of the socially supportive interaction." This hypothesis is not tested by Levinger. . . . In the light of Levinger's hypothesis of emotional reciprocity in the marital dyad it is difficult to see why Levinger would expect differentiation or specialization at the level of initiation. A third hypothesis is thus advanced in the present study—logically consistent it is believed, with Hypothesis (2)—but *contrary* to Levinger's informal and untested hypothesis suggestive of female specialization at the level of initiation.

Hypothesis (3): Emotional role initiation in the marital dyad will be marked by mutuality rather than specialization. That is, neither spouse will be a specialist since emotionality encourages and requires reciprocity.

One further hypothesis is relevant to the present study. Role specialization was predicted earlier in relation to task activities and the sex of the role specialist was related to factors enabling efficient performance of the task. In a consideration of "doing" as distinct from "deciding," the latter need not be related to the funtional factors appealed to in making the predictions about task role specialization. Thus the final hypothesis can be stated:

> Hypothesis (4): Task role initiation will be characterized by either spouse acting as a specialist, or by one spouse initiating the behavior equally often as the other (neither a specialist).

METHOD

Subjects. The sample consisted of 120 married couples who had volunteered to participate in the research upon an appeal for assistance.[1] . . .

Material. Each couple was asked to provide information on "the nature of the marital relationship" [by completing the] Marital Roles Inventory, which consisted of a list of activities for which the respondent was required to provide the identity of the performer of that activity. The activities represented task and emotional behaviors. . . . There were fifteen task activities and twelve emotional activities represented and these included all the activities examined in Levinger's study together with some additional activities. Each activity was listed twice, once in a style of construction that would identify the "doer" of the activity and again in order to identify the "decider" or the "initiator". . . . Information responses for which the spouses showed disagreement were not included in the final analysis. The discord rate in actual practice proved to be very slight (5.45 percent of all responses) and little information was lost due to this practice.

---

[1]Forty of the couples were in the situation where one spouse was taking Psychology I as a course at the University of Sydney in either 1970 or 1971. The other eighty couples were contacted by students taking Psychology I at the same university (in 1971), and the couples contacted had no connection (as students) with the university; typically they were parents of the students or married friends and relations. The sample was drawn from a specified range of socioeconomic indices based upon the occupation of the husband. The index used was formulated by Reiss (1961) and provides a scale ranging from 1 to 100. The sample used in the present study was drawn from the upper half of the range, specifically between indices 100 and 44 for the husband's occupation on the Reiss index. The mean duration of marriage for the sample was 9.15 years, the mean age of the husbands was 34.41 years, for the wives 31.85 years, and more than half of the couples had children. Of the wives, fifty-six were involved in full-time home duties, fifty-one were employed full-time, and thirteen were engaged in full-time studies.

RESULTS AND DISCUSSION

The eight task activities for which husband role specialization is predicted under Hypothesis (1) are listed in Table 1. Physical factors lead to this prediction for activities (1) and (3), traditional expectations are strong for activities (1), (3), and (6) whilst the husband, as the wage-earner in most of the families, is likely to handle financial matters more efficiently and this is a possible factor for activities (2), (4), (7), and (8). A 1×3 chi-squared test of significance, with H_0: $P_1 = P_2 = P_3 = .33$ (where P_1 = column 1, P_2 = column 2, and P_3 = column 3) df = 2 and alpha = .05 (as is the case in all following analyses), indicates that Hypothesis (1) is confirmed in six of the eight activities. No single pattern for disciplining children at the dinner table was evident. The other exception was wife specialization for giving the children pocket money. In the other six activities marked male task specialization is evident as predicted in Hypothesis (1).

The two task activities (9) and (10), for which wife role specialization is predicted under Hypothesis (1) are listed in Table 2. Traditional expectations, and the fact that the wife (if she is not engaged in out-of-home work) is more likely to spend time on such activities as writing letters to relatives and keeping the kitchen in order, are factors that lead to prediction of wife specialization rather than husband specialization.

TABLE 1. REPORTED INCIDENCE OF PERFORMANCE SPECIALIZATION BY MARRIED COUPLES WITH RESPECT TO EIGHT TASK ACTIVITIES IN WHICH MALE SPECIALIZATION IS PREDICTED

Activity	Specialization Husband	Wife	Absence of Specialization	N	Chi-Squared
1. Repairing things around the home	92	5	14	111	123.72*
2. Paying bills when they are due	51	32	20	103	14.23*
3. Putting out the garbage	89	8	9	106	122.28*
4. Obtaining insurance information	74	13	17	104	67.17*
5. Locking up at night	46	10	36	92	22.52*
6. Disciplining children at dinner table	13	16	23	52	3.03
7. Handling money on vacation	74	9	28	111	60.37*
8. Giving children pocket money	9	21	7	37	9.28*

Notes: (1) The activities also studied by Levinger are 1, 2, 3 and 4.

(2) The discrepancy between the reported N and the total sample size of 120 is not entirely due to discarding conflicting responses but is largely due to the irrelevancy of certain activities to some couples—e.g., not having children, not needing to put garbage out, etc.

*indicates that the chi-squared value is significant with alpha .05.

The results confirm these predictions as they relate to two areas of task activity that were also considered in Levinger's study. Levinger reported specialization but did not indicate which member of the marital dyad would be the specialist. Activity (8) in Table 1 also revealed wife specialization and, as a *post hoc* conclusion, it is clear that the wife would be more likely to give pocket money to children since this is often done when the child leaves for school or on some outing—when the father is absent at work.

TABLE 2. REPORTED INCIDENCE OF PERFORMANCE SPECIALIZATION BY MARRIED COUPLES WITH RESPECT TO TWO TASK ACTIVITIES IN WHICH FEMALE SPECIALIZATION IS PREDICTED

Activity	Specialization Husband	Wife	Absence of Specializa- tion	N	Chi- Squared
9. Washing the evening dishes	9	81	18	108	85.50*
10. Keeping touch with relatives	1	71	42	114	65.10*

Note: *indicates that the chi-squared value is significant with alpha .05. Both of these activities were included in Levinger's study.

Table 3 shows the results for the five task activities (11 to 15) for which no prediction of sex specialization is made. In only one of these activities (activity 14) is there evidence of significant specialization according to sex, husband specialization in this case. In all four of the other activities, specialization is either optional (it could be either husband or wife specialization) or is absent. Thus the final prediction in Hypothesis (1) is given considerable support.

TABLE 3. REPORTED INCIDENCE OF PERFORMANCE SPECIALIZATION BY MARRIED COUPLES WITH RESPECT TO FIVE TASK ACTIVITIES IN WHICH THE SEX OF THE SPECIALIST IS OPTIONAL OR IN WHICH SPECIALIZATION IS ABSENT

Activity	Specialization Husband	Wife	Absence of Specializa- tion	N	Chi- Squared
11. Handling the savings account	39	41	27	107	3.21*
12. Obtaining information re purchase of "big items"	36	19	40	95	7.85*
13. Obtaining vacation information and bookings	39	24	33	96	3.56
14. Switching on and adjusting the T.V. and/or radio	52	21	35	108	13.38*
15. Making complaints to salesmen, workers etc.	37	29	30	96	1.19

Note: Activities 12 and 13 were also included in the study by Levinger.
*indicates that the chi-squared value is significant with alpha .05.

Hypothesis (2) is given convincing support by the results detailed in Table 4 for the twelve emotional activities. In all cases specialization is absent to a significant degree and emotional role performance is characterized by mutuality rather than by role specialization as predicted.

Activity	Specialization Husband	Wife	Absence of Specializa- tion	N	Chi- Squared
1. Talking about feelings when bothered or upset	8	43	57	108	35.38*
2. Making an effort to see the other's point of view	15	14	72	101	65.48*
3. Asking about the day's activities	6	17	76	99	85.87*
4. Giving praise when the other has given pleasure	10	14	89	113	105.15*
5. Talking about the activities of the day	10	35	61	106	36.82*
6. Kissing the other first when leaving	28	8	67	103	52.44*
7. Giving comfort to the other when upset	37	12	55	104	26.90*
8. Expressing love and affection	12	13	86	111	97.35*
9. Planning companionate activities	11	14	83	108	92.17*
10. Restoring the peace after a dispute	27	15	58	100	29.54*
11. Showing courtesy to the other	8	2	100	110	164.58*
12. Showing sympathy to the other	9	23	71	103	61.59*

Note: The activities used in Levinger's study were 1, 2, 4 and 5.
*indicates that the chi-squared value is significant with alpha .05.

Emotional role initiation (the "decider" as distinct from the "doer") is not marked by wife initiation as suggested by Levinger, but in accordance with Hypothesis (3) is marked by mutuality. The data in Table 5 illustrate this and confirm Hypothesis (3).

The analysis of task role initiation (Table 6) indicates that initiation behavior is of a different character to performance on the same activities. In the case of the seven task activities that reveal husband specialization, the frequency of husband initiation is considerably less. Only activities (4) and (7) reveal husband specialization in relation to initiation, and there is a substantial reduction in the frequency of this in relation to actual performance. Wife specialization for initiation replaces male specialization in performance for activity (3). The remaining activities reveal equality of initiation (activities (4), (5), (6), and (8)) or no particular pattern of initiation in which either or both partners initiate such activities (activities (1) and (2)). Hypothesis (4) is thus confirmed in these general trends.

The two activities that reveal wife specialization in performance also reveal initiation by the wife. Thus Hypothesis (4) is not given support in the case of these task activities. For the four task activities in which

TABLE 6. REPORTED INCIDENCE OF INITIATION BY MARRIED COUPLES IN RESPECT TO FIFTEEN TASK ACTIVITIES

Activity	Husband Initiates	Wife Initiates	H or W initiate Equally Often	N	Chi-Squared
1 a	25	38	32	95	2.67
2 a	35	31	24	90	2.06
3 a	36	45	15	96	14.81*
4 a	48	14	44	106	19.54*
5 a	22	31	42	95	6.33*
6	10	11	35	56	21.46*
7 a	59	8	40	107	37.24*
8 a	6	16	22	44	8.83*
9 b	7	79	27	113	73.34*
10 b	2	56	44	102	47.29*
11 c	30	13	67	110	41.58*
12 c	17	26	57	100	26.42*
13 c	23	9	55	87	38.34*
14	31	16	57	104	24.82*
15 c	27	26	44	95	6.32*

Notes: a indicates an activity in which male specialization was observed in relation to performance as distinct from initiation.

b indicates an activity in which female specialization was observed in relation to performance as distinct from initiation.

c indicates an activity in which no distinct sex role specialization was observed.

*indicates that the chi-squared value is significant with alpha .05.

TABLE 5. REPORTED INCIDENCE OF INITIATION BY MARRIED COUPLES IN RESPECT TO TWELVE TASK ACTIVITIES

Activity	Husband Initiates	Wife Initiates	H or W Initiate Equally Often	N	Chi-Squared
1	11	25	67	103	49.47*
2	20	11	67	98	55.36*
3	11	27	64	102	43.47*
4	6	20	79	105	85.77*
5	11	41	57	109	30.01*
6	5	27	79	111	78.05*
7	9	15	79	103	87.68*
8	9	16	83	108	92.72*
9	6	13	83	102	106.65*
10	26	15	61	102	33.94*
11	7	9	92	108	130.72*
12	8	22	77	107	74.59*

Note: The activity numbers correspond to those listed in Table 4.

*indicates that the chi-squared value is significant with alpha .05.

no distinct sex role specialization for performance is evident in Table 3, initiation is not found to be subject to specialization either. Activity (14), which had revealed husband specialization for performance, is characterized by equality of interaction in the analysis of initiation as distinct from performance. These results give support to Hypothesis (4).

CONCLUSION

These findings imply that the Bales-Parsons' view of role differentiation cannot be supported in relation to middle-class Australian marriages. Task role specialization is not solely a male prerogative and emotional role performance is not characterized by female specialization but is, as suggested by Levinger, subject to mutuality. Task specialization, it has been shown, is best analyzed in terms of the demands of the problem facing the marital dyad and how these demands can be most efficiently met by the resources of the members of the dyad. Initiation, as distinct from performance, in relation to emotionality, is not characterized by wife dominance as implied by Levinger but is also subject to mutuality —sharing of initiation as it relates to emotional activities. A further implication of the study is that in relation to certain task activities that exhibit performance specialization, initiation behaviors are not subject to this same specialization. One exception to this generalization would appear to be certain task activities marked by female specialization. In such cases female initiation is also evident.

REFERENCES

Barry, W. A.
   1970   "Marriage research and conflict." Psychological Bulletin 73:41–54.
Levinger, George.
   1964   "Task and social behavior in marriage." Sociometry 27(December):433–448.
Mowrer, E. R.
   1969   "The differentiation of husband and wife roles." Journal of Marriage and the Family 31:534–540.
Parsons, Talcott, and Robert F. Bales.
   1955   Family Socialization and Interaction Process. Glencoe, Ill.: Free Press.
Reiss, Albert J.
   1961   Occupations and Social Status. Glencoe Ill.: Free Press.
Rossi, A. S.
   1968   "Transition to parenthood." Journal of Marriage and the Family 30:26–39.
Zelditch, Morris, Jr.
   1955   "Role indifferentiation in the nuclear family: A comparative study," Pp. 307–352 in Talcott Parsons and Robert F. Bales, Family Socialization and Interaction Process. Glencoe, Ill.: Free Press.

Sex Role Differentiation

Joel Aronoff
William D. Crano

An important theme recapitulated throughout much of the literature concerned with the analysis of social institutions has been the attempt to delineate universal patterns of interdependence within the family....

Following Durkheim's original formulation in *The Division of Labor*, ... recent attempts to establish a general interdisciplinary framework for the analysis of the family have held that an essential characteristic of the family as an economic system is the division of labor in the tasks of production (Parsons & Bales, 1955; Stephens, 1963; Biddle & Thomas, 1966; Bell & Vogel, 1968). This differentiation of basic subsistence activities, seen as an invariant feature of the family, is typically thought to arise in the service of the maximal utilization of labor through task specialization. A further regularity concerning task differentiation in the family was developed from Murdock's (1937) findings, which suggested the segregation of economic activities by sex. In Murdock's research, hunting, fishing, mining, and herding were found to fall almost exclusively in the domain of male economic activities, while burden bearing, mat making, cooking, and water carrying were found to be assumed, almost exclusively, by women. In a later theoretical extension of this research, Murdock (1949) generalized these empirical results into a more inclusive principle of social organization and family structure. This theoretical development was grounded in the observation

Excerpts reprinted from Joel Aronoff and William D. Crano, "A Re-examination of the Cross-Cultural Principles of Task Segregation and Sex Role Differentiation in the Family." *American Sociological Review* 40(February 1975):12–20. Reprinted by permission of the authors and the American Sociological Association.

that males, possessing greater strength, could be expected to undertake the more strenuous economic tasks while females, seen as handicapped by the physiological burdens of pregnancy and nursing, were relegated to the simpler tasks that could be performed near the home.[1] . . .

In attempting to locate the study of the family within the context of a more extensive theoretical and empirical perspective, Parsons and Bales (1955) made the useful observation that the nuclear family might well be conceptualized as a small group. . . . An important distinction that regularly emerged in the investigation of small groups concerned the nature of specialist roles exhibited in [Bales's] study of group process. Consistently, Bales found that two contrasting patterns of behavior emerged in his groups, and further, that these behaviors were typically found in two different persons. The role of *task specialist* was assumed by individuals who directed the behavior of group members to the successful completion of the task, while the *socioemotional specialist* was concerned primarily with expressive relationships in maintaining the integrity of the group. In this conceptual scheme, the task specialist was seen as concerned with the instrumental activity of the group, while the socioemotional specialist was primarily oriented toward the expressive activities of group members. . . .

Zelditch (1955), a collaborator and co-author of Parsons and Bales (1955), further refined this analysis of task specialization to the differentiation of roles within the family. . . . Zelditch's basic argument was that both instrumental and expressive specialists were necessary in a group, and both roles could not be assumed at the same time by the same person. Thus, he maintained that the optimal group structure was characterized by a segregation of these activities into two separate roles. Within the family, the allocation of roles was supported by a new biosocial assertion based on a special characteristic of the female—that she nurses the child—as opposed to Murdock's argument which was based on the greater strength of the male. Zelditch argued that nursing the baby established the mother as a source of security, comfort, warmth, and stability, and because of the emotional nature of this special relationship to the child, the mother was more likely to become the family member who specialized in handling the expressive component of the family.[2]

---

[1]This biosocial proposition finds widespread use in the social sciences. See Blood and Wolfe (1960) for an example of its uncritical use in an empirical study of role specialization in the American family, or Stephens (1963) in a more theoretical cross-cultural analysis of the family.

[2]This simple biosocial assertion has been employed by a variety of more focused studies. For example, when Barry, Bacon and Child (1957) attempted to provide a functional basis for their findings that childhood socialization, in a cross-cultural sample, emphasized nurturance, obedience and responsibility in girls, and achievement and self-reliance in boys, they employed Murdock's and Zelditch's argument that biological differences between the sexes direct each to alternative roles in the economic system. Following Murdock's (1937) early breakdown of economic activity, they concluded that the

... Categorization by contrast often leads to false clarity, and nowhere has this problem been more apparent than in the study of this variable in the behavior of small groups.... Gibb (1969) argued that simple dichotomization be avoided and that task variation in groups be viewed as a more continuous variable, conceptualized in terms of the proportion of relevant acts emitted by the various members of the group.... The principle advantages of Gibb's approach, of course, are that it fosters a more precise definition and identification of the behaviors of interest and, in addition, provides for the utilization of the total data pattern (cf. Crano & Brewer, 1973)....

In his early research in this area, Murdock (1937) separately examined each of a large variety of economic activities within societies, and judged the relative contribution, by sex, to each of these activities. In light of the great theoretical impact that these findings have had, it is important to note that this procedure failed to assess the relative economic importance of each activity to the society, or the relative economic contribution by sex across the total range of activities undertaken within a given society.... Thus, Murdock's procedure fails to yield precisely the needed overall degree of economic contribution that is made by sex in a given society.

In a recent examination of a related question, Murdock and Provost (1973) focused their attention on the factors which might underlie sex-linked specialization of economic activities. With a somewhat larger sample than employed in previous research (Murdock, 1937), they report both a replication of the original findings as well as a set of correlations between sex and a number of social factors derived from the Ethnographic Atlas (Murdock, 1967). Although Murdock and Provost coded for the relative importance of each activity for a given society, these results were not presented in their report nor used in a reappraisal of the original findings....

A complete examination of the general theoretical propositions, of course, would require a cross-cultural analysis of the expressive as well as the instrumental role. While the data available in Murdock's Ethnographic Atlas, the data source employed in this study, are ideally suited for an examination of the degree of differentiation in the instrumental role, Murdock has not provided material that can be used to examine the distribution of expressive behaviors across family members. Therefore, this report must focus most particularly on the data that are available for the study of the instrumental role. Even given this restriction, however, the available data enable an initial test of Parsons and Bales'

---

observed differences in socialization were designed to support biological differences and develop in members of a society personality characteristics appropriate for the different economic roles they were destined to play.

proposition concerning the necessary division of instrumental functions in the family.

DATA BASE

... Murdock has presented data on a wide variety of sociocultural traits for 862 societies, divided into six major culture regions: Africa, Circum-Mediterranean, East Eurasia, Insular Pacific, and North and South America. For the purposes of the present report, only a very small subset of this data matrix need be examined, for the present study focuses upon the specific question of the degree to which males and females contribute, differentially, to the subsistence economy of their particular society. Trait variables enabling an investigation of this issue are available in Murdock's Atlas, which contains information concerning (a) the degree to which each of the societies surveyed are dependent upon each of five subsistence activities (Gathering, Hunting, Fishing, Animal Husbandry, and Agriculture), and (b) the degree to which males and females are independently involved in these activities.

... The variables of present interest are rather easily translated to ordinal categories and, given the admission of certain assumptions concerning the distributions of the critical variables, ... it is possible to assume that the data approximate interval scale qualities. This procedure allows for the use of the more powerful parametric statistical techniques.

... The first set of variables to be considered was concerned with the degree to which a society was dependent upon each of the five major subsistence activities (Gathering, Hunting, Fishing, Animal Husbandry, and Agriculture) noted in the Ethnographic Atlas. ...

The second group of variables to be rescaled was concerned with sex role specialization in each of the five subsistence activities. Murdock (1967:162) divided each of these variables into nine nominal categories which referred to the proportional participation of males and females in the various subsistence tasks. ... The endpoints of this new classification are defined by Murdock's M and F categories, which describe activities in which males or females are involved, respectively, to the exclusion of the other sex. ...

This translation of Murdock's nominal classification system to scales of approximately equal-interval quality permits an investigation of the relationship between the degree to which a society is dependent upon a particular subsistence activity and the degree to which males (or females) are involved in this activity. If the degree of societal dependence upon each of the five major subsistence activities was multi-

plied by a factor indicating the extent to which males or females participate in that activity (see Table 1), and the contribution within each
activity summed across the different economic activities present in a
given society, then a reasonable estimate of the relative subsistence
contribution, by sex, would be obtained. . . .

TABLE 1. INTERVAL RESCALING OF MURDOCK'S CATEGORIZATION SYSTEM

Category Description	Murdock's Code	Estimated Participation by Sex	
		Male	Female
Total female participation	F	0%	100%
Predominantly female participation	G	25	75
Sex irrelevant, or equal participation	D, E, I	50	50
Predominantly male participation	N	75	25
Total male participation	M	100	0

. . . For purposes of . . . example, consider the relevant descriptive
data attributed to the Navaho of North America. In his classification of
the subsistence economy of this society, Murdock (1967:147) estimated
that Gathering of small plants accounted for 16–25 percent of the society's food, Hunting for 6–15 percent, Fishing for a negligible 0–5 percent, Animal Husbandry for 26–35 percent, and Agriculture for 36–45
percent. In terms of sex role specification of these subsistence tasks,
Murdock found females to account completely for the food obtained
through Gathering and Fishing, and males completely responsible for
Hunting. Further, females accounted for half the food obtained through
Animal Husbandry, and for one-fourth of the food from Agriculture.
Using the midrange value of each subsistence variable as the best estimate of societal dependence, and multiplying these values by the appropriate female-contribution proportion, revealed that women
accounted for 20.5 percent of the society's food by Gathering (that is,
$100\% \times 20.5\%$ dependence), for none of the food obtained through
Hunting ($0\% \times 10.5$), for 2.5 percent through Fishing ($100\% \times 2.5$),
for 15.25% through Animal Husbandry ($50\% \times 30.5$), and for 10.12
percent by Agriculture ($25\% \times 40.5$), resulting in a total female contribution of 48.37 percent of the Navaho's food.

RESULTS

These same procedures were employed in developing estimates of subsistence contributions by sex for all societies in Murdock's Atlas, within
each culture area. The results of these operations are presented in Table

2. Examination of the results of this table demonstrates that, contrary to the conclusions that may be drawn from Murdock's (1937) original data, women appear to contribute appreciably to the subsistence economy of their respective societies. The worldwide percentage of food contributed by women is 43.88, with a range over specific culture areas of 32.24 to 50.73. These results indicate that even in the culture region where women's contribution is the lowest (32.24 percent) the actual amount of food that they produce is substantial. In terms of production across the important subsistence tasks, these findings provide no support for the theoretical position of a universal principle of task segregation and sex role differentiation in the family. While these data do not bear on considerations of socioemotional specialization, they do demonstrate clearly that women play a most significant instrumental role in the family.

TABLE 2. MEAN PERCENTAGE OF FOOD ACCOUNTED FOR BY WOMEN, BY ACTIVITY, OVER ALL CULTURE REGIONS

Subsistence Activity	Africa	Circum-Med	East Eurasia	Insular Pacific	North America	South America	All Societies
Gathering	7.63	3.64	6.06	8.31	24.22	13.05	12.85
Hunting	0.09	0.47	0.51	0.75	0.24	0.00	0.30
Fishing	3.68	1.77	3.66	8.60	4.75	2.83	4.43
Animal Husbandry	4.68	10.78	7.60	6.24	2.35	3.36	5.11
Agriculture	33.80	15.58	20.28	26.83	7.65	19.56	21.19
Total	49.88	32.24	38.11	50.73	39.21	38.80	43.88

It should be stressed that the totals in Table 2 are not attributable to the presence of a few societies within each cultural region in which women contribute almost exclusively to the subsistence of their group. As demonstrated in Table 3, the variability of female subsistence contributions within each region is distributed about the mean regional value in a manner approximating normality. These data reinforce the validity of the findings of Table 2, and lend credence to the interpretation offered above. Such instrumental contributions on the part of the female are more variable than those of males, whose contributions rarely fall below 40 percent, but are, nonetheless, appreciable.

More important, the data presented in Table 3 allow for yet a more direct examination of the proposal that role differentiation and task specialization by sex are universal principles of family organization. If, in fact, males have assumed the role of instrumental specialist within the family, then women's contributions to the subsistence economy should be minimal. In inspecting this proposition in light of the present findings, "minimal" will be operationally defined as anything less than

Proportion of Society's Food Contributed by Women	Culture Region						Total World Sample
	Africa	Circum-Med.	East Eurasia	Insular Pacific	North America	South America	
0–10	.00	.19	.07	.01	.12	.08	.07
11–20	.04	.17	.07	.03	.09	.05	.07
21–30	.12	.25	.23	.14	.23	.19	.18
31–40	.24	.16	.27	.19	.24	.28	.23
41–50	.24	.16	.27	.27	.18	.26	.22
51–60	.24	.05	.10	.20	.10	.13	.15
61–70	.12	.01	.00	.12	.05	.01	.07
71–80	.01	.01	.00	.04	.01	.00	.01
81–90	.00	.00	.00	.00	.00	.00	.00
91–100	.00	.00	.00	.00	.00	.00	.00

a 41 percent overall economic contribution. Clearly this exceptionally high cutoff point operates in favor of the principle developed by such theorists as Parsons and Bales. Thus, if women characteristically contribute 41 percent or more to the larder of their respective subsistence economies (in terms of the five major economic variables noted by Murdock) over a significant proportion of the world's societies, then there would exist presumptive evidence calling for a rejection of the assumption of universal sex role differentiation and task specialization. The data of Table 3 indicate clearly that such a reassessment is in order, since in nearly 45 percent of all 862 societies surveyed, women's subsistence contributions surpassed the extremely conservative 40 percent cutoff point that was suggested above. . . . Irrespective of the hypothesized impact of biological differences upon levels of contribution to the subsistence economy, it is clear that women contribute a significant share to the total subsistence larder of their society—and this observation holds even though the present analysis does not include that share provided by mother's milk.

For the instrumental role, at least, the implication of these results overall is that the feature that characterizes the family is that of role sharing not segregation. Rather than discovering a universal feature of the family, there has emerged from this research the conclusion that participation in the instrumental role is distributed continuously, and not in a dichotomous fashion.

CONCLUSIONS

In summary, the results presented above provide no support to the theoretical analysis presented by Parsons and Bales. Considering direct subsistence activity as a whole, the principle of task specialization in the family, with women confined to the household arena by assumed biological factors, clearly seems to be incorrect. The second principle of role segregation, with males assuming the role of instrumental specialist in the family, seems equally incorrect, at least as extrapolated from the original findings of Murdock.

REFERENCES

Barry, H., III, M. K. Bacon, and I. L. Child.
1957 "A cross-cultural survey of some sex differences in socialization." Journal of Abnormal and Social Psychology 55(November):327–332.
Bell, N. W. and E. F. Vogel (eds.).
1968 A Modern Introduction to the Family. Glencoe, Ill.: Free Press.
Biddle, B. J., and E. J. Thomas (eds.).
1966 Role Theory: Concepts and Research. New York: Wiley.
Blood, R. O., Jr. and Wolfe, D. M.
1960 Husbands and Wives: The Dynamics of Married Living. Glencoe, Ill.: Free Press.
Crano, W. D. and M. B. Brewer.
1973 Principles of Research in Social Psychology. New York: McGraw-Hill.
Durkheim, Emile.
1947 Division of Labor. Glencoe, Ill.: Free Press.
Gibb, G. A.
1969 "Leadership." Pp. 205–82 in G. Lindzey and E. Aronson (eds.), The Handbook of Social Psychology, Vol. 4. Group Psychology and the Phenomena of Interaction. Reading, Mass.: Addison-Wesley.
Murdock, G. P.
1937 "Comparative data on division of labor by sex." Social Forces 15(May):551–3.
1949 Social Structure. New York: The Macmillan Company.
1967 "Ethnographic atlas: a summary." Ethnology 6(April):109–236.
Murdock, G. P., and C. Provost.
1973 "Measurement of cultural complexity." Ethnology 12(April):379–92.
Parsons, Talcott and Robert F. Bales.
1955 Family Socialization and Interaction Process. Glencoe, Ill.: Free Press.
Stephens, W. N.
1963 The Family in Cross-Cultural Perspective.
Zelditch, Morris, Jr.
1955 "Role differentiation in the nuclear family: a comparative study." in T. Parsons and R. Bales (eds.), Family Socialization and Interaction Process. Glencoe, Ill.: Free Press.

The Marriage
Relationship

Introduction   Nona Glazer

As the American family has gradually lost most of its traditional activities, social scientists have looked for new activities to explain why people persist in marrying and remarrying. In fact, in spite of a rising divorce rate, an increasing proportion of the population since 1900 has actually married. Supposedly, the family exists to provide a socially approved setting for the production of goods and services, sexual relations, reproduction, and the socialization of children. Now, however, production occurs away from the home in the marketplace; extramarital sexual partners as well as pre- and postmarital partners are more easily available; birth control techniques and the preference for small families have limited reproductive activities; even childbearing outside of marriage is increasingly tolerated. The socialization of young children remains one of the few activities still carried on mainly by the family. Aside from socialization, there is one new activity that social scientists consider critical in explaining the persistence of the family: providing emotional support for family members. While important for all members, emotional support is asserted to be the very basis of the husband-wife relationship, especially among middle-class professionals.[1]

While the conjugal family system is being given new importance by social scientists, it is currently being subjected by young people to the most severe criticism it has experienced since the Soviets temporarily abolished obligatory marriage in 1926. Many young people do not agree with social scientists that the family is a natural and inevitable system;

---

[1] Lillian B. Rubin, *Worlds of Pain* (New York: Basic Books, 1976). The persistence of working-class marriage may rest more on fulfillment of traditional gender roles than on a successful search for marital intimacy.

rather they see it as a historically developed system. In America and Europe, young women and men are trying a variety of living arrangements inside and outside of marriage. Heterosexual, homosexual, and bisexual relations; childbearing in and out of marriage; child care by men as well as women; communal living; group marriage; and quasi-extended families not based on kinship are among the alternatives being tried. Those who are experimenting consider it critical to replace the gender roles of the conjugal family system. They believe this may be possible by finding a socially acceptable alternative to the conjugal family itself.

The articles on marriage included in this section treat the husband-wife relationship from a variety of perspectives. What kind of family is seen as normal, what gender roles are seen as desirable has implications for both understanding changes in the family and for recommending family policy.[2] While a husband and wife and their offspring are usually considered "the family," recent changes in living arrangements have led to a rethinking of that concept. A more adequate definition than the traditional one is suggested by Donald Ball, who defines *family* as

> any cohabiting domestic relationship that is (or has been) sexually consequential, i.e., gratification for members or the production of offspring. These are the relationships most often associated with the emotions of love and the home, whether members are conventionally situated or otherwise.[3]

This definition of the family has several important features: (1) the sex of the relating individuals is ignored and, therefore, the division of labor by sex is not basic to the family; (2) permanency is not considered a prerequisite; (3) while domestic cooperation is assumed, economic cooperation is not; (4) the formalization or legal recognition of the relationship is not assumed; and (5) the complementarity of roles in the relationship is not required. Hence, what the "family" is or might be becomes considerably open to the judgment, imagination, and hopes of people.

In the first reading, Peter L. Berger and Hansfried Kellner present a social psychological analysis, in contrast to Parsons' structural one (included in the preceding section), that starts with the problem of *anomie* as posed by Emile Durkheim. They present a picture that fits Eli Zaretsky's analysis (in Part One) of the ideology of the privatized family. They see the middle-class urban family in the industrial West as the

[2]Nona Glazer-Malbin, "The Captive Couple: The Burden of Gender Roles in Marriage," in Don H. Zimmerman with D. Lawrence and Siu Zimmerman, *Understanding Social Problems* (New York: Praeger, 1976), pp. 264–268.

[3]Donald W. Ball, "The Family as a Sociological Problem: Conceptualization of the Taken-for-Granted as Prologue to Social Problems Analysis." *Social Problems* 19(1972):295–305.

place where family members can develop some sense of order and control that they do not experience in society. The husband and wife, they suggest, through sharing their experiences, thoughts, and interpretations, develop a miniature world of their own. They provide themselves with order, an order they come to believe exists outside themselves. Both are stabilized by the sense of who they are, and the couple finds solace in the haven of the domestically constructed social reality. The husband uses the marriage relationship in an additional way: his sense of powerlessness, derived from his everyday experiences in an unfulfilling job, and his cynical view of political action, is mitigated —according to Berger and Kellner—by the sense of control he may feel in the circle of the family, where he can play at being "master."

Several aspects of the Berger and Kellner analysis are especially pertinent to understanding women's roles in the family, as well as to understanding the treatment of women in sociological analysis itself. At first glance, it appears that Berger and Kellner loosen the marriage relationship somewhat from cultural prescriptions by considering it to be developed, through social interaction by the spouses. This is in contrast to Parsons. Parsons considers marriage, basically, a system shaped by explicit culture norms, while Berger and Kellner consider cultural norms to effect the marital relationship but not determine it to the same extent. The latter analysis might suggest that less-differentiated gender roles could be developed; the process of social interaction would be the the the means by which the possibly traumatic consequences of deviating from conventional gender-role prescriptions could be avoided. Marriage in the Berger and Kellner conception provides a setting wherein new ways of behaving could be developed and justified.

The second particularly pertinent aspect of their analysis is this: according to Berger and Kellner, marriage is the key relationship within which *men* can construct a social reality with which they can cope—in contrast to the job and politics—and in which they may have a feeling of being in control. Men return to the confines of most American homes, to wives and children over whom they may exert or feign control. Yet, this analysis ignores women, who appear to have no comparable context into which they can escape from their own everyday frustrations with politics, with repetitive household chores, with small and demanding children, and with the daily isolation in the home from easy contacts with adults. For the 44 percent of married women who work, a job may be an escape from the home, but on the job they experience the same problems as their husbands. Women may play "mistress" over small children, domestic helpers, and pets, but this is hardly different from men playing "master" over secretaries and file clerks, receptionists and telephone operators, cashiers and waitresses whom they encounter on the job and in other daily experiences outside the home. Homemaking and work on the job do not appear to provide the sexes with equivalent structures. The recent diminution in the importance of the "feminine mystique" and of the "work ethic" may be signs that women and men are both becoming aware of their oppression by these socially pre-scribed definitions of how they should relate to each other.

Moreover, it is in the Berger and Kellner analysis of the marriage as a haven for the man that the relation between *culture* as a determinant of social behavior and *social interaction* as a determinant of social real-ity become blurred. It is not the idiosyncratic development of social reality that gives the man the chance to bolster his sagging self-esteem and low morale. The cultural norms prescribe that women have more responsibility for their husband's morale than vice versa; that women have less responsibility for certain critical decisions, such as moving from one community to another, than their husbands; that women have more responsibility than their husbands in the management of the household. These prescriptions long antedate urban, industrial United States and appear to persist in spite of the middle-class ideology of husband-wife equality.

In the next selection, Roslyn Feldberg and Janet Kohen consider how the contemporary American family, rather than being insulated and isolated from the major societal institutions, lives in an "antifamily set-ting." Taking the enclave theory of the family to be *ideology*—not reality, as Berger and Kellner see it—Feldberg and Kohen discuss how the commitments that men are expected to have outside the family, and the division of labor between husband and wife, drive family members apart. Their point is particularly interesting since it directly contradicts the long-held notion that husbands and wives must have different, though complementary, roles in order to have a happy relationship. According to the theory, when both partners fill similar roles, rivalry, jealousy, and competition are created between the spouses. Feldberg and Kohen suggest, however, that the nature of the complementary roles that spouses are expected to play in American society propels women and men into contrasting behavior, which prevents their finding emotional statisfaction in the marital relationship. Each person pursues goals that are difficult to meet and they may be unintelligible to the other partner. Feldberg and Kohen's analyses make sense out of the cycle of marriage, divorce, and remarriage, and explain why personal counseling fails to solve marital problems. "Marriage problems" lie not —at least not *only*—in the inadequacy of the partners, which may respond to personal counseling, but in the incompatibility of the de-mands placed on marital partners by society and by their own personal needs for intimacy and emotional satisfaction.

The black lower-class family in the United States, the topic of the next selection by Kathryn Dietrich, should be particularly interesting to feminists. During the 1960s, the plight of black Americans appears to have been laid squarely in the lap of the black woman. Starting with the work of E. Franklin Frazier, many people came to believe that the black American family was typically matriarchal, that is, dominated by the wife rather than the husband. When it was not so dominated, it was, supposedly, characterized by a woman head of household. Actually, in 1971 a majority of all households (67 percent of all nonwhite families and 88 percent of all white families) were headed by both a husband and wife.[4]

The theory of black matriarchy became notorious following the publication in 1965 of Daniel P. Moynihan's report written to inform policymakers about the social conditions of black Americans. Moynihan concluded that the black family "is the fundamental source of the weakness of the Negro community," faulting the matriarchal structure of the family for failing to prepare black children (especially boys) for success in American society.[5] Hence, black *women* rather than the black experience of discrimination in jobs, education, housing, etc. bear the major responsibility for the plight of blacks. This individualistic approach was actually accepted to the extent that some black groups such as the Black Panthers urged women to be supportive of men by adopting the "subordinate" feminine role. The ideology of male dominance is also a prominent feature of Black Muslim beliefs. What is interesting to feminists is that social scientists, instead of seeing the alleged power of black women in the husband-wife relationship as compatible with the American ideology of egalitarian relationships, exhorted the black family to become more "normal," that is, less egalitarian and more sexist.

Dietrich's study is pertinent in the context of the castigation of black women. Her data on lower-class black families (in a wide variety of American cities) does not support the theory that the black family is, normatively, committed to domination by women. As Dietrich notes, her study focuses on the ideology of black spouses rather than their actual behavior. (Data on actual behavior is difficult to gather, so most studies of the American family involve preferred and/or reported behaviors rather than actual observations of behavior.) Dietrich's study —while hardly conclusive—makes the allegations that black women are responsible for the problems of black Americans suspect since the com-

---

[4]U.S. Bureau of the Census, *Statistical Abstract of the United States: 1972*, 93rd ed. (Washington, D.C.: U.S. Government Printing Office, 1972), p. 38, Table 49.

[5]Daniel P. Moynihan, *The Negro Family: The Case for National Action* (Washington, D.C.: U.S. Government Printing Office, 1965), p. 4.

mitment of lower-class blacks is to the norm of egalitarianism. Is this a lesson in the sexism of social scientists? Perhaps so. It means we ought to view with skepticism notions that the victims—women, blacks, or the poor—are responsible through false values for their fate.

The final selection on contemporary marriage by Lenore J. Weitzman is a summary of the legal meaning of the institution for each sex. The marriage contract is perplexing because of its invisibility: women and men about to marry rarely investigate the laws of their respective jurisdiction about the effect matrimony will have on their names, legal residence, property rights, credit standing, the right to establish a domicile separate from their spouse, and myriad other ordinary features of living. Yet, the marriage laws bind a woman and a man into a contract exactly as if each had signed a mortgage or a contract to purchase an automobile. Equally important, women and men have no idea that contracts abrogating common law about marriage partnerships can be made only with great difficulty and are rarely acceptable to the courts. The "personal choice" ideology in which Americans are such strong believers, thus, is faced with another contradiction in the legal system: marriage is as the law decides, not as Mary and John would have it.

Marriage and the Construction of Reality

Peter Berger

Hansfried Kellner

Ever since Durkheim it has been a commonplace of family sociology that marriage serves as a protection against anomie for the individual. Interesting and pragmatically useful though this insight is, it is but the negative side of a phenomenon of much broader significance. If one speaks of *anomic* states, then one ought properly to investigate also the *nomic* processes that, by their absence, lead to the aforementioned states. If, consequently, one finds a negative correlation between marriage and anomie, then one should be led to inquire into the character of marriage as a *nomos*-building instrumentality; that is, of marriage as a social arrangement that creates for the individual the sort of order in which he can experience his life as making sense.

The process that interests us here is one that constructs, maintains, and modifies a consistent reality that can be meaningfully experienced by individuals. In its essential forms this process is determined by the society in which it occurs. Every society has its specific way of defining and perceiving reality—its world, its universe, its overarching organization of symbols. This is already given in the language that forms the symbolic base of the society. Erected over this base, and by means of it, is a system of ready-made typifications, through which the innumerable experiences of reality come to be ordered. These typifications and their order are held in common by the members of society, thus acquiring not only the character of objectivity, but being taken for granted as *the* world *tout court,* the only world that normal men can conceive of.

Excerpted from Peter L. Berger and Hansfried Kellner, "Marriage and the Construction of Social Reality," *Diogenes,* 46. Copyright 1964 by Diogenes.

The seemingly objective and taken-for-granted character of the social definitions of reality can be seen most clearly in the case of language itself, but it is important to keep in mind that the latter forms the base and instrumentality of a much larger world-erecting process.

The socially constructed world must be continually mediated to and actualized by the individual, so that it can become and remain indeed *his* world as well. The individual is given by his society certain decisive cornerstones for his everyday experience and conduct. Most importantly, the individual is supplied with specific sets of typifications and criteria of relevance, predefined for him by the society and made available to him for the ordering of his everyday life. This ordering or (in line with our opening considerations) nomic apparatus is biographically cumulative. It begins to be formed in the individual from the earliest stages of socialization on, then keeps on being enlarged and modified by himself throughout his biography.

This order, by which the individual comes to perceive and define his world is discovered by him as an external datum, a ready-made world that simply is *there* for him to go ahead and live in, though he modifies it continually in the process of living in it. Nevertheless, this world is in need of validation, perhaps precisely because of an ever-present glimmer of suspicion as to its social manufacture and relativity. This validation, while it must be undertaken by the individual himself, requires ongoing interaction with others who coinhabit this same socially constructed world. In a broad sense, *all* the other coinhabitants of this world serve a validating function. Every individual requires the ongoing validation of his world, including crucially the validation of his identity and place in this world, by those few who are his truly significant others. Just as the individual's deprivation of relationship with his significant others will plunge him into anomie, so their continued presence will sustain for him that *nomos* by which he can feel at home in the world at least most of the time. In everyday life, however, the principal method employed is speech. In this sense, it is proper to view the individual's relationship with his significant others as an ongoing conversation. As the latter occurs, it validates over and over again the fundamental definitions of reality once entered into, not, of course, so much by explicit articulation, but precisely by taking the definitions silently for granted and conversing about all conceivable matters on this taken-for-granted basis. Through the same conversation the individual is also made capable of adjusting to changing and new social contexts in his biography. In a very fundamental sense it can be said that one converses one's way through life.

If one concedes these points, one can [then] state a general sociological proposition: The plausibility and stability of the world, as socially defined, is dependent upon the strength and continuity of significant relationships in which conversation about this world can be continually carried on. Or, to put it a little differently: The reality of the world is sustained through conversation with significant others. This reality, of course, includes not only the imagery by which fellow men are viewed, but also includes the way in which one views oneself. The reality-bestowing force of social relationships depends on the degree of their nearness; that is, on the degree to which social relationships occur in face-to-face situations and to which they are credited with primary significance by the individual.

With these preliminary assumptions stated we can now arrive at our main thesis here. Namely, we would contend that marriage occupies a privileged status among the significant validating relationships for adults in our society. Put slightly differently: Marriage is a crucial nomic instrumentality in our society. We would further argue that the essential social functionality of this institution cannot be fully understood if this fact is not perceived.

We can now proceed with an ideal-typical analysis of marriage; that is, seek to abstract the essential features involved. Marriage in our society is a *dramatic* act in which two strangers come together and redefine themselves. The drama of the act is internally anticipated and socially legitimated long before it takes place in the individual's biography, and amplified by means of a pervasive ideology, the dominant themes of which (romantic love, sexual fulfillment, self-discovery, and self-realization through love and sexuality, the nuclear family as the social site for these processes) can be found distributed through all strata of the society. The actualization of these ideologically predefined expectations in the life of the individual occurs to the accompaniment of one of the few traditional rites of passage that are still meaningful to almost all members of the society. It should be added that, in using the term *strangers*, we do not mean, of course, that the candidates for the marriage come from widely discrepant social backgrounds—indeed, the data indicate that the contrary is the case. The strangeness rather lies in the fact that, unlike marriage candidates in many previous societies, those in ours typically come from different face-to-face contexts—in the terms used above, they come from different areas of conversation. They do not have a shared past, although their pasts have a similar structure. With the dramatic redefinition of the situation brought about by the marriage, however, all significant conversation for the two new partners is now centered in their relationship with each other—and, in fact, it was precisely with this intention that they entered upon their relationship.

It goes without saying that this character of marriage has its root in much broader structural configurations of our society. The most important of these, for our purposes, is the crystallization of a so-called private sphere of existence more and more segregated from the immediate controls of the public institutions (especially the economic and political ones), and yet defined and utilized as the main social area for the individual's self-realization. It cannot be our purpose here to inquire into the historical forces that brought forth these phenomena, beyond making the observation that these are closely connected with the industrial revolution and its institutional consequences. The public institutions now confront the individual as an immensely powerful and alien world, incomprehensible in its inner workings, anonymous in its human character. If only through his work in some nook of the economic machinery, the individual must find a way of living in this alien world, come to terms with its power over him, be satisfied with a few conceptual rules of thumb to guide him through a vast reality that otherwise remains opaque to his understanding, and modify its anonymity by whatever *"human relations"* he can work out in his involvement with it. It ought to be emphasized, against some critics of "mass society," that this does not inevitably leave the individual with a sense of profound unhappiness and lostness. It would rather seem that large numbers of people in our society are quite content with a situation in which their public involvements have little subjective importance, regarding work as a not too bad necessity and politics as at best a spectator sport. It is usually only intellectuals with ethical and political commitments who assume that such people must be terribly desperate. The point, however, is that the individual in this situation, no matter whether he is happy or not, will turn elsewhere for the experiences of self-realization that do have importance for him. The private sphere, this interstitial area created (we would think) more or less haphazardly as a by-product of the social metamorphosis of industrialism, is mainly where he will turn. It is here that the individual will seek power, intelligibility and, quite literally, a name—the apparent power to fashion a world, however Lilliputian, that will reflect his own being: A world that, seemingly having been shaped by himself and thus unlike those other worlds that insist on shaping him, is translucently intelligible to him (or so he thinks); a world in which, consequently, he is *somebody*—perhaps even, within its charmed circle, a lord and master. What is more, to a considerable extent these expectations are not unrealistic. The public institutions have no need to control the individual's adventures in the private sphere, as long as they really stay within the latter's circumscribed limits. The private sphere is perceived, not without justification, as an area of individual choice and even autonomy. This fact has important consequences for the shaping of identity in modern society that cannot be pursued here. All that ought to be clear here is the peculiar location of the private sphere within and between the other social structures. In sum, it is above all and, as a rule, only in the private sphere that the individual can take a slice of reality and fashion it into his world. If one is aware of the decisive significance of this capacity and even necessity of men to externalize themselves in reality and to produce for themselves a world in which they can feel at home, then one will hardly be surprised at the great importance which the private sphere has come to have in modern society.

It is on the basis of marriage that, for most adults in our society, existence in the private sphere is built up. It will be clear that this is not at all a universal or even cross-culturally wide function of marriage. Rather has marriage in our society taken on a very peculiar character and functionality. It has been pointed out that marriage in contemporary society has lost some of its older functions and taken on new ones instead. This is certainly correct, but we would prefer to state the matter a little differently. Marriage and the family used to be firmly embedded in a matrix of wider community relationships, serving as extensions and particularizations of the latter's social controls. There were few separating barriers between the world of the individual family and the wider community, a fact even to be seen in the physical conditions under which the family lived before the industrial revolution. The same social life pulsated through the house, the street, and the community. In our terms, the family and within it the marital relationship were part and parcel of a considerably larger area of conversion. In our contemporary society, by contrast, each family constitutes its own segregated subworld, with its own controls and closed conversation.

Unlike an earlier situation in which the establishment of the new marriage simply added to the differentiation and complexity of an already existing social world, the marriage partners are now embarked on the often difficult task of constructing for themselves the little world in which they will live. To be sure, the larger society provides them with certain standard instructions as to how they should go about this task, but this does not change the fact that considerable effort of their own is required for its realization. The monogamous character of marriage enforces both the dramatic and the precarious nature of this undertaking. Success or failure hinges on the present idiosyncrasies and the fairly unpredictable future development of those idiosyncrasies of only two individuals (who, moreover, do not have a shared past)—as Simmel has shown, the most unstable of all possible relationships.

Every social relationship requires objectivation; that is, requires a process by which subjectively experienced meanings become objective to the individual and in interaction with others become common property and thereby massively objective. The degree of objectivation will depend on the number and the intensity of the social relationships that are its carriers. A relationship that consists of only two individuals called upon to sustain by their own efforts an on-going social world will have to make up in intensity for the numerical poverty of the arrangement. This, in turn, accentuates the drama and the precariousness. The later addition of children will add to the, as it were, density of objectivation taking place within the nuclear family, thus rendering the latter a good deal less precarious. It remains true that the establishment and maintenance of such a social world makes extremely high demands on the principal participants.

The attempt can now be made to outline the ideal-typical process that takes place as marriage functions as an instrumentality for the social construction of reality. The chief protagonists of the drama are two individuals, each with a biographically accumulated and available stock of experience. As members of a highly mobile society, these individuals have already internalized a degree of readiness to redefine themselves and to modify their stock of experience, thus bringing with them considerable psychological capacity for entering new relationships with others. Also, coming from broadly similar sectors of the larger society (in terms of region, class, ethnic and religious affiliations), the two individuals will have organized their stock of experience in similar fashion. In other words, the two individuals have internalized the same overall world, including the general definitions and expectations of the marriage relationship itself. Their society has provided them with a taken-for-granted image of marriage and has socialized them into an anticipation of stepping into the taken-for-granted roles of marriage. All the same, these relatively empty projections now have to be actualized, lived through, and filled with experiential content by the protagonists. This will require a dramatic change in their definitions of reality and of themselves.

In other words, from the beginning of the marriage each partner has new modes in his meaningful experience of the world in general, of other people and of himself. By definition, then, marriage constitutes a nomic rupture. In terms of each partner's biography, the event of marriage initiates a new nomic process. Now, the full implications of this fact are rarely apprehended by the protagonists with any degree of clarity. There rather is to be found the notion that one's world, one's other-relationships and, above all, oneself have remained what they were before—only, of course, that world, others, and self will now be shared with the marriage partner. It should be clear by now that this notion is a grave misapprehension. Just because of this fact, marriage now propels the individual into an unintended and unarticulated development, in the course of which the nomic transformation takes place.

What typically *is* apprehended are certain objective and concrete problems arising out of the marriage—such as tensions with in-laws, or with former friends, or religious differences between the partners, as well as immediate tensions between them. These are apprehended as external, situational, and practical difficulties. What is *not* apprehended is the subjective side of these difficulties, namely, the transformation of *nomos* and identity that has occurred and that continues to go on, so that all problems and relationships are experienced in a quite new way, that is, experienced within a new and ever-changing reality.

Take a simple and frequent illustration—the male partner's relationships with male friends before and after the marriage. It is a common observation that such relationships, especially if the extramarital partners are single, rarely survive the marriage, or, if they do, are drastically redefined after it. This is typically the result of neither a deliberate decision by the husband nor deliberate sabotage by the wife. What rather happens, very simply, is a slow process in which the husband's image of his friend is transformed as he keeps talking about this friend with his wife. The process, if commented upon at all within the marital conversation, can always be explained by socially available formulas about "people changing," "friends disappearing," or oneself "having become more mature." This process of conversational liquidation is especially powerful because it is one-sided—the husband typically talks with his wife about his friend, but *not* with his friend about his wife. Thus the friend is deprived of the defense of, as it were, counter-defining the relationship.

Marriage thus posits a new reality. The individual's relationship with this new reality, however, is a dialectic one—he acts upon it, in collusion with the marriage partner, and it acts back upon both him and the partner, welding together their reality.

The reconstruction of the world in marriage occurs principally in the course of conversation, as we have suggested. The implicit problem of this conversation is how to match two individual definitions of reality. By the very logic of the relationship, a common overall definition must be arrived at—otherwise the conversation will become impossible and, *ipso facto*, the relationship will be endangered. Now, this conversation may be understood as the working away of an ordering and typifying apparatus—if one prefers, an objectivating apparatus. Each partner ongoingly contributes his conceptions of reality, which are then *"talked through,"* usually not once but many times, and in the process become objectivated by the conversational apparatus. The nomic instrumentality of marriage is concretized over and over again, from bed to breakfast table, as the partners carry on the endless conversation that feeds on nearly all they individually or jointly experience.

This process has a very important result—namely, a hardening or stabilization of the common objectivated reality. It should be easy to see now how this comes about. The objectivations ongoingly performed and internalized by the marriage partners become ever more massively real, as they are confirmed and reconfirmed in the marital conversation. The world that is made up of these objectivations at the same time gains in stability.

Futhermore, it is not only the ongoing experience of the two partners that is constantly shared and passed through the conversational apparatus. The same sharing extends into the past. The two distinct biographies, as subjectively apprehended by the two individuals who have lived through them, are overruled and reinterpreted in the course of their conversation. Sooner or later, they will "tell all"—or, more correctly, they will tell it in such a way that it fits into the self-definitions objectivated in the marital relationship. The couple thus constructs not only present reality but reconstructs past reality as well, fabricating a common memory that integrates the recollections of the two individual pasts. Similarly, there occurs a sharing of future horizons, which leads not only to stabilization, but inevitably to a narrowing of the future projections of each partner. Before marriage the individual typically plays with quite discrepant day-dreams in which his future self is projected. Having now considerably stabilized his self-image, the married individual will have to project the future in accordance with this maritally defined identity. The wife, having "found herself" as a liberal, an agnostic and a "sexually healthy" person, *ipso facto* liquidates the possibilities of becoming an anarchist, a Catholic, or a lesbian. At least until further notice she has decided upon who she is—and, by the same token, on who she will be. The stabilization brought about by marriage thus affects the total reality in which the partners exist.

It cannot be sufficiently strongly emphasized that this process is typically unapprehended, almost automatic in character. The protagonists of the marriage drama do *not* set out deliberately to recreate their world. Each continues to live in a world that is taken for granted—and keeps its taken-for-granted character even as it is metamorphosed. The new world that the married partners, Prometheuslike, have called into being is perceived by them as the normal world in which they have lived before. Reconstructed present and reinterpreted past are perceived as a continuum, extending forwards into a commonly projected future.

We have analyzed in some detail the process that, we contend, entitles us to describe marriage as a nomic instrumentality. It may now be well to turn back once more to the macrosocial context in which this process takes place—a process that, to repeat, is peculiar to our society as far as the institution of marriage is concerned, although it obviously expresses much more general human facts. The narrowing and stabilization of identity is functional in a society that, in its major public institutions, must insist on rigid controls over the individual's conduct. At the same time, the narrow enclave of the nuclear family serves as a macrosocially innocuous "play area," in which the individual can safely exercise his world-building proclivities without upsetting any of the important social, economic, and political apple carts. Barred from expanding himself into the area occupied by those major institutions, he is given plenty of leeway to "discover himself" in his marriage and his family, and, in view of the difficulty of this undertaking, is provided with a number of auxiliary agencies that stand ready to assist him (such as counseling, psychotherapeutic, and religious agencies). The marital adventure can be relied upon to absorb a large amount of energy that might otherwise be expended more dangerously. The ideological themes of familism, romantic love, sexual expression, maturity, and social adjustment, with the pervasive psychologistic anthropology that underlies them all, function to legitimate this enterprise. Also the narrowing and stabilization of the individual's principal area of conversation within the nuclear family is functional in a society that requires high degrees of both geographical and social mobility. The segregated little world of the family can be easily detached from one milieu and transposed into another without appreciably interfering with the central processes going on in it. Needless to say, we are not suggesting that these functions are deliberately planned or even apprehended by some mythical ruling directorate of the society. Like most social phenomena, whether they be macro or microscopic, these functions are typically unintended and unarticulated. What is more, the functionality would be impaired if it were too widely apprehended.

There now exists a considerable body of data on the adoption and mutual adjustment of marital roles. Nothing in our considerations detracts from the analyses made of these data by sociologists interested primarily in the processes of group interaction. We would only argue that something more fundamental is involved in this role-taking—namely, the individual's relationship to reality as such. Each role in the marital situation carries with it a universe of discourse, broadly given by cultural definition, but continually reactualized in the ongoing conversation between the marriage partners. Put simply: Marriage involves not only stepping into new roles, but, beyond this, stepping into a new world. The *mutuality* of adjustment may again be related to the rise of marital equalitarianism, in which comparable effort is demanded of both partners.

The purpose of this article is not polemic, nor do we wish to advocate any particular values concerning marriage. We have sought to debunk the familistic ideology only insofar as it serves to obfuscate a sociological understanding of the phenomenon. We wanted to show that it is possible to develop a sociological theory of marriage that is based on clearly sociological presuppositions, without operating with psychological or psychiatric categories that have dubious value within a sociological frame of reference. We believe that such a sociological theory of marriage is generally useful for a fully conscious awareness of existence in contemporary society and not only for the sociologist.

BIBLIOGRAPHY

Philippe Aries, *Centuries of Childhood.* New York: Knopf, 1962.
Peter Berger, *Invitation to Sociology: A Humanistic Perspective.* Garden City, N.Y.: Doubleday, 1963.
Peter Berger and Thomas Luckmann, *The Social Construction of Reality.* Garden City, N.Y.: Doubleday, 1966.
George H. Mead, *Mind, Self and Society.* Chicago: University of Chicago Press, 1934.
David Riesman, *The Lonely Crowd.* New Haven: Yale University Press, 1953.
Alfred Schutz, *Collected Papers, I.* The Hague: Nijhoff, 1962.

Family Life in an Antifamily Setting

Roslyn Feldberg
Janet Kohen

The American ideology of the family emphasizes personal fulfillment as the reason for maintaining family relationships and love as the basis for marriage ... (Theodorson, 1965). Most people in our society do marry, probably expecting what that ideology promises, but they find themselves pressured into organizing their family life along other dimensions. Internal family responsibilities, demands of formal organizations, sex-role stereotypes, and sex discrimination limit couples' choices in the way they organize their family life. The resulting family structure may complicate, if not preclude, finding personal satisfaction within the family....

Divorce is often the consequence, but people do not view their divorces in these terms. Structural problems are largely invisible to people who must cope with the personal consequences of these problems on a daily basis: the spouse who is always tired, always irritable, or always away from the family. Having learned that marriage results from being in love with the right person, they feel that they or their partners are responsible for their disappointments. Divorce comes to be viewed as a matter of mistaken choice, as a personal, not an organizational, failure. The community views divorce similarly and encourages divorced persons to embark on a search for new, more compatible partners. The cycle continues.

This cycle embodies the contradictory relationship between the family and the corporate, capitalist order (Smith, 1973; Vogel, 1973)....

The family is supposed to support the corporate order by socializing children to be workers in that order and by renewing adult workers so that they can return to their jobs and work hard at them. In the family haven, workers are expected to rest, find emotional fulfillment, and renew their commitments to unemployed family members so that they can withstand the strains of their jobs and are motivated to do so. The contradictions are twofold. First, as an institution which reinforces the standards of the corporate order, the family is involved in creating the frustrations and problems that it is later expected to solve or, at least, contain. Second, the family unit's dependence on the corporate order for daily necessities forces family members to organize their relationships around the demands of that order so that the family cannot respond to their individual needs. The family becomes the haven-that-isn't. And the woman, as the overseer of family emotional life, becomes responsible for the consequences of this contradiction. Our analysis centers on the second contradiction. . . .

IDEOLOGY OF THE FAMILY

As societies industrialized, many of the traditional family functions were transformed to external organizations.[1] Although the contemporary family still shares responsibility for these functions, it alone is assigned responsibility for the emotional-nurturant needs. Most people view the family primarily as an emotional unit, oriented to individual well-being, and expect it to be the one group in which they will find stable interpersonal relationships that offer support, sharing and intimate communication. . . . Love has become the most important basis for marriage and public control over the choice of marriage partners has been minimized.

The allocation of responsibilities in the family reflects societal beliefs about the innate, complementary attributes assumed to define the sexes. This division of labor prescribes a role for males that makes them marginal to the central function of the family, the emotional-nurturant one. Men are believed to be best at instrumental tasks and consequently have major responsibility for the family's relationship to external organizations. In contrast, females are believed to be innately capable of understanding and ministering to emotional needs. They are thought to achieve their fulfillment through bearing and caring for children and

---

[1]Unless specified otherwise, the term *family* will be used interchangeably with *married couples*. While the ideology and structure of the family have important implications for children, the arguments raised here deal with the effects of this contradiction on adult choices to enter, maintain, or leave a marital relationship.

nurturing others.... The female's presumed superiority is translated into responsibility.

Assumptions about the family are integral to the cultural ideology that affects all organizations in the society. The ramifications of this relationship appear in many areas. As long as the family alone is believed to care for and promote people's well-being, formal organizations can be based on principles that ignore or conflict with that well-being.... Men are expected to be deeply involved in formal organizations because of their economic and political responsibility for their families. Emotional or nurturant interests in their families are considered voluntary, personal responses. Women who participate in extra-familial organizations are assumed to be engaged in activities of secondary importance to their family role (Siegal & Haas, 1963; Bart, 1972)....

FAMILY STRUCTURE

Although people's beliefs affect the way they organize their activities, family structure is not a summary of personal choices. The extent to which family life can represent personal interests depends on the control family members can maintain over their responses to each other. The limits of this control are inescapable because family activities can't be performed without resources obtained from external organizations. These resources are available according to the hiring practices, business hours, and other demands of these organizations, not according to family members' choices of what would be best for them. The consequences of this dependence are far-reaching, affecting even tasks such as child rearing, which appear to be purely internal family matters....

Family life is based on paid work that is done outside the family, generally by the husband/father. The paycheck is a double link. It connects the family to external organizations and the man to the family. Through the paycheck the goods and services of other units are purchased. By providing the financial basis for these purchases, the man contributes to the family and secures his place in it.... The organizations that control the paycheck determine who will work, at what hours and for what pay—indirectly they control the basic arrangements of family life and the standard at which the family lives....

Partly because it is performed outside the family and partly because it is paid, outside "work" is highly valued and visible. The home-centered work of the family is much less visible, hidden by walls and by absence of pay.[2] ...

---

[2]Feldberg and Kohen's lengthy discussion of housework has been abbreviated. The reader is referred to "Housework" in Part Four.—THE EDITORS

While housework is often underplayed and trivialized, child care is dramatized as the essence of the family and particularly as the most meaningful activity of the woman. . . . Both the women and the community often view shared child care as a failure of the woman to meet her responsibility and as detrimental to the child. . . . Both [housework and child care] are assigned to the woman because of her supposed superiority in emotional and nurturant skills and her "internal," domestic orientation; but success in either depends on her ability to deal with "external" organizations and her cognitive, physical, and organizational skills. . . .

Families must also respond to the social and legal agencies on behalf of their members. The family must deal with police or courts, mental and medical hospitals, social treatment agencies and educational institutions. In addition, family members are expected to participate in and support religious institutions, to be apprised of and engage in local and national politics, and to update their work skills. . . .

While family activities are often shaped by demands which conflict with family ideology, the division of labor obscures the conflict. The sexual division of labor gives substance to the internal/external dichotomy, masking the way that household patterns are shaped by "external" pressures and the fact that the energies of family members are devoted largely to organizational, not family, tasks. . . .

THE FAMILY AS AN EMOTIONAL UNIT

If people believe that the family is an expression of personal choices, then it is reasonable for them to seek personal fulfillment in the family. Doing so highlights the conflict between what is satisfying for each spouse and what is required for family maintenance. Work which provides routine necessities takes priority; emotional well-being must be continually compromised. . . .

Most couples expect to spend some time together. . . . The sex-based division of labor can foster conflict rather than harmony even in activities meant to be relaxing. What creates leisure often creates housework. Wives are usually expected to plan, prepare, serve and clean up whether it's dinner, a party or just beer and popcorn in front of the TV. A night out must be preceded by arrangements for the children, their meal, their bath, their babysitter. . . .

The conventional division of labor creates other problems too. Responsibility for resolving tension and creating emotional harmony is assigned to women on the basis of sex role stereotypes. Since men must adapt to external organizations which generally ignore emotional needs, they often have relatively little experience, skill or commitment in providing psychological support. . . .

The husband's one-sided contribution not only results in direct clashes, but also reinforces the traditional role allocation, leaving the woman with almost total responsibility for the stability of the family and the emotional well-being of its members. . . .

The allocation of emotional work to the woman has implications for her self concept. Since family structure is not conducive to meeting emotional demands as they arise, the woman is structurally positioned to fail. When emotional needs and crises go unresolved in the home, the woman, as the adult primarily responsible for this area of family life, may question her self worth. At the very least, she is unlikely to find the fulfillment she sought in family life. . . .

The difficulties family members face in trying to be an emotional unit manifest the contradiction between the external order and family life.

THE MOVE TO DIVORCE

For many people, this contradiction results in divorce. The pattern of their marital breakups is determined by the structure of relationships within the family. For men, the major gain from the family is an emotional one. He contributes the money essential for the family survival and expects services and emotional gratification in return. When he is unsatisfied with the exchange, he can either seek a divorce or begin to develop alternative relationships. For the woman the emotional tie is strengthened by the economic security she obtains for herself and her children through marriage. The breakup of the marriage means the loss of both. . . . When the major bond between spouses is an emotional one, the continuity of the marriage depends on the very satisfactions that are most readily jeopardized by the external order's demands on family life.

The societal response to divorce remains consistent with the ideology of the family. It explains divorce as a consequence of personal failure, ignoring the realities of family life. . . . (Marsden, 1969)

The services available to troubled spouses also reflect this perspective. Several varieties of personal and family counseling are offered but little recognition is given to the structural impediments of family life such as disruptive work hours, the eventlessness of house-wifery, too little money, or a location which creates continual scheduling difficulties. . . .

If structural problems are so important, why do they remain obscure? Why do couples view their own divorces as a result of personal failure? The reasons are found in the screen which the ideology of family fosters for the marital couple. They expect their family relationships to provide for their personal interests and private lives. The inevitable conflicts which derive from responding to the imperatives of external organizations occur within the private territory of the family and become visible as personal conflicts of husband and wife. They are further obscured by the sex-based division of labor in the family. The man is insulated from the internal work of the family by the wife/mother who arranges family activities around the demands of his schedule, particularly his employment, and creates the illusion that his activities dovetail with her own and those of the children. . . .

For the woman the relationship between structural problems and personal ones is even more complex because love mystifies her work. . . . [Her job] is an expression of her love for her husband and children. The better she manages, the less visible her work is and the more loving she is thought to be. . . .

For both spouses, marital and individual problems are easily identified, particularly when expressed in anger, drinking, physical abuse, or mental illness, and they become the focus of attention. While the family deals with its immediate situation, the problems remain personal and their social bases are not explored. . . . The high rates of marriage and remarriage indicate not the success of the family, but the strength of the ideology and of the desire to get what that ideology promises. . . .

CONCLUSIONS

Two types of change are needed. First, the ideologies of the family must be changed so that people are free to develop alternatives as they come to assess the family's potential and limitations as an emotional resource. This is a complex change involving related beliefs surrounding sex roles, motherhood, and the privacy of the family. Second, the corporate order must be changed. Since the structure of family life and of other organizations is an outgrowth of the same industrial development, the problems of family structure cannot be approached in isolation. Only when all organizations of the social order are made to respond to the various needs of those who staff and use them, will it be possible to create new family structures. . . .

REFERENCES

Bart, Pauline.
1972 "Are you a housewife or do you work? Women in traditional roles," in Women: Resources for a Changing World. Cambridge, Mass.: Radcliffe Institute, Radcliffe College.
Siegal, A. E., and M. B. Haas.
1963 "The working mother: A review of the research." Child Development 34:513–542.
Smith, Dorothy E.
1973 "Women, the family and corporate capitalism." Pp. 2–35 in M. L. Stevenson (ed.), Women in Canada. Toronto: New Press.
Theodorson, G. A.
1965 "Romanticism and motivation to marry in the United States, Singapore, Burma and India." Social Forces 44(September):17–27.
Vogel, L.
1973 "The earthly family." Radical America 7:9–50.

ADDITIONAL READINGS

Gintis, Herbert.
1972 "Alienation in capitalist society." Pp. 274–284 in R. C. Edwards, Michael Reich, and T. E. Weisskopf (eds.), The Capitalist System. Englewood Cliffs, N.J.: Prentice-Hall.
Holmstrom, Lynda L.
1972 The Two Career Family. Cambridge, Mass.: Schenkman.
Marsden, Dennis.
1969 Mothers Alone: Poverty and the Fatherless Family. London: Allen Lane, Penguin Press.

The Myth
of Black
Matriarchy
Katheryn Thomas Dietrich

A review of the recent profusion of literature about family power yields relatively little empirical research that had dealt specifically with the lower-class black family. . . .

While the black matriarchy has been exposed as a myth in the black middle classes (Scanzoni, 1971), Robert Staples (1971) is one of the few sociologists to denounce assumptions of matriarchy as mythical in the black lower classes as well. . . . The following sociological problems in reference to the decision-making dimension of conjugal power are still viable: How pervasive is female dominance of conjugal decision-making in lower-class black families and is it normative?

. . . Evidence suggesting that lower-class black families are more likely to be female-dominated than white middle-class families does not indicate that female-dominance pervades most lower-class black families. . . . Whereas the black male is predicted to have weak conjugal power because of his inability to adequately perform the provider role for the family, the bargaining advantage that the black male may enjoy in the marital situation because of his scarcity in the black population may well offset his bargaining disadvantage as an inadequate provider.

. . . This article reports research on aspects of conjugal decision-making and decision-implementation in seven black, predominantly lower-class populations. These populations are of varying population densities and from three different regions of the U.S. . . .

Excerpts reprinted from Katheryn Thomas Dietrich, "A Re-examination of the Myth of Black Matriarchy." *Journal of Marriage and the Family* 37(May 1975):367–374. Copyright 1975 by the National Council on Family Relations. Reprinted by permission.

An additional purpose of this study is to compare the perceived allocation of conjugal power by area of decision and between decision-making and decision-implementation. . . .

METHODS

Data Collection. Identical measurement procedures were used in collecting data [in 1970 and 1971] about black families in five metropolitan areas (Houston, Texas; East Chicago, Indiana; Toledo, Ohio; Champaign-Urbana, Illinois; Las Vegas, Nevada), one nonmetropolitan urban area (Center, a town of 5,000 population in East Texas), and two rural villages (less than 1,000 population in East Texas). The families studied were restricted to those in which a child under eighteen years of age resided in the home. An additional requirement was that the families contain a female homemaker who was under sixty-five and, unless she was the mother of one or more of the children living in the home, over eighteen. All households or randomly selected households in selected low-income census tracts of the communities were screened to determine if they met the above criteria. The female homemakers in the eligible families served as the sources of information about the families. . . . This analysis is restricted to those families in which husbands resided in the households at the time of the interviews.

The main breadwinners in the large majority of the families were employed as unskilled or semiskilled laborers or were unemployed. Most of the husbands and wives had not graduated from high school. About half of the families were in or near poverty, according to a poverty index by which income was evaluated in relation to family size, age of family members, and consumer price indices for the study areas.

Operationalization of Power in Decision-Making and Decision-Implementation. Power in decision-making was operationalized as the wife's perception of the mate (husband, wife, or both together) who "mainly decides": (1) Which friends you see the most? (2) The best place for the family to live? (3) About the wife working outside the home? (4) How to handle the children? (5) How the money is used? Decision implementation in two corresponding decision-areas was operationalized by the wife's perception of who (husband, wife, or both together) "mainly": (1) Handles the children when both parents are at home? (2) Handles money matters (pays bills, spends for what the family needs, etc.)?

These measures of decision-making and decision-implementation . . . have a number of limitations, as do all extant techniques of operationalizing conjugal power. [It has been demonstrated] that measures such as these, which request retrospective recall of the exercisers of power, are more likely to elicit the person "who is perceived as the authority on that issue" than "actual role performance." Authority refers to the person whom cultural or social norms designate as the "ex officio 'rightful' person" . . . to make, or implement, the decision. . . . Whereas this study cannot get at such important issues as how much actual power is granted the wife by default of the black male, the measures should shed light on what are the "normative" conjugal relationships in reference to decision-making and decision-implementation in black lower-class families.

Types of Comparisons. Conjugal distributions of power in decision-making and decision-implementation are analyzed in three ways: (1) by composite indices of decision-making; (2) by separate decision area; (3) by indices of the interaction of decision-making and decision-implementation. . . .

The composite decision-making index was derived from two preliminary indices, an index of relative husband-wife authority (RA), and an index of degree of shared authority (DS). These indices, in turn, provided the base for a four-fold classification of conjugal power distribution:

> (1) *Wife Dominant Type,* wherein the wife's range of authority is considerably larger than her husband's. (2) *The Syncratic Type,* consisting of couples between which there is nearly a balance of relative authority and the shared range is equal to or greater than the combined ranges of husband and wife. (3) *The Autonomic Type,* wherein there is also an approximate balance of relative authority, but the husband's and wife's ranges together are greater than the shared range. (4) *The Husband Dominant Type* . . . in which the husband's range is considerably greater than that of his wife (Centers et al., 1971).

The index of interaction between decision-making and decision-implementation consists of nine classifications: (1) *Husband Autonomy,* "the husband does and decides about the activity by himself"; (2) *Wife Autonomy,* "the wife does and decides about the activity by herself"; (3) *Husband Leadership,* "they do it together, the husband decides"; (4) *Wife Leadership,* "they do it together, the wife decides"; (5) *Husband Autocracy,* "the wife does it, the husband decides"; (6) *Wife Autocracy,* "the husband does it, the wife decides"; (7) *Syncratic Cooperation,* "they do and decide about it together"; (8) *Syncratic Division of Functions,* where "the *husband does it* and both decide"; and (9) *Syncratic Division of Functions,* where "*the wife does it* and both decide."

RESULTS

By Composite Indices of Decision-Making. These indices reveal a predominance of egalitarian decision-making structures (syncratic or autonomic authority types) in every study population (Table 1). Egalitarian structures accounted for almost three-fourths of the families in Champaign-Urbana, East Chicago, and Las Vegas and slightly over half of the families in Toledo and the Texas study populations. The modal authority type in every study population was the syncratic (i.e., decision-making was shared). Only in rural Texas was another authority type, wife-dominant, equally predominant.

TABLE 1. COMPOSITE DECISION-MAKING SCORES

	Champaign-Urbana	East Chicago	Las Vegas	Toledo	Houston	Center, Texas	Rural Texas	Total of Study Populations
	%	%	%	%	%	%	%	%
Authority types:								
Wife Dominant	20.0	21.2	13.7	16.4	34.7	25.5	33.3	24.2
Syncratic	60.0	66.2	53.7	54.5	43.0	38.3	33.3	48.3
Egalitarian								
Autonomic	10.0	6.3	17.9	5.5	10.0	19.2	24.3	13.6
Husband Dominant	10.0	6.3	14.7	23.6	12.4	17.0	9.1	13.9
X RA	9.8	9.7	10.0	10.0	9.3	9.8	9.5	9.7
X DS	2.9	3.6	3.7	3.3	2.7	2.7	2.2	2.9

Wife-dominant authority types were more prevalent than husband-dominant authority types in all but two study populations. Nevertheless, both wife-dominant and husband-dominant authority types were infrequent response patterns. Proportions of wife-dominant authority types ranged from about a third of the decision-making structures in Houston and rural Texas to less than a fifth in Las Vegas and Toledo. This means that, either by sharing or as an autonomous main agent, the husband was perceived as an active participant in decision-making in two-thirds or more of the families in every study population.

By Decision-Area. Similar response patterns were observed in all of the study populations with respect to allocation of decision-making and decision-implementation by area of decision. Given these similarities, the data of the various study populations have been combined to facilitate comparisons of responses by the different decision areas.

Examination of areas of decision-making reveals that husband-wife sharing of decision-making was the majority response with respect to every area of decision except about the wife working (Table 2). However, comparison of "husband" versus "wife" responses and mean power scores (when "wife" responses are weighted 1, "husband and wife" = 2, and "husband" = 3) shows the balance of normative decision-making power tended to favor the wife in four decision-areas and the husband in only one decision-area.

Reports of wife power were greatest by far with respect to decisions about her working. This was the only area of decision-making in which the modal response was wife alone. In fact, wife as the sole main decision-making agent was named almost twice as often with reference to her working than to any other type of decision.

TABLE 2. ALLOCATION OF DECISION-MAKING AND DECISION-IMPLEMENTATION BY AREA OF DECISION

Decision Area	Main Agents			Total	N	X*	s
	Wife	Husband	Both				
	%	%	%	%			
Decision-Making							
Friends	19.9	11.9	68.2	100.0	548	1.9	0.6
Where to Live	14.1	26.5	59.4	100.0	552	2.1	0.6
About the Wife working	41.8	24.3	33.9	100.0	551	1.8	0.8
How to Handle the Children	23.9	11.9	64.2	100.0	553	1.9	0.6
How to Use the Money	19.7	13.6	66.7	100.0	552	1.9	0.6
					Grand Mean=1.9		
Decision-Implementation							
Handling the Children	36.8	20.2	43.0	100.0	551	1.6	0.6
Spending the Money	45.2	17.2	37.6	100.0	553	1.8	0.5
					Grand Mean=1.8		

*Mean power was derived by weighing the responses as follows: Wife=1; Husband and Wife=2; Husband=3.

Reports of husband-power, on the other hand, were greatest with respect to decisions about where to live. Nevertheless, husband as the sole decision-maker was not the modal response for even this decision-area. Indeed, the husband alone was named almost as often as the main decision-maker with respect to the wife working as where to live. In decisions about the wife working, however, the husband was named much less as a sharer of decision-making than he was in other areas of decision.

Comparison of decision-making and decision-implementation shows that decision-implementation was perceived to be shared less than decision-making with reference to both spending money and handling children. Reports of wives' participation in decision-implementation was much greater (twice or more) than reports of husbands' participation. Decision-implementation, therefore, was perceived more likely to be dominated by the wife than was decision-making. Wives' perceived domination of decision-implementation was more pronounced with respect to spending money than handling children.

Despite the greater reported participation of wives in contrast to husbands in decision-implementation and most areas of decision-making, the roles of the husbands were not perceived by the black wives to be neglibible or even marginal in any decision-area. By virtue of shared or autonomous participation, the husband was generally perceived as a main decision-making agent and as a main decision-implementing agent in reference to every decision area.

Patterns of Interaction of Decision-Making and Decision-Implementation. Response patterns were strikingly similar with respect to the decision-areas of handling children and spending money when decision-making and decision-implementation were considered jointly. "Syncratic cooperation" (sharing of both decision-making and decision-implementation) was the modal response pattern, comprising about a third of the families, with respect to both decision-areas (Table 3). Syncratic division of functions where decision-making was shared but the wife implemented the decision (WaBd) was the next most common response pattern for both decision areas. This latter pattern appeared slightly more frequently with regard to decisions about spending money than handling children. Similar proportions of families (about a sixth) were also characterized by wife-autonomy with respect both to spending money and handling children. The remaining patterns of decision-making and decision-implementation were infrequent with respect to both decision-areas.

TABLE 3. CONJUGAL INTERACTION PATTERNS IN REFERENCE TO HANDLING CHILDREN AND USE OF FAMILY MONEY

		Decision Area	
Pattern	Designation	Handling Children	Spending Money
		%	%
HaHd*	Husband Autonomy	6.7	6.0
WaWd	Wife Autonomy	16.3	16.1
BaHd	Husband Leadership	4.0	3.1
BaWd	Wife Leadership	5.1	2.4
WaHd	Husband Autocracy	1.3	4.5
HaWd	Wife Autocracy	2.6	1.3
BaBd	Syncratic Cooperation	33.9	32.2
WaBd	Syncratic Division	19.2	24.4
HaBd	of Functions	10.9	10.0
Total		100.0	100.0
N		551	552

*a=acts, or implements decision
d=decides

SUMMARY AND CONCLUSIONS

The similar response patterns observed in the diverse lower-class, black populations lend credibility to the thesis that wife-dominance of decision-making and decision-implementation is not normatively prescribed in lower-class black families—at least not by the purported usurper of power, the black wife. Either as sharers or as autonomous agents, husbands were perceived to be main participants in decision-making in two-thirds or more of the families in every study population. Husbands' main roles in decision-making were evident in every decision-area. Moreover, husbands were also perceived to be main participants—shared plus autonomous participation—in implementing decisions about handling the children and spending money.

In both decision-making and decision-implementation, the husband's role was primarily perceived to be that of a sharer rather than an autonomous agent. Sharing of decision-making was the majority response with respect to all decisions except decisions about the wife working, and syncratic authority type was consistently the modal decision-making structure. When interaction of decision-making and decision-implementation was considered, the predominant structures were syncratic cooperation (BaBd) and syncratic division of functions where decision-making was shared but decision-implementation was performed by the wife (WaBd).

... The wife was perceived as a more active participant than the husband. The balance of normative decision-making power favored the husband in only one decision-area, where to live; it favored the wife in the four remaining decision-areas. Wife-power was especially great in decisions about her working. Wives were even more likely to dominate decision-implementation than decision-making when the two decision-areas of handling children and spending money were considered. Wives' perceived participation in decision-implementation was greater with respect to the latter decision-area. ... Further research is needed ... to more adequately identify the relevant familial-decisions among lower-class blacks and to determine the relative importance of these decisions to the family as a whole and to the individual family members. In addition, power with regard to conflict resolution needs to be explored, and husbands' as well as wives' perceptions of power should be tapped.

REFERENCES

Centers, Richard; Bertram H. Raven; and Aroldo Rodrigues.
  1971   "Conjugal power structure: A re-examination." American Sociologi-
         cal Review 36(April):264–278.
Scanzoni, John H.
  1971   The Black Family in Modern Society. Boston: Allyn and Bacon.
Staples, Robert.
  1971   "The myth of the black matriarchy." Pp. 149–159 in Robert Staples
         (ed.), The Black Family. Belmont, Calif.: Wadsworth.

ADDITIONAL READINGS

Moynihan, Daniel P.
  1965   The Negro Family: The Case for National Action. Washington, D.C.:
         U.S. Department of Labor.
Parker, Seymour, and Robert J. Kleiner.
  1969   "Social and psychological dimensions of the family role performance
         of Negro males." Journal of Marriage and the Family 31(Au-
         gust):500–506.

Legal Equality
in Marriage
Lenore J. Weitzman

TRADITIONAL LEGAL MARRIAGE: STATE-IMPOSED INEQUALITY

The legal marriage contract is unlike most contracts: its provisions are
unwritten, the terms are unspecified, and the terms of the contract are
typically unknown to the contracting parties. One wonders how many
men and women entering marriage today would freely agree to the
provisions of their marriage contracts if they were given the opportunity to read the contracts and to consider the rights and obligations to
which they were committing themselves. However, no state gives them
the opportunity to read the terms of their marriage contract, nor does
any state ask them if they are willing to assume the duties, rights, and
obligations it specifies. All states simply assume that everyone who gets
married will want to—or have to—abide by the state-imposed "unwritten" contract known as legal marriage.

What is in this unwritten contract? The four essential provisions of the
traditional marriage contract are those that (1) recognize the husband
as head of the household, (2) hold the husband responsible for support,
(3) hold the wife responsible for domestic services, and (4) hold the wife
responsible for child care. Each of these provisions is rooted in common
law, and each remains alive in 1975.

The Husband Is Head of the Family. In the common law of England, the husband and wife were merged into a single legal identity,
that of the husband. As Blackstone explained:

This article is adapted from "Legal Regulation of Marriage: Tradition and Change," *California Law
Review* 62, no. 4(1974):1169–1288, copyright by Lenore J. Weitzman. Revised and printed with the
permission of the author.

By marriage, the husband and wife were one person in law . . . [T]he very being or legal existence of the woman is suspended during the marriage, or at least is incorporated and consolidated into that of the husband, under whose wing, protection, and cover she performs everything.[1]

Under this doctrine of coverture, a married woman lost the control of her real property to her husband, as well as the ownership of her chattels. She could not make a contract in her own name either with her husband or with third parties, nor could she sue or be sued in her own name.[2] If she worked, her husband was entitled to her wages. If she and her husband were to separate, her husband would invariably gain custody of the children. In fact, the concept of the unity of the husband and wife as a single person even prevented her from full criminal responsibility for her own conduct. Criminal acts done in her husband's presence were assumed to be committed under her husband's command, and he was therefore held responsible for them.[3]

Most legal barriers to *property* were removed by the passage of the Married Women's Property Acts in the nineteenth century.[4] However, today, one hundred years later, the basic legal obligations between husband and wife remain bound by English common law—and thus remain fundamentally the same. The first of these is the basic common law assumption that a woman assumes her husband's identity upon marriage.

When a woman marries today, she still loses her independent identity: she assumes her husband's name, his residence, and his status— socially and economically. The married woman's loss of identity is clearly symbolized by the loss of her birth name. Married women who have tried to retain their birth names have had difficulty voting, running for office, obtaining a driver's license, and securing credit.[5]

As recently as 1972, the United States Supreme Court upheld an Alabama law requiring a married woman to use her husband's surname on her driver's license.[6] Many states are now adopting a more progressive attitude, however, and are holding that common laws do not require a woman to assume her husband's name even though such a

---

[1]Sir William Blackstone, *Commentaries on the Laws of England,* Vol. 1 (1765; reprint ed., Boston: Beacon Press, 1962), p. 442.

[2]Max Radin, "The Common Law of the Family," in *National Law Library,* Vol. 6 (New York: P. F. Collier, 1939), pp. 79–175.

[3]Homer Clark, *The Law of Domestic Relations* (St. Paul, Minn.: West Publishing Co., 1968), p. 223.

[4]Leo Kanowitz, *Women and the Law: The Unfinished Revolution* (Albuquerque: University of New Mexico Press, 1969), p. 40.

[5]Barbara Brown, Thomas Emerson, Gail Falk, and Ann Freedman, "The Equal Rights Amendment." *Yale Law Journal* 80(1971):871.

[6]Forbush v. Wallace, 405 U.S. 970 (1972).

custom might be followed by the majority of married women.[7] Yet in other states, a married woman who does not want to assume her husband's surname may still have to contend with laws and administrative regulations that restrict her freedom to do so.

The second area in which a woman assumes her husband's identity is in her domicile—the legal term for a person's residence. A married woman is required to accept her husband's choice of residence. If she refuses, she is "considered to have deserted him." If "deserted," the husband has valid grounds for divorce. In some states, a wife found guilty of desertion is "at fault" in the divorce action and can be deprived of her right to seek alimony. The location of a person's legal domicile also affects a broad range of legal rights and duties, including the place where he or she may vote, run for public office, serve on juries, receive free or lowered tuition at a state school, be liable for taxes, sue for divorce, register a car, and have his or her estate administered.[8] For example, a woman who is, and has always been, a state resident, and therefore receives free tuition at the state university, may suddenly be charged out-of-state tuition if she marries a male student whose legal domicile is in another state.

There are other areas in the law that recognize the husband as head of the household with his wife's identity subordinate to his. Some of these are found in administrative regulations regarding unemployment insurance, social security benefits, federal survivors and disability insurance, and public assistance.[9] Other regulations, such as those governing consumer credit, are derived from legal principles but have acquired an authority of their own. The result is a series of social customs and regulations that surround and enlarge the husband's strictly "legal" rights as head of the household and, consequently, further diminish those of his wife.

The Husband Is Responsible for Financial Support. The courts in our country have a strict, conservative view of the necessity of a clear division of roles within the family, holding that the "husband has a duty to support his wife, that she has a duty to render services in the home, and that these duties are reciprocal."[10] All states, even those with community property systems, place the prime burden of family support on the husband: he is to provide necessities for both his wife and his children.[11] In contrast, a wife is *never* held responsible for her husband

---

[7]Stuart v. Board of Supervisors of Elections, 226 Md. 440, 295 A.2d 223 (1972).

[8]Herma H. Kay, *Sex-Based Discrimination in Family Law* (St. Paul, Minn.: West Publishing Co., 1974), p. 127.

[9]Colguitt Walker, "Sex Discrimination in Government Benefit Programs." *Hastings Law Journal* 23(1971):277.

[10]Clark, *Law of Domestic Relations*, p. 181.

[11]Kay, *Sex-Based Discrimination*, p. 133.

in two-thirds of the states; and in the remaining minority of states, a wife is held responsible for her husband's support only if he has become incapacitated or a public charge.[12]

One effect of placing the primary support obligation on men is to further reinforce the husband's position as head of the household and, more specifically, his authority over family finances. While the husband's obligation for support does not alone bestow upon him the mixed blessings of financial authority and financial responsibility, most of his financial power stems directly from this obligation. For example, in most states, because the husband has the primary responsibility for family support, he has the power to manage and control family income and property. In some states, again because of his responsibility for support, his permission is necessary before his wife can open a business or trade in commodities.[13] The husband's financial powers are also used to justify granting married women credit in their husbands' name. This is especially harmful to the wife in the event of a divorce. She (*not he*) automatically loses "her" credit rating and is then forced to begin again and reestablish her credit by proving that she is financially responsible.

An underlying assumption behind the husband's legal responsibility for support is the implication of the continued economic incapacity of the wife. As Professor Kay has recently noted:

> The support laws embody the legal view that a married women is
> an economically nonproductive person dependent upon others for
> the necessities of life ... [T]he married woman continues to be
> treated as a legal dependent, like the children and insane person,
> with whom the law formerly classified her.[14]

This automatic assumption of a wife's dependency is clearly anachronistic in 1975. Today, 44 percent of all married women are in the labor force and are actively contributing to the financial support of their families.[15]

Such absolute laws have the effect of perpetuating unnecessary sex stereotypes in the lives of individual men and women. The modern man becomes bitter and resentful when the courts force him to support a woman who is well employed or wealthy. On the other side, the employed wife feels insulted because the law assumes she is incapable of supporting herself and doesn't recognize her important contribution to the family's income. The legal adherence to these sex stereotyped roles appears to be unrealistic and unnecessarily rigid in modern-day mar-

---

[12]Kay, *Sex-Based Discrimination*, p. 139; Clark, *Law of Domestic Relations*, p. 186.
[13]Kanowitz, *Women and the Law*, p. 57.
[14]Kay, *Sex-Based Discrimination*, pp. 140–141.
[15]U.S. Department of Labor, *1975 Handbook on Women Workers* (Washington, D.C.: Government Printing Office, 1971), p. 18.

riages when many women voluntarily share the burden of financial support with their husbands.

The law diverges from social reality in a second respect. In practice, the spousal support obligations of the husband are rarely enforced because the courts have been reluctant to interfere with an ongoing marriage. In the leading case in this area, McGuire v. McGuire,[16] the wife complained that her husband had not given her any money or provided her with clothes for the past three years. Although he was a man of substantial means, her husband had also refused to purchase furniture and other household necessities (beyond the groceries that he paid for by check). The court, however, refused to consider the wife's complaint because the parties were still living together and the court did not want to "intrude" on the marital relationship.

If a wife does not receive the court's assistance in obtaining support during her marriage, then it becomes meaningless to speak of the husband's legal obligation to support his wife. The Citizens' Advisory Council on the Status of Women aptly describes the present situation: "[A] married woman living with her husband can, in practice, get only what he chooses to give her."[17]

Women do not fare much better after divorce, although the husband's theoretical responsibility for support continues with his obligation to provide alimony for his former wife. Alimony was originally awarded by the English ecclesiastical courts, which gave only divorce *a mensa et thoro* (from bed and board), authorizing the husband and wife to live apart but not freeing them from the marital bond.[18] An alimony award under these circumstances was an enforcement of the husband's continuing duty to support his wife. Since the husband retained control over his wife's property, and employment opportunities for women were absent, alimony alone provided a woman's essential means of support.

The survival of alimony today, despite recent changes in women's status and labor force participation, reflects the law's continued assumption of the wife's dependency on her husband (and perhaps its cognizance of the realistically poor employment opportunities of a middle-aged woman who has devoted her productive years to full-time housework and child care). Because the law encourages a woman to give up her independent earning potential in favor of marriage, the provision for alimony is based on the assumption that women have done just this—and are, as a result, incapable of independent financial survival.

[16]McGuire v. McGuire, 1975 Neb. 226, 59 N.W.2d 342 (1953).

[17]*The Equal Rights Amendment and Alimony and Child Support Laws* (Washington, D.C.: Government Printing Office, 1972), p. 38.

[18]Chester G. Vernier and John B. Hurlbut, "The Historical Background of Alimony Law and Its Present Statutory Structure." *Law and Contemporary Problems* 6(1939):197.

Yet, if a woman relies on the law's promise that her husband will continue to support her, she will find her expectations thwarted. Even though most states continue to hold the husband theoretically liable for alimony, in fact, alimony is actually awarded in less than 15 percent of all divorce cases.[19] Although the myth of "alimony drones" and wives "taking their husbands to the cleaners" persists, it should be emphasized that for over 85 percent of the divorced women in the United States, alimony is just that—a myth.

The Wife Is Responsible for Domestic Services. As we have already noted, legal marriage assigns specific roles to both husband and wife. The man exchanges financial support for his wife's service as a companion, housewife, and mother. The services a man can legally expect from his wife are enumerated in Rucci v. Rucci:

> ... [S]he has a duty to be his helpmate, to love and care for him in such a role, to afford him her society and her person, to protect and care for him in sickness, and to labor faithfully to advance his interests [citations omitted]. Likewise, she must perform her household and domestic duties, ... without compensation therefor. A husband is entitled to the benefit of his wife's industry and economy.[20]

In the past century, the courts have been remarkably consistent in upholding the wife's domestic obligations above all else. Because "a husband is *entitled* to the benefit of his wife's industry and economy," the courts have reasoned that a wife *owes* domestic services to her husband, and they have therefore refused to honor contracts whereby a husband agreed to pay his wife for her domestic services. The law states that "one of the implied terms of the contract of marriage is that the wife's services will be performed without compensation." On the other hand, if a woman does not want to devote herself exclusively to homemaking, and instead chooses a full-time job or career, the law does not accept her decision to change roles. By law, she is still obliged to cook, clean, and maintain comforts for her husband even though this results in a clear inequality: she must handle two jobs, one at work and one at home, while her husband has only one.

The law's assumption that a wife "owes" her domestic services to her husband undermines the value and importance of the wife's labor in building the family wealth and property, both during the marriage and at the time of dissolution. As Professor Kay has noted, "When a woman's labor is seen as a service she owes her husband rather than a job deserving the dignity of economic return," the contribution and value of the

[19]Stuart Nagel and Lenore J. Weitzman, "Women as Litigants." *Hastings Law Journal* 23(1971):190.

[20]Rucci v. Rucci, 23 Conn. Supp. 221, 181 A.2d 125 (Super. Ct., 1962).

housewife is greatly underestimated.[21] Although there is "much rhetoric about the value of homemaking and child rearing," the law does little to ensure that these tasks are accorded the "status, dignity, and security they deserve."[22]

Recognition of the housewife's contribution to the marriage may be even more important at the time of divorce. In many states, the woman discovers that her contribution to the family wealth and property is ignored upon dissolution. Although marriage is considered a partnership in theory, when the partnership profits are divided, the woman's contribution is often devalued. In the forty-two states with separate property systems, the man owns whatever property he has acquired during the marriage. Many of these states—such as the State of New York, referred to in the following quote—simply disregard the wife's contribution to this "family property" at the time of divorce:

> The system disregards the division of labor in the family and leaves the wife without family assets.... At current prices, the replacement value of a wife's services may not be an insignificant sum. There also are such intangibles as a wife's help and encouragement in furthering her husband's career.[23]

Thus the woman who has contributed to the growth of her husband's business, career, property, or income during the marriage generally finds that her contribution to the partnership is unrecognized in law. Upon dissolution, the partnership is treated as a one-man business, and she is cheated out of a fair share of her half of the effort.[24]

It is a strange irony that the law seems to punish a woman who has devoted herself to being a mother and a wife at the same time that the law encourages all women to assume these roles. The law thus puts women in a double bind: the legal structure of marriage seems to provide incentives and rewards for women to remain in domestic roles, but upon divorce women are penalized for having remained in these roles.

The Wife Is Responsible for Child Care. The fourth provision of the state-imposed marriage contract places almost total responsibility for child care, both during marriage and after dissolution, upon the wife.

---

[21]Kay, *Sex-Based Discrimination*, p. 142.

[22]Citizens' Advisory Council on the Status of Women, *Recognition of Economic Contribution of Homemakers and Protection of Children in Divorce and Practice* (Washington, D.C.: Government Printing Office, 1974), p. 6.

[23]Henry H. Foster and Doris Jonas Freed, "Economic Effects of Divorce," *Family Law Quarterly* 8(1974):174–175.

[24]A recent report by the Citizens' Advisory Council on the Status of Women (1974) urges a careful evaluation of the economic effects of divorce laws to insure that the homemaker's contribution to the marital property is not ignored. They have specifically urged states adopting no-fault divorce laws to change their laws on the division of property, alimony, child support, and enforcement so that the law explicitly recognizes the contribution of the homemaker.

The woman's role as mother remains at the very core of our legal conceptions of her place in society, and it is likely to meet the most resistance to change. It provides a "fertile ground for stereotype and the most stubborn and intractable bastion of discrimination"[25] The continued legal assumption that the woman is the natural and proper caretaker of the young is most clearly reflected in child custody dispositions. Woman continue to be awarded custody of their children in over 90 percent of the cases.[26]

The practice of automatically giving the mother custody of the children may not take sufficient, if any, account of the needs of the individual children and parents involved. Because it is assumed that all mothers will want custody of their children, there is a strong social pressure for women to assume this role without thinking about it, and its consequences. Since custody awards to the mother are so routine, the woman who admits that she would prefer not to have her children is viewed suspiciously and made to feel deviant and guilty. She may therefore be coerced into a role that is harmful both to her and her children. Once again, the law seems to be based on stereotyped assumptions about the proper roles of men and women. Women who may not want to be full-time mothers are coerced into it, and fathers who want to have custody are prevented by the legal priorities given to women.

A second negative consequence of the practice of routinely awarding child custody to the mother is that it has the ultimate effect of causing the mother to bear the greater, if not the total, financial burden of child support. When a mother is awarded custody, she is expected to perform child-care services without pay. The father's obligation is limited to direct support for the child. Even the Uniform Marriage and Divorce Act, which represents the enlightened vanguard in family law, makes no provisions for a custodial parent to be compensated for his or her labor in taking care of the children.

Although the father, as a noncustodial parent, is typically ordered to pay child support, most fathers do not support their children as ordered.[27] Indeed 62 percent fail to comply fully with the court-ordered payments in the first year after the order, and 42 percent do not make even a single payment.[28] By the tenth year, 79 percent of the fathers are in total noncompliance. Yet, despite the alarmingly high rate of noncompliance, legal action against nonpaying fathers is rarely taken.[29]

---

[25]Brief of Appellees, Geduldig v. Aiello, 94 S.Ct. 2485 (1974).

[26]William J. Goode, *Women in Divorce* (New York: Free Press, 1965), pp. 29, 209.

[27]Nagel and Weitzman, "Women as Litigants," p. 190.

[28]Kenneth Eckhardt, "Deviance, Visibility, and Legal Action: The Duty to Support," *Social Problems* 15(Spring 1968):470.

[29]Eckhardt, "Deviance, Visibility, and Legal Action," p. 470.

CHANGES IN FAMILY PATTERNS:
CHALLENGES TO TRADITIONAL LEGAL MARRIAGE

In the past 200 years, there have been profound transformations in our society that have impelled corresponding changes in the nature and functions of the family. With the increasing industrialization and urbanization of our socity, the central role of the family has shifted from a productive economic unit to a socioemotional one in which the family's role as the major source of psychological and social support for its individual members has increased. Sharing, companionship, and emotional solace in the marital bond have become primary for most couples in our society—and this type of family seems to require a very different type of legal marriage. However, despite these profound changes in our society in the internal structure of marriage and in the relations between husbands and wives, the legal structure of marriage has remained stagnant and, consequently, is a rigid and outmoded vestige of the old social system.

In this section I shall examine the ways in which the traditional marriage contract is challenged by three major changes in American family patterns: the increase in egalitarian family patterns, the increase in divorce, and the increase in remarriage throughout the life cycle. Each of these changes points to the need for a more flexible legal model, a model that is more suited to the nuclear family unit and to the diverse roles modern husbands and wives must assume.

The Increase in Egalitarian Family Patterns: The Modern-Day Partnership. Social scientists have noted a trend toward more egalitarian family patterns, those in which authority and decisions are more equally shared by the husband and wife, or responsibilities are assumed by one spouse or the other on the basis of ability and individual temperament. A significant thrust toward these more egalitarian family patterns is coming from women's increasing dissatisfaction with the traditional role of the housewife and mother, and their resulting demands for more independence, greater participation and compensation in the labor force, and more sharing of domestic chores by husbands and children.[30] This trend toward more egalitarian relationships within the family provides a fundamental challenge to each of the provisions of the traditional marriage contract.

The first provision of the traditional contract, that of recognizing the husband as head of the family, is inconsistent with an egalitarian family form in which both authority and responsibility are increasingly shared. Decisions on financial matters such as budgeting, purchasing, saving,

---

[30]C. Foote, "Changes in American Marriage Patterns." *Eugenics Quarterly* 1(1954):246.

and the "general struggle for survival" are now being made jointly or apportioned on a less sex-stereotyped basis.

The second provision of the traditional contract, that of holding the husband primarily responsible for family support, is similarly challenged by changing social reality. Married women now constitute 60 percent of the female labor force, and these 20 million married women certainly contribute to the financial support of their families. Today, when 44 percent of all married women are in the labor force, social reality strongly contradicts the legal assumption that the husband should and does support his family alone.

The third provision, that which holds the wife solely responsible for domestic services, is also challenged by the egalitarian family norm. Today an extended range of domestic responsibilities are increasingly being shared or alternated between husband and wife. A growing number of married couples are interchanging household roles, with men playing a greater role in cooking, shopping, and cleaning, and women assuming more responsibility for family budgets, working in the garden, and fixing things around the house.

The final provision of the legal marriage contract, that which holds the wife responsible for child care, may also be challenged by changing family patterns. Parenthood is coming to be defined more and more as the joint enterprise of both husband and wife. This is true not only because women are insisting that men share some of the load, but also because many young professional men themselves no longer accept as their fate the compulsive male careerism that dominated the 1950s.[31]

The Increase in Divorce. Traditional legal marriage is intended to be permanent; it is a union for life. The religiously based legal concept of marriage derives from the Christian doctrine that marriage is indissoluble, a holy union of man and woman that is meant to last for the duration of the joint life of the parties: "We take each other to love and to cherish, in sickness and health, for better, for worse, until death do us part."[32]

In contrast to the legal system's naive assumption that "people fall in love, marry, and live happily ever after" is our society's steadily increasing divorce rate and a rapidly diminishing probability that any marriage will last until the death of one of the parties. Since the 1860s, there has been a continual upward trend in the rate of divorce, with a dramatic 80 percent increase in the divorce rate in the past ten years and a 9 percent increase from 1971 to 1972 alone.[33]

---

[31]Arlene Skolnick, *The Intimate Environment: Exploring Marriage and the Family* (Boston: Little, Brown, 1974).

[32]Max Rheinstein, *Marriage, Stability, Divorce and the Law* (Chicago: University of Chicago Press, 1972), p. 3.

[33]National Center for Health Statistics, *Monthly Vital Statistics Report*, Vols. 21 and 22 (Washington, D.C.: Government Printing Office, 1973).

Today there is at least one chance in three that a woman who is now thirty-five years old will be divorced. Moreover, current trends seem to indicate that the divorce rate will continue to rise. There is a growing acceptance of divorce as "normal" and a lessened social stigma attached to divorce. There are increased alternatives available to women, especially economic alternatives, which allow the possibility of a viable existence outside their present marriage.[34] Finally, there are rising expectations for happiness in marriage that make it more difficult for both men and women to justify remaining in an unsatisfactory marriage.[35]

The social reality of divorce points to the need for a legal system that recognizes that individuals may want to plan for a marriage that lasts for a period shorter than a lifetime. Instead of assuming a permanent commitment, legal marriage could include provisions for marriage contracts, term marriages, limited-purpose marriages and, most important, spousal protection both during marriage and upon dissolution, for persons wishing such alternatives.

The Increase in Marriage Throughout the Life Cycle. The traditional marriage contract assumes that all marriages are first marriages of the young. The ideal scenario is one of a young couple starting to build their lives together: they share the hard work in their early years and reap the benefits in their later years. The model assumes joint investments of time and energy in the job, home, and family. The couple's efforts begin to pay off in middle age, and they are assured happiness and security in their old age together.

The assumption of a first marriage is evident when one considers the omissions from the traditional marital obligations. While there are provisions for the husband's support of his wife and children, there are no provisions for balancing these obligations against those he may have to a former spouse or to the children of a former marriage. Nor is there any consideration of a wife's similar dual obligations to both a former and a present husband and children. Also ignored or omitted are provisions for balancing the competing interests of the first and second families with respect to property. In addition, while most states have automatic provisions, by statute or common law, for the surviving spouse to inherit a fixed share of the mate's estate, there is no recognition that a former spouse may have played a greater role in building the estate and should, therefore, be given a proportionate interest in it.

The legal assumption of a single marriage of young people is challenged by the high rate of remarriage after divorce and the resulting

---

[34] William J. Goode *World Revolution in Family Patterns* (New York: Free Press, 1963), p. 81.
[35] Hugh Carter and Paul P. Glick, *Marriage and Divorce: A Social and Economic Study* (Cambridge, Mass.: Harvard University Press, 1970), p. 55.

large number of people who form second and third marriages in their middle years. Persons entering a second marriage are likely to have different concerns from those beginning their first marriage, and these concerns need to be recognized by the legal system. Most persons entering a second marriage bring with them some responsibilities and obligations from their first marriage. They are likely to be older, to possess more property, and to be more concerned with how that property will be distributed at death. In addition, persons entering a second marriage are likely to have children and may want to structure their lives so that they can remain social, economic, and psychological parents to them.

Support and property obligations to former spouses will also be of concern to those entering a second marriage. Questions of life and accident insurance, medical coverage, retirement benefits and pension rights, shared investments in careers, real estate, business, and other property will also arise. Some may want to specify how income and property will be apportioned between first and second spouses; others will want to ensure the inheritance rights of each spouse as well as those of all their offspring.

In addition to those who remarry in middle age, there is a growing number of people who are remarrying closer to and after retirement. These people have entirely different problems which are similarly neglected by the present legal system.

The current increase in both divorce and remarriage reflect a movement towards a pattern of serial monogamy, or serial family formation, in American society. Serial monogamy refers to the pattern in which many people will go through the formative phase of establishing a new family with a new spouse more than once. Recognition of the increased importance of serial monogamy may well transform our legal and social expectations of a "normal" age-related family life cycle, and may profoundly alter the role of marriage for individuals and for our society as a whole. Clearly there is a need for a more flexible legal system to meet the challenge of these changing family patterns.

PATHWAYS TO CHANGE:
INDIVIDUAL CONTRACTS AND THE EQUAL RIGHTS AMENDMENT

There are two routes for challenging and altering traditional legal marriage. The first is through individual marriage contracts that seek to redefine the spousal obligations within—or as an alternative to—legal marriage. The possibilities for and structure of such contracts are discussed elsewhere.[36] A second (but by no means mutually exclusive) route to restructuring legal marriage may be found through the passage of the Equal Rights Amendment (ERA) to the United States Constitution. The ERA, if properly enforced, would eliminate the sex-based responsibilities that the traditional legal marriage imposes on husbands and wives. Let us briefly examine the probable effects of the Equal Rights Amendment on each of the provisions of the traditional marriage contract.

The first provision of the traditional contract, that which establishes the husband as head of the family, would clearly be illegal. The married women's loss of identity and the traditional network of legal disabilities imposed upon her with marriage would have to disappear.[37] For example, since name and domicile regulations continue to subordinate a woman's identity to her husband's, these and any other laws that require a married woman to assume her husband's identity would become a legal nullity. No married woman could be required by law to take her husband's name upon marriage. In addition, married women would have to be granted the same independent right to choice of domicile as married men now have.[38]

Since the ERA would prohibit enforcement of sex-based definitions of conjugal functions, it would invalidate the provisions of the traditional contract that assign specific roles to husbands and wives. The Equal Rights Amendment clearly prohibits legislation that dictates different roles for men and women within the family.[39] Thus, the second provision of the traditional marriage contract, that requiring the husband to be solely responsible for family support, would be illegal. The responsibility for family support would no longer fall on men alone. Each spouse would be equally liable "based on current resources, earning power, and nonmonetary contributions to the family welfare."[40] Similarly, the ERA would require that alimony be available to both husbands and wives, although laws could be passed to grant special protection to any spouse who had, in fact, been out of the labor force for a long time in order to make a noncompensated contribution to the family's well-being. Such laws would tend to benefit the traditional wife and would provide legal recognition of her contribution to the family. Thus, the ERA would not remove the housewife's right to support either during marriage or after divorce. It would only extend this right to men

[36]Lenore J. Weitzman, "Legal Regulation of Marriage: Tradition and Change," *California Law Review* 62, no. 4(1974):1169–1288.

[37]Brown et al., "Equal Rights Amendment," p. 937. For further documentation of the legislative history, see 118 *Congressional Record* S4372 (daily ed., March 21, 1972), and S. Rep. no. 97-689, 92d Cong., 2d sess. 49 (1972).

[38]Brown et al., "Equal Rights Amendment," p. 941.

[39]Brown et al., "Equal Rights Amendment," p. 953.

[40]Brown et al., "Equal Rights Amendment," p. 946.

if they have assumed the "housewife" role while their wives supported the family.

The third provision of the marriage contract, that of requiring a wife to do housework, to provide affection and companionship, and to be available for sexual relations, would likewise be prohibited as yet another example of sex-based assignment of family roles. These obligations could be required of wives only if they were also required of husbands. Although it is likely that such obligations would be removed from the laws of most states, some states might require domestic services of both spouses.

Finally, the fourth provision of the traditional contract would have to fall, as wives could not be held responsible for child care unless equal obligations were imposed upon all husbands. It is probable that most states would extend these obligations to husbands so that both parents would be responsible for their children's care. In addition, it is likely that most states will hold men and women equally responsible—according to their financial ability—for child support after divorce.

Thus, the Equal Rights Amendment would nullify the existing marriage contract and would require that marital rights and duties be based on individual functions and needs. In both marriage and divorce this would mean that spouses would be treated equally or on the basis of their individual capacities. Today's network of legal disability for married women would have to disappear. Some women have feared that the passage of the ERA would eliminate all the protections they currently enjoy in law. This would not be so. If a woman has spent her productive years in homemaking and child care, then it would be reasonable to award her alimony on the basis of her past functions and her need.[41]

Although the ERA will not remove the possibility of support for the homemaking spouse, it is useful to recall that the law's promise of support for divorced women has often been a hollow guarantee. Over 85 percent of the married women in this country have not received the law's guaranteed support upon divorce. Similarly, most divorced women have not received court-ordered child support. Thus, it is difficult to think of the ERA threatening rights that have rarely existed in practice.

On the very positive side, the Equal Rights Amendment allows for and encourages a complete redefinition of marriage as a true partnership. This modern conception of marriage might well include provisions for compensating a spouse who contributes, as the housewife does, to building the family's wealth and property.[42] Another possibility under the ERA would be the treatment of housework as a bona fide occupation

---

[41]S. Rep. no. 92-689, 92d Cong., 2d sess. 17–18 (1972).
[42]This theory is further developed in Weitzman, "Legal Regulation of Marriage," p. 1185, fn. 82.

with compensation and fringe benefits. With the fall of the wife's traditional obligation to provide domestic services, the law could then recognize the wife's services as an independent contribution to the marriage. Further, married women could be covered as independent workers under social security. Even more important, when it comes to divorce, the value of their contribution to the building of family wealth and property would be recognized by law.

The Equal Rights Amendment thus provides a unique opportunity for revitalizing legal marriage and for bringing it into line with social changes in family patterns that have already taken place. Once the amendment is passed, all states will have to remove each of the sex-based provisions of the traditional marriage contract, and will thereby allow husbands and wives to create a true partnership—and a new legal equality—within legal marriage.

The Job Market

Introduction   Helen Youngelson Waehrer

In today's job market, women share many of the same disabilities experienced by other groups with minority status. Although woman's inferior economic position parallels her general inferior social position, it is her economic disadvantages that cause her the most obvious hardships.

Women today face lower earnings, lower-status jobs, more limited occupational opportunities, and a higher chance of unemployment than men. A significant contribution to women's inferior economic situation is the division of the job market into men's jobs and women's jobs with little interchange between these sex-typed jobs. Women are not only distributed differently among occupations, but they are segregated into a relatively narrow range of all occupations (see the Manpower Report of the President in Part One). The sex typing of jobs becomes most apparent when men's and women's jobs are compared at the same level of schooling. Juanita Kreps notes:

> A male high school graduate has three times as good a chance of becoming a manager (the top industry classification) as a female with similar education. Among college graduates, the male's probability for employment in this select group is four times as great as that of college educated women.[1]

She further notes that, at the high school level,

---

[1] Juanita M. Kreps, "The Occupations: Wider Economic Opportunity," in Mary Louise McBee and Kathryn A. Blake (eds.), *The American Woman: Who Will She Be?* (Beverly Hills, Calif.: Glencoe Press, 1974), pp. 72–73.

... the male-female trade-off in jobs seems to be craftsmen and blue-collar workers for clerical and kindred workers. Among college graduates, the sex division places males as professionals, managers, proprietors, and salesmen, with women primarily in professions and clerical work.[2]

Women's proportionately large representation in the professions is explained by their predominance in the low-status professions of elementary and high school teaching and nursing, whereas men predominate in the higher-status fields of medicine and law.

In recent years, some women have gained employment opportunities by moving into male-dominated occupations such as skilled blue-collar trades, law, and banking.[3] These gains have been more than offset, however, by the influx of men into such fields as library science, nursing, elementary school teaching, and social work—occupations traditionally held by women.[4] Indicative of this loss by women of administrative positions is the statement made in a report on the sex balance among head librarians, which noted that "the overwhelming majority of new, young administrators were male."[5]

Nonwhite women are an especially disadvantaged group because they face both sex and racial discrimination. In comparison with other groups of workers, they receive the lowest relative median earnings[6] and experience the highest rate of unemployment.[7] In recent years they have made some gains, as an increasing proportion of young black women are turning to clerical work rather than domestic service; however, their full-time median earnings still remain considerably lower than those of white women.

Contrary to popular thought, women's overall economic position has worsened during the last fifteen years despite the vocal concern for women's economic equality and the existence of legislation promoting equal pay and equal job opportunity. The segregation of women into low-status, low-paying jobs remains virtually unchanged, while in the period from 1962 to 1973 women's full-time median earnings relative to men's has deteriorated in most occupational groups.[8] Women's overall relative full-time median earnings fell from 61 percent to 56

[2]Kreps, "The Occupations," p. 73.

[3]Women's Bureau, 1975 Handbook on Women Workers (Washington, D.C.: U.S. Government Printing Office, 1975), pp. 92–93.

[4]James W. Grimm and Robert N. Stern, "Internal Labor Market Structures: the Female Semi-Professions." Social Problems 21(June 1974):690–705.

[5]W. C. Blankenship, "Head Librarians: How Many Men? How Many Women?" in Athena Theodore (ed.), The Professional Women (Cambridge, Mass.: Schrankman, 1971), p. 99.

[6]Census Bureau, A Statistical Portrait of Women in the U.S., Current Population Report, Special Studies Series P-23, no. 58 (Washington, D.C.: Government Printing Office, April 1976), p. 74.

[7]Census Bureau, Statistical Portrait of Women, p. 72.

[8]Women's Bureau, 1975 Handbook on Women Workers, pp. 131–132.

percent of men's between 1960 and 1974.[9] Moreover, the rates of unemployment for women have been increasing relative to men. In 1974, the unemployment rate of women was 31 percent higher than that of men; in 1960, the unemployment rate of women was only 9 percent higher than men's.[10]

The readings in this section attempt to document the barriers to women's economic equality with men in the job market. They focus on the issues of wage discrimination, occupational segregation by sex, and unemployment.

Trying to determine how much of the observed male/female earnings differential is attributable to direct wage discrimination (pay differences not caused by relative productivity differences) has been the focus of a number of empirical studies.[11] Although a comprehensive theory of wage discrimination has not yet been constructed, these studies attempt to estimate the amount of discrimination by concentrating on those existing theories that can be tested. Such empirical tests estimate the amount of wage discrimination as a residual, since discrimination itself is not visible. Thus discrimination must be estimated from the amount of unexplained wage differential after accounting for other factors (such as education, age, years of work experience, etc.) that reflect differences in productivity.

In the first selection, Victor Fuchs discusses his study of male/female wage differentials based on a national sample of 1960 data. Using Gary Becker's theory of discrimination,[12] Fuchs attempts to test whether the observed differences in wages are caused by direct wage discrimination on the part of employers, employees, or customers (see the discussion by Blau and Jusenius in Part Two). On the basis of his results, Fuchs suggests that occupational segregation, not direct wage discrimination, is a significant cause of the observed female/male wage differences. Fuchs notes, however, that this conclusion just shifts the problem from explaining wage differences to explaining occupational segregation by sex. He suggests that most of the 40 percent unexplained wage difference is due to gender roles that affect women's occupational choices, the amount and type of training they receive, and their intermittent participation in the job market.

It is difficult to compare Fuch's results with the findings of other studies because of differences in data base, statistical methods em-

---

[9]Women's Bureau, *1975 Handbook on Women Workers*, p. 131.

[10]Women's Bureau, *1975 Handbook on Women Workers*, p. 65.

[11]For a review of empirical studies based on national samples, see Hilda Kahne, "Economic Perspectives on the Roles of Women in the American Economy." *Journal of Economic Literature* 13(December 1975):1259–1261.

[12]Gary S. Becker, *The Economics of Discrimination*, 2nd ed. (Chicago: University of Chicago Press, 1971).

ployed, and factors taken into account in the estimation of unexplained wage difference. Although there seems to be general agreement that occupational segregation by sex is a significant source of women's lower relative earnings,[13] the studies differ about the source of this segregation. Some agree with Fuchs, ascribing the cause to gender roles, while others emphasize that discriminatory practices by firms discourage women from having high aspirations, from seeking training, and from devoting time to searching for jobs.[14]

The study of relative gains in women's and men's earnings due to additional years of schooling is the focus of the next selection, by Albert Niemi, Jr. Although the article is highly technical, its inclusion is important because it demonstrates that women's alleged lack of education does not explain their low earnings. Indeed, women's earnings are lower than men's even when both have the same level of education. Using the human capital approach, which assumes that an investment in formal schooling, training, etc., will bring returns in the form of increased earnings over one's lifetime, Niemi calculates the lifetime earnings that women and men could *expect* (i.e., rate of return) according to their level of education. He then compares the *expected* earnings with the *actual* earnings of women and men at three educational levels —high school, college, and postcollege. Niemi finds that the actual earnings neared the expected rate of return for men with college and postcollege educations. For women, however, the findings are somewhat different. While the rate of return has increased relative to women's investment in additional education, women's actual earnings have declined relative to men's actual earnings, even when the levels of education are comparable. Niemi ascribes this differential in women's earnings to occupational segregation, not to education. This would suggest that the sex typing of jobs must be eliminated to insure equality of income.

Robert Gubbels, in the third selection, contributes to an understanding of the complex set of factors fostering the continuation of job segregation in most industrialized countries.[15] He details the barriers that inhibit women from entering jobs traditionally held by men. He discusses such barriers as protective labor legislation and the different definitions of appropriate working conditions for men and women; the socialization of women that prepares them for marriage and motherhood rather than for the job market; and those prejudices and beliefs that influence people to practice sex discrimination. Gubbels

[13]Kahne, "Economic Perspectives on the Roles of Women," p. 1261.

[14]See Isabel Sawhill, "The Economics of Discrimination Against Women: Some New Findings," *Journal of Human Resources*, 8(Summer 1973):383–396.

[15]For a theoretical discussion of the causes of sex segregation, see the articles by Blau and Jusenius, and by Reich et al. in Part Two.

concludes by asserting that these barriers will not be broken unless legislation prohibiting the denial of jobs based on sex is vigorously enforced.

A woman's more frequent movement in and out of the labor force during her work life makes her more vulnerable than a man to fluctuations in the general level of economic activity. Women have high unemployment rates—like blacks and teenagers, they are among the last to be hired and the first to be fired—and are prone to "hidden unemployment." Women are more likely than men to drop out of the labor force when jobs become scarce. Betty MacMorran Gray cogently discusses the consequences of "hidden unemployment" for women, and the reasons why a full-employment, growth economy is necessary for an improvement in women's economic position.

In the final selection, Elizabeth Almquist attempts to separate the interacting effects that sex discrimination and race discrimination have on the economic condition of black women. Her study is, in part, a response to recent assertions that the economic problems of black women are due mainly to their race rather than their sex. After discussing women as a caste within American society, Almquist develops and applies a model for assessing the separate effects of sex discrimination and race discrimination on the rates of unemployment, occupation patterns, and the earnings of black women. Her results show that sex discrimination contributes more than race discrimination to black women's inferior economic situation. Almquist concludes that the elimination of sex discrimination as well as race discrimination will be required if nonwhite women are to achieve full economic equality with men.

Differences in
Hourly Earnings
Between Men
and Women

Victor R. Fuchs

The fact that men earn more than women is one of the best established and least satisfactorily explained aspects of American labor-market behavior. The lack of satisfaction does not stem from a dearth of hypotheses, but rather the reverse. It is claimed that men are stronger than women; that they invest more in themselves (in on-the-job training, apprenticeships, and so on) after formal schooling is completed; that they are more firmly attached to the labor force; that women place more importance on the nonmonetary aspects of a job than do men; and last, but not necessarily least, that women suffer from discrimination at the hands of employers, fellow employees, customers, and society at large. . . .

The principal focus [of this paper] is on determining the size of the sex differential in hourly earnings for all nonfarm employed persons and on analyzing how this differential varies across industries, occupations, and other subgroups. The assumption underlying the research strategy is that the *pattern* of variation can shed some light on the *causes* of the differential. . . .

The basic source of data is the One-in-One-Thousand sample of the 1960 *Census of Population and Housing.* . . .

Total annual earnings in 1959 are calculated for workers in each classification. Total hours are estimated by multiplying (for each worker) the weeks worked in 1959 and the hours worked in the Census week

Excerpts reprinted from Victor R. Fuchs, "Differences in Hourly Earnings between Men and Women," *Monthly Labor Review* 94(May 1971):9–15. Washington, D.C.: U.S. Department of Labor, Bureau of Labor Statistics.

in 1960 and summing across all the workers in a classification. Average hourly earnings for each classification are obtained by dividing total earnings by total hours. When there are only a few workers in a classification the estimates of hourly earnings are subject to considerable sampling error; therefore, results for groups containing fewer than 50 observations are usually omitted or are marked accordingly.

The differential is expressed in the form of female earnings as a percentage of male earnings. These percentages are based on comparison of group means using simple and multiple regressions on dummy variables.

DISCRIMINATION AGAINST WOMEN

For nonfarm employed, average female hourly earnings were 60 percent of male earnings in 1959 (see Table 1). Adjustment for color, schooling, age, and city size has very little effect on this differential. Adjustment for length of trip to work, marital status, and class of worker raises the ratio to 66 percent. The length-of-trip variable is of particular interest because it reflects the different pressures on women that cut into their market earnings. It is well known, and confirmed by this study, that jobs located in residential areas pay less on average than do comparable jobs not located in residential areas. Regardless of sex, employed persons who work at home or walk to work earn about 26 percent less than do those who must travel to their jobs, other things being equal. Women typically have greater responsibilities in the home, and we might expect them to seek employment nearer home.

The variation in the size of the differential by marital status is quite large and suggests some of the processes that contribute to differences in earnings. The differential is largest for men and women who are married with spouse present. In such cases the man's incentive and ability to devote himself to work in the market is greatest, and that of women is usually the smallest.

Analysis of earnings for different classes of workers also helps to shed some light on the nature and extent of discrimination against women. Consider first the hypothesis that the employer or supervisor is the principal source of discrimination. If so, we would expect the male-female differential in earnings to be smallest for the self-employed, because no discrimination of this type is possible. Also, a smaller differential might be expected for private wage and salary workers than for government workers because the competitive pressures for profits and survival would tend to exert more discipline in the private sector.

**TABLE 1. FEMALE AVERAGE HOURLY EARNINGS RELATIVE TO MALE
FOR ALL NONFARM EMPLOYED AND SELECTED SUBGROUPS, 1959**
(In percent)

Characteristic	Unadjusted	Adjusted for color, schooling, age, and city size	Adjusted for color, schooling, age, city size, marital status, class of worker, and length of trip
All	60	61	65
Length of trip to work:1			
Short trip	64	63	65
Medium trip	63	63	66
Long trip	59	62	65
Marital status:			
Married, spouse present	58	59	61
Never married	88	82	83
Other	69	67	68
Class of worker:			
Self employed	41	45	58
Private wage and salary	58	59	64
Government	81	77	79
Age:2			
Less than 25	83	82	82
25-34	69	69	73
35-44	58	59	62
45-54	58	57	61
55-64	57	54	61

NOTE: The source of all tabular material is the One-in-One-Thousand sample of the 1966 Census of Population and Housing. All calculations are by the author.

1Short trips═work at home or walk to work. Long trips═place of work in different county or city than place of residence. Medium trips═all other.

2Whites only.

The results presented in Table 1 strongly reject this hypothesis. The male-female differential in earnings is definitely largest for the self-employed and smallest for government employees. The data could be interpreted as saying that there is less employer discrimination in government, but this fails to explain why the differential is larger for the self-employed than for private wage and salary workers. The observed pattern of earnings differentials and employment distribution *is* consistent with the hypothesis of discrimination by customers. (For example, customers at an auto repair shop may not be willing to let a female mechanic work on their cars, regardless of her training and experience. Or, many customers in expensive restaurants often prefer waiters to waitresses.) Government could be expected to be least sensitive and the self-employed most sensitive to that type of discrimination.

The sharp decrease in the female-male earnings ratio with increasing age is one of the most striking findings of this study. It supports the hypothesis that much of the overall differential is related to the more casual attachment of women to the labor force and to sex differences in postschool investment. This interpretation is confirmed if we look at the differentials by age and marital status. . . . Women who have never married—who are much more likely to stay in the labor force and who have more incentive to invest in themselves after formal schooling is completed—have an age-earnings profile which is very similar to that of men. At young ages there is not much variation in the size of the sex differential by marital status, but for married women with spouse present (and "other" women to a lesser extent), the differential increases with age. The pattern of differentials in average annual hours shows clearly the way marital status (and its concomitant demands on women for work outside the market) affects their earnings potential.

DIFFERENCES ACROSS INDUSTRIES

The male-female differential in hourly earnings varies considerably across industries . . . analysis of this variation may help to shed light on the differential itself. For instance, a finding that the differential is related to institutional industry characteristics such as unionization or establishment size would tend to support the employer discrimination hypothesis. If, however, differences in the differential can be explained primarily by differences in worker characteristics such as schooling and age, the discrimination hypothesis tends to be refuted.

In order to avoid considering atypical situations, the analysis is restricted to industries with at least 50 males and 50 females in the One-in-One-Thousand Sample. These 46 industries account for 81 percent of all women and 54 percent of all men. Most of the excluded industries employ very few women; some employ fewer than 50 (thousand) of either sex.

In the regressions . . . the dependent variable is female hourly earnings as a percentage of male. The most significant independent variable, in either the simple or multiple regressions, is female "expected" earnings as a percentage of male ["expected" hourly earnings based on all industries earning ratios for 168 color, age, sex, and schooling classifications and the distribution of employed persons in each group]. This tells us that the pattern of the differential across industries is highly correlated with the pattern of differences in mix of schooling, age, and color.

Furthermore . . . the differential is *not* related to extent of unionization or size of establishment. If employer discrimination was a major factor in the sex differential, we might expect that it would vary across industries in an erratic fashion or be related to such institutional variables as unionization and establishment size.

The age-profile variable is also significant. This is a measure of the extent to which earnings of white males rise with age, and I interpret it as revealing the extent to which there is a labor-market effect relative to postschool investment in human capital. The sex differential in earnings is higher in industries with the steep age profiles because men are more likely than women to undertake such investment.

The higher the percentage of female employment the lower are earnings, but this is true for men as well as women. There is no support for the hypothesis that men dislike working in the same industries as women and must, therefore, be given special compensation to do so.

DIFFERENCES ACROSS OCCUPATIONS

When sex differentials across occupations are examined, one of the most striking findings is how few occupations employ large numbers of both sexes. Most men work in occupations that employ very few women, and a significant fraction of women work in occupations that employ very few men.

Although there are significant differences in schooling between white men and black men, their occupational distributions are much more alike than are those of white men and white women.

It should not be thought that the difficulty in finding many occupations that employ both large numbers of men and women is attributable to the small size of the average occupation. There are 100 occupations that employ over 100,000 persons, but only 46 of them employ as many as 35,000 of each sex.

The results of regressions across these occupations are in general similar to those reported for industries. One new variable, which measures the extent of variation of earnings of individual males, proves to be highly significant. This variable can be interpreted as a measure of the heterogeneity of the occupational classification. The more homogeneous the occupation, the smaller will be the individual variability. We find that women's earnings are particularly depressed in occupations in which there is great individual variability among males. This suggests that the more detailed the occupational classification the smaller would be the observed sex differential in earnings. Indeed, I am convinced that if one pushes occupational classification far enough one "explain" nearly all of the differential. In doing so, however, one changes the form of the problem. We would then have to explain why occupational distributions differ so much.

SUMMING UP

The difference in hourly earnings between men and women has been and is very large. When most jobs required heavy labor, the difference might have been explained by differences in physical strength, but, given the present occupational structure, it is implausible to attribute a 40 percent differential to inherent differences in physical or mental ability.

In my opinion, most of the 40 percentage points can be explained by the different *roles* assigned to men and women. Role differentiation, which begins in the cradle, affects the choice of occupation, labor-force attachment, location of work, postschool investment, hours of work, and other variables that influence earnings. Role differentiation can, of course, result from discrimination. We have not found, in this preliminary study, evidence that employer discrimination is a major direct influence upon male-female differentials in average hourly earnings. Discrimination by consumers may be more significant.

Given the changes that have been and are occurring in our society—such as the reduction in infant mortality, the improvements in family planning and the shift from an industrial to a service economy—it appears to many (including this writer) that some reduction in role differentiation is desirable. Such reduction would require the combined efforts of men and women at home and in school, as well as the marketplace, and probably would result in a narrowing of earnings differences over the long run.

Differences
in Return
to Educational
Investment

Albert W. Niemi, Jr.

... This article is concerned with sex variation in returns to schooling in 1960 and 1970 for three population groups (total, white, and black) and three completed levels of education (high school, college, and postcollege). It is shown that the expected rates of return on female educational investment are sufficiently high to warrant further spending. However, it is also demonstrated that high rates of return to female schooling are not sufficient to lead to parity with male income levels and, during the past decade, the income of females relative to males has declined in most age-education cells.

METHODS FOR ESTIMATING RETURNS TO EDUCATION

The pioneering work regarding the calculation of returns to education was done by Gary S. Becker,[1] and I have closely followed his procedures. ... The internal rate of return, r, is implicitly defined by the following:

$$C = \sum_{j=1}^{n} (Y_j - X_j)/(1 + r)^j,$$

Excerpts reprinted from Albert W. Niemi, Jr., "Sexist Differences in Return to Educational Investment." *Quarterly Review of Economics and Business* 15(Spring 1975):17–25. © 1975 By the Board of Trustees of the University of Illinois. Reprinted by permission.

[1]Gary S. Becker, *Human Capital: A Theoretical and Empirical Analysis* (New York: Columbia University Press, 1964).

where C = the cost of education, X and Y = earnings streams resulting from different levels of completed education, and j = the number of years of observation. Thus r is the rate of discount that equates the present value of the higher earnings streams associated with advanced levels of completed education to the present value of the costs of obtaining that higher education. The value of r was calculated and the results were rounded to the nearest one-quarter of a percent. Expected future earnings with a high school education were compared with future earnings with an eighth-grade education; expected earnings with a college degree (four years) were compared with expected earnings with a high school education; and expected earnings with a postcollege degree (five years or more) were compared with expected earnings with four years of college. It was assumed that an individual with a high school education entered the labor force at age eighteen; an individual with four years of college entered the labor force at age twenty-two; and an individual who remained in school after college entered the labor force at age twenty-four. In all cases, the benefits of education were measured to age sixty-five.

The costs of education were defined as the sum of direct costs plus opportunity costs. For high schools, it was generally assumed that there are no direct costs, and the cost of obtaining a high school degree was equal to the income forgone during the period in which one is pursuing his education. Becker argued that education occupies most individuals for three-fourths of the year and, therefore, opportunity costs should be viewed as equal to three-fourths of the earnings of those who entered the labor force with a lower level of completed education. I have used three-fourths of the mean income of eighteen through twenty-four years olds who entered the labor force with eight years of education as a measure of the opportunity cost of going to high school.

The direct costs of a college education were defined to include expenditures for tuition, fees, books, and miscellaneous expenses incurred because of enrollment in college. Data on tuition and required fees are available from the U.S. Office of Education. Average annual student charges were provided for public and private institutions by type of program: four-year university, four-year college, and two-year college. The charges for public and private four-year programs were weighted by enrollment to obtain an estimate of the average expense for tuition and required fees. The average cost for all students served as the basis for the Variant 1 estimates of returns to college education. In addition, a Variant 2 measure was provided that used the average costs of a public education. Expenditures for books and miscellaneous items were each estimated at $75 in 1960 and $100 in 1970. The opportunity cost of attending college was estimated as equal to three-fourths of the mean earnings of high school graduates between the ages of eighteen and twenty-four.

The costs of postcollege education were calculated in a fashion similar to the procedure followed for a four-year college education. Average charges for tuition and required fees were obtained from the Office of Education. Three variants of direct expenses for graduate study were used: Variant A represented the average cost of all institutions; Variant B represented the average cost for public institutions; and Variant C assumed that financial aid compensated for all direct costs of graduate study. Figures on postcollege educational attainment revealed that two years was the average length of time spent in school beyond college. Opportunity costs of postcollege education were taken to be equal to three-fourths of the mean income earned by individuals between twenty-five and thirty-four who had completed four years of college.

The expected future earnings streams associated with each completed level of education must be adjusted to take into account taxes and mortality. The tax adjustment is necessary to reduce that portion of future higher income levels that will be taxed away. The mortality adjustment is necessary to take into account the probability that an individual will not live to retirement age and receive the total extra income associated with higher educational attainment. Some studies of returns to education have also attempted to adjust the earnings data for secular productivity growth and ability, but no adjustment for these factors was attempted in this article. It would be difficult to derive appropriate percentage rates of secular productivity growth for different sex and racial groups. Becker used three measures of secular growth (0 percent, 1 percent, and 2 percent) and found that each increase of 1 percent in secular growth tended to raise the internal rate of return to college by approximately 1 percent. Native ability is difficult to measure and I have not attempted to isolate the portion of the calculated internal rate of return due to native ability. Fred Hines and his coauthors[2] calculated internal rates of return to education with and without an adjustment for secular growth and native ability. They found that the adjustments tended to cancel each other out and resulted in virtually no net change in the rate of return.

In addition to adjusting for taxes and mortality, I have also adjusted income to take into account intraracial sex differences in labor force participation rates. This adjustment was necessary because many females work on a part-time basis and the census income-education data

---

[2]Fred Hines, Luther Tweeter, and Martin Redfern, "Social and Private Rates of Return to Investment in Schooling, by Race-Sex Groups and Regions." *Journal of Human Resources* 5(Summer 1970):318–340.

include all who earned any income. The adjustment for sex differences in annual hours worked involved weighting female income in each age-education cell by a coefficient constructed as the ratio of male/female annual hours worked. The internal rates of return calculated on the basis of the adjusted income data yielded results that can be looked upon as the potential rate of return to education for full-time female workers. I have also calculated the internal rates of return using the unadjusted census income data, and these results provided an estimate of the actual earned rate of return on female education.

ESTIMATED RETURNS TO EDUCATIONAL INVESTMENT

The calculated rates of return for 1960 and 1970 appear in Table 1. In examining the results, it should be reiterated that the adjustment for labor force participation rate differences involved a conversion of female earnings to male participation rates within racial groups. Therefore, it was inappropriate to compare the adjusted rates of return of white and black females. The results in Table 1 show that during the past decade there has been some increase in returns to both males and females on spending for advanced education and there also has been a significant narrowing of sex differences in returns to college and post-college. Adjusted returns to white females exceeded male returns only for postcollege education. On the other hand, in 1960 black females earned higher rates of return than black males on all levels of education, especially college. Sex differences for blacks have narrowed considerably during the past decade, but in 1970 female returns to college still substantially exceeded male returns.

MARKET DISCRIMINATION AGAINST FEMALES

The calculated rates of return in Table 1 suggest that investment in education, particularly college education, is rational for both males and females. However, the recent relative increase in the rate of return on female investment in education has not brought any improvement in the relative earnings position of women. Within given age and education cells, females continue to earn substantially less than males. Becker's analysis of discrimination provided us with a useful summary measure of earnings variation.[3] An average market discrimination coefficient (ADC) can be defined as follows:

---

[3]Gary S. Becker, *The Economics of Discrimination*, 2nd ed. (Chicago: University of Chicago Press, 1971), chaps. 1 and 8.

TABLE 1. INTERNAL RATES OF RETURN TO HIGH SCHOOL, COLLEGE, AND POSTCOLLEGE EDUCATION, 1960 AND 1970

Sex and racial group	High school	College		Postcollege		
		Variant 1	Variant 2	Variant A	Variant B	Variant C
1960						
All males	6.25	7.75	8.00	1.75	2.00	2.00
All females (adjusted)*	6.25	5.75	6.25	7.00	7.50	7.75
All females (unadjusted)*	7.50	5.50	6.00	7.00	7.50	8.00
White males	6.25	7.75	8.00	1.75	2.00	2.00
White females (adjusted)	5.75	5.50	6.00	7.25	7.50	8.00
White females (unadjusted)	7.25	5.25	5.75	7.00	7.50	8.00
Black males	5.50	4.75	5.25	6.00	6.25	6.50
Black females (adjusted)	6.50	8.00	8.75	6.25	6.50	7.00
Black females (unadjusted)	8.00	8.25	9.25	6.00	6.50	7.00
1970						
All males	6.00	8.00	8.50	3.75	4.00	4.25
All females (adjusted)	5.75	7.75	8.25	7.00	7.25	7.75
All females (unadjusted)	6.75	6.76	7.25	7.00	7.25	8.00
White males	5.75	8.00	8.50	3.75	4.00	4.00
White females (adjusted)	5.25	7.25	7.75	7.25	7.50	8.00
White females (unadjusted)	6.50	6.50	7.00	7.25	7.50	8.00
Black males	6.75	6.00	6.50	6.00	6.25	6.75
Black females (adjusted)	6.75	8.50	9.25	5.75	6.00	6.25
Black females (unadjusted)	8.25	8.50	9.25	5.75	6.00	6.50

*The adjusted estimates were calculated on the basis of the earnings data which take into account sex differences in annual hours worked; the unadjusted estimates were calculated without adjusting for labor force participation differences.

$$ADC = (Y_m{}^i/Y_f{}^i) - 1,$$

where Y = mean income, i = the ith age-education cell, m = males, and f = females. If there is no market discrimination, $Y_m{}^i = Y_f{}^i$, and the $ADC = 0$; if there is market discrimination against females, $Y_m{}^i > Y_f{}^i$, and the $ADC > 0$; and if there is market discrimination against males, $Y_m{}^i < Y_f{}^i$, and the $ADC < 0$.

The estimated *ADC*s in Table 2 have been calculated from the mean income adjusted for sex differences in labor force participation rates. For whites, the results show that a very large sex earnings difference exists for each education level and, despite the recent relative improvement in female rates of return on education, the past decade has witnessed an increase in the size of the *ADC* in favor of males in virtually every age-education cell, especially in college and postcollege. The *ADC*s for blacks are much smaller than those for whites, especially for advanced levels of education, but they still indicate an earnings discrepancy in favor of males. During the past decade, some slight progress toward equality of earnings by education was made by black females.

TABLE 2. AVERAGE DISCRIMINATION COEFFICIENTS BY RACE, AGE, AND EDUCATIONAL ATTAINMENT, 1960 AND 1970

	1960				1970			
Age group	Eight years	High school	College	Post-college	Eight years	High school	College	Post-college
	Total population							
18-24	.33	.19	...	...	.42	.31	...	...
25-34	.85	.73	.75	.40	.83	.82	.63	.35
35-44	1.00	1.07	1.29	.78	1.07	1.06	1.27	.83
45-54	.94	.91	.97	.65	1.08	1.08	1.31	.96
55-64	1.19	1.01	.97	.59	1.19	1.00	1.13	.92
	White population							
18-24	.32	.19	...	...	.44	.31	...	...
25-34	.79	.72	.77	.41	.85	.86	.67	.36
35-44	1.00	1.08	1.33	.79	1.08	1.09	1.34	.85
45-54	.90	.91	.98	.65	1.08	1.10	1.33	.99
55-64	1.19	1.02	.98	.59	1.19	1.01	1.14	.93
	Black population							
18-24	.27	.19	...	...	.18	.19	...	...
25-34	.80	.53	.21	.11	.51	.48	.16	.10
35-44	.97	.72	.30	.31	.77	.57	.22	.33
45-54	1.03	.72	.21	.33	.90	.59	.21	.28
55-64	.96	.84	.13	.40	1.01	.64	.14	.25

SUMMARY

The results in Tables 1 and 2 may appear somewhat paradoxical. Table 1 shows that white female returns to education have approached those for males; however, the *ADC*s in Table 2 suggest that a very high earnings differential exists within given age-education cells. The procedure involved in estimating the rate of return to education solves for the rate of discount that equates expected future earnings due to education with the costs of obtaining that education. The major component of education costs is the income forgone by not entering the labor force at an earlier date. Because of the low-paying occupations open to females, the opportunity costs are very low and, therefore, the calculated internal rates of return are high.

Most studies of sex earnings differences argue that low female earnings result largely from the operation of a sex-segregated labor market that concentrates females in low-paying female-dominated occupations. . . . A review of 1970 census data suggests that occupational stratification [by sex] is severe for all levels of education, but it does appear that the range of available job opportunities widens with increased education. I classified as female-dominated those occupations in which females provided more than 50 percent of total employment. It was found that 81 percent of high school graduates, 76 percent of college graduates, and 65 percent of postcollege graduates were employed in female-dominated occupations. Fifty percent of all females with a high school diploma were employed in clerical occupations. Highly educated females were heavily concentrated in noncollege teaching, where 50 percent of college and 48 percent of postcollege educated females were employed.

Thus, in spite of the high internal rates of return to female educational spending, the income and occupational outlook for females does not appear to improve substantially as a result of increased educational attainment. The labor market appears to be slightly less sex-segregated for females with postcollege training, but the differences in occupational stratification [by sex] among educational classes are minor and all females, regardless of educational attainment, are faced by a great deal of market segregation. There is a large body of literature concerning the rationality and sources of market discrimination, and this question is beyond the scope of this article. What does seem clear from the results presented here is that returns to female education are sufficiently high to warrant continued educational investment. At the same time, however, it should be made clear that in most cases increased education will not promote parity with male earnings but instead will shift the employment opportunities of females from one sex-segregated set of occupations to another.

The Supply and Demand for Women Workers

Robert Gubbels

QUALIFICATIONS DEMANDED AND THE TYPES OF APPLICANT

It is no easy task to determine the qualifications demanded; the situation in these matters is always fluid, and varies both in time and space. The situation may differ from one country to another, for many reasons, ranging from the degree of technical development to social habits and prejudices. The qualifications demanded may also vary in time, since women workers occupy a very special place on the labor market. In most countries they are still largely marginal and constitute an "emergency reserve" to be called upon in periods of full employment or overemployment.

For the last ten years or so, as a result of full employment, the number of women workers has increased in most industrialized countries.

But if we started to head for a contraction in the volume of employment, if appreciable unemployment were to manifest itself, the employment of women workers would no doubt decline substantially. There are very few people who find it natural that "women should work while men are idle." This is true both of employers and workers and of the women themselves.

These reservations must be kept well in mind and it must be recognized that they underlie all discussion of the subject: an economic crisis would reopen the whole issue.

Excerpts from Robert Gubbels, "Characteristics of Supply and Demand for Women Workers on the Labour Market," *Employment of Women*, Regional Trade Union Seminar, Paris, 26–29 November, 1968 (Paris, France: Organization for Economic Cooperation and Development, 1970), pp. 99–111.

With this premise, it can be said that, for some years past, the main characteristics of demand have been the following:

An Increase in Volume. The demand for labor has been expanding almost permanently over the last ten years or so.

Thus, over the last decade (1951–1961) the proportion of women in the total work force has increased in all OECD countries, except France, Portugal, and Turkey.

One of the essential features in this trend is the increase in the number of married women going out to work. In the old days, the working woman was essentially a woman on her own, unmarried, widowed, divorced or separated. Nowadays, a constantly increasing number of married women are found in the working world. In the United States, for example, they account for about 60 percent of the female work force, and one-fifth of them have one or more children aged five or under.

Married women also form a majority of the female work force in Canada, France, the United Kingdom and Sweden.

Greater Insistence on Trade Skills. This is true of the whole work force, men as well as women. A job that was filled twenty years ago, without calling for trade certificates, would now be reserved for candidates who could prove a certain amount of theoretical knowledge. It is true to say that, except for pure laborers' jobs, the insistence on trade skills has increased very appreciably.

This trend is no doubt linked up with technical development and the perfection of production methods. This shift in the qualifications required of manpower in general has been less marked in the case of women, but it is nevertheless perceptible, and it is reflected in particular in the establishment of a certain number of training courses under the auspices either of the authorities, or of firms themselves.

Simultaneously, the implementation of an active manpower policy and full employment imply a fall in *unemployment through maladjustment* represented by the conjunction of unfilled manpower requirements of firms and a mass of workless without the required type or standard of skill.

Assuming that the industrialized countries experience no grave economic crisis, it can be expected that the reduction of unemployment through maladjustment will be the main social objective for the next few years.

It is along these lines that we must consider the fairly widespread idea that the future solution is a division of labor between men and women, the men specializing in the "blue-collar" jobs and the women in the "white-collar" jobs.

To some extent, this trend seems in line with the present position.

There are obviously far more men in industrial jobs in the strict sense, while women are mainly employed in the tertiary sector, in offices, shops and the like.

It is impossible to exaggerate the disadvantages and dangers of a solution of this kind, which would introduce a factor of rigidity into the labor market. Furthermore, technical evolution, and the long-term lightening of tasks that it entails, should throw open to constantly increasing numbers of women a certain number of industrial jobs from which they are at present virtually excluded. The objection will no doubt be raised against this view that the women themselves prefer "white-collar" jobs in the tertiary sector. But this is largely the result of the marginal position accorded to them in industry. We shall revert to this point in the second part of this paper.

It is clear that the lack of vocational training among women, which condemns most of them to unskilled jobs and confines them to a certain number of trades, is precisely a barrier to that interchangeability that is so desirable.

If women have always constituted a reserve on the labor market, the whole nature of that reserve has changed, since it is increasingly the result of a cleavage in vocational training; *women nowadays are no longer only economically marginal, they are also technically marginal.*

THE BARRIERS TO INTERCHANGEABILITY

If, therefore, total interchangeability is the ideal to be aimed at, it is in the interest, not only of the women themselves, but also of the economy in general. The aim is that the division of labor in society should no longer coincide with the division of the sexes.

We must therefore inquire into the barriers to this evolution. This will lead us to consider in turn a certain number of factors of different kinds that contribute to creating or maintaining the cleavage.

The Physical Barriers. The first objection that obviously leaps to the mind is the physical differences between men and women.

It is nevertheless important to make it clear that most of the studies undertaken in this field fail to show any essential difference between them from the point of view of work.

There are no grounds for attributing to either sex special aptitudes or characteristics that would make them a different economic unit. The only really unquestionable difference in aptitude relates to muscular strength.

Researches conducted by the International Labor Office indicate that the muscular strength of women is about 65 percent of that of men.

It must nevertheless be clearly recognized that, in industrial societies, muscular strength is becoming less and less important particularly because, in general, technical progress lightens the tasks and does away with the heavier jobs; the mechanical excavator has driven out the navvy.

A more serious obstacle is obviously the impediments arising from pregnancy and childbirth. And this means not only the stoppages of work involved—since men may also experience similar stoppages, for example for military reasons—but a certain number of counterindications in the case of pregnant women, such as vibrations, toxic fumes and the like.

Less essential, though still real, are the various arrangements, particularly sanitary, resulting from the segregation of the sexes. If a manufacturer, for example, introduces women into a factory previously occupied by men only, he will have to provide separate conveniences in the form of lavatories, showers, cloakrooms and the like, which may involve considerable expense and, in some cases, may be enough to deter the engagement of women.

The Legal Barriers. For many years past we have witnessed the elaboration of a whole body of legislation designed to protect women workers and safeguard them from some of the particularly harmful consequences of working life.

The practical effect of this legislation is to bar women from a certain number of jobs. Examples are the legislation on nightwork or the prohibition of underground employment of women in mines. In the same category may be ranged a certain number of special provisions, which vary widely from one country to another, governing the employment of women in certain jobs. The most typical case is the driving of lorries and heavy vehicles, which is subject to regulations that are extremely variable in different countries.

The justification for these various protective measures is a highly controversial issue that hinges on the meaning to be attached, in this context, to the word *progress;* is progressive legislation that which protects women and by so doing introduces discrimination or is true progress to be found in absolute and complete equality subject to the special reservations noted above in the matter of pregnancy and childbirth?

Whatever the answer, there seems little doubt that, in their day, the various protective enactments represented substantial progress.

Since then, however, it is clear that there has been an evolution and the line of approach for the future is now to strengthen protective measures for *all workers,* men and women alike. This will gradually make the special protection for women workers superfluous. It may be emphasized in this connection that Sweden, for example, has recently repealed its legislation prohibiting women from night work and underground work in the mines, and has replaced it with very strict regulations on these two types of work for all workers. It is, moreover, worth noting that, contrary to widespread opinion, the most troublesome shift is not the night shift but what is called the afternoon shift, which generally runs from about 2:00 P.M. to about 10:00 P.M. This is the most inconvenient shift because it rules out any possibility of social life and introduces the greatest upsets into family life.

But the objection will no doubt be raised that the prohibition of night work for women is also based on moral reasons and is designed to protect them against the "dangers" they may encounter both at work and on the way to and from work.

The Technical Barriers. A third category of barriers is connected with machine and tool design. Machines and tools are very generally designed and constructed to be handled by men and not by women. Many of the difficulties in transferring a job from a man to a woman arise out of this fact.

It is obviously difficult to put a woman behind a machine that has been designed to fit the size of a man's hand, a man's height, and so forth.

These difficulties are obviously overcome in theory. The fact nevertheless remains that, in practice, they often have serious consequences.

Cultural and Technical Barriers. Among the factors that militate against interchangeability, a large place must be allotted to all those connected with habit and prejudices. Habits and prejudices are all the harder to eradicate since they always purport to be based on reason and "experience."

Among these, pride of place must obviously be given to discrimination in the matter of vocational training. It is, for example, quite exceptional for parents to attach the same importance to the education of their daughters and of their sons. The girls are brought up and educated to be wives and housewives rather than for any professional occupation; even when they do follow a course of study, a great many of them are very naturally channelled to schools that offer quite negligible career possibilities, such as schools of dressmaking or domestic science and the like. Even when they go on to higher education, there is still a certain segregation; girls are, for example, extremely rare in the polytechnic faculties.

On the same plane may be placed the relative absence of social infrastructure that makes it so problematical for a mother to go out to work unless she has the benefit of quite exceptional circumstances (relations, neighbors, et cetera).

This lack of social infrastructure, in addition to the practical difficulties it involves, also has moral and psychological consequences; a mother who is obliged to go out to work will often have a feeling of guilt because she is not giving her children the care and attention they are entitled to expect from her.

All these factors frequently lead to the abandonment, or at least the interruption, of work outside the home if some mishap upsets the precarious arrangements made for looking after the children, or as soon as family circumstances make the woman's wages less vital.

It is clear that this risk will always make the employer hesitate. He knows that everything may be upset until the woman reaches middle age when the children become independent and she can at last experience a certain occupational stability.

The barriers to interchangeability resulting from what may be called "the image of woman" or the idea of "womanliness" can be placed on the same footing.

In our society, only too often, a man does not regard himself as a real man, unless he is doing "a man's job." A woman is only "a real woman" if she is doing "a woman's job." These ideas flow from a purely man-made traditional image of woman.

The same can be said of the traditions that reserve a certain number of jobs for women or exclude them from certain others.

Examples are very numerous. It is only relatively recently that women have been admitted to plead at the bar or deal on the stock exchange. Even today, a woman engineer is an exception. Similarly, certain jobs and certain trades are still closed to women. A woman crane-driver is unheard of and, with one outstanding exception, we know of no ship-building yard in which women are accepted. And yet, during the War, we found women doing these jobs from which they are excluded and, when all is said and done, they did no worse than their male counterparts. And, furthermore, the work in no way lessened their attraction. But once the War was over everything reverted to normal.

It may be noted, in passing, that in nearly all cases, these jobs that are deemed "unwomanly" are highly paid.

The prevailing conception continues to be that of the division of labor and of functions; the man is the breadwinner, the woman contributes "a little extra" that allows for some luxuries or tiding over temporary difficulties, and this pattern is made to fit all women, even those who live on their own and have no other resource except that "little extra."

The Sociological Barriers. A last category of barriers is connected with social habits and behavior. An example is the hostility of the male workers themselves, who will often be opposed to the transfer to women of jobs previously "reserved" for them.

To this must be added the fears or feeling of inferiority of the women themselves, who often acquiesce in this state of affairs.

Yet other factors come into play, and in a recent paper at the Sixty-second Congress of the American Sociological Association, sociologist Cynthia Epstein clearly demonstrated the extremely complicated mechanism that results in maintaining the existing cleavage. An instance is what she calls the "protégé system" under which top management is generally co-opted; a man will train his assistants, initiate them into his work and brief them, to such an extent that, if one day the question of his succession arises, whoever has the power of appointment is in practice left with very little latitude; the decision has been ready-made for them. But in practice, and for many reasons, a department head, for example, would hesitate to take on a woman as his direct assistant—in the first place because he can never be certain that she will not one day quit her job for family reasons, and secondly because working in such very close collaboration might raise psychological problems between a man and a woman, who may, moreover, each have his own marriage partner.

Family Obstacles. Among the factors of discrimination, mention must also be made of a certain instability that may arise out of family circumstances; in general, a woman is constrained to work in the same region as her husband. If he is transferred away, or has to move, she has to give up her job and look for another. This is an additional factor in arousing a certain apprehension among employers and creating a definite reluctance to take on women workers.

THE CLEAVAGE

This whole combination of factors leads in practice to a veritable cleavage. Women are restricted to a certain number of jobs and trades with common characteristics. It is perfectly possible to typify women's jobs and to define the work generally done by women as follows:

1. Women's work is unskilled or almost unskilled work, calling for:
   a) great resilience;
   b) manual dexterity, generally acquired in other trades.
2. Women's work is fragmented and purely operative.
3. Women's work is poorly paid.
4. Women's work involves no responsibilities.

It is important to emphasize at the outset that in practice manual dexterity is an element that is generally undervalued in all job-evaluation systems.

Muscular strength, in contrast, is always highly prized. The out-and-out application of the principle "equal pay for equal work" inevitably means a revision of trade classifications. But it must be borne well in mind that modern technical evolution is calculated to lessen the role of physical strength while dexterity and concentration are becoming more and more important. In this sense, it could be said that industrial work is tending to become more and more "women's work." It should also be emphasized that another reason for low pay is the exclusion, already referred to, of any work involving responsibility, either for material, or for the work of others. Thus, for example, in the clothing industry, traditionally a favored sector for women workers, with some exceptions, it is men who are cutters, thus assuming great responsibility for the material. The women are merely makers-up, "apprentices" or "improvers."

All this boils down to the fact that, in practice, segregation is the rule. The statistics, moreover, bear this out; in nearly every trade where they are represented, women are in the majority.

Some Concrete Cases. A certain evolution is, however, beginning to take shape. Investigation brings to light a certain number of transfers, which we shall first list and than analyze.

MOTOR REPAIR AND MAINTENANCE. Women service-station attendants have been fairly common for some years. What is less common, but is nevertheless found, is the employment of women for garage work proper, both the maintenance and repair of vehicles.

DRIVING BUSES, TAXIS, TRUCK-LIFTS AND TRAVELLING CRANES. Another sphere in which women workers are tending to take a considerable place is everything to do with vehicle driving. An example is the truck-lifts used to transport goods and supplies inside a factory. In several countries a fairly large number of women are beginning to be employed on this work. A similar case is that of travelling cranes; women operators are found, especially in Sweden and France. On the other hand, there are no women crane drivers proper.

ARC WELDING. This job was commonly done by women during the War, but the old practice was resumed after the War. A certain tendency can be noted to bring women back to this work, especially in Sweden, Japan and Canada.

WOMEN MACHINISTS IN GENERAL. The woman machinist is, of course, nothing new, but the evolution that is taking place relates mainly to the type of work done. So far, women machinists have done purely repetitive work, calling for nothing but simple manual dexterity.

Women are now sometimes found assigned to creative work, such as working to plans. There are, however, two limitations on this evolution; first of all, women are excluded from work that involves lifting heavy objects. Secondly, they are excluded from work on the machine itself; a woman machinist is only very rarely authorized, at any rate officially, to adjust and maintain her own machine. But this is often a decisive criterion in trade qualifications, as well as affecting wage rates.

WORKING TO PLAN.   Wiring, assembly, welding, molding, et cetera, have traditionally been women's work, but so far the work done has been purely repetitive work. Women are now sometimes entrusted with working to plans.

OPERATING AUTOMATED PROCESSES.   Examples are found of women controlling automated processes. In Sweden there is a chemical plant and an automatic rolling mill entirely operated by women.

POLICE, SURVEILLANCE, ET CETERA.   Women in posts of authority, marked for example by a uniform and, where appropriate, the use of weapons, have hitherto been limited to very special jobs, such as Customs searchers, vice squads, et cetera. The situation is tending to change in this respect and armed women surveillance officers, women detectives and women traffic police are becoming relatively numerous.

PROGRAMMERS.   The increasingly intensive use of electronics in the form of computers, ordinators, electronic brains, et cetera, has meant the creation of new jobs, among which women have carved themselves an appreciable place. This is not a question of punched card operators, whose work is similar to shorthand typing, but various jobs of a mathematical character involved in the operation of the equipment.

This is a very important development since these jobs are quite foreign to the conventional definition of women's work, especially in the matter of remuneration.

NEW JOB OPENINGS

The typology set out above, corresponding to the conventional characteristics of women's work, is therefore in the process of evolution. This evolution has, moreover, impressed public opinion, since it is manifest in everyday life in the form of women taxidrivers, tram drivers, policemen, and so forth. But the visible character of the evolution under way might induce an error of judgment as to its true scope and character. It is therefore important to emphasize that in practice this evolution has two aspects. There is, first of all, a transfer to women of traditionally masculine activities, or in other words, as the result of a certain number of factors, in the forefront of which we must place technical progress, there are jobs whose characteristics have changed and which have evolved so as to conform to the type outlined above. This case is relatively frequent. The most typical case is the job that used to be done by highly skilled workers but is considerably simplified by the introduction of new apparatus. It thereby loses its "masculine" characteristics and thus quite naturally becomes open to women. In other words, it becomes "a woman's job."

In this case, it can be said that the line of cleavage shifts but does not disappear.

A traditionally masculine job becomes a woman's job; this does not necessarily mean any fundamental evolution in the matter of cleavage. Nor can it be regarded as a feminine "conquest." In practice, nothing fundamental is changed by an evolution of this kind. Simultaneously, however, a much more profound, but also much slower, evolution is also taking place towards the disappearance of the cleavage or to use a word that is not yet in established usage, but is evocative, in the direction of *mixity*. In this case, and in this case only, we can talk of a fundamental evolution. It exists, but we must recognize quite clearly that it is infinitely less clear-cut and less decisive than might be imagined. One woman cosmonaut does not mean that the condition of women as a whole has evolved.

Nevertheless, tenuous as it is, this evolution unquestionably exists and we can see women doing totally new jobs that were formerly closed to them.

This evolution is the result of various factors, the first of which, already referred to, is technical progress, which normally lightens the task and thus breaks down the main physical barrier to the "mixity" of jobs. In any event, this phenomenon is well known, and there is no need to dwell on it further.

On the contrary, it would be much better to emphasize that what is believed to be a quite general rule, is nevertheless subject to a certain number of exceptions. It may happen that technical progress makes a job heavier. In the textile industry, for example, certain entirely new machines are fitted with reels that are so heavy that they cannot be handled by the women who traditionally did this work. As a result, jobs previously done by women have had to be transferred to men. Similarly, in general, the perfecting and improving of tools sometimes means an increase in their weight. An example recently noted is that of multiple head screwdrivers, which have become so heavy that most women workers have had to be replaced. No doubt all these are only exceptions, but it is as well to bear clearly in mind that the lightening of jobs by technical progress is no more than a general rule that may be subject to a certain number of exceptions.

Another factor that has contributed towards creating new job openings for women has been the labor shortage in recent years. This is obviously the decisive factor: the business chief who needs labor to meet his commitments to his customers will override tradition, prejudice, or any other similar consideration. The labor shortage has unquestionably been the driving force behind the evolution in countries where it has been particularly marked, such as Sweden and Japan. It is, moreover, significant to note the strange similarity in this respect between countries that are otherwise so different; not only are the jobs transferred substantially the same, but in addition, when business chiefs are questioned about their projects, the experiments contemplated are also largely similar. This convergence of evolution is obviously not merely due to hazard. It is partly the result of identical technical evolution (sometimes, even, the equipment is purely and simply standardized internationally). Account must also very probably be taken of contacts within the world of employers, exchange of experience, et cetera.

But another factor, of a more sociological character, has contributed towards the launching of interpenetration; outlooks are changing. Women, especially among the younger women, no longer find it quite natural that some jobs should be reserved for men. A minority among them are beginning to recognize their capabilities. Men, for their part, are slowly beginning to accept the evolution.

Furthermore, the well-known phenomenon of middle-aged women going back to work has also played its part. It is common knowledge that, for some years past, there has been a very marked tendency for women who have passed the age of childbearing to return to work. The presence of these middle-aged women on the labor market has a great many consequences, especially in our present context. In practice they have generally very little geographical mobility, their life is organized, their home well established, the husband in a steady job. For this reason, if they want work, they must adapt themselves to the local openings. Where appropriate, they will therefore be candidates even for jobs that are not "women's jobs," if only they are open.

Experience in fact shows that there is a substantial proportion of middle-aged women among the cases of transfer.

All the factors summarized above constitute what might be called the components of sociological determinism, or in other words, they will all take effect, in the absence of any external influence. They represent "the force of events."

If, as is probable, the rate of technical progress continues and if, at the same time, the rate of economic development is maintained (or in other words, if we succeed in staving off unemployment), it can be said that the evolution, which is still only in its first infancy, will gain momentum. But we must not burke the fact that this evolution will be slow, extremely slow. The question whether this slowness is acceptable and whether a gradual painless evolution is preferable to a rapid evolution, which by its very speed involves numerous upheavals, is essentially a question of policy. It is therefore outside the competence of the economist and the sociologist, who can do no more than formulate it, and analyze its components and its applications. But in the last analysis, the decision will depend on an option, and that option will depend on the overall view that is taken of society. We reiterate that this means that the problem is a political one.

This being said, it is clear that if a rapid evolution is desired, it would be illusory to rely purely and simply upon social and economic determinism. A rapid evolution calls for measures of compulsion such as those recently taken in the United States, where the Civil Rights Act prohibits outright any discrimination based on sex and forbids employers to exclude women from any job whatsoever.

Sex Bias and Cyclical Unemployment

Betty MacMorran Gray

... How does capitalism, unable to use an increasing quantity of women workers, systematically disuse women workers? Unemployment is awkward, especially when it spirals up against the background of the American dream. During busts, the numbers of unemployed rise to embarrassing highs. However, what might be called the "statistical-industrial complex" comes to the rescue of capitalism. Often it can obscure the awkward highs as effectively as a cloud can obscure the top of the Empire State Building. The statistical-industrial complex defines the labor force as being made up of people who are *at work, or eligible for and actively seeking work.* Consequently, it counts only those people as being either employed or unemployed. The logic is faultless, but the reality behind it—the reality of the definition itself—is awry. Economists estimate that the number of people who want jobs and don't have them at any given time is considerably higher than the official reports—how much higher depends on which economist you read.

Who are the workers who don't make the official reports—the hidden unemployed? In the main, they are the woman (sometimes called "married," sometimes "adult"), the teenager, the old man and the old woman —almost a group, a rather touching one, from a Faulkner novel. It is easy for the statistical-industrial complex to count them, *at will,* as either in or out of the labor force. It is easy to hide them, for they come from and go to some place—presumably, the home, the school, retirement.

Excerpted from Betty MacMorran Gray, "Economics of Sex Bias," *The Nation,* June 14, 1971, pp. 742–744. Reprinted by permission of the publisher.

It is difficult to hide white adult males and increasingly difficult to hide black adult males. Either they are working or they are hanging around, visibly and embarrassingly. During booms, the woman, the teenager, the old man and the old woman can be counted in; they are dubbed "Madam" and "Sir," the "emergency labor force," the "secondary labor force," the "peripheral labor force." During busts, they can be counted out. When they are counted out, not only are they not being used in increasing numbers but they are being systematically *disused:* the counting out compensates in large part for a major defect in the system of capitalism—for its cyclical fluctuations which lead to cyclical unemployment.

How do we know that, during a bust, the woman, the teenager, the old man and the old woman don't go back, happily, to cooking the chicken in the pot, to the Bunsen burners and the playing fields, to Florida? How do we know that their numbers are significant? We don't know about them all, but we have many clues about many. Here are three, from diverse years and sources.

1. In 1944 and 1945, as the full employment years of World War II were coming to an end; the Women's Bureau surveyed 13,000 women who were employed in war-production areas and who represented all occupations, except domestic service. The bureau found that more than half of the women who had been housewives at the time of Pearl Harbor, and three-quarters of the girls who had been students, wanted to stay, after the war, on the job or on another job; wanted to stay within the labor force.

In 1947, however, J. Frederic Dewhurst, explained in the Twentieth Century Fund's semiofficial, indeed semibiblical, *America's Needs and Resources,* that "Reemployment of returning servicemen and of workers laid off by munitions industries has been facilitated by the withdrawal of emergency war workers from the labor market." Indeed, 6 million of the 7 million members of the emergency labor force—which, according to Dewhurst, was made up of married women, young people of from fourteen to nineteen, and superannuated-retired-marginal workers—"withdrew" within a year after the war's end.

2. In 1955, the Bureau of the Census experimented with a new definition of unemployment. The bureau believed that the new definition might prove more objective than the existing one and more in accord with the actual labor force behavior of jobless people; that it might include, in addition to those actively seeking work, the inactive (people who wanted work, but who judged there was no point in trying—at Macy's, at the machine shops).

The bureau turned up one million inactive unemployed. And the bureau stated, "Most of the additional persons who would be classified as unemployed under the proposed new definition were *teenagers and adult women.* (Emphasis added.) If those million had been added to 1955s officially unemployed, they would have raised the total by one-third. The statistical-industrial complex failed to adopt the new definition; it is still using the old one.

3. The woman, the teenager, the old man and the old woman, according to multitudinous reports, are forever "withdrawing from," "leaving" or "dropping out of " the labor force—at moments convenient for capitalism. A random example: "Last month's improvement [in unemployment] was due to a drop in unemployed women, presumably because they had left the labor force," wrote *The New York Times* on December 2, 1962. Another: "49,000 people, many of them students and housewives, dropped out of the work force [of Massachusetts] after the Christmas holidays," *The Boston Globe* reported almost a decade later, on February 25, 1971.

In such observations, the woman, the teenager, the old man and the old woman sound, in their labor-force behavior, as obliging as Fielding's Sophia who "took the first Opportunity of withdrawing with the Ladies," as content as baseball fans leaving a doubleheader, as ready as pears to drop out of a tree. It is likely, however, that the terminology of the statistical-industrial complex is as slippery as that of the Pentagon; that, for instance, "withdrawing" resembles "Vietnamization." A general comment (in a "Crisis of Confidence" editorial): "The Bureau of Labor Statistics is suddenly stopped from explaining its data when such an analysis might remind the American public that all is not well with the economy," from *The New York Times* of April 13, 1971.

The Disadvantaged Status of Black Women

Elizabeth M. Almquist

Racism and sexism pervade American culture, creating an unusually disadvantaged status for black women. With notable exceptions, discussions of the unique status of black women are almost totally absent from standard social science literature. This implies either (1) that black women are unworthy objects of social science interest, or (2) that we have assumed that the topic is logically exhausted by examining sex differences/sexism and race differences/racism.... I shall be concerned to stress the sexual one, but this does not mean that I will ignore the importance of racism. Indeed I will raise fresh evidence of racism in American society, because the major thrust of this paper is to inquire about what types of data are necessary to test the race versus sex question and to examine such data as are available on the issue. It is possible that the interaction of race and sex produces further disadvantages than those that accrue from the sum of the variables taken individually. If interaction effects are strong, then black women appear as a unique group whose interests are solely allied with neither black men nor white women.... [Some] argue that blacks form a caste in American society, that black women in the labor force are disadvantaged because of their race, and that the feminist movement appeals largely to white housewives. Each of [these] claims needs to be clarified if not rejected. In the process of posing the race versus sex question, I shall be concerned to stress that the system of male-female

Excerpted from Elizabeth M. Almquist, "Untangling the Effects of Race and Sex: The Disadvantaged Status of Black Women." *Social Science Quarterly* 56(June 1975):127–142 (Austin: University of Texas Press), by permission of the author and publisher. Copyright © 1975 by the Southwestern Social Science Association.

relations in the United States also constitutes a caste system, that black women in the labor force are more disadvantaged because of their sex than because of their race, and that the women's liberation movement has a very wide appeal, engendering much support from black women as well as white.

WOMEN AS A CASTE

A caste system is a "hierarchy of endogamous divisions in which membership is hereditary and permanent." These divisions, called jati, are unequal in prestige and status; in fact, Heller (1969) sees the prestige differential as the predominant factor of inequality from which all other inequality tends to flow. Furthermore, the units are closed, mobility is ideally prohibited, and the system relies nearly exclusively on ascription for recruiting members. Each jati possesses a fairly well-developed subculture that includes elaborate rituals and specialized beliefs. Members of different castes are enjoined from engaging in commensuality, including communal eating. This restriction on free intermingling reaches its apex in the ban on intermarriage.

In all these respects, the system of black-white relations in America fits, more or less closely, the concept of caste. But so does the system of male-female relations. Men and women are born into separate groups. Membership is permanent for all, with the possible exception of those who undergo complex surgical procedures. . . .

The best argument against the existence of a male-female caste system is the fact that men and women do intermingle freely—they do in fact dine together and marry one another. . . . In America, marriage is clearly an institution where the two spouses are unequal. A few instances to the contrary, women are incapable of conferring their general social status on the men they marry; in fact, quite the opposite occurs. Within the marriage, men maintain a degree of informal power over the wife even when she has considerable educational and occupational accomplishments. . . .

While nothing in the law requires it, women have almost universally been given the custody of children when a marriage is dissolved. They assume the day-to-day responsibility for the children and frequently the financial burden as well. . . . The low frequency of awarding alimony holds despite the fact that lawyers are trained to attempt to disguise child support as alimony because women pay the taxes on alimony while men pay income taxes on money designated for child support.

When marriages continue unbroken, women do not exercise an effective claim on their husbands for support. . . . Wifebeating may not be specifically illegal in many states. Simultaneously, the wife is compelled by law to submit to the sexual advances of her husband. Moreover when a woman is killed or maimed in an accident, the husband may sue the perpetrator of the accident for loss of consortium; wives do not often have a similar right.

Other aspects of the law emphasize the inequality between husband and wife. A married woman's domicile automatically is that of her husband. If he moves to a separate domicile or deserts her, "this can affect her rights to vote, to run for public office, to serve on juries, or to have her estate properly administered." A number of states have laws that restrict a married woman's rights to make contracts, to engage in an independent business without court approval, to sign for a loan, or dispose of her property without her husband's consent. Only nine states have community property laws; in the remainder, the wife is financially at the husband's mercy, since all money earned by the husband belongs to him.

The argument presented in this paper thus far is as follows. One might believe that males and females belong to the same caste because they intermarry. Bans on intermarriage signify membership in unequal castes. By the same logic, two Brahmin men could not be members of the same caste because they cannot marry each other. In my view, the right to intermarry is not the *sine qua non* of caste equality. . . . It is true that some members of the female caste in America enjoy a certain amount of access to the privileges and prerogatives held by some members of the male caste. However, the actual marital situation joins two unequal individuals, the male member of the married pair generally wields the greater amount of power in the interpersonal relationship, and family law institutionalizes [this] inequality. . . .

WOMEN AS AN UNEQUAL POWER GROUP

Now the argument needs to be extended further. Contrary to what Heller argued, ritual purity and prestige are not the central components of caste. Power is the predominant factor of inequality in all caste systems. . . .

As a caste, women enjoy less political and economic power than the male caste. If intermarriage with the members of the male caste does produce, in some cases, monetary and status advantages, these are hardly translatable into tangible benefits outside the family and the arena of consumption. . . . Women do not control a major share of the nation's wealth. . . . Nor do women exert much control in the church, the world of work, or in the peace-keeping forces. . . .

When women enter the labor force, they are largely directed and supervised by men. . . . Finally, a brief glance at the legislative branches of government shows that only 3 percent of U.S. representatives are women and none is a senator. Women comprise only 8 percent of the 7,438 state legislators.

A MODEL FOR ASSESSING THE EFFECTS OF RACE AND SEX

For every disadvantage that women have, a similar example could be found for blacks. To forestall a flurry of charges and countercharges, what obviously is needed is a method of identifying disadvantaged conditions of black women and for sorting out "pure" sexual causes from "pure" racial causes. . . .

The method used here has most of these virtues, but it may sacrifice the analysis of interaction effects for the sake of simplicity. It was originally devised to identify racial and sexual components in black women's lower earnings, but it applies to other types of data equally well. For each characteristic or situation chosen (unemployment rate, earnings, representation in Congress), a score, index, or rate is computed for each of the four race-sex groups—white males, black males, white females, and black females. Ordinarily it is calculated so that high scores (for example, mean earnings) represent an advantaged status and low scores represent a disadvantaged status. Then four comparisons are drawn:

1. Black males are compared to white males
2. Black females are compared to white females
3. White females are compared to white males
4. Black females are compared to black males

Differences observed in the first two comparisons are due to race differences and/or racism. Differences observed in the third and fourth comparisons are due to sex differences and/or sexism. Then one may simply determine whether the two figures for racial differences exceed the two figures for sexual differences, or whether in fact the sexual disparities outweigh the racial disparities.

In most of the situations selected, white males enjoy the most advantaged position, black females have the least, and black males and white females are arrayed in between. A fifth comparison can be drawn— black females can be compared to white males. If black females differ from white males more than the combination of the differences between white males and black males (racial gap) and between white males and white females (sexual gap), then we may assume that there is an interaction effect, that the handicaps of race and sex together produce further disadvantages than the simple additive effects of race and sex. This last assumption may prove too crude empirically, but it does give something of a check on interaction effects.

In spite of the fact that a high score does not connote an advantage, the analysis of unemployment rates illustrates the use of the method. From Table 1 it can readily be seen that the two race differentials exceed the two sex differentials. Thus in spite of the fact that women have an inflated unemployment rate because they enter, leave, and re-enter the labor force more frequently than men, it appears that race is a greater determinant of unemployment rates than sex is. In addition, the difference between black females and white males equals 5.3 points. This exceeds the combined differences between white males and females (1.4) and between white males and black males (2.8) by 1.1 points, suggesting that there is an interaction effect for black women. Their high rates of unemployment cannot be explained by simply adding the separate effects of race and sex.

TABLE 1. UNEMPLOYMENT RATES BY RACE AND SEX

	Sex		Sex Differentials
	Male	Female	
Race			
White	2.9	4.3	—1.4
Black	5.7	8.2	—2.5
Race differentials	—2.8	—3.9	

Source: "Employment and Unemployment in 1973," Special Labor Force Report 163, U.S. Department of Labor: Bureau of Labor Statistics, 1974.

THE MODEL APPLIED: EMPLOYMENT PATTERNS AND EARNINGS

The four race-sex groups differ markedly in their patterns of distribution among the many occupations that compose the current labor force (see Table 2). The Index of Dissimilarity can be computed as an indicator of the extent to which the labor force is segregated by race and sex. When any two groups are compared by means of the Index, the result represents the percentage of one group that would have to change jobs to have the same occupational distribution as the other group. When the Index was computed, the following results were obtained.

1. Black males—White males 35.3
2. Black females—White females 29.3
3. White females—White males 39.3
4. Black females—Black males 40.3

There are several noteworthy aspects of these results. First, they seriously underestimate the extent of racial and sexual segregation because

TABLE 2. OCCUPATIONAL DISTRIBUTIONS OF THE FOUR RACE-SEX GROUPS 1970

Occupation	White Males	Black Males	White Females	Black Females
Professional, technical	14.2	5.2	15.3	10.3
Managers and administrators	11.4	2.7	3.8	1.3
Sales workers	7.3	1.8	7.5	2.2
Clerical	7.2	7.2	34.8	18.4
Craftsmen, foremen	20.4	13.2	1.8	1.3
Operatives, except transport	12.3	17.2	12.5	14.2
Transport equipment operatives	5.2	8.8	0.4	0.4
Laborers, except farm	5.4	13.6	0.9	1.3
Farmers and farm managers	2.9	0.7	0.2	0.1
Farm laborers and foremen	1.5	3.1	0.4	0.8
Service workers, except private household	6.9	13.8	14.2	22.5
Private household workers	0.1	0.4	2.1	15.3
Occupation not reported	5.3	12.3	6.1	11.9
Total	100.1	100.0	100.0	100.0
Total N (in thousands)	(43,501)	(4,091)	(25,471)	(3,329)

Source: U.S. Bureau of Census, Census of Population, 1970: General Economic Characteristics. Final Report PC(1) United States Summary (Washington, D.C.: U.S. Government Printing Office, 1972).

only the twelve major occupational categories were used. Gross (1971) has shown that the Index of Dissimilarity, calculated for males and females, using detailed occupational categories, has hovered around 65 and 70 for each of the decades between 1900 and 1960. In his view, to the extent that any integration has been accomplished, this is occasioned more by males entering female fields than by women penetrating the male-dominated occupations.

In the current results, differences among the various Indexes are not large; nonetheless, a distinctive pattern emerges. The gaps between groups paired on the basis of sex are larger than those between the groups compared on the basis of race. Hence sexual segregation exceeds racial segregation. Black females are less perfectly integrated with black males than they are with white females; in fact, the lowest Index is between white and black females. Taken together with the evidence presented in Table 2, this suggests that black women share a great deal of labor force experience with white women.

Black women altered their occupational distribution considerably between 1960 and 1970. The Index of Dissimilarity between black women for these two decades was 22.8, suggesting that nearly one-fourth of black women were in different fields in 1970 than they were in 1960. Their movement has largely been away from domestic work and into the secretarial and clerical fields and to some extent into the professions. Hence black women are more closely integrated with white women in 1970 than they were in 1960. To the extent that black men changed their labor force distribution over the decade, they entered fields long held by white men. Whites changed their occupational distributions very little. As a result, the labor force is less race-segregated in 1970 than it was in 1960, but it is essentially no less segregated by sex.

Several differences between the occupational patterns of black males and females merit special attention. Moynihan (1967), Bernard (1975: 241), and Bock (1971) have all claimed that black women have an easier time finding work and that they enjoy a certain "unnatural superiority" over black men. Besides the fact that they have failed to take account of black women's unemployment rates, they have mostly based their claims on black women's heavier concentration in the professions. Among blacks, 11.30 percent of the females but only 5.86 percent of the males were professional, technical, and kindred workers. So it is true that, proportionately, nearly twice as many black women as black men are professionals. And the female-male differential is much larger for blacks than for whites. However, the ranks of the black female professionals are swelled by a large number of nurses and teachers. Eliminating nurses, dieticians and therapists, and teachers (other than college) reduces female professional workers from 11.30 percent of the black female labor force to only 3.99 percent. Eliminating the same occupations for black males only reduces the percentage of professional workers from 5.86 percent to 4.43 percent of the black male labor force. Were it not for these two occupations, which rank in the lower middle section of the professions [in terms of status], black males would actually have a slight lead over black females in the professions.

Moreover, males and females are unevenly distributed among professional jobs, with black males being overrepresented in the high-status and high-paying fields and females being overrepresented among the low-prestige and low-paying fields. Women are 61 percent of the total black professionals, yet they are only 9 percent of the architects, 5 percent of the engineers, 15 percent of the judges, 13 percent of the lawyers, 16 percent of the physicians and dentists, and 23 percent of the life and physical scientists. On the other hand, women are 85 percent of the black librarians, 95 percent of the nurses and 77 percent of the noncollege teachers. These distributional differences hold despite the fact that black professional women have attained higher educational levels than black professional men.

A major indicator of black women's disadvantaged status is their earnings. Table 3 shows that white women earned less than black men, and while the sex differentials generally exceed the race differentials, the results are not totally unambiguous. However, when the various groups are standardized to one another on the separate variables of age, education, occupation, and region of the country, the results support the hypothesis that sex-based gaps in income exceed race-based gaps

| | Sex | | |
	Male	Female	Sex Differentials
Race			
White	$10,458	$5,280	$5,178
Black	6,404	4,077	2,327
Race Differentials	4,054	1,203	

Source: U.S. Bureau of the Census, *Census of Population: 1970, Subject Reports, Earnings by Occupation and Education,* Final Report PC (2)—88. Data are for year-round workers only.

in income. The differences in earnings that remain after standardizing are as follows:

1. Black males standardized to white males $1,772
2. Black females standardized to white females . . . .$ 0
3. White females standardized to white males $4,570
4. Black females standardized to black males $2,501

In these results, the racial disparities in income were lowered considerably after subtracting the compositional effects of occupation, education, and region, but the sexual disparities in income remained quite wide. In fact, these findings suggest that if black women had the same occupational, educational, and regional distributions as white females, they would be earning the same amount of money. Clearly racial discrimination is still present, since black men would earn $1,772 less than white men even if they had the same distributions as white men. If the differences that remain after standardization provide some sort of index of discrimination, then sexual discrimination exceeds racial discrimination.

These findings comport well with the results Suter and Miller (1973) obtained. Using a complex regression analysis and controlling on several variables, they concluded that women are simply unable to convert their educational and occupational attainments into earnings at the same high rates men do. Similarly, Sawhill (1973) found that differences in education, occupation, industry, unionism, age, and other variables explained 52 percent of the income gap between blacks and whites but only 17 percent of the much larger gap between women and men. The remaining income discrepancy between women and men was quite large and was mainly attributable to wage discrimination.

THE WOMEN'S MOVEMENT: WHAT'S IN IT FOR BLACKS?

If [race is more important than sex], we would expect black and white women to differ considerably on several key issues, and for black women to show little interest in or support for the new feminist movement. Several pieces of evidence contradict these ideas. First, national surveys show that black and white women would support a woman for president in equal numbers, while black women are somewhat less favorably disposed to abortion rights than are white women. . . . Second, black and white women have joined forces in the National Welfare Rights Organization to fight together for decent treatment for ADC families. Third, evidence from another national survey reveals that women from all educational levels, all ages, social class backgrounds, and labor force statuses support the new feminist movement in equal proportions. Fifty-eight percent of black women, but only 42 percent of white women reported that they felt "warm" toward the women's movement. Black women have forged two national organizations of their own—the National Black Feminist Organization and Black Women Organized for Action. . . . The feminist movement has [wide] concerns. It is committed to rooting out sexism—the policies, practices, and procedures that discriminate against women—*whoever practices them.* Feminists are seeking protection against rape, control over reproduction, and passage of the Equal Rights Amendment. Their search for quality day care, for equal pay, for fair employment practices, for impartiality in the granting of credit, and for the recognition of the value and dignity of housework, will ultimately redound to the benefit of all women, white or black.

CONCLUSION

. . . Women's caste status is very apparent in their low status in the labor force, in their lack of representation in the various branches of government, and in their relatively powerless situation in the nuclear family. Even when they enter male-dominated occupations, their sexual status is highlighted and emphasized. They do not pass readily into the dominant caste.

The statistical survey of the labor force reveals that black women are disadvantaged in three important ways: their unemployment rates are extremely high, they have difficulty in obtaining high-level jobs, and they experience a great deal of wage discrimination (unequal pay for equal work). In the case of unemployment, race, and the interaction of race and sex produce the disadvantaged condition. In employment and earnings, the sexual handicaps and sex discrimination surpass racial discrimination. . . . Juxtaposing the labor force status of black women with that of black men clearly yields evidence of sex-based handicapping as well. Black women's patterns of participating in the labor force resemble those of white women more than any other group. And when the appropriate contrasts are drawn, there is considerable evidence which points to the prevalence of sex discrimination over race discrimination.

REFERENCES

Bernard, Shirley.
   1975   "Women's economic status: Some cliches and some facts." In Jo Freeman (ed.), Women: a Feminist Perspective. Palo Alto, Calif.: Mayfield Publishing.
Berreman, Gerald D.
   1960   "Caste in India and the United States." American Journal of Sociology 66(September):120–127.
Bock, E. Wilbur.
   1971   "Farmer's daughter effect: The case of Negro female professionals." Pp. 599–611 in Athena Theodore (ed.), The Professional Woman. Cambridge, Mass.: Schenkman.
Gross, Edward.
   1971   "Plus ca change . . . ? The sexual structure of occupations over time." Pp. 39–51 in Athena Theodore (ed.), The Professional Woman. Cambridge, Mass.: Schenkman.
Heller, Celia S. (ed.).
   1969   Structured Social Inequality. New York: Macmillan.
Jackson, Larry R.
   1970   "Welfare mothers and black liberation." The Black Scholar 1(April):31–37.
Moynihan, Daniel P.
   1967   "The Negro family: The case for national action." Pp. 39–124 in Lee Rainwater and William L. Yancey (eds.), The Moynihan Report and the Politics of Controversy. Cambridge, Mass.: M.I.T. Press.
Sawhill, Isabel V.
   1973   "The economics of discrimination against women: Some new findings." Journal of Human Resources 8(March):383–396.
Suter, Larry E., and Herman P. Miller.
   1973   "Income differences between men and career women." American Journal of Sociology 78(January):962–974.

PART FOUR
Myths about Women

Myths hide the reality of everyday life. Myths are, however, not simply benign fairy tales in which the Princess kisses the frog to discover a handsome Prince, and everyone lives happily ever after. Most of our contemporary myths insure the opposite, that people live *unhappily* ever after.

Myths about Women

Introduction The Editors

Myths divert our attention from trying to understand the social world
and encourage us to accept a set of half-truths. This has grave consequences if the myths are taken as guides to everyday action and social
policy. Two articles in the preceeding part—on family life in an antifamily setting, and on lower-class black American matriarchy—suggest some of those consequences. People, believing that marital
happiness is a personal responsibility, unconnected with the organization of the society in which the family exists, try repeatedly (and often
unsuccessfully) to find personal fulfillment in the marital relationship.
Second, the probably mythical matriarchy in the black lower-class
family was actually a basis in the 1960s for the development of educational programs (costing millions of dollars) to prepare young blacks for
the competitive, work-centered American life, since black mothers presumably had failed to do so. (It could be argued easily that it would have
been more useful for the federal government to have devoted its resources to a full employment program or to raising minimum wages
instead.)

The many, and contradictory, contemporary myths about the American woman start from the premise that she has a better life than any
woman at any time or in any place. She is seen as lolling in front of the
television while her husband is hard at work. She is seen as controlling
the nation's wealth. She is seen as living parasitically on alimony and
child support, preferring her freedom to the hard demands of being a
housewife and mother. Contradictorily, she is seen as a parasite within
marriage, too, preferring to stay home where she is free to follow her

interests in needlework, tole painting, and bridge rather than seeking employment to supplement the family income. And, when she does work, it is supposedly to find "personal satisfaction, or perhaps, have an extramarital fling."

In the selections that follow, some of the common myths about women are contradicted. Each selection presents some empirical data that dispute assertions used to justify particular political and economic acts of discrimination against women, or to justify not developing programs to meet the needs of the contemporary American woman.

The Myth. *The United States is a country devoted to the preservation of the family. Women, after divorce, live a life of idleness maintained by alimony and child-support awards.*

Americans are proud of asserting that, in this nation, unlike in socialist societies, the family is the stronghold of society. Support for that assertion may come from the legal system, which is so protective of the privacy of the family that, as Weitzman notes in her selection in Part Three, the courts will not intervene usually in the marital relationship except when the couple legally separates or files for divorce. Furthermore, in vetoing the child-care bill, which would have made low-cost child care available to working mothers, President Nixon spoke of the dangers of "communalism" to the survival of the American family. Yet, the lack of commitment to the family shows quite clearly in U.S. social policy or, rather, in the absence of a social policy on the family and in the relatively little attention given to families in trouble.

Perhaps in the case of divorced mothers and their children (the topic of the selection by Ruth A. Brandwein, Carol A. Brown, and Elizabeth Maury Fox), the situation is made difficult because such families deviate from the conventional belief that a family must include husband, wife, and offspring. The favorable treatment of male-headed families, in contrast to female-headed families, shows the prejudice against *women* being divorced: male-headed families arouse the sympathy of society while, as Brandwein, Brown, and Fox point out, the divorced mother has little in the way of support services available to her. She must struggle along, economically, without much financial support from either the father of her children or society. What might society do? Low-cost, well-run child-care facilities; caretakers for the sick child of the working mother; food services; housecleaning, shopping, and household equipment repair services are just a few of the services that could be provided for the single parent. Establishing neighborhood centers from which such service-providing workers might visit local homes to help the single parent carry out the multiple responsibilities of mother, father, and labor force worker would contribute to making the assertion of our "family-centeredness" true. To this should be added services such as children's allowances, medical care for children, school scholarships, and other devices to insure that raising children would not be financially devastating to single-parent families.

The Myth. *Women do not work in the home.*

The second selection on the family surveys the literature on housework. Nona Glazer summarizes the findings on the work week of the employed and nonemployed housewife, a work week that has remained surprisingly long in view of the technology and conveniences that housewives supposedly enjoy. Housework has too readily been dismissed as trivial, as making no contribution to the well-being of society. An examination of the varied estimates of housewives' services contradicts this, however, and suggests that the work of housewives is intrinsic to the continuation of capitalism. Wives supply services that the private market is loath to provide. Incorporating such services into the marketplace is not likely to be the answer, however, because, at least in capitalist societies, such a move would turn all activities into market exchange relationships and possibly increase the economic neediness of poorer families.

The Myth. *Because women are less competent than men, they reduce the standards of quality in any field they enter.*

According to popular belief, women are not hired in high-status, high-paying fields (e.g., university teaching, corporate management, medicine) because they are less competent than men; if women are hired in these fields, performance standards will drop. The reason women are incapable of doing such high-prestige work, it is asserted, is because their family and home responsibilities require too much of their attention, making it impossible for them to concentrate enough time and energy on their careers. The article by Leigh Bienen, Alicia Ostriker, and J. C. Ostriker refutes this argument as it pertains to academic women. Their data show that women are at least as competent as men in similar positions and, therefore, that hiring and promoting women will not reduce standards of academic excellence. Bienen and colleagues also show that academic institutions do, in fact, discriminate against women in hiring, promotion, and pay. Instead of evaluating women on the basis of their qualifications, university administrators continue to simply assume that women are less productive than men.

The Myth: *Women control the wealth of the nation.*

Since the 1920s, many reports have circulated in magazines and newspapers to the effect that women are the major shareholders in some corporations or that women are often the main beneficiaries of large estates;[1] thus women must be in control of great wealth. This myth is

---

[1] Robin Barlow, H. E. Brazer, and J. Morgan, *Economic Behavior of the Affluent* (Washington, D.C.: Brookings Institution, 1966).

symbolized by giving the post of treasurer of the United States to a woman! Some recent studies show that women do not have quite the wealth attributed to them. Women retain less control over their wealth than do men because women tend to delegate management of their assets to others. A study by the New York Stock Exchange concluded that, although shareholders are evenly divided between men and women, much of the stock held by women was put in their names by their husbands in order to limit the husbands' liabilities and taxes and to avoid certain aspects of community property laws.[2] In the final reading, Robert Lampman presents other data to suggest that women are not as wealthy as popular belief makes them.

The Myth. *Men are the breadwinners of the family.*

A man is supposedly the family breadwinner, the sole person providing his family with the economic necessities. A woman supposedly works outside the home to earn extra money for the vacation to Hawaii, the new refrigerator, or Christmas presents. Little recognition is given to the important contribution the earnings of working women make to the economic well-being of their families. Contrary to popular belief, most women work to provide their families with a decent standard of living, their husband's income alone not being sufficient. In fact, a woman's earnings often make the difference between her family's living above or below the poverty level. Also, the myth of the male breadwinner ignores totally the increasing number of women who are the heads of families and provide the sole support for their families. The selection from the Women's Bureau discusses the contribution women's earnings makes to the level of family income by documenting the gains in family income when the wife works at a paid job.

---

[2]"Shareownership—1970: Census of Shareowners, New York Stock Exchange." New York: New York Stock Exchange, 1970.

The Social Situation of Divorced Mothers and Their Families

Ruth A. Brandwein
Carol A. Brown
Elizabeth M. Fox

In the United States today over 3.5 million families with children are headed by a single parent; over 85 percent of these parents are women (Census Bureau, 1970:402). While extensive literature exists concerning the absence of the father in female-headed families, little attention has been paid to the remaining parent, the mother.... We wish to focus primarily on the legally separated and divorced mothers, since unwed mothers and widowed mothers have somewhat specialized and more well-defined statuses. However, since studies often fail to differentiate among the types of female-headed families, we have reviewed a number of studies which included all types.

Related to the paucity of studies on mothers is the assumption throughout the literature that the female-headed single-parent family is deviant and pathological.... Such families are called "broken," "disorganized," or "disintegrated" ... rather than recognized as widespread, viable alternative family forms....

This is stigmatization—the labeling of these families as deviant and the assumption of negative effects on family members. Evidence of stigmatization and the effects of negative sanctions upon women single parents and their children will be an underlying theme of this paper.

Stigmatization is multifaceted. Stigma is ascribed to divorced and separated women for their presumed inability to keep their men. The societal myth of the gay divorcee out to seduce other women's husbands leads to social ostracism of the divorced woman and her family. There are expectations of neighbors, schools, and courts that children from broken homes will not be properly disciplined, will have sex role confusion, and will be more likely to get into trouble. The mothers themselves may incorporate society's attitudes, feeling insecure and guilt ridden regarding their childrearing abilities. They may seek solutions in attempting the "superwoman" role, or in fleeing to remarriage.

Further evidence of negative social attitudes towards these families is the virtual absence of social supports such as public provisions for day care and housekeeping services. The major exception, Aid to Families with Dependent Children (AFDC), provides only minimal financial assistance at the price of further stigma and loss of dignity.

This review will attempt to evaluate critically the scattered findings on divorced women as single parents and on the family units they head, and to re-examine effects of stigma on these families, as seen both in societal attitudes and in professional writings about female heads of families.... We will consider how family functions are fulfilled in the single parent family.

FAMILY FUNCTIONS

We will ... review ... research on changes in family organization and behavior which take place when the family structure and resources change. The four major areas of family functioning we will consider are (1) economic functions, (2) authority, (3) domestic responsibilities (child care and housework), and (4) social and psychological supports.

Economic Functions. Divorce and poverty are intimately related. The poorer a family is, the more likely the parents are to divorce....

Yet are divorced mothers poor only because they were poor *before* divorce, or does poverty also *follow from* divorce? Research indicates that poverty of the female-headed family may also result from divorce. Winston and Forsher (1971) report a study of divorced mothers receiving AFDC payments which shows that their ex-husbands' occupations, and apparently their ex-husbands' incomes, were not concentrated in low-income categories, but paralleled the occupational distribution of men as a whole.

In 1969 the median income of families with children headed by women aged 25 to 44 was $4,000 a year, compared to a median for all two-parent families of $11,600.... In 1969 the percent of all male-headed families who were poor was 6 percent for whites, 20 percent for nonwhites. Among female-headed families the rates were 32 percent for whites, 58 percent for nonwhites (Ferris, 1971). Looking at the other end of the income distribution, only 9 percent of female-headed families of all races had incomes over $10,000, while 55 percent of two-parent families had this or more.... The higher income of two-parent families results in part from the fact that both parents may be working. This economic strength of the two-parent family is denied both single mothers and single fathers.

... Kriesberg's (1970) study of mothers in poverty shows that "among the mothers who are husbandless due to separation or divorce ... whether or not they are poor is not related to their socioeconomic origins.... The economic fortunes of a husbandless mother are largely determined by contemporary circumstances." ...

Much of the downward economic mobility among divorced mothers can be viewed in terms of economic discrimination against women. A mother at every class and income level is expected to depend for the major part of her and her children's support on the income of her husband and economic opportunities for a woman without a husband are limited as a result. Women are given less job training, and are concentrated in low income, insecure occupations.... Even working wives have to depend on their husbands for the bulk of family income—the median proportion of family income contributed by the wife's earnings was 27 percent in 1970.... Thus the departure of the husband usually means the departure of the main financial contribution to the family....

SOLUTIONS TO ECONOMIC PROBLEMS.   The most common solution of the problem is for the mother to begin (or continue) working.... The labor force participation rates for women with *preschool* children in 1971 is as follows: married mothers, 30 percent; separated mothers, 41 percent; divorced mothers, 62 percent (Waldman & Gover, 1972). The rates for all married versus all divorced women were 41 and 70 percent respectively....

Women regardless of marital status do not earn the incomes men can earn. Median earnings of full-time, full-year employed women average 55 percent of men's earnings both for the labor force as a whole and within the same occupational categories.... The assumption that women do not or should not support a family provides justification for these low wages. Low wages in turn make it extremely difficult for most mothers alone to support a family....

Although legally men are required to support their children following divorce, and in some instances their wives as well, evidence shows that the majority of men do *not* continue to provide support. Goode (1948) ... showed that one-third of men are not even ordered to make payments, 40 percent who are ordered to pay never or rarely made the payments, and an additional 11 percent made them only irregularly. A more recent study showed that a majority of judges in a nationwide sample award less than 35 percent of husband's income to the wife and family. . . . A Wisconsin study in the late 1960s showed that "within one year after the divorce decree, only 38 percent of the fathers were in full compliance with the support order. . . . Forty-two percent of the fathers made no payment at all." . . . By the time four years had passed, 67 percent of fathers had ceased providing any money (Citizens' Advisory Council, 1972). The Uniform Desertion and Non-Support Act valid in most states allows a criminal complaint to be made against the father only if the family is "in destitute or necessitous circumstances." The courts are generally apathetic or opposed to taking legal action against men for nonsupport. . . .

Another institutionalized form of outside income available to divorced mothers, besides husbands' support payments, is public welfare. . . . In this case the state replaces the husband in regulating the wife's activities, her work, sexual behavior, etc. . . . Since welfare benefits are calculated to provide only minimum subsistance income, benefits do not raise families out of poverty. Average payments nationally in January 1973 were $168 a month or $2,016 a year for a mother and 2.5 children. The state with highest payments, New York, gave only $284 a month, or $3,408 for such a family.

SUMMARY. In sum, economic discrimination against women, and the reluctance of ex-husbands or outside agencies to aid mothers in supporting themselves and their children, often forces the families of divorced mothers to suffer severe economic hardship. Since women usually keep the children following divorce, the parent least able to support them is left with the major economic responsibility.

Authority. The social conditions to which women as a whole are subject affect the divorced mother and her family not only with respect to her economic resources, but also in terms of the authority and respect she commands.

Men are accorded the right to be "head of the household." . . . Mothers and children are expected to be under the protection of, and dependent upon, the man of the family. . . .

We have uncovered little empirical evidence to document the extent of discrimination against women as heads of families in their roles as gatekeeper and authority. However, there is evidence that women in general are taken less seriously and are respected less than men. . . .

Evidence is accumulating concerning financial discrimination that in effect denies "head of household" status to divorced mothers. . . . Credit granting institutions, in keeping with policies toward married women, will often refuse credit to a divorced woman, or grant it only in her ex-husband's name. Banks frequently deny mortgages or other loans to a divorced woman, sometimes insisting that the ex-husband or the woman's father sign for her and thus partially control her property. . . . Landlords may refuse to rent to families without adult males, with the result that a woman as head of household may have to pay more than a man for equivalent housing. . . .

We have not found any studies determining whether providers of services respond differentially to men and women. On the one hand, they may respond more quickly to women out of charitable motives; on the other hand, they may respond more slowly because they have less respect for women's demands.

We can conjecture that solo mothers, but not solo fathers or mothers with husbands, might have to deal with the attitudes and actions of men concerning sexual exploitation of a woman who "doesn't belong to anyone" and who therefore, in their minds, has no protection. . . .

The mother may also lack the training and ability for the role of authority, protector, and counselor for the children. . . . Certainly her competence is questioned by the larger society, Smith (1970) . . . found that juvenile authorities were less likely to remand children in their mother's custody than in their father's. . . . To the extent that social institutions *give* the woman less authority over her children, she *has* less. Smith . . . found that parents with little expertise or low perceived "legitimate right to exert influence" were listened to less by their children.

As a final point, the powerlessness of divorced mothers should be seen in proper perspective. Married mothers do not have that much power either. . . . There is evidence that many divorced mothers perceive the divorced state as an increase in power and independence. . . . Cavan (1964) found that remarriage rates were higher among lesser educated women, indicating that women may be pushed into remarriage by their inability to support themselves without it, rather than drawn in by its positive attractions.

Domestic Functions. Two major internal domestic tasks have to be performed—housekeeping and child care. American social structures tend to require that these be the full-time job of a wife, and that they be incompatible with earning a living for the family. . . .

The physical isolation of the nuclear family increases domestic work and child care for the mother, and decreases the opportunity for labor sharing. . . . Housing and land use patterns also restrict alternatives to nuclear family living arrangements. . . .

Housework and child care must be performed whether the single parent is a man or a woman. However, the same outside supports may not exist for both sexes. In Washington, D.C., the welfare department at one time provided free homemaker services to a single father, but permitted equal services to a single mother only if she were mentally incompetent, chronically ill, or physically disabled. . . . Additionally, a single father's income may permit him to buy services that a single mother cannot afford.

Helping women with the task of child care is not generally seen by policy makers as a valid reason for creating day care programs. Programs are usually justified in terms of developing the child's potential, removing the child from a poor home situation, or providing workers to industry. . . . Social institutions have traditionally made little effort to solve the problems of aiding women with child care. Instead, their policies have often had the effect of keeping women at home. . . .

The lack of child care options feeds back on economic deprivation. Without child care, the mother may not be able to work, thus eliminating an important source of family income; if the mother does work, her children may be inadequately cared for. If child care must be paid for, this expenditure further reduces an already decreased income. . . .

The amount of child care a divorced mother uses to permit social activities is not known. Marsden (1969) and Goode (1948) indicate that the women in their samples simply do not get out of the house for social activities as often as they had when married.

While pressures to maintain the mother in her isolated domestic role remain strong, alternatives can be found. Apartment houses with built-in services make neighborly sharing more convenient. Communes may be a counter trend to the isolation of nuclear family units. . . . Other types of informal organizations such as baby-sitting cooperatives and play groups may make up some of the gap. Furthermore, the isolation of the nuclear family has recently been discovered to be less total than was once assumed. . . . The doubling up of households sometimes found among divorced mothers may ease the strain also. . . .

However, limitations of housing continue to make extended cooperation difficult. Few apartments, for example, have space suitable for day care centers. The U.S. Office for Child Development refused to fund one such center in a proposed housing development for single parents, on the grounds that the mothers might become too dependent on such housing.

Emotional Supports. The function of emotional support is not as amenable to precise analysis as the other functions. The kinds of supports family members provide or need cannot easily be quantified. We can speak only generally about social factors that provide a favorable or unfavorable psychological climate for family living.

SOCIAL CLIMATE. Goode's seminal work (1948) found that the divorced woman has no clearly defined status. She and her family exist in a social limbo. . . .

Single-parent families headed by women are blamed for many social problems. . . . The women involved believe society sees them as abnormal and they themselves accept the label. The divorced mothers also believed that they might be inadequate parents. . . . Otto Pollak (1964) in a discussion of broken homes as a social problem explained the difference between unmarried and divorced mothers as the inability of the first to "get a man" and of the second to "keep her man." Writers have observed that the difference in payments to widows and to divorcees under programs for mother-headed families reflects the value policy-makers place on the relative worthiness of the mothers.

Both Goode (1948) and Marsden (1969) found that women they interviewed were ashamed of being divorced and denied that the divorce was their fault. Marsden (1969) also found an order of prestige among female heads of families, with widows considering themselves highest and unwed mothers lowest. . . .

INTERPERSONAL SUPPORT. On the positive side, the attitudes of friends and relatives, especially the mother's family, and the amount of personal support they offer is important. . . . Goode (1948) found that half of the divorcees studied kept their old friends and the remainder were on the whole satisfied with the new friends they made. Marsden (1969) found that for one-third of families studied the impact of father absence was softened by a relative, friend, lodger, neighbor, or boyfriend. Bernard (1964) found that none of his respondents were without some assistance from kin, however minimal. However, he also found that regardless of relative economic circumstances, women who seemed to handle their daily affairs "cheerfully and with humor" had a network of friends and relatives to draw upon. . . .

Formal institutions and agencies appear unwilling and unable to provide emotional supports. Weiss (1973) found that when low-income solo mothers turned to social service agencies, hospitals, churches, and guidance clinics, "they there found service to be accompanied by actions or comments injurious to their self-esteem, and support and guidance to be virtually unobtainable." . . .

The importance of positive emotional support from other people cannot be overemphasized when children are a 24-hour responsibility. As Glasser and Navarre (1964) have pointed out, children cannot provide emotional support—their love is demanding of the parent, rather than supportive. A great, and often overlooked, strength of the two-parent family is the presence of two *adult* members, each providing the other with aid in decision making, psychological support, replacement during illness or absence—someone to take over part of the burden. The solo parent not only has to fulfill all family functions, but has no relief from her or his burden. . . .

... Much more research is needed to carefully define exactly how parents in a two-parent family do provide emotional support and working relief to each other. However, the indirect evidence cited above suggests that the resources available to the mother for sharing the family responsibilities and the daily griefs and joys of family life with other adults (not necessarily the father) may be critical to the survival of the family unit.

SUMMARY AND CONCLUSIONS

Over 10 percent of families in the United States are headed by one parent. Nearly 90 percent of these single parents are women. While there are a number of categories of single-parent families with children under 18, the most prevalent and increasing is that of divorce and permanent separation. Divorce by couples with children is a rapidly increasing phenomenon.

With the growth of the women's liberation movement has come an increasing body of literature cataloging discrimination against women in employment, education and income, and describing the differential socialization of the sexes for, and access to, positions of leadership and competence. However, little of this research has been applied to the situation of women who have responsibility for heading a family.

Scattered in various disciplines we have found studies comparing socioeconomic status for married and divorced women, studies of the effects of father absence on children—particularly boy children, studies of roles with and without sex role stereotyping, and the effects of stress upon families. Yet we found little attention paid to the husbandless mother or to the female-headed family as an operating social system following divorce. Little or no attempt has been made in the social science literature to integrate these various pieces of knowledge into an understanding of how women cope in the single-parent situation, what effect various constraints have upon them and what variables determine women's abilities to overcome these constraints.

Over and over the literature assumes that the single-parent state is temporary. Although many women, especially those under 30, do remarry, a greater proportion, especially after the age of 30, remain divorced (Carter and Glick, 1970). Divorced men are more likely to remarry than are their ex-wives. Because of the assumption that divorcees will remarry, society does not feel obligated to provide supports for single parents. Because societal supports are largely unavailable, husbandless mothers come to view remarriage as the only viable alternative to a difficult situation. The situation will remain difficult as long as policies are based on these circular assumptions.

REFERENCES

Bernard, Sydney.
  1964 "Fatherless familes; their economic and social adjustment." Papers in Social Welfare Number 7. Waltham: Florence G. Heller Graduate School for Advanced Studies in Social Welfare, Brandeis University.

Carter, Hugh, and Paul C. Glick.
  1970 Marriage and Divorce: a Social and Economic Study. Cambridge:- Harvard University Press.

Cavan, Ruth S.
  1964 "Structural variations and mobility." Pp. 535–581 in Harold T. Christensen (ed.), Handbook of Marriage and the Family. Chicago:Rand McNally.

Census Bureau.
  1970 Census of the Population: General Social and Economic Characteristics. Washington, D.C. PC(1)-C1.

Citizens' Advisory Council on the Status of Women.
  1972 Memorandum: The Equal Rights Amendment and Alimony and Child Support Laws. Washington, D.C. (January).

Ferris, Abbott.
  1971 Indicators of Trends in the Status of American Women. New York- :Russell Sage Foundation.

Glasser, Paul, and Elizabeth Navarre.
  1964 "Structural problems of the one-parent family." Journal of Social Issues 21 (January):98–109.
  1965 "The problems of families in the AFDC program." Children 12 (July):151–157.

Goode, William J.
  1948 After Divorce. Glencoe Ill.:The Free Press.
  1963 World Revolution and Family Patterns. New York:The Free Press.

Kriesberg, Louis.
  1970 Mothers in Poverty. Chicago:Aldine.

Marsden, Dennis.
  1969 Mothers Alone: Poverty and the Fatherless Family. London:Allen Lane, The Penguin Press.

Pollak, Otto.
  1964 "The broken family," in Nathan E. Cohen (ed.), Social Work and Social Problems. New York:National Association of Social Workers.

Smith, Thomas.
  1970 "Foundations of parental influence upon adolescents: an application of social power theory." American Sociological Review 35 (October):860–873.

Waldman, W. E., and K. R. Gover.
  1971 "Children of women in the labor force." Monthly Labor Review 94(7):19–25.

1972   "Marital and family characteristics of the labor force." Monthly Labor Review 95 (April):4–8.

Weiss, Robert S.

1973   "Helping relationships: relationships of clients with physicians, social workers, priests and others." Social Problems 20 (Winter):319–328.

Winston, Marian P., and Trude Forsher.

1971   Nonsupport of Legitimate Children by Affluent Fathers as a Cause of Poverty and Welfare Dependence. Santa Monica:Rand Corporation.

Housework:
A Review
Essay
Nona Glazer

The invisibility of women in scholarship has drawn a good deal of commentary in recent years, but hardly anywhere has the sociological acumen failed as embarrassingly as in its inability to recognize women's work—housework—as work. In *The Sociology of Housework*, Ann Oakley (1975) summarizes the underlying sociological axioms that support the invisibility of women's work:

1. Women belong in the family, while men belong "at work."
2. Therefore, men work, while women do not work.
3. Therefore, housework is not a form of work.

I would add several complementary axioms to these:

4. Monetary and social rights belong to those who work—to those who are economically productive.
5. Women do not work but are parasitic.
6. Therefore, women are not entitled to the same social and economic rights as men.

Ignoring woman's work provides a rationale for her second-class status both inside and outside the home. Recent scholarship, compatible to varying degrees with a feminist concern, has begun to center on a discernible set of issues, each of which I shall consider.

Excerpted and revised from Nona Glazer-Malbin, "Housework." *Signs: Journal of Women in Culture and Society* 1(Summer 1976):905–934. Reprinted with permission of the University of Chicago Press.

HOUSEWORK AS THE DIVISION OF LABOR

Beginning in the mid-1950s with the Blood and Wolfe studies of the husband-wife relationship, sociologists have usually studied housework because of a concern with the possible relation between the wife's working outside the home and the marital division of labor. The main theoretical perspective that has been used to explain the division of labor—the wife's responsibility for "traditional" feminine tasks and the husband's responsibility for "traditional" masculine tasks—is an assumed rational imperative (based on the biological differences between the sexes). Hence, Blood and Wolfe (1960:48) write:

> To a considerable extent, the idea of shared work is incompatible with the most efficient division of labor. Much of the progress of our modern economy rests upon the increasing specialization of its division of labor.

The questionable theoretical framework is complemented by methodological difficulties of sampling, of the definitions of housework, and of measurement.

The findings of such studies are frequently interpreted as indicating a shift toward greater participation by husbands in household tasks over the last decades. This shift has occurred, it is said, in response to the wife's being in the labor force. However, other studies suggest that the shift has been greatly exaggerated, with the husbands of employed wives doing very little housework compared with that of their wives. Indeed, the husbands of employed wives do about the same amount of housework as the husbands of nonemployed wives.

THE MONETARY VALUE OF HOUSEWORK

Only the low status of women and the disparagement of housework can explain why economists have found it so difficult to calculate the contribution of housework to economic well-being. Although Marxian economists have a theoretical reason, neoclassical or institutional economists, for whom housework has economic utility, have no such justification for failing to estimate the monetary value of housework.

Economists finally began to calculate the estimated monetary value of housework because of male demands. A number of court suits over the loss of wives' services prompted American economists finally to overcome the so-called weighty problems of gathering data on the time women spend doing housework and to calculate the estimated monetary value of their work. (Of course these same economists had overlooked for nearly forty years the time-budget studies done in the 1920s.)

There are a variety of methods for estimating the monetary value of the work of the American housewife. Pyun (1969) combines two approaches: an opportunity approach, which uses estimates of the housewife's possible earnings in the labor force, given her educational attainment, and a market cost approach, which considers the cost of hiring her substitute(s). Consider a hypothetical white woman who dies at the age of forty-one. At the time of her death, she was the mother of three, a full-time homemaker, and the holder of a degree from an eastern liberal arts college. Pyun estimates that it would cost $82,640 to replace her services for the next eleven years, until the age when she would have completed her child-rearing responsibilities. Economists also use the market cost approach alone, and utilize varying wage bases for estimating replacement costs. Even if the housewife's value is based on low-paid, low-status occupations such as dishwasher, cook, or charwoman, her replacement value is higher ($4,705 for 1972) than if her work is considered simply the equivalent of a domestic worker ($3,935 for 1972). If higher status, better paid occupations—e.g., interior decorator, nursery school teacher, caterer—are considered to be the marketplace equivalents of her work, then her replacement cost can rise as high as $13,364 for 1973 (Galbraith, 1973:33).

The models used in the computation of costs (e.g., the cost of a woman's leaving the labor force to care for a child) have been criticized for being aggregate choice models. Galbraith considers an aggregate choice model of limited use since it avoids consideration of the impact of the individual choice by collapsing all family members into the category "household." In this model, the cost of a woman's foregoing employment to do housework is seen as affecting only her family rather than as having a potential effect on her, too. For example, her willingness to remain out of the labor force may lessen her future employability (for instance, a licensed nurse forfeits her right to practice in the State of Oregon after five years of not being employed.)

THE INEVITABILITY OF DOMESTICITY

The analysis of cross-cultural data is relevant to the question of whether or not women are inevitably domestic, responsible for housework as well as child care and excluded from power and authority. Beginning with the statements of Judith K. Brown (1970; 1973) about women and Sharlotte N. Williams (1971) about primates, anthropologists question increasingly the universal domestication theme. Peggy Sanday (1974:-192) contrasts women's roles and women's status in twelve quite different societies. In some of the societies women's status in the public domain is high, while in others it is low. Sanday's research points up the fact that there are societies in which women have attained high status in the public domain.

Ester Boserup (1970) has attacked the myth of inevitable domesticity by her examination of women's economic role in African societies. The power of African women was eroded by the presence of Europeans acting on the basis of their own cultural myths about "women's place," which excluded women from significant participation in and control of the political economy. Ernestine Friedl (1975) reviews the position of women in hunting and gathering societies and in horticultural societies. Friedl concludes that childbearing and child rearing are accommodated *to* women's role in the public economy (not vice versa), that it is not women's contribution to subsistence but her control over the products of her work that is crucial for her political and personal power.

There are two especially useful discussions of women's domesticity in industrial society: Martin and Voorhies (1975) examine women in a variety of technological levels of society; Oakley (1974) investigates women's status in industrial society. Both studies dispel the myth that since Adam and Eve women have been confined to the household except for minor aberrations. "Women's place is in the home" is a relatively new proscription, a by-product of the transfer of production for the market from the home to the factory.

HOUSEWORK AND SOCIAL ROLES: THE HOUSEWIFE

Helena Z. Lopata (1971) provides us with the first comprehensive study of American housewives as occupants of social roles. She treats seriously and at length the varied experiences of women in the city and suburbs around Chicago during a decade that began in the 1950s. Lopata studies housework as an aspect of the housewife role, which she examines over the life cycle, rather than as a static role. How women gain the necessary knowledge to be a homemaker; who assists the housewife with her jobs (family members as well as commercial workers); the frequency with which jobs involve interaction with others in the community; the division of labor in the marital relationship; women's perceptions about being a housewife and doing housework—these are among Lopata's topics. She suggests that the role of the housewife in the United States is similar to that of a lower-class European housewife: she is a drudge and a menial rather than, as in the European aristocratic style, a manager, a coordinator, a hostess of soirees, and a participant in the mainstream of the life of the society.

A somewhat contrasting view of the housewife and housework emerges from Ann Oakley's (1975) study of housework. As far as I know hers is the only full-fledged sociological study of housework and is a companion volume to her *Woman's Work*. The contrast between the creativity and innovativeness that characterize the women Lopata studies and the dissatisfaction with housework that Oakley found in the British sample is dependent on the distinction between doing *housework* and being a *housewife*. Oakley finds that women are dissatisfied with the first and yet satisfied with the second. Oakley limits her study, insofar as possible, to women's reactions to *housework* as work. She discovers the fragmentation, monotony, and isolation that women dislike about housework. She examines children's influences insofar as these interfere with doing housework, since the demands of being a good mother may contradict the demands of being a good housekeeper.

HOUSEWORK AND THE POLITICAL ECONOMY

An Institutional Analysis. John Kenneth Galbraith (1973) sees women as exploited, as, in his words, "crypto-servants." His interpretation of women's social position is an interesting departure from conventional economics because he is concerned with the *ease of consumption* rather than with the problem of choice among goods and services. The problem of choice in the neoclassical model assumes that consumption itself is problem-free, but Galbraith believes that rising standards of consumption are attractive only if the consumers themselves do not have to expend much time and energy preparing the goods for final consumption. Whether or not modern economies, rather than the special character of capitalism, have forced women into this menial role is open to argument; it is also open to future events. The only major attempts to relieve women of private responsibility for housework that have met with some success appear to be in situations of privation (e.g., the People's Republic of China, the early years of the kibbutzim movement) or in some of the short-lived communes that have sprung up in the United States. Most of the communes in the United States have been characterized by a division of labor by sex that assigns "inside" labor to women and "outside" labor (farmwork, construction, etc.) to men. An exception to this may be some of the contemporary secular communes whose members are committed to the ideology of sex equality and whose structure, according to Rosabeth Moss Kanter (1975), supports new conceptions of gender roles.

A Radical Analysis. Marxian analyses approach the question of women and housework by examining capitalism, an approach that led initially to the conclusion that women would cease to be oppressed with the advent of socialism. Given the dreary picture of the European socialist societies, where women have not been relieved of housework responsibilities, many Marxians now recognize that factors other than the organization of the economy need to be considered. Juliet Mitchell notes that four structures—socialization of children, reproduction, and sexuality as well as production—must be understood to grasp women's condition in modern society. Women "produce" children in the home "in a sad mimicry" of how their husbands produce commodities in their work outside the home, but Mitchell does not examine housework itself. Housework itself is considered in Margaret Benston's analysis.[1] She uses the concepts of "exchange-value" and "use-value" to explain how women's exclusion from commodity production (or her minimal participation through intermittent employment in low-paying jobs) and the continued private nature of housework are the bases of the housewife's inferior position.

Mariarosa Dalla Costa (1972) sees the condition of women's work in the home as isolating them from the experience of social labor, from contacts with other women doing the same work, and from knowledge about the world outside of family responsibilities. In addition, women benefit only partially from modern capitalism; for example, while we tend to see the modern kitchen as the best of modern technology (especially in the United States), it is not the best that is available given our technical sophistication. Dalla Costa sees women's housework as *productive* labor in that it reproduces labor. This includes, especially, bearing and rearing children but also involves helping men to prepare for another day of work. At the same time, the economic dependency of women (and children) locks men into wage labor. Seeing as she does the problems facing workers under capitalism (boring work, low wages, cyclical unemployment), Dalla Costa does not believe that entering the labor force will emancipate working-class women. Nor does she see paying housewives as likely to change women's status—on the contrary, it would freeze them into the home, into doing "woman's work."

Some Marxians, such as Wally Secombe (1974), object to describing the activities of housewives as *productive labor,* reserving this term for a particular aspect of the theory of capitalism. According to Marxian theory, *production* in capitalism means the creation of surplus value. The workers sell their labor power to the capitalist, who pays them a wage sufficient for survival but less than the value their labor has added to the product. In other words, the workers' labor is only partially

---

[1]See Part Two for articles by Juliet Mitchell and by Margaret Benston.

compensated for. The portion that is not compensated for is called *surplus value*. According to Marx, the capitalist's appropriation of this surplus value is *exploitation*. Using this analysis, it can be reasoned that the housewife is not exploited (another technical term) because her goods, although they have use-value, do not enter the commodity market but instead are consumed in the home. However, the housewife is oppressed. She is oppressed by her economic dependency on her husband, whose health and well-being as well as goodwill are crucial to her own well-being. She is oppressed by being isolated from other women like herself because of her home duties, by having to perform work that she and others see as trivial, and by being seen by herself and others as "parasitic" since her housework brings her no money.

Secombe objects to seeing housework as productive labor for several reasons. First, the housewife does not relate to either the means of production or the means of exchange, which she did in the precapitalist world. While labor in the home may add value (to the commodities being consumed), the value does not enter the marketplace because the housewife does not create *surplus* value. Thus, service that does not produce surplus value is not considered economically productive—which is the reason the Eastern European socialist countries exclude even the market costs of services from the GNP. I am not convinced that this is a reasonable view of work in the labor force—that services cannot be considered an equivalent of commodities—nor am I convinced that the direct control by the capitalist of a worker's time is somehow more real than the indirect control by the capitalist of the activity of women in the household. If the labor of the domestic worker is necessary for production and necessary for the reproduction of labor (i.e., for bearing and rearing children and for preparing men to work each day for wages), then the capitalist's criterion of a monetary value seems irrelevant.

Whether or not the radical analysts agree on the exact meaning of housework under capitalism, they agree that the housewife works for the maintenance of capitalism rather than simply being a worker for her family. This is important: if housework is seen as being for the family only, then we study the housewife and suggest research questions and social policy that focus on the husband-wife relationships, which is what has been done. The answer to the question, "Who must pay for housework?" is easy: "The husband!" Thus, it has been suggested by various critics of contemporary women's position that a wife is entitled to half of her husband's wages or, alternatively, that husbands pay wives for housework on some hourly or weekly basis. Husbands (and children) are seen as the beneficiaries of the domestic work of wives, a view that privatizes the family, turning each family into a small-scale production unit. This view supports the conventional division of labor between the sexes by implying that it is the husband who exploits his wife if he demands that she be responsible for housework (and fails to share work in the home with her to any substantial degree regardless of her status in the labor force). The wife's assuming responsibility for the housework is "in exchange" for the husband's assuming responsibility for the financial support of her and their children.

Many American sociologists do see the husband and wife as a complementary unit. The marital relationship is then examined using concepts such as balance and exchange. The division of labor *for* the marital couple becomes an issue of balancing the man's activities against the woman's activities, the man's interests against the woman's interests, and so on. If, in contrast, we conceptualize women's work as supporting capitalism (considering it either as labor or as "productive" labor), we pose a different set of questions about the family. Our analysis shifts from exploring the relationships between husband and wife, in the home, to asking how their relationships to institutions outside the home affect husband-wife relationships. We deprivatize the family in our research. As sociologists we appear to believe that the family is isolated from society, somewhat in the same way that ideology leads family members to see themselves as constructing a private world away from the turmoil of modern industrial-urban life. In the broadest sense, then, a Marxian analysis means developing a "sociology" of the family (relatively neglected for the past several decades) as a complement to the "social psychology" of the family.

CONSTRUCTING THEORY: HOUSEWORK AND A SOCIOLOGY FOR WOMEN

I want to end this review with a brief reference to Dorothy E. Smith's critique of a sociology *of* women, and her model for a sociology *for* women.[2] A sociology *for* women begins by inquiring into how the everyday world is experienced by women, as described by women, rather than attempting to squeeze women's experiences into preexisting rational-administrative models of the world. The subsequent steps involve connecting the everyday world, as seen by women, to the larger social context of the political economy. A sociology for women would connect the world that women experience as housewives (as well as wives and mothers) to the less immediately apprehended world that shapes their everyday experiences. We may then succeed in connecting personal troubles to public issues.

[2]See Part One for the article by Dorothy E. Smith.

Blood, Robert O., Jr., and Donald M. Wolfe.
1960   Husbands and Wives: The Dynamics of Married Living. New York: Free Press.

Boserup, Ester.
1970   Woman's Role in Economic Development. London: George Allen and Unwin.

Brown, Judith K.
1971   "A note on the division of labor by sex." American Anthropologist 73:805–806.
1973   "Leisure, busywork and housekeeping." Anthropos 68(5):881–888.

Dalla Costa, Mariarosa.
1972   "Women and the subversion of community." Radical America 6(January-February):67–102.

Friedl, Ernestine.
1975   Women and Men: An Anthropologist's View. New York: Holt, Rinehart and Winston.

Galbraith, John Kenneth.
1973   Economics and the Public Purpose. Boston: Houghton-Mifflin.

Gilman, Charlotte Perkins.
1972   The Home, Its Work and Influence. Urbana: University of Illinois Press. First published in 1903.

Lopata, Helena Z.
1971   Occupation: Housewife. New York: Oxford University Press.

Martin, M. Kay, and Barbara Voorhies.
1975   Female of the Species. New York: Columbia University Press.

Oakley, Ann.
1974   Woman's Work: A History of the Housewife. New York: Pantheon Books.
1975   The Sociology of Housework. New York: Pantheon Books.

Pyun, Chong Soo.
1969   "The monetary value of a housewife: An economic analysis for use in litigation." American Journal of Economics and Sociology 28(July):271–284. Reprinted in Nona Glazer-Malbin and Helen Y. Waehrer (eds.), Woman in a Man-Made World. First Edition. Chicago: Rand McNally, 1972.

Sanday, Peggy R.
1974   "Female status in the public domain," in Michelle Zimbalist Rosaldo and Louise Lamphere (eds.), Woman, Culture and Society. Stanford, Calif.: Stanford University Press.

Secombe, Wally.
1974   "The housewife and her labour under capitalism." New Left Review 83(January-February):3–24.

Vanek, Joann.
1974   "Time spent in housework." Scientific American 231(November):14, 116–120.

Williams, Sharlotte Neely.
1971 "The limitations of the male/female activity distinction among primates: An extension of Judith K. Brown's 'A note on the division of labor by sex.'" American Anthropologist 73:805–806.

Sex Discrimination in the Universities

Leigh Bienen
Alicia Ostriker
J. P. Ostriker

> "We shall be left with the blind, the lame, and the women."
>
> Nathan Pusey

BACKGROUND

It is an unpleasant fact that the basically decent, liberally-educated people who administer universities and colleges in the United States have, on a widespread and systematic basis, practiced discrimination against women in hiring, promoting, and to a lesser extent in setting salaries. In the five years from 1968 to 1973, despite all governmental and private group pressures, the fraction of faculty women has increased by *less than 1 percent,* although the number of women Ph.D.s produced only in the years 1960–70, who would have affected hiring from 1968–73, increased dramatically and was more than the total from all previous years since 1926.

Richard A. Lester's book, *Antibias Regulation of Universities: Faculty Problems and Their Solutions,*[1] ... ignores the weighty documentation amassed in recent years concerning discrimination at universities, and actually argues that the only real stumbling block is a deficient supply of qualified women academics. Moreover, he states that the problem of

---

Excerpts reprinted from Leigh Bienen, Alicia Ostriker, and J. P. Ostriker, "Sex Discrimination in the Universities: Faculty Problems and No Solution." *Women's Rights Law Reporter* 2(March 1975):3–12. Reprinted by permission.
[1](New York: McGraw-Hill, 1974); hereinafter cited as Lester.

rectifying discrimination should be left essentially in the hands of those who have been in charge in the past, and that compliance with antidiscriminatory government regulations will damage American universities and result in a lowering of standards.

Lester's argument has two principal threads. First, American colleges and universities are eager to hire, promote and pay appropriate salaries to qualified women if they can find them; this point is argued by assertion. Second, the supply or "pool" of women candidates for positions is relatively inferior in quality as well as in numbers to the pool of male candidates; this argued largely by innuendo. If these propositions were true, it would certainly follow that enforcement by government of increased hiring of women would reduce scholarly standards and erode the principle of academic liberty in American higher education. But in fact neither position is close to the truth. . . .

THE ACADEMIC MARKETPLACE

Much of Lester's argument rests on a rosy but idealized picture drawn of American academic life. . . . Decisions on hiring, promotion and pay are governed in Lester's version of the academic marketplace by an objective searching for scholarly excellence and productivity. . . .

Deans of faculty should know that even prestigious universities are not perfect meritocracies. Mediocre departments exist and tend to perpetuate themselves by hiring and promoting mediocre colleagues. Much hiring occurs through old-boy networks and through the tendency of departments to employ former students or candidates from the chairman's alma mater on the grounds that such candidates will be "effective colleagues." None of these problems is a secret; all relate directly to fair employment issues. Yet the author fails to mention that such considerations have been and continue to be important in decisions to hire or promote. . . .

The actual evidence of discrimination, much of which was presented in the hearings before the House Special Subcommittees on Education and Labor in June 1970,[2] is clear. The result has been that nationally women tend to be in the lower ranks of the lower-prestige institutions. Numerically they constitute 26 percent of two-year college faculties, 23 percent of four-year college faculties, and 15 percent of university faculties. The overall fraction of faculties that is female is 20 percent, not far from the appropriately weighted fraction of advanced degree holders. This indicates that most women who receive advanced degrees

[2]U.S. Congress, House, Subcommittee on Education of the Committee on Education and Labor, *Hearings on Section 805 of H.R. 16098.* 91st Cong., 2nd sess., pt. 1, June 1970.

do find some type of faculty job and that they remain in academic life. They do not drop out. But their comparative distribution by rank and type and institution presents striking differences. Women are heavily concentrated in the lower ranks. They are seven times more likely to be in the low ranking instructorships than in the full professorships (6 percent of the full professors at universities are women, as opposed to 42 percent of the instructors). And they have had twice or three times as much difficulty in entering the higher prestige and higher paying universities as the community two-year institutions. Given the essentially equal scholarly performance of men and women (see Table 2, infra), the gross inequalities in rank distribution highlight past discriminatory hiring practices.

Not surprisingly, recent studies show that income disparities between men and women faculty members are substantial; in 1968–69 the difference in their mean salaries amounted to approximately $2,400 or 20 percent.[3] Most of the discrepancy was attributable to differences in rank distribution, as shown by Table 1, and so is evidence of bias only insofar as discriminatory hiring and promotion practices have relegated women to inferior ranks and lower-salaried institutions. However, an unaccounted-for residual salary gap was also found. In an updated version conducted for the American Council on Education, a residual income disparity amounting in 1970 to $1,000 was found, even after allowing for differences in seniority, rank, and various measures of scholarship, which could not be attributed to anything but sex bias.[4]

We note that the distribution of women among various types of institutions and among ranks in these institutions is quite different from men. The elite institutions, about which Lester is particularly concerned, show the greatest discrepancies between women and men with respect to overall numbers and rank distribution.... This academic year, 1974–75, the total number of women faculty members in the ranks of associate and full professor at Princeton, Yale, Harvard, and Columbia is 55 out of 1429, or 2.7 percent, a modest increase over the 1.0 percent reported in 1969–70.[5]

Of course, these figures give only prima facie evidence of discrimination. Can the low position of women in academic life be explained by their own inadequacy rather than by discrimination? This seems to be Lester's position, necessitated by the fact that he is defending existing

---

[3]Helen S. Astin and Alan E. Bayer, "Sex Discrimination in Academe," in Alice Rossi and Ann Calderwood (eds.), *Academic Women on the Move* (New York:Russell Sage, 1973).

[4]Reported from data collected by Michael Faia. Income differentials for men and women faculty members are compared for 1969 and 1973 in *Chronicle of Higher Education*, Aug. 5, 1974, p. 9.

[5]The aggregate figure was calculated from official figures obtained directly from Harvard, Yale, Columbia, and Princeton universities. Percentages were calculated on the basis of the number of women in the ranks of associate and full professor in the college or faculty of Arts and Sciences in each unversity.

TABLE 1. WOMEN'S SHARE OF FULL-TIME FACULTY JOBS

	All Ranks	Prof.	Assoc. Prof.	Asst Prof.	Instructors
All Institutions	22.3%	9.8%	16.3%	23.8%	39.9%
Public					
Institutions	22.7	10.0	15.8	23.7	39.2
Universities	17.1	6.7	12.3	20.0	44.4
Other Four-Year	23.2	12.7	17.4	24.7	44.0
Two-Year	32.3	21.2	24.3	31.3	35.1
Private					
Institutions	21.2	9.5	17.2	24.1	42.5
Universities	14.5	5.4	12.9	19.0	41.0
Other Four-Year	23.6	12.3	19.1	25.7	41.5
Two-Year	45.4	31.5	34.3	41.3	53.8

Sourse: National Center for Educational Statistics (1973).

prerogatives. As a result he ignores four forms of evidence that discrimination per se exists. First, the personal experience of women undergraduate and graduate students, documented in testimony before Congress, supports the conclusion that bias against women students influences grades, scholarships, and fellowships. But more insidious is the atmosphere of scorn created for "women's brains"; there is testimonial evidence of active discouragement by their advisors of women who intend to pursue academic careers. It is difficult to believe that faculty prejudice can exist at the student level and not affect hiring and promotion practices. . . .

Second, a 1970 study of hiring decisions in departments of psychology[6] and a 1971 study of hiring decisions in departments of physical science[7] indicate that chairmen in these two fields do show bias against women in hiring situations. . . .

Third, when we compare doctorates granted to women by departments in elite institutions with positions held by women in these same departments we find that the best universities are training women in higher proportions than they are willing to hire and advance them. Harvard, Yale, Princeton, and Columbia in 1962–63 granted 16 percent of their Ph.D.'s to women but at present less than 2–3 percent of their tenured ranks are filled with women.[8] Since high-prestige departments hire from each other as a rule, we may conclude either that they are granting Ph.D.'s to unworthy students or that they are discriminating in hiring. . . .

---

[6]L. S. Fidell, "Empirical Verification of Sex Discrimination in Hiring Practices in Psychology." *American Psychologist* 25(December 1970):1094–1098.

[7]Arie Y. Lewin and Linda Duchan, "Women in Academia." *Science* 173(Sept. 3, 1971):892–895. See also Letters, *Science* 176(May 5, 1972):457–459.

[8]Patricia Wright, *Earned Degrees Conferred, 1962–63, Bachelor's and Higher Degrees* (OE-54013-63) (Washington, D.C.: U.S. Government Printing Office, 1965).

Fourth, Astin and Bayer, in their classic study, "Sex Discrimination in Academe," conclude that "[s]ex is a better predictor of rank than such factors as number of years since completion of education, number of years employed . . . or number of books published." They also conclude that "when women are statistically matched with men on the variables that determine rewards, they . . . fall below men in rank and salary." . . .

THE SUPPLY OF QUALIFIED WOMEN

Lester's second proposition is that the supply of women scholars is presently inadequate, not only in numbers but in quality, to meet the high demands set by American institutions of higher learning. He develops this idea by inference rather than evidence; or rather he seems to assume that the relative inadequacy of women candidates is such an obvious matter that no very substantial proof is required. The only evidence presented is where he purports to show that among teaching faculties in universities women spend less time on research and have a lower scholarly output. However, although he does note that a larger fraction of women than men work in essentially nonresearch fields like nursing and education, and that only 19 percent of the women as opposed to 42 percent of the men in his sample have a Ph.D. or equivalent degree, he fails to disaggregate the figures and compare men and women with the same degree and academic rank who are in the same field. Thus he is able to conclude that women are significantly less productive than men. In fact the opposite is true as Table 2 indicates. Productivity of female Ph.D.'s as measured by the mean number of articles published is slightly greater than that of males in the physical sciences, slightly less in the social sciences and humanities and overall insignificantly different. Certainly the differences between the average female and the average male, whatever the sign of the difference, is so much smaller than the variance within each group as to make implications of female inferiority unfair to say the least.

Lester repeatedly refers to the well-known handicaps women encounter in pursuing careers as if, mistaking cause for effect, these handicaps made women worse candidates for jobs. It might be more reasonable to predict that women who successfully jump the hurdles prior to the Ph.D. degree will be *superior* in academic qualifications and ambitions to men, whose way has been made relatively easy. He implies, without evidence, that family commitments reduce the reliability and performance level of women academics. First he admits the obvious, that women Ph.D.'s are as qualified as men at that degree level. Then

TABLE 2. PRODUCTIVITY MEASURES: ARTICLE AND BOOK PUBLICATION, BY FIELD, SEX AND MARITAL STATUS

	Published at Least One Article	Mean Number of Articles	Published at Least One Book	Mean Number of Books
Sciences				
Women				
Unmarried	83.3%	5.8	10.1%	1.1
Married	75.4	6.3	6.2	2.6
Married w/children	91.9	7.8	9.5	1.7
Men	88.8	6.1	10.2	1.5
Social Sciences				
Women				
Unmarried	59.3	4.0	23.1	1.8
Married	61.5	4.2	20.9	2.1
Married w/children	66.9	3.9	19.9	1.5
Men	55.9	4.6	30.3	1.8
Humanities				
Women				
Unmarried	47.0	2.8	22.6	1.3
Married	69.7	3.7	22.9	1.6
Married w/children	69.7	3.4	32.8	1.6
Men	50.0	4.3	27.7	1.6
Education				
Women				
Unmarried	51.2	3.5	23.5	1.6
Married	57.4	5.4	35.3	1.7
Married w/children	39.6	3.9	26.0	2.0
Men	44.2	5.1	22.2	1.8
Combined				
Women				
Unmarried	57.9	4.1	21.1	1.6
Married	66.2	5.3	20.2	1.9
Married w/children	63.9	4.3	21.8	1.7
Men	57.5	5.2	23.1	1.7

Source: Rita James Simon et al., "The Woman Ph.D.: A Recent Profile." *Social Problems* 15 (1967):231.

he establishes the unremarkable fact that married women do more housework than men. Finally he concludes that "married women are not likely to devote as much time and effort to increasing their earnings capacity." Earlier he had argued, similarly without any supporting evidence, that "because on the average female faculty devote less time and energy to professional development (especially research) than men and more time to home responsibilities, a smaller percentage of women really qualify for the higher ranks." Since Ph.D. women are as productive as men in manufacturing research books and papers (see Table 2), we are left with the puzzling problem concerning the distractions from which men must suffer to bring them down to the level of women who bear the burden of extra household responsibilities. Perhaps Lester should have devoted a parallel section of his book to the question of whether or not drinking beer and watching sporting events on television, both practices known to correlate with male gender, greatly or only slightly handicap the research potential of the average male faculty member.

For other evidence of the lack of supply of qualified women he rather astonishingly takes the very data which show the drone-position of women on national rank and pay scales—women being hired abundantly to do the proletarian labor of teaching low-level courses with heavy course loads which discourage commitment to research, women hired mainly as instructors, as lab assistants, as research associates, not eligible for promotion, kept on indefinitely as good cheap labor—as if this demonstrated a low level of female capability rather than a high degree of discrimination. Lester's argument seems to be that if women are getting low pay, and not being promoted—does this not *prove* they are less able?

If we look at existing evidence which Lester ignores, it points in the opposite direction, indicating that increased utilization of women under a strict merit system would raise the standards of American education. Studies indicate that women doctoral recipients have somewhat greater academic ability than their male counterparts,[9] and that married women receiving their Ph.D.'s are more capable academically than single women. Women's durability on academic jobs is slightly though not significantly greater than men's, although their rates of promotions and their salaries, and hence their incentives to stay, are lower.

Despite the myth of the dropout woman Ph.D., 91 percent of the women who received doctorates in 1957–58 were working, 81 percent full time; and 79 percent had not interrupted their careers in the ten years after obtaining the doctorate. In contrast, only 81 percent of all male Ph.D.'s are in the labor force, and only 69 percent work full time in their field of study.

Studies attempting to measure teaching effectiveness tend to indicate no difference between male and female teachers.[10] Despite the almost universally accepted belief that women do not produce, the evidence shows that women with Ph.D.'s publish as much as male Ph.D.'s.[11] Furthermore, in most fields, married women were publishing as much or more than both men and unmarried women, although their status and salaries lagged consistently behind both. . . . It must be noted further that women have achieved this degree of academic success despite the

[9]National Research Council, Office of Scientific Personnel, *Careers of Ph.D.'s Academic and Nonacademic, A Second Report of Follow-ups of Doctoral Cohorts 1935–1960* (Washington, D.C.: National Academy of Sciences-National Research Council, 1968), and Harmon, "High School Ability Patterns: A Backward Look from the Doctorate." *Scientific Manpower Report No. 6* 1 (1966).

[10]Jane W. Loeb and Marianne A. Ferber, "Women on the Faculty at the Urbana-Champaign Campus," in Rossi and Calderwood *Academic Women on the Move*, p. 247.

[11]Rita James Simon et al., "The Woman Ph.D.: A Recent Profile." *Social Problems* 15(Fall 1967):221–236.

fact that in our society they have been discouraged from desiring academic success.

CONCLUSION

In sum, Lester's insistence that an overly rapid advancement of women faculty threatens university standards, when he presents no evidence that this fear is realistic, and when such evidence as does exist indicates that (*a*) theoretically, antidiscriminatory policies should improve rather than reduce standards, and (*b*) in fact, women of superior qualifications are being passed by, appears either naive or disingenuous.

Women and
Wealth
Robert J. Lampman

CHARACTERISTICS OF TOP WEALTH-HOLDERS

The median age of the 1953 top living wealth-holders was 54 years (Table 1). Over half of the number were between 40 and 60 years of age. While top wealth-holders made up only 1.04 percent of the total population and only 1.6 percent of the adult population they accounted for 3.5 percent of the men over 50.

TABLE 1. SELECTED CHARACTERISTICS OF TOP WEALTH-HOLDERS, 1953

Characteristic	Both Sexes	Men	Women
Number of persons	1,659,000	1,144,000	514,000
Median gross estate size ($)	112,800	116,800	105,200
Average gross estate size ($)	182,000	162,400	220,500
Share of top wealth (percent)	100	60	40
Median age (years)	54	52	57

Excerpted from Robert J. Lampman, *The Share of Top Wealth-Holders in National Wealth, 1922-56: A Study by the National Bureau of Economic Research* (Princeton, N.J.: Princeton University Press, 1962), pp. 17-20.

Approximately 1.4 million of the 1.7 million top wealth-holders are heads of households, the 0.3 million being (according to our estimate) the number of married women and dependent children in the group. We find that a minimum of 2.28 percent of households and 2.35 percent of married couples have at least one member owning $60,000 of gross estate (Table 2). This compares closely with the Survey of Consumer

Excerpted from Robert J. Lampman, *The Share of Top Wealth-Holders in National Wealth, 1922–56: A Study by the National Bureau of Economic Research* (Princeton, N.J.:Princeton University Press, 1962), pp. 17–20.

Finances finding that 3 percent of spending units in 1950 had $60,000 or more of total assets.

TABLE 2. PERCENTAGE OF TOP WEALTH-HOLDERS IN TOTAL POPULATION AND IN SELECTED GROUPS, 1953

| | Top Wealth-Holders | | |
	Both Sexes	Men	Women
All persons	1.04	1.44	0.64
Adults (20 and over)	1.60	2.26	0.98
Persons (65 and over)	3.00	4.00	2.50
Married persons	1.40	2.30	0.70
Widowers and widows	2.69	3.10	2.60
Households with at least one top wealth-holder	2.28		

The association of age and size of estate is quite clear for men; that is, average estate rises with age and median age rises with estate size. . . . (The latter association is remarkably slight, however. See Table 3.) For women, on the other hand, this relationship is much more irregular.

TABLE 3. MEDIAN AGE OF MALE TOP WEALTH-HOLDERS IN NON-COMMUNITY PROPERTY STATES, BY GROSS ESTATE SIZE, 1953

Gross Estate Size (thous. dollars)	Median Age (years)
60 to 100	54
100 to 200	53
200 to 500	53
500 to 2,000	56
2,000 and over	67

Women top wealth-holders have gradually increased, both in numbers and in wealth, relative to men so that they comprised one-third of all top wealth-holders in 1953 (while only one-fourth in 1922) and held 40 percent of the wealth of the group (Table 1). Women have a larger average estate size than men, although within most age groups there is no clear difference by sex, and although men have a higher median estate size than women.

The information on top wealth-holders furnishes little support for the popular idea that women own the greater part of American wealth. The type of property in the holding of which women come closest to men is corporate stock. While men, it is estimated, held $63 billion worth of stock, women held $54 billion worth. This was the case for the basic variant wealth, but in the total wealth variant, which takes into account personal trust funds, it is probable that women have over half the corporate stock.

One factor that contributes to the increasing importance of women as wealth-holders is the relative population growth in community property states, which now include Arizona, California, Idaho, Louisiana, Nevada, New Mexico, Texas, and Washington. In these eight states ownership is, in many cases, divided by law between husband and wife. Hence, the executor of the estate of the first spouse to die must report for estate tax purposes only half the property acquired after the marriage. Despite this legal provision, this group of eight states has almost exactly the share of top wealth-holders to be expected from its population, that is 18 percent of the wealth-holders and 18 percent of the population. They have somewhat less of the estate tax wealth than would be expected from their per capita income rank, however. A disproportionate number of the married female top wealth-holders are in community property states. This finding would suggest that if the family were the wealth-holding unit rather than the individual, considerably more than 18 percent of the top wealth-holding families would be found in community property states.

Women's
Contribution
to Family
Income

Women's Bureau

INCOME OF FAMILIES

The economic status of women is greatly affected by the income of the families of which they are a part, since most Americans—about 91 percent or nearly 190 million persons in 1973—live as part of a family. In 1973 the 55 million U.S. families had a median income of $12,051 (see Table 1). Between 1952 and 1973, the level of median incomes for families tripled, reflecting an average annual rate of 5.5 percent in current dollars and 3 percent when expressed in terms of constant purchasing power, which takes into account changing prices.

In 1973 the City Worker's Family Budget[1] considered $12,626 as necessary for an urban family of four, including two children, to enjoy a moderate standard of living. For four-person families in 1973, the median income was estimated at $13,710.

A significant portion of the rise in overall family income levels is attributed to the increase in labor force participation by wives in husband-wife families from about 26 percent in 1952 to about 42 percent in 1973. Average family income has also shifted upward as a greater

Excerpts reprinted from Women's Bureau, *1975 Handbook on Women Workers*, Bulletin 297 (Washington, D.C.: U.S. Department of Labor, 1976), pp. 137–141.

[1]Family budgets are computed for three different levels of living—higher, intermediate, (moderately low), and lower, and are also available at different levels for a retired couple. See *Handbook of Labor Statistics, 1973*, Bureau of Labor Statistics, U.S. Department of Labor. A Revised Equivalence Scale for Urban Families of Different Size, Age, and Composition is also available to convert four-person family budgets for use with families of different composition. See Table 149 in the *Handbook of Labor Statistics, 1973*, p. 339. The City Worker's Family Budget consists of a family of four—an employed husband aged thirty-eight, a wife not employed outside the home, an eight-year-old girl, and a thirteen-year-old boy.

TABLE 1. MEDIAN INCOME OF FAMILIES, BY TYPE
OF FAMILY AND RACE, 1973

Selected characteristics	Median Income of All Families	Median Income of Families Headed by Year-Round Full-Time Workers
All families	$12,051	$14,614
Type of family (all races)		
Male head	12,965	14,965
Married, wife present	13,028	15,000
Wife in paid labor force	15,237	17,292
Wife not in paid labor force	11,418	13,675
Other marital status	10,742	13,453
Female head	5,797	8,795
Type of family (head of household white)		
Male head	13,253	15,305
Married, wife present	13,297	15,353
Wife in paid labor force	15,654	17,586
Wife not in paid labor force	11,716	13,911
Other marital status	11,585	13,907
Female head	6,560	9,516
Type of family (head of household black)		
Male head	9,549	11,730
Married, wife present	9,729	11,776
Wife in paid labor force	12,266	13,817
Wife not in paid labor force	7,148	9,297
Other marital status	6,767	10,415
Female head	4,226	7,095

Source: U.S. Department of Commerce, Bureau of the Census: Current Population Reports, P-60, No. 93 (Advance report).

proportion of family heads were employed in professional and technical occupations and a smaller percentage in farm jobs.

Income of Husband-Wife Families and Contribution of Working Wives. Median family income was $13,028 in 1973 for the 46.8 million husband-wife families. In the 19.5 million families where the wife was in the paid labor force, the median was $15,237—17 percent higher than for all husband-wife families, and 33 percent above the $11,418 median in families where the wife had no paid work. It is significant that in only 36 percent of husband-wife families was the husband the only earner in 1972. In more than half of husband-wife families, the wife had earnings, and in about one-eighth of the families, persons other than the husband or wife had earnings (see Figure 1).

A significant change occurred in the income distribution of husband-wife families in the 1952–73 period as the number of such families with working wives more than doubled. In 1973 nearly two-fifths of all husband-wife families had incomes of $15,000 or more, and the wife worked for pay in nearly 54 percent of these families. In 1952 the wife

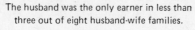

The husband was the only earner in less than three out of eight husband-wife families.

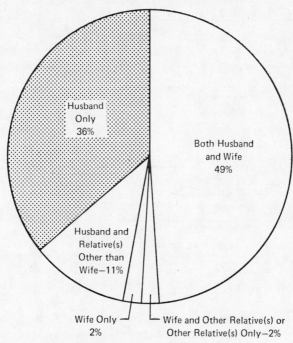

Husband Only 36%

Both Husband and Wife 49%

Husband and Relative(s) Other than Wife—11%

Wife Only 2%

Wife and Other Relative(s) or Other Relative(s) Only—2%

Source: U.S. Department of Commerce, Bureau of the Census.

Note: Families with no earners are not included.

was in paid employment in less than 34 percent of husband-wife families with comparable incomes (measured in constant 1973 dollars).

The earnings that women make and contribute as part of family income enable many families to significantly increase their standard of living. Working wives in white families had mean earnings of $4,125 in 1973, accounting for nearly one-fourth of total mean family income (see Figure 2). Black wives' mean earnings were $4,129 and accounted for nearly one-third of total mean family income in 1973.... Wives who worked year-round full-time (all races) in 1973 had median incomes of $6,364, and their income accounted for 38 percent of family income.

Income of Families Headed by Women. About 6.6 million families, or 12 percent of all families in the United States, were headed by women in 1973. The number of families headed by women increased by more than 50 percent in the 1955–73 period. Moreover, the number

FIGURE 2. CONTRIBUTION OF WORKING WIVES TO FAMILY INCOME

The higher the family income, the more likely the wife worked during the year . . . . At each income level, about one-fourth of the family income came from the wife's earnings in 1973.

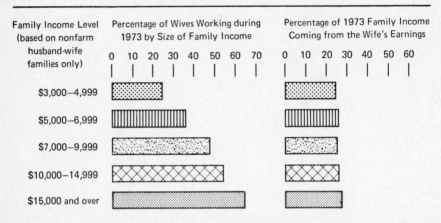

Family Income Level (based on nonfarm husband-wife families only)	Percentage of Wives Working during 1973 by Size of Family Income	Percentage of 1973 Family Income Coming from the Wife's Earnings

Source: U.S. Department of Commerce, Bureau of the Census.

increased by a million in the 1970–73 period; this was nearly equal to the increase in number (1.1 million) that occurred in the entire 1960–70 decade.

The median income of families headed by women was $5,797 in 1973. Families in which the female head was a year-round full-time worker had a higher median income—$8,795. However, this was still substantially below the $13,675 median income of families in which the male head worked year-round full-time but the wife did not work outside the home.

Nearly one out of five women who headed families was under twenty-nine years of age in 1973, compared with one out of ten in 1960. Among the factors responsible for this change are the different age distribution of the population, higher divorce and separation rates, and growing economic independence of women owing to increased labor force participation.

Families Living in Poverty. Despite the continuing rise in family income, there were about 4.8 million families, or nearly 9 percent of all families in the nation, living in poverty in 1973. Whereas families headed by women were 12 percent of all families, they constituted 45 percent of all low-income families.

The Council of Economic Advisers has concluded that perhaps the most important issue concerning poverty status in this country is the increasing identification of poverty with the female-head family. The number of low-income families headed by men declined sharply between 1959 and 1973, while there was a 14-percent increase in the number of low-income families headed by women. Since 1959, families headed by women have become a greater proportion of all low-income families—23 percent in 1959, 30 percent in 1966, and 45 percent in 1973.

A total of 18.3 million persons were in families below the low-income level in 1973. In addition, there were about 4.7 million unrelated individuals (persons living alone or with nonrelatives) below the low-income level, and women accounted for 3.2 million, or about two-thirds, of them. About one-third of these women were black. More than half of all of the unrelated individuals were sixty-five years of age or older.

About 9.5 million children, or 14 percent of all children under eighteen years of age in the United States, lived in poverty in 1973. . . . More than half of all children living in poverty were part of families headed by women.

PART FIVE

Toward Sex Equality

What do American women want? There is no one answer. Social class, ethnicity, race, education, religion, and politics are some factors that make it unlikely that women can readily share one view of their own condition or degree of contentment with their lives. Women also vary in their acceptance of the women's movement and, among supporters, in their acceptance of different perspectives within it; even those who want changes disagree about what those changes ought to be.

Toward
Sex Equality

Introduction

Nona Glazer

Alice Rossi[1] proposes several models of sex equality that are useful for thinking about the current movement. Rossi suggests three models: pluralism, assimilation, and hybrid, which derive, like Hacker's analyses in Part Two, from theories of minority group relations.

In the *pluralist* model, groups that are different from the mainstream of the society—blacks from whites, women from men, Catholics from Protestants—are encouraged to develop and maintain their distinctiveness. In this view, women may be considered different from men on any number of grounds; certain social roles and behaviors are considered appropriate for women but not men. Rossi suggests there are too many barriers (for example, white Anglo-Saxon men dominate the economic and political systems) for this model to mean equality—sexually, racially, or ethnically. In addition to Rossi's observations of limitations, one might ask whether the pluralist model, including ideas such as the "feminine mystique," may not really be an ideological justification of *in*equality.

The *assimilation* model of equality essentially perceives women as being allowed to do what men do. Hence, the life-styles of men—in sex, work and play, politics and civic affairs, clothing and grooming—must be open to adoption by women. Rossi suggests that this style is both uncritically accepted as an ideal and impossible for women to adopt. The life-style of men, which women wish to imitate, depends on the existence of a wife who carries out all of the background activities that

---

[1]Alice Rossi, "Sex Equality: The Beginning of Ideology." *The Humanist* (September/October 1969):3–6, 16. See also Alice Rossi, "Equality Between the Sexes: An Immodest Proposal." *Daedalus* 93(Spring 1964):607–652.

make that life-style possible. The wife accepts responsibility for the children, the home, the everyday chores inside and outside of the household; she coordinates family activities and makes sure these do not conflict with any of her husband's obligations; she plans appropriate entertainment and carries out the necessary attendant duties. All of these leave her husband free to pursue a career or an interest in politics or civic affairs. Women cannot achieve this life-style, notes Rossi, until they, too, have "wives."[2]

Finally, there is the *hybrid* model, the least developed and most promising approach to sex equality. This model rejects both the assumption that women and men are basically different and ought to retain the social differences, and the assumption that the present organization of society and the life-styles of men are the most desirable. Instead, the hybrid model proposes a society in which the sexes live similar lives, but lives markedly different from the ones either lives now. The intense devotion of American men to career advancement, their preoccupation with the sexual exploitation of women, and their obsession with making money are among the themes that are being critically questioned and are believed by some to be socially undesirable. What the new society will be cannot be detailed aside from suggesting that both sexes will get relief from the burdens of their sex-defined roles, for certainly it must be a model that is developed over time and with experience.

Many reactions to the contemporary women's movement and the demands now being made for social changes can be clarified by comparing them with these three models.

First, not all women are involved, even in minor ways, in demanding changes in their current social position. Pluralism is the model of sex equality used by women who accept the traditional homemaker role and who may consider changes in women's roles to be distasteful and undesirable. Some of these women may believe that they are inferior to men, that it is men, not women, whom society discriminates against.[3]

Black women may also be accepting the pluralist model when they contend that the women's movement, from the National Organization of Women to women's communes, weakens the more important struggle for human rights. If they see racism and black matriarchy as having prevented black men from achieving manhood, then they may believe that black women must work for the improvement of blacks—and black men, in particular—rather than for women. While the Black Panthers, the Black Muslims, and the National Alliance for Business differ widely

---

[2]See Judy Syfers, "I Want a Wife." *Ms.* 1(Spring 1972):56.
[3]See the testimony of Mrs. Lynne S. Grace, Chevy Chase (Md.) housewife, before the Senate Judiciary Committee. U.S. Congress, Senate, Committee on the Judiciary, *Hearings on the Equal Rights Amendment*, S.J. Res. 231 (Washington, D.C.: U.S. Government Printing Office, 1970), pp. 352–363.

in their political visions, their programs appear, in effect, to lower the status of the black woman. Their implied ideal marriage seems very close to the white Anglo-Saxon Protestant relationship of a dominating male breadwinner and a dependent, supportive female childbearer and homemaker: black manhood vindicates black womanhood, too, as men can now be relied on for protection and economic support. Books such as *Total Woman* or *Fascinating Womanhood* offer women an exaggerated version of a traditional "feminine" role as a key to personal and marital happiness.[4]

Second, some socialist women believe that the current women's movement weakens the efforts to establish a new society with a more humane political economy. A new economic system supposedly would itself bring the necessary preconditions for developing equality between the sexes. The implied content of sex equality, in such political analysis, fits within the assimilation model, for although social organization is radically altered, there is no indication that gender roles—for men as well as women—would be. Women would gain "men's rights" without men necessarily acquiring any of women's current responsibilities: the responsibility for housework, child care, and other traditional "women's work." The argument persists that a radical change in the political economy would bring about sex equality, even though existing socialist countries have only lessened rather than eliminated inequality between women and men. Radical men, who also protest that women's liberation deflects from "real" problems and who are eager to be democratic and just (except, often, in their relations with women), seem to be supporting some version of a pluralist model.

Arguments that advise women to wait are familiar: women repeatedly are urged to step aside—for the general good of their husbands, for their children, for the benefit of special causes (such as the enfranchisement of black men after the Civil War and the unionization of men during the nineteenth and twentieth centuries). Must a gain in competence and stature for men require an absolute loss in competence and stature for women? Has the women's rights movement retarded other rights movements? No evidence can be shown to support either of these objections to an improved status for women.

Third, the hybrid model is advocated by many kinds of women. The search for personal and sexual fulfillment, frequently discussed in the "consciousness-raising" groups of the women's liberation movement, sometimes leads to demands for the reorganization of gender roles and for the reorganization of social institutions. Some politically radical women have come to see that social policies specifically directed at

---

[4]Marabel Morgan, *Total Woman* (Old Tappan, N.J.: Revell, 1973); Helen B. Andelin, *Fascinating Womanhood* (Santa Barbara, Calif.: Pacific Press, 1963).

women's social condition are explicit needs in any program of radical social change: patriarchy itself must be eliminated in order for changes in the political economy to lead to sex equality.

The men's liberation movement also seems to use the hybrid model in arguing that men, too, are victims of society. From this perspective, men have noted that they have been denied certain "feminine" prerogatives—the right to be emotional, to admit to weaknesses and to emotional needs, to be a nurturing and openly loving parent, to be emotionally close to a person of the same sex, and so on. While such analyses draw attention to real problems that men face in a competitive and bureaucratized society, there has been a singular neglect by men of any analysis of men's power over women. Hence, the men's liberation movement has largely neglected to investigate such questions as how men continue to victimize women, how men themselves resist sharing male privileges with women, how men manage to resist changing their relationships with women toward sex equality. Nor have they tried to find out why it is so difficult for men even to see women as being subordinate to them or to see that the study of women as subordinates is a legitimate part of the search for human understanding.

What social changes are advocated by women? Some resist all changes except those that would broaden the traditional protective legislation, such as alimony laws that supposedly favor women, or labor laws that limit the hours women may work. Others advocate changes ranging from legislation for equal economic rights through social equality in interpersonal relations, to broad institutional reorganization. Nearly all women share a concern—usually formulated in terms of the assimilation model—about economic problems such as limited job opportunities, low earnings, and little training opportunity for women, even though the current movement originated among white, college-educated, middle-class women rather than among working-class, poor or black women.

In sharp contrast, there are some women who believe that women do not readily think of themselves except in relation to men since, unlike other oppressed minorities, women live with rather than apart from their oppressors. For this reason, radical feminists favor a separation of the sexes, hoping women can use it, as other minorities have, to develop a positive identity. While the model of sex equality is pluralist, it may be a precursor for the development of a hybrid model, for some women favor the separation only partly and/or temporarily—in politics and the classroom, for example. Others see a temporary need to separate themselves from men in sexual relations and living arrangements. Still others support a total separation from men, at least until women are, in fact, equal to men.

The final readings in this volume are about how societies may move toward sex equality. The first two readings, by Nancy Barrett about Sweden and by Judith Stacey about the People's Republic of China, discuss how government policy has been designed to change the power and prestige of women. In both cases, a mixture of the *assimilationist* and *hybrid* models is used. Both attempts are very recent; Sweden made its commitment explicit only in 1965, while the People's Republic of China made its commitment about thirty years ago (in 1948). Thus, the Chinese have been involved (off and on, as other problems have loomed) in programs aimed at establishing the equality of women and men somewhat longer than the Swedes. However, unlike Sweden, China has had to work on other serious problems at the same time. Sweden is a highly industrialized society, with the highest standard of living, longest life expectancy, lowest infant mortality, etc., in the world. As Barrett notes, it has long been committed to the establishment of social equality. Sweden has moved to fulfill that ideal by developing extensive social welfare programs through long-term social planning and the regulation of profits of private corporations. This commitment has, however, occurred within the context of a quite patriarchal society, with traditional notions about the relationship between the sexes.

In contrast, the Chinese government was established only in 1948, after years of bitter civil war, colonial exploitation by Western powers, and partial occupation of its territory by the Imperial Japanese army. China was and remains a peasant society, with about 80 percent of its 800 million citizens (20 percent of the world's population) engaged in agriculture and living in the countryside. The government has had to face a combination of problems. Among these have been a need (*a*) to industrialize; (*b*) to modernize agriculture in order to feed the population; (*c*) to develop basic services (e.g., medical care delivery, schooling, etc.); and (*d*) to create a *citizenry* in place of the traditional Chinese familism (a social pattern in which the family or clan rather than the nation is the major unit). Work on these problems had to go on, moreover, in a setting of hostility (rather than helpfulness) on the part of most Western countries, especially the United States, and eventually even China's former ally, the Soviet Union.

Eight years (in Sweden) and twenty-nine years (in China) is too soon to justify dismissing the possibility that government commitment to social policies can move toward sex equality. Barrett's disappointment in the Swedish experiment seems to be short-sighted, to lack an understanding of the problems of social change: a policy does not automatically guarantee that hundreds of years of subordination of women will be wiped out.

Certainly, the experience of both of these countries points up the difficulties of changing people's behaviors and attitudes. Governments in both countries have operated on the belief that both *capitalism* and *patriarchy* prevent the establishment of social equality, of which *sex* equality is just one kind. Sweden, by its welfare policies and the development of a *mixed economy,* and the People's Republic of China, by establishment of a *socialist* economy, provide an economic context without which it is highly improbable that society can move toward sex equality.

In the last selection, the Hungarian sociologists Mihaly Vajda and Agnes Heller present the most systematic hybrid model in their discussion of how changes in sex roles are limited by the conventional nuclear family. They are especially interested in the political relations between men and women and in the relations between parents and children; they suggest the broad outlines for an alternative life-style and living arrangements for a socialist society, concentrating on the individualistic choices that would be available in a socialized economy.

Have Swedish Women Achieved Equality?

Nancy S. Barrett

Five years ago, the government of Sweden embarked on one of the most radical social experiments that any country has ever undertaken. Recognizing what many sociologists and psychologists had argued for years—that women would not be able to achieve full economic equality without fundamental changes in the traditional sex roles—Sweden began a purposeful campaign to change the institution of the family and the attitudes that are associated with it.

The Swedish experience is taking place against a social background that differs in important respects from that of the United States. In Sweden, a small, prosperous country with a homogeneous population, there is a deeply rooted egalitarianism that is difficult for Americans to appreciate. This is reflected not only in the acceptance by nearly all groups in the country of the welfare state and the policy of international neutrality but also in the commitment of the trade unions to wage contracts that reduce inequalities between high-paid and low-paid workers. But this egalitarian spirit in social relationships is mixed with European traditionalism that in some ways makes the Swedish family and its attendant sex roles a much more rigid institution than the American family. In the United States, on the other hand, the heterogeneity of the population has produced a conservatism in organized labor that instinctively reacts against any sizable group of potential new entrants

Excerpted from Nancy S. Barrett, "Have Swedish Women Achieved Equality?" *Challenge*, November/December 1973, pp. 14–20. Copyright © 1973 by International Arts and Sciences Press, Inc. Reprinted by permission.

into the labor force. However, American women seem to have more status and independence within the family than do Swedish women, and this fact softens backward attitudes toward women's labor force activity.

THE SWEDISH EXPERIMENT

The Swedish experiment was, in many ways, the logical result of several decades in which the attitude of married women toward work had changed in almost every industrialized country....

Since the mid-1930's, under the leadership of the democratic socialist government, various laws have been enacted prohibiting discrimination on the basis of sex and providing social benefits, including day nurseries, for working mothers. In 1960, different pay scales for men and women were officially abolished by trade unions. But the 1968 change in social policy, aimed explicitly at the family structure, was dramatic even for a country that had long since reached a consensus on the welfare state.

The policy reflected a widely held opinion among sociologists and psychologists that the problem of achieving economic equality for women was related to the conventional view that a woman's first responsibility is to her home. This produces divided loyalties on the part of women toward home and job, and prejudicial attitudes of employers and coworkers can often be traced to the belief that "A woman's place is in the home"—even if that belief is a rationalization.

As part of a policy of fundamental change, there has been a concerted effort in Sweden to discourage the development of sex-based stereotypes in the education system. Schoolbooks, advertisements and vocational brochures have been refocused to show women in positions of authority over men. Women have been encouraged to apply for jobs traditionally held by men, and men to take jobs usually held by women. In order to free men to assume more household responsibilities, the work week was to be gradually shortened and more opportunities were to be provided for part-time work and more flexible hours.

Another set of measures was designed to force women into the labor market. The rights of women to be economically supported by marriage were abolished along with sex differences in eligibility for public support. Joint taxation of married persons' incomes was eliminated, removing the tax incentive for women to remain at home; and it was explicitly stated that men and women were equals and economically independent....

It is true that labor unions have been successful in narrowing the gap between male and female wages. As shown in Table 1, average hourly earnings for full-time female production workers in mining and manufacturing were 82 percent of the male rate in 1971, compared with 69 percent in 1960. Women's wages increased by an average of 12.5 percent in 1971 over 1970; the equivalent gain for men was 9.8 percent. Still, the figures do not take into account the fact that 83 percent of employed women work outside the manufacturing sector.

TABLE 1. SEX DIFFERENCES IN EARNINGS IN SWEDEN*

Year	Men	Women	Women/Men
1950	043	042	70.3
1960	100	100	68.8
1965	149	162	74.9
1966	162	181	76.5
1967	275	198	77.6
1968	187	213	78.2
1969	203	234	79.1
1970	226	263	80.0
1971	248	296	82.0

Source: Statistika Centralbyran, Am 1972 :65.
*Average hourly earnings of workers in mining and manufacturing (1960=100).

For all occupations, Swedish women earn much less than Swedish men, as shown by their heavy concentration in the low-income categories. In the teaching profession, in which women represent 75 percent of the labor force, 98 percent of those in the lowest pay category are women. There are similar differences among other government employees, despite all the ringing statements about equality.

As shown in Table 2, about 85 percent of Swedish women are concentrated in a few female-dominated occupations, despite the effort to eliminate sex-typing of jobs. A measure of occupational dissimilarity based on an analysis of the thirty-nine standard occupational classifications in Sweden shows a slight move toward greater *inequality* between men and women from 1965 through 1972. Although there was a shift toward the higher-paying occupations for both groups, men moved faster than women. Women have taken jobs traditionally held by men (it is not uncommon to find a female bus driver in Sweden), but women have not gained representation in important policymaking positions. It is still unusual to find women in authority over men, particularly men of the same age and education. Women are still grossly underrepresented in trade unions, in Parliament, and in managerial positions in both public and private enterprise.

TABLE 2. OCCUPATIONS WITH MORE THAN 10,000 WOMEN IN SWEDEN

Occupation	Number of Women	Percent Women in the Occupation
Shop assistant	127,898	80
Secretary, typist	74,592	96
Farmer	62,351	54
Cleaner	57,346	91
Nurse's aid	56,381	98
Maid, child's nurse	52,221	100
Special office employee	50,713	68
Clerical assistant	36,422	82
Sewer	35,909	98
Bookkeeper, cashier	35,638	70
Waitress	28,884	89
Teacher (grades 1-6)	27,980	75
Nurse	25,658	100
Kitchen assistant	24,904	95
Telephone operator	21,497	99
Shopkeeper	18,905	29
Hairdresser	17,728	74
Home helper	17,578	100
Textile worker	14,352	55
Cook	13,960	82
Cattleman	13,206	73
Packing man	12,603	66
Lab technician	11,517	57
Cashier	11,337	98
Home economist	10,583	77
Total	860,163	
Women in other fields	105,364	

Source: Population census.

In Sweden, as elsewhere, women typically have higher unemployment rates than men. And the official measure of unemployment, which requires that individuals be actively seeking work to be counted, may understate the number of women who would work if they could find a job....

One reason why Swedish women earn less than men is that they tend to work fewer hours. In 1972, 44 percent of the employed women and 56 percent of the married women with jobs worked fewer than 35 hours per week; by contrast, only 9 percent of the men worked short hours. The difference reflects varying labor force experience rather than choice. A 1972 study of the part-time labor force indicated that three times as many women as men said that they would have worked more if work had been available. This underemployment was estimated to represent 2.7 percent of the total female labor force against only 0.6 percent of the total male labor force. In addition, even where part-time work is voluntary, the fact that most part-time employees are women suggests that men do not share equally in household responsibilities....

On the whole, the evidence suggests that Swedish women have had difficulties in overcoming the effect of their traditional sex roles. Although social policy has encouraged—and in some cases forced—women into the labor force, the attempt to change occupational sex roles does not seem so far to have been a notable success. Certainly there has been no major shift of men toward part-time work; neither has there been the general reduction in the work week that the 1968 plan envisioned. Family surveys indicate that even those few husbands who share at all in housework undertake at most about a fourth of it.

The number of publicly supported day-care facilities in Sweden has increased rapidly since 1965, but the implications for both children and mothers are far from clear. Women Social Democrats in the Swedish Parliament see the provision of more and better day-care facilities as the outstanding issue in social policy.... This, however, involves a concession that the burden of responsibility for child care still rests with women and is, in some sense, an admission that the Swedish government policy has failed to modify traditional views on sex roles.

Another disturbing aspect of the Swedish experiment is that women who venture out into the working world are faced with the same prospect of low-paying, low-status jobs that they have always had. Changes in the structure of taxes and in income-linked social benefits have in many cases forced women to work when they would have preferred to remain at home. And because equalization of wages in manufacturing has resulted in a relative deterioration of men's take-home pay, many Swedish families now claim that they can no longer afford to live on a single income.

Despite the benefits of sexual equality, the effects of urging women into the labor force are at best uncertain if they are accompanied by a deterioration in the quality of family life. Pamphlets distributed by the women's committee of the Swedish Labor Market Board disconcertingly suggest that working women should avoid "complicated cooking" and that "there are nowadays so many prepared things to buy, for instance frozen food, ready-made dishes and canned nutriment." In addition, institutionalized child care has mixed—and largely unknown—effects on children.

THE FORCE OF TRADITION

Talking with Swedish women, one gets the impression that they are less concerned with job satisfaction than they are disturbed at being forced to work. Swedish women, particularly professional women, seem to be much less achievement oriented than their American counterparts. They are more reluctant to engage in outright competition with men and, despite improved prospects for continuous employment during childbearing years, have fewer career expectations. This may explain why Swedish women have not made more sizable inroads into the male-dominated professions and into the power structure in general.

Indeed, nowhere does this reluctance to compete with men show up more strongly than in the radical feminist organizations themselves. Feminism seems almost to have been an afterthought in Sweden—voicing ideological principles rather than pushing in any practical way to revolutionize social relationships.

The gains that Swedish women have made were to be expected, given the active social support for women's rights. But the Swedish experience is on the whole disappointing: despite explicit recognition that equality cannot come without some change in family relationships, traditional attitudes and values remain deeply ingrained. Revolutionary claims aside, the channels through which sex discrimination is transmitted are still very much the same in Sweden as in the United States. And perhaps the problem is greater in Sweden because of the European traditionalism that pervades sex roles within the family.

It is perhaps useful to keep in mind the contrast between racial discrimination and discrimination based on sex. The channels that have kept blacks in an inferior position in the United States—lack of education, geographical location, and other factors related to the external environment—do not explain male-female differences. Women have not been systematically excluded from equal education and cultural opportunities, and they live in the same regions as men. Prejudicial attitudes toward working women are not based on some irrational feeling of genetic superiority, but are part of the family system on which society is based. This has led some people to justify sex discrimination on moral grounds, a justification that is not possible with respect to race. So, as the Swedish experiment to date has shown, the problem of the economic inequality of women may prove the more intractable of the two.

The Chinese
Family Revolution
and Feminist
Theory
Judith Stacey

Woman's oppression starts right at home. The family is the central institutional context for the transhistorical, transcultural oppression of women. Feminists and socialists have focused on the modern nuclear family as a particularly pernicious incubator of male supremacy....

China provides us with an especially rich and fascinating case study for building feminist family theory. In traditional China, even more than in most preindustrial societies, family life was the indisputable nexus of the social system. Further, the Chinese family was a virtual citadel to patriarchy. Few family systems can compete with the Confucian for degradation and brutality toward women. From female infanticide to crippled feet to childbride sale, wife-beating, polygyny, and more, Chinese women tasted no end of bitterness in their short, mostly poverty-ridden lives. Today the situation is unrecognizably transformed. In the context of a socialist revolution, mainland Chinese women have perhaps moved closer to equality with men than have women in any other contemporary society. At the same time, the Chinese family system has undergone a dramatic transformation in the direction of the modern conjugal family—both in practice and ideology. And while the economic, political, and social hegemony of the family has been categorically eclipsed by party, state, and commune, the modern Chinese family remains a remarkably strong, reputedly harmonious, and peculiarly unquestioned element in Communist Chinese society.

Excerpts reprinted from Judith Stacey, "When Patriarchy Kowtows: The Significance of the Chinese Family Revolution for Feminist Theory," *Feminist Studies* 2, nos. 2/3 (1975):64–112 by permission of the publisher. "When Patriarchy Kowtows" is a condensation from a more comprehensive and comparative treatment of the history and social significance of the Chinese family revolution.

The patriarchal, patrilineal, patrilocal family was the central and most important institution in the traditional Chinese social structure. Even more than in most traditional societies, it was a matter of Confucian principle that the needs and interests of the individual be subordinated to those of the family group. The interests of the entire patriarchal household (as well as of its past and future lineage) were intimately affected by the selection of the bride. A man was not acquiring a mate; the lineage was receiving a social, economic, and biological contribution to its celestial destiny. . . .

The entire Chinese family system was linked to an agrarian economy. Most families were nearly self-sufficient economically, and only slightly less so socially. Division of labor by sex was extreme, with women relegated almost exclusively to internal, domestic chores. In a land of abject poverty and below subsistence-level agriculture, it has been estimated that women supplied only 16 percent of the agrarian labor power. . . . Only in the southern rice cultures were peasant women allowed to play a noticeable role in productive activity, and, not surprisingly, there they were far more likely to retain the use of their feet as well as some degree of movement and influence.

Although the Western fantasy depicts relations of highly cultivated tenderness among Chinese relatives, in fact Chinese family life was marked by a shocking degree of brutality. The Confucian emphasis on filial piety and loyalty was a euphemistic prescription for absolute subordination of young to old and, more important for our purposes, of female to male. Indeed, as Marjory Wolf points out, the structure of the Chinese family looks very different depending on which sex's perspective you choose to view it from. The dominant male perspective conjures an unbroken lineage with power, property, and esteem passing in orderly and gradual fashion from generation to generation. From the female perspective, family life had to appear dramatically opposite. During her lifetime a Chinese woman lived in two distinctly different families—her natal and her marital homes. Instead of an unbroken lineage, the woman was never in her lifetime fully a member of any family. Her name was not even recorded in her father's genealogy, and when she died only her family surname was entered in the genealogical charts of her husband's family. . . .

In countless other ways woman's subhuman status in the traditional family was brought home to her. Inheritance patterns barred her from any control over or rights to property. After her marriage she discarded her given name. She played a subordinate role in public ceremonies and was generally secluded from social life. In a system characterized by filial piety, woman's life was described by the three obediences—to her father during childhood, to her husband during marriage, and to her son during widowhood. Marriages were arranged with neither the participation nor the knowledge of the principals. At marriage the bride was abruptly torn from the relatively sympathetic, possibly loving environment of her natal home and given over to the position of slavelike obedience and often terror among total strangers that awaited her in her husband's household.

   . . . The plight of women and youth of both sexes formed a reservoir of dissatisfaction waiting to be channeled when the floodgates fell. That for two thousand years women were successfully prevailed upon to acquiesce in a system that ruthlessly sacrificed their bodies, minds, and spirits to the patriarchal altar is an unhappy testament both to the forces of coercion and to the effectiveness of patriarchal socialization. The literature leaves little doubt that coercion was a major buttress of traditional social order, and doubly so in the case of female subordination. With her feet literally mangled expressly to restrain as well as to objectify her person, indoctrinated into subservience while barred from education, required to enter into a marriage arranged by others, and most importantly, denied access to either inheritance or gainful employ so that she remained in a state of complete economic dependency, the Chinese woman had little objective stake in preserving the traditional family order. What stake she felt subjectively is a far more complicated question. Certainly there is evidence of individual rebellion and resistance. . . . However, it would be a mistake to deny the less inspirational side of the story—that, in response to two thousand years of subjugation . . . submissiveness, docility, and even extreme self-denigration were far from uncommon among women. To acknowledge the fact that women often willingly participated in their own oppression is not to mitigate the critique of Confucian patriarchy, but to recognize the far less tangible, but equally problematic, realm of social psychological domination.

THE DECLINE OF THE TRADITIONAL FAMILY

A trickle of Western missionaries had penetrated China since the seventh century, but their numbers and ideological impact did not attain significance until after the British victories in the mid-nineteenth-century Opium wars. As the dynastic curtain was forcibly parted in the late nineteenth and early twentieth centuries, Western traders and industrialists began to mine the markets and resources of the immense Manchu empire. Particularly in the urban areas, the combined effects of Western commerce, industry, and ideology were disastrous for the already badly strained family and social structure.

Universalistic job criteria, specialization, and competition were disabling enough, but the opportunity for even a small proportion of women and youth of both sexes to be employed outside the home was probably the decisive factor in the undermining of traditional authority. Industrial capitalists found a ready pool of cheap labor in women of the poorer classes. ... With the increasing economic and physical autonomy of even small numbers of women and youth, all the restrictive familial regulations and customs came to be questioned. As the family began to lose its role as a productive unit, the material basis for arranged marriage, polygyny, footbinding, ancestor worship, veneration of elders, and the double standard began to vanish.

The trend toward the modern nuclear family appeared first among the urban working classes. At the same time, upper classes were subjected to Western ideological influence. For the first time, educational privileges were extended to upper-class girls, and bourgeois women entered the university and the professions. While economic conditions were creating the material basis for the physical emancipation of working-class women, women of the upper classes felt the stirrings of cultural emancipation. ...

The "family revolution" in pre-Liberation China consisted of a series of spontaneous, uncoordinated, sporadic attacks on the Confucian patriarchal order. Although they directly affected the lives of a small minority, student protests, individual experimentation, and legal reforms patterned on Western models chipped away at tradition. ...

COMMUNIST POLICY BEFORE LIBERATION

The women's movement in China was nurtured by war and affected by its vicissitudes. In the course of the Communist movement's twenty-eight-year-long struggle to liberate the homeland, its policy toward women and the family underwent many fits and starts. In 1922 the young CCP [Chinese Communist Party] issued a proclamation for women's rights which established a special women's bureau. Little attention was paid to this at first, probably because there was scant female participation in the early Chinese party. Moreover, both women and men among the early radicals considered women's issues secondary to the proletarian struggle.

... The Kiangsi Soviet became an early testing ground for policies on women and the family. There the central executive committee passed its first two marriage laws in 1931 and 1934. The marriage laws, patterned after those of the Soviet Union, were essentially liberal. They established the principle of free association in marriage. Women received the right to retain custody over children. By requiring the registration of marriage and divorce with local government, the state entered the marriage sector for the first time. The 1934 law, which protected Red Army soldiers from divorce by their wives, reflected aspects of the experience of the Party in implementing the earlier code. Even though the earlier law had not been vigorously enforced, the right to divorce aroused considerable enthusiasm among peasant women and widespread resistance from the men.

Throughout the revolutionary period Party policy and practice veered a shaky course between the exigencies of the class and sex wars. Needing to attack the traditional family, if only to liberate women to mobilize their political and economic support, afraid to antagonize the men upon whom the "liberated" women were justifiably wont to vent their long pent-up fury, the CCP leadership was racked with conflict and dissension on this issue. . . .

Although the struggle for women's emancipation was never as central nor as militant as that for land reform, women in the liberated areas derived significant benefits from both these programs during the War for Liberation. Land reform granted women equal rights to land—the first condition for peasant women's economic independence. Women, quick to grasp the implications of land reform for their status within the family, participated actively in reform struggles. Further, as the war expanded, and male labor power in the villages dwindled, women were forced to take up the slack. Women's associations developed mutual aid teams, undertook sabotage and intelligence operations, devised makeshift hospitals, and strained to maintain the subsistence economy for the duration. Their growth in consciousness and morale must have been stupendous.

FEMINIST CONTROVERSIES

There is no denying the enormous strides Chinese women made under Communist leadership. To pit feminism against the goals of a socialist revolution is to make a prematurely divisive distinction. Socialism is not now, and was not then, exclusively a male project. . . .

Chinese women were caught on the horns of a strategic dilemma familiar to feminists. When they tried to participate as equal members of an integrated movement, they were required to overlook their specific oppression as women. Yet when they organized autonomously around women's issues, they were considered divisive to the cause of class solidarity.

There is disagreement over which horn Chinese women favored. Did they perceive their oppression primarily in sexual or in economic terms? Underlying this question are shades of the contemporary political dispute over whether sex or class is "the basic contradiction." It is difficult to make generalizations, particularly ex post facto, of subjective perceptions. From the available evidence it seems that Chinese women were variously aware of the dual nature of their oppression. There, as elsewhere, bourgeois women tended to focus on their status as women. Radical women, it would seem, accepted, and even helped formulate, the Party analysis that sexual equality would follow from economic liberation. Yet given the practice of democratic centralism, it is not possible to speculate how many Party women silently shared ... misgivings about this approach. Peasant women probably ran the political gamut from sex to class hatred or indifference. Yet there is reasonable cause to assume they were at least as concerned with liquidating the patriarchy as they were with establishing socialism.

FEMINISM AND THE FAMILY IN THE PEOPLE'S REPUBLIC

Political History.   When the victorious CCP adopted its first national marriage law on May 1, 1950, it was making official policy out of the social processes of family reform that had long been underway. What had been sporadic and uncoordinated experimentations now became a matter of explicit legal doctrine and intense propaganda. The May 1 law officially put an end to all the patriarchal, authoritarian abuses of the Confucian family order. It explicitly repudiated "the arbitrary and compulsory feudal marriage system, which is based on the superiority of man over woman." The bill was a victory for the monogamous, conjugal family based on principles of free association and sexual equality. Polygamy, concubinage, child betrothal, marriage by purchase, infanticide, and illegitimacy were abolished. Divorce, remarriage, inheritance, and property rights were guaranteed to women as well as men.

In the twenty-four years since the passage of that revolutionary bill, CCP policy on women and the family has been through a variety of stages and formulations. Every three to four years policy on the family seems to vacillate along the lines of the broader political struggle. As Party strategy shifts from the political to the economic front of the socialist transformation, woman and family policy steers a choppy course between emphasis on the special aspects of women's oppression and the submergence of women's liberation within the broader class struggle. The vicissitudes of family reform recall the preliberation tension between sex and class antagonisms. Accordingly, Chinese family life in the People's Republic has been through alternating periods of upheaval and restabilization.

While it is possible to chart the approximate course of official Party policy, a social history of actual family life must be sketchy and impressionistic. We have little more to go on than the accounts of Westerners whose visits have been widely scattered in time, geography, and perspective, and whose access to primary material has been limited. Bearing this limitation in mind, it seems reasonable to divide the postliberation era into six periods.

1. From liberation until approximately 1953, the family revolution was a political priority. This early period was marked by concentrated political mobilization around the issues of land reform and the marriage law. So intensive was the agitation that the marriage law soon came to be known to the masses as the "divorce law." Women and men of all ages participated enthusiastically in land reform struggles, but, as in the earlier period, many men and older women put up serious resistance to the marriage bill. Women inundated the courts with their divorce suits. They were the plaintiffs in 76.6 percent of the 21,433 divorce cases of the thirty-two cities and thirty-four rural county-seats reported in the *Jen-min Jeh-pao* (*People's Daily*) of September 29, 1951. They were answered by the same brutality and obstruction that their sisters in the liberated areas had experienced earlier. Beatings, confinement, and murder were the fate of many young women who sought to exercise their new freedoms. Nor, as official Party statements recognized, were local Party cadre aloof from this violent, obstreperous behavior. The peasant women came to say: "To get a divorce, there are three obstacles to overcome: the obstacle of the husband, of the mother-in-law, and of the cadres. The obstacle of the cadres is the hardest to overcome."

2. The inadequacy of the economic base was, most likely, as much responsible for the retrenchment of the second period (1953–1957) as were the alarming female suicide and murder rates. During this period of the first five-year plan, political agitation was discouraged, as Communist policy concentrated on economic development. The Party attempted to justify a time of reaction, or restabilization, if one prefers, on issues of family reform by pronouncements that women had already achieved liberation. Divorce policy underwent the most dramatic reversal—one from which it has never since recovered. Divorce became, and remains, exceedingly difficult to obtain, on the principle that if one makes one's own bed, one must lie in it. Or in the words of a village secretary: "Even if the marriage is childless, people still consider divorce immoral, because now that people can choose whom they will marry, they will have chosen each other, and should put up with the consequences."

3. The Great Leap Forward (1958–1961) was particularly well-

named from the point of view of feminist progress. The establishment of the people's communes represented an important structural innovation for women, replacing the family as the source of an individual's economic and social security. There is evidence that the communes were a popular response to local need rather than an edict from Peking. Women had everything to gain from the innovation. . . . Not only were labor opportunities for women limited, but, before the institution of the commune, wages were paid to the family rather than to the individual. With collectivization, the countryside experienced its first labor shortage. Women were called upon to fill the gap. It was an instance when the needs both of the society and of women's emancipation were in close harmony. To free women for productive activity such social services as canteens (collective dining halls) and nurseries were introduced. A new era for women and socialism appeared close at hand.

4. Predictably, in the fourth period (1962–1965) China entered a second phase of retrenchment. The Liu Shao-chi faction assumed Party leadership, economic development was once more the national priority, and restabilization of the family was again the order of the day. The Party issued a handbook on *Love, Marriage and the Family,* which put forth the official ideology on the family. Marriage, it was asserted, is the single appropriate response to love, an emotion which it would seem was expected to be guided primarily by the dictates of political priorities . . . Communist stories of this period, in contrast to those published during the Great Leap Forward, also resurrect some of the Confucian family virtues. Respect for elders, the closeness of the father-son relationship, and semiarranged marriages are common themes in these stories. . . . In the villages, many women seemed to accept their familiar subordinate status.

5. The Cultural Revolution (1966–1968) was, in part, an attempt to shake the masses out of their lethargy. . . . *Women of China* began publishing articles attacking arranged marriages, betrothal gifts, and extravagant wedding celebrations. Women were encouraged to participate in the widespread political criticism and fervor that marked the period, but the official woman's movement was disbanded. International Women's Day disappeared from Chinese calendars. Women were asked once more to throw in their revolutionary lot with men. . . .

The Cultural Revolution was a complex event from a feminist point of view. The massive politicization and particularly the renewed emphasis on women as equal revolutionary agents was crucial to women's progress, but during the two-year suspension of all normal social activity, education and the birth control campaign were among the casualties. Despite official propaganda to the contrary, youthful marriages also increased—perhaps in response to the suspension of schooling and the general relaxation of social control. Since a history of sex discrimination in education and inferior literacy rates are key factors in women's continued subordinate status, the two-year holiday was a very mixed blessing. Yet the Cultural Revolution broke the stranglehold on the family. Women, and men, seemed to gain a renewed respect for women's productive, political, and cultural capabilities—an ideological triumph it would be foolish to minimize.

6. It is difficult to so neatly categorize the period since the Cultural Revolution. The earlier pattern would suggest that once more political and feminist issues would recede, economic concerns become paramount, and family life enjoy renewed emphasis. . . .

Yet it would be incorrect to characterize the post-Cultural Revolutionary period as thoroughly reactionary on feminism. Women continue to be exhorted to assume full membership in the revolution. Recent issues of *Peking Review* are instructive for ascertaining the official line on women's emancipation. Most of the articles on women take the form of inspirational autobiographical addresses, intended to reaffirm faith in women's steady progress under Chairman Mao, the CCP, and the socialist road.

. . . The current emphasis on shared housework, communal facilities, family planning, equal status, and increased political leadership roles for women bodes well for feminism. It demonstrates that there is official ideological backing for all of those reforms. Secondly, the scapegoating device indicates the awareness of the Party that women's emancipation depends on ideological struggle as well as structural reforms. By exhorting women to participate in criticism campaigns, the Party is indirectly encouraging a revival of women's consciousness-raising activity, reminiscent of the earlier "speak bitterness" campaigns.

The Current State of the Family Revolution. By now it should be clear that the family revolution in modern China has been an integral aspect of a long, complex process of broad social change. It has taken close to a century for the Chinese Revolution to transform a decaying semifeudal social order governed by a system of bureaucratic despotism —with the patriarchal lineage as its social cement—into a powerful modernizing society that guarantees security, dignity, and opportunity to all its members, through the most egalitarian example of a socialist system the world has yet seen.

In the course of that process the Confucian patriarchal family is perhaps the most dramatic, unmourned casualty. It has been replaced by a particularly Chinese variant of the increasingly universal pattern of modern conjugal family life. . . .

On the level of structural change, the first striking fact is that kinship is no longer the central organizational fact of life in China. Through the socialization of the forces of production, the family has been transformed from a self-sufficient unit of production to a unit of consumption whose members are highly integrated into the larger social order. Hence, the family has lost its former significance as the sole source of its members' economic security. Even more than in other industrializing nations, the family has also forfeited many of its educational, religious, medical, and recreational responsibilities. In China, the work team, production brigade, commune, neighborhood association, state, and Party now provide more assurance of an individual's right to eat, work, study, survive, and prosper than the family ever did or could. . . .

Most of the other important structural changes in the Chinese family read like a catalog of modern, nuclear family features. The husband-wife relationship has replaced the father-son as the pivotal relationship in the family structure. Polygamy, betrothal by purchase, arranged marriages, ancestor worship, infanticide, prostitution have disappeared with varying rates of haste. Youth has begun to eclipse its elders in social status and authority. However, children are still required by law to support their aged parents—probably as much a reflection of the limitations of the Chinese economy as of the traditional veneration of the aged.

The acceptable age for marriage in China has been raised, both by statute, and increasingly, by custom. The marriage law prohibited marriage by females under eighteen and by males under twenty, and intensive propaganda has been directed toward delaying the event considerably longer. Although reports of actual practice vary, there is evidence that rural women typically marry between the ages of twenty-one and twenty-three to men who are twenty-three to twenty-five, while in the cities marriage is typically delayed a couple of years longer. At the same time the trend has been toward having fewer children. . . .

Private life has been officially assigned a very feeble second place in the People's Republic. In countless interviews, cadres make this point explicit: "One's private life is a small matter; it's the state, the society, that's important." . . .

In view of this apparently widespread sentiment, it is not surprising that political criteria are expected to dominate selection of one's marriage partner, and decisions concerning divorce. The emphasis in marital relationships is comradeship. Reason dictates passion, and it is considered the height of good sense to seek out a hard-working, frugal, even-tempered, service-oriented mate.

Closely related to this highly rationalistic and political approach to love is the much-remarked-upon asceticism that seems to pervade contemporary China. We have already referred to the apparent near-universality of premarital chastity in China. Monogamy, fidelity, and exclusive heterosexuality are equally esteemed sexual values, so much so that adultery is punishable by law. [Although] birth control devices are readily available, so that sex and reproduction can reasonably be separated, sexual freedom is considered a product of bourgeois decadence. . . .

Nevertheless, it is the apparent near-absence of sexual experimentation in China that sits most mysteriously on Western consciousness. Add to this the homogeneity of life patterns—the total absence of viable alternative life styles to that of the monogamous nuclear family—and you have a morality which few foreign individualists are prepared to covet.

. . . The lack of tension in the family is probably a function of the absence of power relationships created by the loss of economic functions. Family roles are stripped of power when they do not determine the individual's access to economic security. Further, family equanimity is probably helped along by the segregation of social networks of individual family members. Individuals in China are tightly integrated into small extrafamilial groups—typically the work group, school, or neighborhood association—which meet weekly under the direction of an activist to discuss all manner of public and personal issues. . . .

There is no denying that Chinese women and the Chinese family have come a very long way. But we would be remiss to overlook the limitations which remain to China's progress toward sex equality and family reform. The most obvious inequity is the serious underrepresentation of women in positions of high-level leadership in the Party and in the military. . . .

Secondly, despite impressive gains, sex-typing is far from dormant in Chinese economic and social life. Women uniformly perform the traditionally female tasks. All nursery and kindergarten teachers are women. Domestic production inside and outside the home is typically defined as women's work. . . .

It has been difficult to overcome the culturally embedded conviction that family work is woman's work. Economic and theoretical factors reinforce the difficulty. Even today women are not yet fully integrated into the productive work force. . . .

In urban areas the situation is different, but not dramatically superior. Urban men appear to participate more often in household chores, communal child-care facilities in factories and neighborhoods are more widely available than in the countryside, women factory workers receive paid maternity leaves, and women play central leadership roles in the urban residents' committees. However, women are the first to be laid off when employment drops, and they are concentrated in the low-wage neighborhood "housewife" industries. Although their familial burdens are lighter than those of their rural sisters, urban women retain more responsibility than do their husbands for child care and domestic chores.

Although sex-typing is far from eliminated, it appears that a conscientious attempt is being made to open traditionally male-defined roles to women.... However, men do not seem to be entering traditionally female occupations. Moreover, sex differences are accepted as natural and desirable by most Chinese. They believe women are better with children and seem to let it go at that.

Perhaps the critical area of discrimination against women concerns their unequal access to economic rewards. Women in China do receive equal pay for equal work; but they do not have the opportunity to perform what is considered equal work. As long as they retain primary responsibility for household and child-care tasks, this is likely to remain the case. The commune work-point system is a critical structural factor in perpetuating this inequity in rural China.... Because the family remains the critical income unit, women are apt to shoulder the household responsibilities in order to free their husbands for the more lucratively awarded work-point jobs. In turn, the emphasis on physical criteria and experience reinforces the tendency to sex-type work force and domestic tasks.

The halt of the communalization movement in the early 1960s probably accounts for much of this double bind. The unsuccessful attempt fully to socialize domestic work sent traditional woman's work, and thus woman's identity, back to its original family base....

The other side of this dilemma is that work performed in the home continues to be regarded as individual rather than socially productive labor. Hence it receives no work points from the collective....

A final factor cries out for examination. Of the traditional oppressive "4 P's" in China (patriarchy, patriliny, patrinomy, and patrilocality), one remains an index and buttress of male supremacy. The majority of Chinese marriages continue to be patrilocal.... This immediately places many Chinese women at a social, political, economic, and psychological disadvantage. They lack the local reputations and experience to win them positions of responsibility and power. They lose seniority at work. They must build from scratch the loyalties and friendships which they will need to support them in their domestic and public trials.... It is not only the practical consequences of patrilocality which are significant for women. There is evidence that women and men alike accept the asymmetrical arrangement unquestioningly. It is thought to be "natural," like sex differences, and that is simply that.

CONCLUSION

After surveying the history of family revolution in China one cannot help but feel that the transformation in the status of Chinese women is little short of miraculous. It is true that New China has participated in the universal trend of social evolution from a form of the self-sufficient extended family to the highly interdependent conjugal family system. In China, as elsewhere, the family has lost its exclusive responsibility and control over the socialization, employment, inspiration, and nurturance of its members. Yet the People's Republic variant of the modern conjugal family is unique. The Chinese family today appears to be stronger, more harmonious, more agreeable to its participants than does the family life of any modern society we know about.

In sum, the positive political lessons of the Chinese family revolution teachings are essentially these:

1. Socialism has proven itself to be an important aspect of women's liberation. The relationship between women's economic contribution, security, and recognition are closely related to their social status and to family reform.

2. Structural reforms in familial relationships can contribute impressively toward eliminating women's oppression. The most effective reforms are those which remove power relationships from the family.

3. Women seem to progress most during periods of militant political activity. Periods that concentrate on rapid economic development are often reactionary for feminism.

There are negative lessons to be drawn as well:

1. Sexual equality must cut both ways. It is not sufficient that formerly "for men only" doors be opened to women. As long as traditionally female roles go unchallenged, sexism keeps its heavy foot safely in the corridor. It seems particularly important for women to be delivered of their primary identification with children and their responsibility for domestic work.

2. The social evaluation of work requires considerable reconsideration. So long as physical strength, intergenerational experience, and a public arena are significant criteria, women's access to status is likely to be disadvantaged.

3. Sexism is deeply ingrained in the human psyche. Although psy-

chological differences by sex are social products, they have been part of human society long enough to develop a semiautonomous existence of their own. The barely noticed persistence of patrilocality in China is evidence of the depth of sex conditioning.

4. Women must make their own revolution in their own name. It cannot be handed us by "another" revolution. We must find some way as women to form our own base of power.

Perhaps, if one is absolutely truthful, there is at least as much we cannot learn from the Chinese. China made its revolution starting from a very different place from where we must start. Our revolution must be one that takes account of our long tradition of bourgeois individualism and that gives equal measure to personal liberation.

SUGGESTED READINGS

Boserup, Ester.
    1970   Woman's Role in Economic Development. London: George Allen and Unwin.
Cohen, Charlotte.
    1970   "Experiment in freedom: Women in China," in Robin Morgan (ed.), Sisterhood is Powerful. New York: Vintage Books.
Crook, Isabel, and David Crook.
    1966   The First Years of Yangyi Commune. London: Routledge and Kegan Paul.
Curtin, Katie.
    1974   "Women and the Chinese Revolution." International Socialist Review 35(March):8–11, 25–40.
Davin, Delia.
    1973   "Women in the liberated areas." P. 78 in M. Young (ed.), Women in China. Ann Arbor, Mich.: Center for Chinese Studies.
de Beauvoir, Simone.
    1958   The Long March. Cleveland: World.
Freedman, Maurice.
    1970   Family and Kinship in Chinese Society. Stanford, Calif.: Stanford University Press.
Karol, K. S.
    1968   China: The Other Communism. Tr. by Tom Baistow. New York: Hill and Wang.
Myrdal, Jan.
    1965   Report from a Chinese Village. New York: Pantheon Books.
Myrdal, Jan, and Gun Kessle.
    1970   China: The Revolution Continued. New York: Pantheon Books.

Rowbotham, Sheila.
1973   Women, Resistance and Revolution: A History of Women and Revolution in the Modern World. New York: Pantheon Books.
Salaff, Janet.
1973   "Institutionalized motivation for fertility limitation." Pp. 93–144 in M. Young (ed.), Women in China. Ann Arbor, Mich: Center for Chinese Studies.
Sidel, Ruth.
1973   Women and Child Care in China. Baltimore: Penguin Books.
1974   Families of Fengsheng: Urban Life in China. Harmondsworth, England: Penguin Books.
Suyin, Han.
1972   The Crippled Tree. New York: Bantam Books.
Wolf, Margery.
1972   Women and the Family in Rural Taiwan. Stanford, Calif.: Stanford University Press.
Yang, C. K.
1965   Chinese Communist Society. Cambridge, Mass.: MIT Press.

Family Structure and Communism

Mihaly Vajda
Agnes Heller

The abolition of private property and the destruction of alienated collective authority, which are recurring themes of Marxian communism, are a function of ... positive value presuppositions. Neither is a goal in itself. Both are means and processes meant to bring about a "humane" society, since the end of private property and the state are fundamental preconditions for the elimination of (1) the fetishization of human relations into relations among things, (2) the subordination of men to other men (social division of labor), and (3) the relation of men to other men as mere means....

Does the process of total social transformation automatically satisfy the preconditions which would permit the realization of its goal; that is, the positive and nonalienated regulation of human relations? Does purely political and economic activity create the types of men necessary for a really *free* society? The communist transformation of the relations of production and the transformation of alienated power structures into "social," local governing structures can be accomplished only if *our conscious revolutionary intentions* are also directed toward transforming everday life. Indeed, all these factors are mutually conditioning. The transformation of production relations and the dissolution of power relations are unimaginable without the conscious revolutionary reconstruction of everyday life, and *vice versa*.

Engels posed this problem in his *Origin of the Family, Private Proper-*

Excerpts reprinted from Mihaly Vajda and Agnes Heller, "Family Structure and Communism." *Telos* 7(Spring 1971):99–111. This essay was originally written in Hungarian. English translation by Andrew Arato. Reprinted by permission, *Telos,* Department of Sociology, Washington University, St. Louis.

ty, and the State. According to him, the destruction of private property and the withering away of the state must necessarily accompany the dissolution of the monogamous family. Engels argued that in a communist society the monogamous family would turn into a marriage partnership but added that nothing certain can be said in advance about this development since the new forms are yet to be worked out.

It has been suggested that within communism it is possible to separate the task of bringing up new generations from the constant framework of intimate relations between men and women (that is, in the form of child care centers organized by the state or by the whole of society as the basic units for forming new generations). This notion is not only utopian but also implies the impoverishment of human life in at least one essential respect. Thus, it stands in opposition to the value presuppositions of communism: it would eliminate from life the internal connections of adults and children as organic parts of universal human relations. Furthermore, it implies the introduction of a new division of labor, the separation of a stratum of educators. The rejection of this view, however, is also connected with the rejection of the alternative that the children's upbringing must always take place within the framework of the monogamous bourgeois family.

The original structure of both types[1] of bourgeois family is in a state of transition. Today, as a result of changes in the structure of modern capitalism, the majority of bourgeois families are no longer organized around production but around consumption. Thus, even within capitalism, the economic function of the family is diminishing. The phenomena usually described as the "dissolution of the family" or "crisis of the family form" are probably connected to this change. What are these phenomena? (1) The end of monogamy in the strict sense. Divorce *de jure* (or at least *de facto*) is universally accepted, although some attention has been paid to its socially negative characteristics. The most dramatic manifestation of this phenomenon was the suggestion in Sweden and Denmark to legally abolish marriage as an institution. (2) The almost complete *de jure* elimination and the *de facto* reduction of male authority in marriage. This is connected to so-called women's emancipation, the gradual widening of the circle of occupations open to women, the achievement of political equality by women, et cetera. (3) The transformation of moral norms relating to sexuality, which improves the situation of women and is connected to the increase in divorces. (4) The practical disappearance of the multi-generational family: the narrowing of the family to the "nuclear family."

From the viewpoint of the basic value of free choice of human ties,

---

[1]The petit bourgeois family function was that of a *productive unit*; the upper bourgeois family was as a property holding unit.

this process must be considered positive even if it leads to insoluble conflicts which society is powerless to solve even when it seeks to eliminate them in an organized manner. One such basic conflict flows from the contradiction between the freedoms of divorce and raising children. The financial problems involved are easily solved if the society is sufficiently affluent. This is not as serious a problem as the disruption brought about by divorce in the lives of many children.

Another basic problem resulting from this disintegration is loneliness. The nuclear family reduces the possibility of intensive, many-sided relationships (in societies where, almost without exception, human ties outside the family are merely functional). This problem is all the more serious in the case of old people who are left alone. In many families, if the old people live with the nuclear family, they either serve it or become a burden for it; and if they do not live with the family, they are abandoned to complete loneliness. The same problem arises with divorced people, especially women who must raise children. Such a task obviously interferes with entering into new relations.

Sexual revolution as a slogan and as a movement expresses and stimulates this process of disintegration, although its main aim is the formation of free human relations. For the sake of this aim, the "sexual revolution" strives toward the complete dissolution of the bourgeois family. Naturally, as in all human relations, the free choice of sexual relations and the freedom to choose them again and again is a basic precondition for the development and universalization of individuality. At the same time, the sexual revolution restricts the program of establishing human ties to the free choice of sexual partners. It fails to analyze the relationship between sexuality and other types of intense ties: first and foremost, the relations between adults and children. The sexual revolution offers no solution toward the formation of the basic units of a new society. It is one-sided even in terms of its restricted analysis of sexual relations. Beginning with the assumption that the historically available types of sexual relations are not free, it prefers promiscuity and disregards the fact that the most substantial, intense, and many-sided human relations (for example, love, friendship, et cetera) originate in the lives of couples. ... The solutions to the two problems of sexuality and family must be sought together, but it would be regressive to seek the solutions in some new type of bourgeois family.

Independently of its economic function, the basic social function of the bourgeois family is to shape a type of personality that guarantees the frictionless operation of bourgeois society. The Marxist theory of society presupposes an immediate connection between the structure of personality and the totality of social relations. It assumes as natural that the transformation of the production and property relations, political structures, et cetera, of a given society will produce the type of man adequate to the new society. The theory does not examine the concrete mechanisms which shape character types corresponding to social conditions. As a result, it ignores that family which plays no basic role in the organization of production; it examines the relations between family structure and society only as a moment of production or of property relations. . . .

Because of inborn characteristics, a basic human personality is formed and fixed in early childhood. We will call this "psychic character." The belief that the whole human personality can go through *perceptual* and *radical* changes during the entire life span is implicitly or explicitly present in Marxism. However, this is an unfortunate inheritance from sensualism. What can and often does change is *moral character*, and even this does not change independently of the psychic character: for example, a negative psychic character precludes a radical moral catharsis. Accordingly, psychic character is primarily formed in the family, which also transmits basic moral preferences to the child. Later on, however, these moral preferences can be modified through choice, unlike psychic character, which cannot.

The bourgeois family must guarantee that the psychic character of the men who grow up within it are adequate to the demands of bourgeois society. This, of course, need not be accomplished consciously. Indeed, in most cases the task is accomplished even if the dominant family ideology is openly *antibourgeois*. . . .

The two parents constitute the basic environment of the small child. Upbringing in the nursery and in the day care center always relates back to the family. It is "natural" for the child to love his parents before anyone else. Indeed, parents "must" be loved and honored: society expects it. Until the moment of adulthood, the child's deepest emotional ties are with his parents, and he must seek his moral ideals in them. The day care center, and later the school, provide other moral ideals, but never in relation to everyday life and activity and never with such immediacy that they can direct the child in his activities. . . . Without going into situations where one or both parents have generally negative moral character yet society demands that the child love *these* parents (although in extreme cases of blatantly brutal or criminal parents society does not demand it), it suffices to point out that in this situation the child becomes totally homeless: he belongs nowhere.

The bourgeois family is authoritarian: it is not a community. Even today in the great majority of families, because of tradition and his social situation, the man is the authority independently of the means to exercise this authority. There are families where, because of her place in society or the strength of her personality, the woman has authority. This does not change the fact that the family is authoritarian. As a result, the contemporary family is not adequate to teach the child how to live and act in a community.... Second, a real community cannot be formed because of the small number of children. Even in those unusual cases where the family has many children, they are not of the same age and the age difference creates a kind of "natural hierarchy." This happens because older children often become the representatives of parents. The children's authoritarian social conduct is prepared by this structure....

Within the family, the instinct of self-preservation becomes a desire to own or to have. Even when it is not a unit of production and does not have private property that provides an income, the bourgeois family is based on community of property. Because of its authoritarian structure, the use of the family's property is a function of the decision of the family authority. This can lead to a struggle for the use of property within the family and at the same time to a defense of the family's material interests against every other family and group....

Originally, the proletarian family was *not* a bourgeois family. It was not bourgeois even in Marx's time, when the material conditions of the proletariat prevented it from developing the preconditions for a "normal" bourgeois family life.... The gradual improvement of the conditions of the proletariat permitted the "bourgeoisification" of its family structure and encouraged the development of the predominant family type: the monogamous bourgeois family. Bernstein saw this well and approved of it: everyone must be brought up as a *Bürger*. He also correctly saw the connection between this process and the development of reformist tendencies within the working-class movement. Those who live in a bourgeois way do not wish to fundamentally change bourgeois society but instead try to reform it so as to guarantee higher standards of living. Even in great economic crises, the proletarian who grows up in a petit bourgeois family becomes a rebel, not a revolutionary....

Naturally, the negative role of the bourgeois family in the formation of psychic and moral character does not seem to be entirely a function of the family structure. This restriction applies specifically to the "possessive orientation" and the particular "collective unconsciousness." But, in the first place, there seem to be factors which cannot be transcended within the given family structure, for example, the essentially authoritarian relationship between child and parent and the absence of community in everyday life. Secondly, and this is the crucial point, certain habitual norms and value preferences have historically become attached to the contemporary family in such a way that their elimination from the family structure as it is seems almost impossible.

Thus, a revolutionary transformation of the family structure aimed at the denial of these habitual norms and value preferences seems more promising.

The Marxism of the Second International considered the total social process and the formation of psychic character to be immediately related: it was convinced that the transformation of the former leads mechanically to the transformation of the latter. Originally, Bolshevism did the opposite. Thus, in the period immediately following the October Revolution it seemed natural that decisive changes must occur in the relations between man and woman and in the basic forms of communal living, since the creation of proletarian authority and the liquidation of the ruling classes does not automatically imply these changes. There were fundamental changes in family law, along with decisive attempts to completely transform everyday life. . . .

The ideology that became predominant in the 1930s and restored many theoretical conceptions of the Second International also restored social democratic conceptions of family structure. Conscious steps were taken to restore or to strengthen the bourgeois family structure. Although they might have felt it instinctively, they were not conscious that this tendency strengthened the authoritarian character of the whole system. When other socialist countries came into being, the transformation of the family structure was definitely not on the agenda. There was concern only with those aspects of the bourgeois family which were directly connected with all of society, while the family ideal itself remained untouched. . . .

In the history of Marxist theory, however, a different conception has been developed which now plays an important role in Western European leftist movements. This conception does not consider the shaping of a "new man" merely as a result of ideological "influences" nor does it view this aim simply as the mechanical result of the transformation of the total social structure. Rather, it considers the development of a new psychic character in relation to the democratic transformation of the *units of social production*. . . . Naturally, the democratic transformation of the structure of the workshop is also one of the basic preconditions of communism. However, even this provides no answer to our problem. That is: (1) The more developed a society, the later an individual enters production. Thus, the young increasingly begin work with a fixed psychic and moral character. (2) The more developed a society, the less time is spent in production. Indeed, the reduction of working time is a goal, although the formation of many-sided relationships is also related to production. (3) Even if professions and skills are freely chosen, it is still impossible to determine production from the individual viewpoint. Democracy at the level of production can become natural and free from manipulation only if democratic life and norms of action have *already* become natural for the individual entering production. . . .

A solution to this problem is possible only through a *radical transformation of the family*. What criteria must be met by the new family structure? (1) It must be a democratically structured community which allows the early learning of democratic propensities. (2) It must guarantee many-sided human relations including those between children and adults. (3) It must guarantee the development and realization of individuality. The basic precondition of this is the free choosing and rechoosing of human ties even in childhood. (4) It must eliminate both the conflicts originating in monogamy and those originating in its dissolution. This is the type of solution to be sought in the new type of family, which we will call the *commune*.

The following will outline how we conceive of family structure in communist society. It is useless to work out details since, as always, the organizations of the future cannot be realizations of prior "plans." Furthermore, in the same way that there are many different types of monogamous families, the "collective family," or the commune, will also take on a variety of guises. In fact, since it is a matter of putting together a much more complicated structure than the monogamous bourgeois family, it is likely that the number of variations will be greater.

This commune is the "successor" of the bourgeois family. Thus it is not the basic economic or political cell of communist society. The whole organization of society is completely independent of the commune, which is the *organizational center of everyday collective life*.

Thus, our commune has nothing in common with Fourier's phalanx or other similar plans for communes functioning as productive units or communities based on the sharing of the same living space. Since it functions *only* as a family, the realization of our commune is *not* independent of the sociopolitical situation and of the *overall* realization of communism. This commune would help bring about communist transformation by producing the type of men and frameworks needed for such transformation. Although its immediate function is the solution of the conflicts discussed, the commune creates the preconditions for communist changes in the economic and political structure so that they become *irreversible*. This does not mean that the organization of communes "must wait" at least *until* the beginning of communist social transformation. On the contrary, the two processes must begin together. If the situation favors this solution, it may be possible for the transition to communes to precede the full process.

The commune is a freely chosen community. Its members choose to be in it and are accepted by *all* other members of the community.

Individuals enter the commune: every adult member of the entering families becomes a commune member as an individual. Of course, the membership must be small enough to guarantee that the affairs of the commune can be conducted through immediate democracy. In the commune, all forms of personal individuality must be respected. Three conditions are necessary for the fuctioning of the commune. These are: (1) the obligation to work (all able members of the commune must work and participate in the social division of labor). Thus, even in the present context, it is not permissible within the commune that a high-earning man supports a woman with whom he has a stable attachment. (2) No one is relieved of collective tasks within the commune. (3) Everyone must be somehow engaged with the commune's community of children, regardless of whether or not he has children of "his own." Aside from this, the community does not interfere in the lives of its members, their occupation, free time, and human relations. Of course, as in every community, there will be preferred forms of human conduct. Except in extreme cases, however, moral preferences will not become moral imperatives. In extreme cases, the commune will expel the member.

According to our notion, the commune does not have value preferences concerning sexual relations. Until now in civilized societies, value preferences relating to sexuality had their main source in two factors. The first is the consciousness of property or ownership: the woman is the man's private property or, in a more modern version, the man and the woman are each other's property. The second factor is the need to take care of children. Since the commune is based on the denial of private property relations, the first factor is naturally dropped. In relation to the second, the solution lies in the commune, which will take care of children born in or belonging to it even if their parents choose a different partner, or if one or the other leaves the commune. What is the concrete meaning of the absence of value preferences regarding sexuality in the commune? It means that both life-long relations of couples and promiscuity are possible within the confines of the same commune. The commune does not make promiscuity obligatory. This is important, because in past years similar organizations have not only opted for promiscuity, but have been directly built on it. This, however, entails as much limitation of the individual's free self-development as does monogamy. Under these conditions, the dissolution of the relations of couples not only leaves the children's life unchanged, but also reduces the negative aspects of contemporary divorce for adults. Here, it is not a question of the reduction of pain, since it is not a question of life. Rather, it is a question of the possibility that after the end of a relation, the divorced partners can stay in their original community without remaining alone.

The commune solves the problem of loneliness in cases other than those involving divorce. Unattached people can find a community with married people since, given the present family structure, marriage partners can also be lonely. Because of lack of time, spatial separation, et cetera, married people can lack varied and many-sided human relations even if there are other people with whom they would gladly associate. Naturally, the loneliness of the old and their feeling of superfluousness disappears in the commune.

Communal living reduces human relations based on mere habit and routine. Within the context of the contemporary family, people often continue living with each other because they are used to it, cannot imagine a better solution, and want to avoid the problems brought about by divorce. These problems disappear in the commune.

The commune is not a closed unit which hinders the formation of rich human ties outside of it. External ties will develop spontaneously, since the commune is neither a productive nor a political unit. To the extent that there are many communes, fluctuation of membership among them will be natural.

Obviously, the commune will hold no "officially" declared ideology. But it is also obvious that a community of people who have freely chosen each other will have some common ideological outlook, especially in view of the fact that, at least in the present context, the commune implies the *revolutionary* transformation of life in one fundamental respect. As a result, ideological problems in the commune are likely to generate internal conflicts.

"Liberation" from housework does not seem possible in the foreseeable future, and the service industry, in spite of its growth, is not a solution. The modernization of the household helps, but it does not solve the problem. Within the commune, however, it is possible to substantially reduce the time spent running the household, even under present economic and technological conditions: larger households are much more economical and conducive to the use of machines. This alone increases the amount of free time which, in the commune, can also be used in radically different ways. Whereas in the monogamous family parents with small children are tied to the house, such is not the case in the commune, and the "house" itself allows a *diversified* use of free time. Even "within the house," free time should not be restricted to consumption but should be active, cultural, and conducive to personal development. Of course, the forms this development will take cannot be determined in advance, but within such a cultural context a community is likely to advance. This is shown by historical examples such as the cultural effects of the trade union communities of the old working-class movements. This advancement, of course, occurs only when the community does not restrict the unfolding of individuality, which we have postulated in principle.

As already mentioned, the commune's most basic advantage concerns children. Everything discussed so far concerns "finished" persons for whom the commune guarantees the solution of already existing problems. But the destruction of the bourgeois family is fundamental because it eliminates many negative factors determining the formation of psychic character. Before investigating this problem, however, it is important to outline the commune's community of children. In the commune, children are not "collectively" raised, but they belong to a real *community of children.* The judgment of children's conduct, their entrance into the division of labor, and the bestowing of reward and punishment, that is, the regulation of children's relations, is a function of age levels and should be not an adult task but one of the community of children. This does not mean that the relations between adults and children are not close and diversified; but they are not unambiguously authoritarian as in the bourgeois family. Children should be aware that they decide their fate in many ways. This leads to the early development of democratic inclinations so that children can become full members of the community of adults at a relatively early age. Even with very small children, for whom the authoritarian aspect of adult-child relations cannot be eliminated, it is crucial that *every* adult and older child in the commune, rather than just their "biological parents," be somehow occupied with them. Thus, from birth, they lack fixed emotional preferences. While growing, the child increasingly chooses adults to whom he is more attracted and to whom he feels connected by fundamental inner ties. The opposite is also true. The commune's adult members are not necessarily most strongly attracted to their "own" children. Thus, they can choose the children whose temperament, character, and intellect are "nearest" or most "attractive" to them. Both adults and children do not *have to* love anyone, nor *must* one love anyone *the most.* As with every other emotion, *love* also is a function of choice. This lessens the "mine"/"yours" dichotomy on the emotional level.

Of course, unlike the case of children born within the commune, free choice of emotional ties is illusory for members entering the commune with children. This can result in conflicts for people brought up in the old family structure. Yet, we should recall the common experience of people who feel they could love a child as "their own" if the child had been brought up in their environment. On the other hand, parents often cannot confront their children's faults, since they are afraid that exposure of these faults would leave them with nothing. The latter is not always the case today in families with many children.

The commune's community obviously makes demands on the children's community: there are the *same* demands made on adults, for example, the obligation to work (study) and obligatory participation in the community's common work. In this context, even if the adult community is forced to appear authoritarian, it is not in the sense of "family head," since the adults require the performance of obligations similar to their own. In addition to deemphasizing the "mine"/"yours" dichotomy, the child community also hinders the development of private property psychology in other contexts. In the children's world, unlike the adults' world, all personal property is eliminated. Many existing child communities show how this can be accomplished.

The psychic character of children who grow up in the circumstances will be conducive to democratic life. They will *never accept as natural* a situation in which they do not have a voice in determining their fate. At the same time, they will not develop a need to oppress other men. It could be argued that existing children's communities are characterized by cruelty. These communities, however, consist of children who grew up in bourgeois families and who want to "live out" power instincts that were developed and at the same time repressed in the family. A more serious objection is that children's communities might hinder the development of individuality. To avoid this, the commune must create the preconditions to enable children as well as adults to follow their own wishes and tastes after satisfying their communal obligations. Each child must be able to play as he wants, read what he wants, and spend his free time as he wishes.

On the other hand, the development of free individuality is greatly enhanced by children confronting a large number of adults. If adults are basically of positive moral character, as in the case of the nuclear family, the children have the opportunity to choose as the ideal of everyday conduct those adults whose psychic and moral character is adequate to their particular gifts. Thus, communes which satisfy their social functions will have definite material preconditions. First, the commune cannot be closed: each individual member must be free to leave the commune at any time. Second, the community must have the right to expel a member if necessary. The preconditions of this must be assured: society must guarantee available apartments which can be occupied by departing members at any time. Also, the normal functioning of the commune requires a certain level of material prosperity. "Communes based on misery," at least under European conditions, necessarily dissolve. Yet no great "affluence" is necessary for the establishment of the commune, especially since housekeeping, common library, collective child education, et cetera, substantially reduce individual expenses. As long as the commune operates within a commodity-producing society, material problems must be carefully regulated so that they create as few conflicts as possible. Since the commune cannot be isolated from society at large, this problem can be solved only by reduction of income differences. As long as the communist solution to the problem of income is not completed, the commune can only reproduce in itself the larger problems in this area.

The commune can also change or dissolve as a result of other conflicts. Since the commune is the organizational center of the everyday life of communist society, existing noncommunist societies hinder the development of communes and aim at their dissolution. The ideal type of commune described is also laden with conflicts; but these are not the conflicts of a society built on possession. They are "truly human" conflicts. However, the influence of existing societies can result in the reproduction of old conflicts and structures. Thus, the development of a very strong particular identity within individual communes is to be expected. This identity can be the cause or effect of competition or even of animosity among communes. Other important problems can result from the fact that individual communes would probably consist of people occupying the same position in the social division of labor. This can cause significant differences in the standards of living of the various communes and results in the preservation of cultural differences.

It is utopian to believe that the commune *alone* can solve the most basic social problems. No isolated political or economic transformation can be final or prevent the reproduction of old social structures. Thus, for example, workshop democracy can easily be deformed and transformed into manipulated democracy. An isolated solution to the problem of the family is no exception and, if it remains isolated, the commune will definitely be deformed. Thus, a basic social task of commune members is to assist in communist transformation in *every* social sphere. Similarly, without the revolution of the family, structural changes in a communist social direction cannot become irreversible. The formation of a new psychic character can take place only within the revolutionized family. This is the only locus of mass education for individuals who are to take an active part in the direction of social affairs, not only in times of great social crises but "every day."

NAME INDEX

Blood, Robert O., Jr., 249n, 255, 361, 368
Bock, E. Wilbur, 341, 344
Bogoras, Waldemar, 131, 132, 134
Boserup, Ester, 363, 368, 413
Boulding, Kenneth E., 5n, 13n
Bourlière, Francois, 161n
Bowen, W. B., 181n
Braito, Rita, 120, 124, 126
Brandeis, Louis, 82
Brandwein, Ruth A., 184, 347, 350–59
Braverman, Harry, 44n, 80n
Brazer, H. E., 348n
Brecher, Jeremy, 210, 215
Brenton, Myron, 122, 124
Brewer, M. B., 250, 255
Broverman, Donald, 5n
Broverman, Inge, 5n
Brown, Barbara, 288n
Brown, Carol A., 347, 350–59
Brown, Judith K., 109, 128–36, 233, 362, 368
Bruton, Brent, 120, 124
Buettner-Janusch, John, 161n
Burgess, Ernest W., 49n, 144, 147

Cain, Glen G., 184
Calderwood, Ann, 372n
Carter, Hugh, 297n, 357, 358
Cavan, Ruth, 354, 358
Centers, Richard, 281
Child, I. L., 249n, 255
Clancy, Kevin, 7n
Clark, Alice, 41n, 75n
Clark, Colin, 6n
Clark, Homer, 288n
Clarkson, Frank E., 5n
Cohen, Charlotte, 413
Cohen, Yehudi A., 160n
Cole, G. D. H., 79n
Commons, John R., 210, 215
Confucius, 49
Constantinople, Anne, 118, 124
Coult, Alan C., 163n
Craddock, Alan E., 233, 239–47
Crano, William D., 233, 248–55
Crook, David, 413
Crook, Isabel, 413
Curtin, Katie, 413

Dahrendorf, Ralf, 11
Dalla Costa, Mariarosa, 365, 368
Daniels, Arelene K., 5, 29
Davies, Margery, 44n

Davin, Delia, 413
Davis, Angela, 67, 70
Dean, Dwight, 120, 124, 126
de Beauvoir, Simone, 101, 156n, 172, 413
Decter, Midge, 47n
Defoe, Daniel, 43
Delcourt, Marie, 122, 124
Denmark, Florence L., 3n
De Schlippe, Pierre, 132, 134
Dewhurst, J. Frederic, 333
Dexter, Elisabeth A., 41n
Diamond, Esther E., 118, 124
Didion, Joan, 19n
Dietrich, Katheryn Thomas, 260, 279–86
Doeringer, Peter B., 183, 201n, 212, 215
Douglas, Jack D., 29
Duchan, Linda, 373n
Dunlop, John T., 201n
Durkheim, Emile, 5n, 128, 135, 232, 248, 255, 257, 262

Eckhardt, Kenneth, 294n
Edgerton, Robert B., 117, 124
Edgeworth, F. Y., 196
Edmond, Wendy, 51n, 108n
Edwards, Richard C., 13n, 82n, 184, 186, 208–15
Eifler, Deborah, 108n
Ellul, Jacques, 40n
Emerson, Thomas, 288n
Engels, Frederick, 26, 28, 65, 66, 69, 99, 101, 112, 113, 148–55, 156–67, 171, 219, 415, 416
Epstein, Cynthia, 7n, 326
Erhardt, Anke A., 1n
Etzioni, Amitai, 28
Eve, 39, 43, 363

Faia, Michael, 372n
Falk, Gail, 288n
Faulkner, William, 332
Fawcett, Millicent, 196
Feldberg, Roslyn, 184, 187, 259, 272–78
Ferber, Marianne A., 376n
Ferris, Abbott, 351, 358
Fidell, L. S., 3n, 373n
Finegan, T. Aldrich, 8n, 181n
Firestone, Shulamith, 55, 70, 101, 111n
Fisher, Ann, 107n
Fisk, Norman, 117, 125

Fleming, Suzie, 51n, 108n
Flexner, Eleanor, 45n
Fogarty, Michael P., 7n
Folsom, Joseph 141, 146
Foote, C., 295n
Forde, C. Daryll, 131, 135
Forsher, Trude, 351, 359
Fourier, Charles, 170, 171, 176, 421
Fox, Elizabeth M., 347, *350–59*
Franklin, Benjamin, 43
Franklin, Raymond S., 184
Frazier, E. Franklin, 260
Freedman, Ann E., 82n, 288n
Freedman, Maurice, 413
Freeman, Alma, 122, 124
Freeman, Jo, 107n, 111n
Freud, Sigmund, 47, 233
Fried, Morton H., 156n
Friedan, Betty, 46
Friedl, Ernestine, 103n, 363, 368
Fuchs, Victer G., 185, 304, 305,
    307–12

Galbraith, John Kenneth, 183, 213,
    215, 362, 364, 368
Garai, Josef F., 116, 124
Garfinkle, Harold, 11
Gelber, Sylvia M., 5n
George, C. H., 61, 70
Gibb, G. A., 250, 255
Gilman, Charlotte Perkins, 69, 101,
    231, 368
Gintis, Herbert, 278
Glasser, Paul, 356, 358
Glazer-Malbin, Nona, 49n, 257n
Glazer, Nona, 51n, *101–14*, 182, 184,
    187, *231–33, 256–61*, 348,
    360–69, 388–93
Glick, Paul C., 47n, 230n, 297n,
    357, 358
Goffman, Erving, 11
Goode, William J., 49n, 294n, 297n,
    352, 355, 356, 358
Gordon, David M., 13n, 82n, 83n,
    184, 186, 205n, *208–15*
Gordon, Michael, 47n
Gornick, Vivian, 7n, 108n
Gough, Kathleen, 112, *156–68*
Gove, Walter, 7n
Gover, K. R., 352, 358–59
Graham, Alma, 2
Graves, Robert, 43n
Gray, Betty MacMorran, 181,
    332–34, 306
Griffiths, Martha, 38
Grimm, James W., 303n

Gronau, Reuben, 182n
Gross, Edward, 340, 344
Gross, Leonard, 109n
Gubbels, Robert, 305, *320–31*
Gump, Janice P., 123, 124
Gusinde, Martin, 133, 134, 135

Haas, M. B., 274, 278
Hacker, Helen Mayer, 101, 110,
    137–47, 388
Hacker, Sally L., 2n
Hamilton, Henry, 41n
Hamilton, Peter, 29
Harré, Romano, 19, 28
Hartley, Ruth E., 122, 124
Hartmann, Heidi, 52–53, *71–84*
Hegel, G. W. F., 65
Heller, Agnew, 393, *415–26*
Heller, Celia S., 184, 336, 344
Henley, Nancy, 2n
Hill, Ann C., 82
Hill, Georgianna, 75n
Hill, W. W., 117, 125
Hines, Fred, 315
Hitchcock, John T., 130, 135
Hochschild, Arlie Russell, 19, 28,
    101, 102, 104
Hockett, Charles F., 160n
Hoffman, Lois W., 8n, 105n
Hokado, Elizabeth, 108n
Holmstrom, Lynda L., 278
Holter, Harriet, 114, 125
Horner, Matina S., 105, 120, 125
Howell, F. Clark, 161n
Huang, Jen Lucy, 129, 135
Huber, Joan, 101n, 121, 125
Hughes, Helen MacGill, 3n
Hurlbut, John B., 291n
Hutchins, B. L., 75n
Hutchinson, Anne, 43
Hymer, Stephen, 74n

Jacklin, Carol, 106, 107
Jackson, Larry R., 344
Jemison, Mary, 132
Jenkin, Noel, 118, 125
Jenness, Diamond, 131, 135
Johnson, Shirley B., 8n, 187n
Johnsen, Virginia E., 47, 108n
Jones, Howard W., Jr., 122, 125
Josephson, Eric, 1
Josephson, Mary, 1
Jung, Carl G., 118, 122, 125
Jusenius, Carol L., 181, 185, 186,
    194–207, 304

Kaberry, Phyllis, 130, 133, 135
Kagan, Jerome, 116, 123, 125
Kahne, Hilda, 180n
Kanowitz, Leo, 40n, 288n
Kanter, Rosabeth Moss, 5n, 107n,
    364
Karol, K. S., 413
Kay, Herma H., 289n, 290, 292
Kellner, Hansfried, 11, 257, 258,
    259, *362–71*
Kerr, Clark, 201n
Kessle, Gun, 413
Kleiner, Robert J., 286
Kohen, Janet, 184, 187, 259, *272–78*
Kohlberg, L., 2n
Komarovsky, Mirra, 120, 125
Kreps, Juanita M., 302
Kriesberg, Louis, 352, 358

Lakoff, Robin, 111n
Lambert, William, 130, 136
Lamphere, Louise, 73n
Lampman, Robert J., 349, *378–80*
Laslett, Barbara, 49n
Laub, Donald R., 117, 125
Leacock, Eleanor B., 101n
Leibenstein, Harvey, 182n
Leibowitz, Arleen, 8n
Lenin, V. I., 176
Lenski, Gerhard, 11
Lester, Richard A., 370–72, 374–75,
    377
Levi-Strauss, Claude, 73, 117, 125,
    129, 135
Levinger, George, 239, 240, 241,
    243, 245, 247
Lewin, Arie Y., 373n
Lewin, Kurt, 138, 145, 146
Lilith, 43
Lin Piao, 49
Lipman-Blumen, Jean, 2n, 101n,
Lippert, Julius, 131, 135
Lipset, Seymour Martin, 1
Liu, Shao-chi, 407
Livernash, E. Robert, 201n
Livingstone, Frank B., 160n
Lloyd, Cynthia, 6n, 7
Locke, Harvey J., 49n
Loeb, Jane W., 376n
Lopata, Helen Z., 101n, 108n, 363,
    364, 368
Lowie, Robert H., 160n
Luckmann, Thomas, 271
Lukács, Georg, 70
Lundberg, Lars-Olaf, 398

Lyndon, Susan, 47n
Lynn, Naomi, 107n

McClung, Nellie, 24, 28
Maccoby, Eleanor, 106, 107, 123,
    125, 130, 135
MacEwan, A., 13n
MacIntosh, Anita, 182n
McKern, Sharon, 161n
McKern, Thomas W., 161n
Madden, Janice Fanning, 8n, 199
Malamud, Rene, 122, 126
Malinowski, Bronislaw, 129, 135
Mandell, Ernest, 184, 216, 217, 218
Mannheim, Karl, 1, 5n, 40n
Mao Tse-tung, 408
Marcuse, Herbert, 176
Marsden, Dennis, 276, 278, 355,
    356, 358
Marshall, Gloria, 130, 135
Martin, M. Kay, 363, 368
Marx, Karl, 5n, 11, 26, 27, 28, 56,
    61, 65, 66, 151, 161, 170, 171,
    366, 419
Masters, William H., 47, 108n
Matasar, Ann, 107n
Matthiasson, Carolyn J., 104n
Mead, George Herbert, 11, 26, 28,
    271
Mead, Margaret, 101, 129, 130, 135
Mednick, Martha T. Shuch, 105n
Merryweather, Mary, 79n
Merton, Robert, 11, 101
Miles, Catherine C., 116n, 127
Mill, John Stuart, 65, 99, 101
Miller, Herman P., 342, 344
Millet, Kate, 64, 70, 101, 156n
Millman, Marcia, 5n, 7, 107n
Mincer, Jacob, 181, 182, 185, 197n,
    189–93
Minturn, Leigh, 130, 135, 136
Mitchell, Juliet, 55, 70, 101, 113,
    166–79, 219, 220, 365
Money, John, 1n
Moran, B. K., 7n, 108n
Morgan, J., 348n
Morgan, Lewis Henry, 133, 136,
    156, 157, 160, 164n
Morgan, Marabel, 390n
Morgan, Robin, 44n
Morris, Desmond, 161n
Moss, H., 116, 125
Moss, Zoe, 48n
Mosteller, Frederick, 120, 126
Mowrer, E. R., 239, 247

Moynihan, Daniel P., 260, 286, 341, 344
Mueller, E., 118, 126
Muller, Viana, 77n
Munroe, Robert L., 129, 136
Munroe, Ruth H., 129, 136
Murdock, George Peter, 128, 129, 131, 133, 136, 162n, 163n, 248–53, 255
Myrdal, Gunnar, 101, 109, 110, 141, 146
Myrdal, Jan, 413

Nagel, Stuart, 292n
Navarre, Elizabeth, 356, 358
Niemi, Albert W., Jr., 305, *313–19*
Nilsen, Alleen Pace, 108n
Nixon, Richard M., 347
Norton, Arthur J., 47n
Norton, Eleanor H., 82n
Nottingham, Elizabeth K., 45n
Nye, F. Ivan, 8n

Oakley, Ann, 13n, 107n, 360, 363, 364, 368
Oakley, Anne, 114, 126
O'Connor, James, 70
Okun, Arthur M., 201n
Oppenheimer, Valerie K., 181n
Ortner, Sherry B., 73
Ostenso, Martha, 24, 25, 28
Ostriker, Alicia, 348, *370–80*
Ostriker, J. P., 348, *370–80*
Overzier, Claus, 117, 126

Parelman, Allison, 107n
Park, Robert E., 143, 144, 146, 147
Parker, Gail, 69, 70
Parker, Seymour, 286
Parsons, Talcott, 11, 19, 28, 101, 174, 175, 177, 232, 233, *234–38*, 239, 240, 241, 247, 248, 249, 250, 254, 255, 258
Patai, Raphael, 43n
Perry, George L., 201n
Piaget, Jean, 117, 126
Piercy, Marge, 44n
Pierson, Frank C., 201n
Pinchbeck, Ivy, 75n
Piore, Michael J., 183, 201n, 205n, 212, 214, 215
Pohly, S. R., 118, 126
Polacheck, Solomon, 197n
Pollak, Otto, 356, 358

Pospisil, Leopold, 129, 136
Postgate, Raymond, 79n
Powers, Edward A., 120, 124, 126
Provost, C., 250, 255
Pusey, Nathan, 370
Putney, Emily James, 42n
Pyun Cheng Soo, 362, 368

Radin, Max, 288n
Rapoport, Rhona, 7n
Rapoport, Robert N., 7n
Raven, Bertram H., 286
Reagan, Barbara B., 3n
Redfern, Martin, 315n
Reich, Michael, 82n, 176, 181, 184, 186, *208–15*
Reiss, Albert J., 242n, 247
Reiter, Rayna, 71n
Reynolds, Joyce E., 117, 124
Rheinstein, Max, 296n
Rice, David G., 109n
Richardson, Herbert W., 118, 126
Riesman, David, 176, 271
Robinson, Joan, 199
Roby, Pamela, 7n
Rodrigues, Aroldo, 286
Rosaldo, Michelle Z., 73n
Rose, Frederick G. G., 133, 136
Rosen, Ruth, 5n
Rosenberg, Benjamin, 116, 127
Rosenberg, Marie, 107n
Rosenkrantz, Paul, 5n
Ross, Catherine, 108n
Ross, Heather L., 8n, 182n
Ross, Susan C., 82n
Rossi, Alice S., 101, 102n, 239, 247, 372n, 388
Rowbotham, Sheila, 414
Rubin, Gayle, 71n
Rubin, Lillian B., 256
Rugh, Roberts, 122, 126
Rush, Dr. Benjamin, 43
Ruskin, John, 64

Safilios-Rothschild, Constantina, 109n
Salaff, Janet, 414
Samuelson, Paul, 182
Sanday, Peggy, 362, 368
Sanford, Nevitt, 117, 123, 126
Santos, Fredericka P., 182n
Sawhill, Isabel V., 8n, 182n, 305n, 342, 344
Scanzoni, John H., 183n, 279, 286
Scheinfeld, Amram, 116, 124

Woock, Robert, 1
Wortis, Rochelle Paul, 8n, 108n
Wright, Arthur, 149
Wright, Patricia, 373n
Wrong, Dennis A., 103n

Yang, C. K., 414

Zaretsky, Eli, 23n, 49–52, 55–70,
  187, 257
Zelditch, Morris, Jr., 232n, 239, 247,
  249
Zetkin, Clara, 176
Zimmerman, Don H., 49n, 257n
Znaniecki, Florian, 101

SUBJECT INDEX

Abortion, 47
Adultery, 152, 159
Affirmative Action programs, 4, 183
Aging, double standard of, 48
Aid to Families with Dependent Children (AFDC), 351
Alimony, 336, 347–48
  and Equal Rights Amendment, 200, 299
  and law, 291–92
  origins of, 291
Androgyny, 122–23
Anglo-Saxon law. *See* Common law
Angus Downs aborigines, 134
Assimilation of sexes, 145, 388–89
Authority in family, 281, 287–89, 299, 535–54

Birth names, use of, 288–89
Black Muslims, 389
Black Women Organized for Action, 343
Blacks:
  family structure of, 260–61, 279–86
  in female labor force, 90, 383
  and myth of matriarchy, 279–86
  returns to educational investment for, 316
  and sex and race discrimination, 306, 339–42

status of compared to status of women, 141–43, 142 (table)
  and women's movement, 342–43
Bourgeois family:
  decline of, 63–65
  as an economically independent unit, 61–62
  trends in, 416–17
Bunting v. *Oregon*, 82
Bureaucratization, and labor market segmentation, 211–12

Capitalism:
  emergence of, 74–84
  and family life, 56, 272–78
  and occupational segregation, 52–53
  and sociological discourse, 18
  and status of women, 57–58
Cash crop farming, 25
Caste/class approach to sexual inequality, 111–13
Catholic church, 41–42. *See also* Religion
Child care:
  in communes, 422–25
  and Equal Rights Amendment, 200
  and labor force participation, 87–89, 94
  and law, 293–95
  in precapitalist societies, 130–34
  as a universal women's role, 33–34

Child care facilities, 347, 398
Child custody, 294, 336
Child labor laws, 66, 78
Child support, 247–48, 294–95, 352–53
Childless marriages, 94
Children:
  effect of on construction of social reality, 267
  effect of on labor force participation of mothers (fig.), 88
Chimpanzees. See Great apes
China:
  divorce in, 404
  status of women in, 48–49, 173, 364, 392, 400–414
Cigarmakers International Union, 81
Citizens Advisory Council on the Status of Women, 293n, 353, 358
Civil War (U.S.), role of women in, 44
Civilization stage of cultural development, 158–59
Cognitive development theory, 2
Common law (England), 387–88. See also Family law
Communes, 421–26
Community property laws, 337, 380–81
Consumer role:
  family in, 222
  linked with human meaning, 66, 68
  wife in, 13–14, 35–36
Contraception:
  in China, 173
  effect on sexual freedom, 45–46
Contravention, 144
Conversation, functions of, 263–64, 268–69
Courtly love, 159
Cuckolds, 152
Cultural evolution theory (Engels), 156–68
Cultural Revolution (China, 1966–68), 48, 407–8

Decision making:
  allocation of, by area of decision (table), 283
  in black families, 282–85, 282 (table)
  conjugal interaction patterns in (table), 284
  measures of, 280–81

Developmental change model of gender role change, 123
Discrimination:
  average coefficients of, by race, age, and educational attainment (table), 318
  and cyclical unemployment, 332–34 and definition of minority group, 137–39
  and human capital approach, 198
  method of measuring, 338–39
  and occupational segregation, 37
  overcrowding hypothesis of, 195–97
  statistical, 203–4
  in universities, 370–80
Division of labor by sex:
  anthropological perspectives on, 73–74, 128–36
  in colonial farm families, 79
  and compatibility of productive functions with child care, 130
  determined by culture, 33, 160
  and development of language, 160
  and economic interdependence of sexes, 130
  and family problems, 275–76
  and family roles, 273–74
  and housework, 361
  sociological explanations of, 231–33
  into task and socioemotional specialist roles, 239–55
  universality of, 129–30, 362–63
Divorce:
  division of property in, 293
  in early Communist China, 404
  and economic functions of the family, 351–53
  and emotional supports, 355–57
  and external organizations, 276–77
  and housework, 354–55
  increase in, 296–97
  after Russian Revolution, 173
  societal response to, 276
Divorce insurance, 51
Domestic industrial system:
  role of women in, 75–76
  See also Family factory system
Domestic labor. See Housework
Domicile, establishment of, 288
Dual labor market analysis, 205–6

Earnings, 93–94
  comparison of by race-sex (table), 342

and external control of family
structure, 274
female, relative to male (table),
309
sex differences in, in Sweden
(table), 396
wifes legal rights to, 288
Earnings differential, 93, 185–87,
303–4, 351–52
and discrimination, 304
and distance from job, 308
and education, 305
explained by human capital
approach, 197–99
across industries, 310–11
explained by internal labor market
approach, 202–3
and marital status, 208, 310
between men and women (table),
309
and occupation, 311–12
by race and sex, 341–42
and self-employment, 308–9
in Sweden, 396
in universities, 372–73
Economics, theoretical approaches
to women in, 30–38, 182–84
Economy, defined, 40, 55
Education:
as a change strategy, 178–79
and earnings differentials, 305
and labor force participation,
89–91, 97–98, 98 (table)
and labor market segmentation,
213
methods for estimating returns to,
313–16
and occupational segregation, 97
returns to, and discrimination,
316–18, 317 (table)
Egalitarian marriage, 282–84,
296–97, 300–301
Equal Rights Amendment, 298–301
Everyday world:
as beginning of inquiry, 23–25
defined, 22
of women vs. men, 10–11
Exchange value of housework, 188,
216–18
Expressive leader, 232, 234–38

Family:
and capitalism, 56, 61–70
commune as alternative to, 421–26
consumer role of, 67–68
defined, 257

effect of corporations on, 50,
259–60
effect of factory system on,
63–64
effect of government on, 50
as emotional enclave, 49, 63–64,
175, 221–22, 235, 257–59, 270,
275–76
functions of, 56–57, 235–36
and gender role intensification,
236–37
medieval, 74
pairing, 149–50, 157
Roman, 150–51
as separate from social institutions,
49
and socialism, 56
as a socializing agent, 235–36
success of, and external
institutions, 272–78
in traditional China, 400–402
See also Bourgeois family;
Matriarchy; Nuclear family;
Patriarchy; Proletarian family
Family counseling, and family
structure, 276
Family factory system:
avoidance of in U.S., 79–80
breakdown of under capitalism,
76–77
and family authority structure,
76
Family income:
contribution of working wives to,
382–83
median, trends, in, 381
median, by type of family (table),
382
Family law:
and use of birth name, 288–89
challenges to, 295–98
and child care responsibility,
293–95
and domicile establishment, 289
and Equal Rights Amendment,
298–301
on family authority, 287–89
and financial support, 289–92
and housework, 292–93
and property ownership under,
25, 287
and remarriage, 297–98
and women's rights, 40, 43, 153,
336
Family patterns, trends in, 295–98
Family structure:
and communism, 415–26

controlled by external
organizations, 274–75
and gender roles, 234–38
Farmwives, 24–25
Father role, 164
Federal programs, wife's rights to
benefits from, 289
Female-headed families:
income of, 53, 383–84
and myth of black matriarchy,
279–86
Femininity, measurement of, 116–19
Feminism:
and blacks, 242–43
in China, 404–5
impact of on scholarship, 6–8
in nineteenth century, 65
Financial support laws, 289–92
Ford (Motor Company), 212

Gender role models:
change in, 122–23
dichotomization of, 115–19
Gender roles:
androgyny as a model for change
in, 122–23
approach to study of sex
inequality, 107–9
assumptions about, 114–27
as bipolar, 117–18
continuity of, 118
developmental change model of,
123
distinguished from sex role,
114–15
extent of differences in, 116–19
in the family, 248–55
and family structure, 234–38,
248–55
intensification of, and nuclear
family, 236–37
multidimensionality of, 118
normal distribution, use of in
measuring, 118
and "playing dumb," 120
and role reversal, 122
and specialization in subsistence
activities, 251–55
and success avoidance, 120–21
uses of, 119–22
Generation gap, 69
Generic terms, 1–3
Great apes, family structure of,
161–62
Great Depression, 45
Great Leap Forward, 407

Gross National Product, exclusion of
housework from, 229
Group marriage, 157, 162–63
criticism of Engels's views on,
162–63
Guilds:
breakdown of, 76
participation of women in, 52, 63,
76

Hetaerism, 150–51, 159
Homosexuality, legalization of, 178
Housework:
and divorce, 293, 354–55
and Equal Rights Amendment,
300
exchange value of, 188
industrialization of, 219–21,
224–25
inevitability of, 34–35, 361–63
and law, 292–93
and leisure, 275
managerial aspect of, 21
monetary value of, 188, 293,
361–62
and political economy, 64–67
radical analysis of, 365–67
and religion, 63
and social roles, 363–64
and sociology for women, 367–68
time spent on, 46, 219
use value vs. exchange value of,
217–19
Human capital, 185
and occupational segregation,
197–99
Husband's earnings, effect of on
labor force participation of
women, 89–90
Hybrid model of sex equality, 390

Ideology, defined, 40
Illegitimacy, 47
Incest prohibitions, 164–66
Income:
contribution of working wives to
(fig.), 384
distribution of by earners (fig.),
383. See also Earnings
differential
independent, 34
median, of families (table), 382
median, of full time women
workers (table), 93
Index of Dissimilarity, 339–40

Industrial Workers of the World
(IWW), 210
Industrialization:
emergence of, 74–84
and family functions, 273
and family structure, 41–43, 402–3
of housework, 219–21
and "personal life," 67
Inheritance:
in matrilineal families, 149–50
in patrilineal families, 157–58
Institutional approaches to sex
inequality, 103–4, 183, 201–7,
364
Instrumental leader, 232–38
Internal labor market approach:
and occupational segregation,
201–5, 264
and productivity, 204–5
and statistical discrimination,
203–4
Iroquois, 132–33, 164n

Job interchangeability between
sexes, barriers to, 322–26
Job satisfaction, 96
Job skills, 321–22

Knowledge as a social relation,
16–17

Labor force participation of women,
85–98
and age, 86–87, 87 (table), 330
and children, 87–89, 88 (fig.), 94,
352
and earnings, 92–93
and education, 89–90, 96–98, 98
(table)
full-time vs. part-time, 92
and husband's earnings, 89–90
and job satisfaction, 96
and job skills, 321–22
and labor supply, 189–93, 222–23
and life expectancy, 93–95
and life-style changes, 93–95
and marital status, 46, 87–89, 87
(table), 94, 229–30, 321
and median family income,
381–82
and occupational aspirations,
95–96
and occupational distribution,
90–93

and qualifications demanded,
320–22
rates of, 90 (table), 91 (table)
and race, 90
stages of, 53
static nature of, 174
study of, 184–85, 189–93
as a threat to male jobs, 79
during wartime, 44–45, 46, 224
Labor market activities, research
topics in, 180–81, 185–87
Labor market segmentation theory,
82–83, 186–87, 208–15
and bureaucratization of authority,
211–12
defined, 208–9
and education, 213
origins of, 209–13
political implications of, 214–15
social functions of, 214–15
systemic forces reinforcing,
213–14
and unions, 213
and welfare capitalism, 212
Labor supply:
and labor force participation of
women, 44–45, 46, 189–93, 224,
321, 332–34
and opportunities for women, 80
and sex assignment of jobs,
329–30
Labor unions. *See* Unions
Land reform, and status of women
in China, 404
Language, place of women in, 2. *See
also* Conversation
Law. *See* Common law; Family law
Legislation, as a strategy for change,
183. *See also* Equal Rights
Amendment; Protective
legislation
Leisure:
as economic concept, 5–6, 33,
189–93
and housework, 275
Life expectancy, changes in, 94–95
Life-style, changes in, 94–95
Logoli, division of labor among, 129
Lower Barbarism stage of cultural
development, 157
Lower Savagery stage of cultural
development, 157
Lunga, division of labor among, 133

McGuire v. McGuire, 291
Macrosociology, 11

Marginality:
of housework, 219
of women, 145–47
Marital Roles Inventory, 242
Marriage:
childless, 94
and construction of social reality,
262–71
egalitarian, 282–4, 296–97
emotional specialization in,
239–47
function of conversation in,
268–69
group, 157, 162–63
and labor force participation,
87–89, 94, 229–30, 321
as a legal contract, 261
as a partnership in bourgeois
families, 62–63
use of in measuring social
distance, 140–41
process of nomic transformation
in, 267–69
parental consent for, and private
property, 153
as sign of a successful woman,
228–30
and task specialization, 239–47
Marriage contracts, 298–99
Married Women's Property Acts,
288
Mary cult, 41
Masculinity, measurement of,
117–20. See also Gender roles
Maternal death rate, 46
Matriarchy:
and blacks, 279–86
prevalence of, 163–65
Matrilineality, 148–50, 157, 167
Matrilocality, 163–65, 167
Medieval family, 74
Men's liberation movement, 391
Microsociology, 11
Middle Barbarism stage of cultural
development, 157
Middle Savagery stage of cultural
development, 157
Minority group:
defined, 137
subjective and objective
components of definition of,
137–39
women as, 137–46
Minority group status:
as different from minority group,
138
of women, 109–11, 139–40

Monogamy:
and adultery, 152
origins of, 151, 158
and prostitution, 151–52
prevalence of, 167
Monopsony, and occupational
segregation, 185, 199–200
Mother, socioemotional specialist
role of, 249, 276. See also
Expressive leader
Muller v. Oregon, 82
Murdock's categorization system,
rescaling of (table), 252

National Alliance for Business, 389
National Black Feminist
Organization, 343
National Center of Health Statistics,
119, 126
National Civil Federation (NCF),
210
National Organization of Women
(NOW), 389
National Welfare Rights
Organization, 343
Neoclassical economics, 182–83
Neuroticism, 232–33
New Women, 45
1975 Handbook on Women Workers,
46n, 185n
Nomic apparatus, defined, 263
Nonmarket activities, research topics
in, 181–82, 187–88
Nuclear family:
as emotional enclave for children,
235
functions of, 235–36
and gender role intensification,
236–37
and industrialization of housework,
224–25
as a socializing agent, 235–36

Occupation:
defined in relation to home
responsibilities, 37
and earnings differential, 311–12
opportunities for in Sweden, 398
as sign of successful person,
228–30
Occupational aspiration of women,
96
Occupational distribution:
for four sex-race groups (table),
340

of men and women workers, 91–92
Occupational segregation, 185–87, 302–3
  and age, 330
  and barriers to interchangeability of jobs, 322–26
  and capitalist control of production, 80, 83
  in China, 410
  and dual labor market analysis, 205–6
  in early factory system, 78–84
  and education, 319
  factors fostering, 305–6
  human capital approach to, 197–99
  institutional approach to, 201–7
  internal labor market approach to, 201–5
  and labor shortages, 329–30
  monopsony model of, 199–200
  neoclassical approaches to, 195–201
  overcrowding approach to, 195–97
  patriarchy as a source of, 52–53
  and protective legislation, 37
  by race and sex, 339–42
  and status, 229
  in Sweden, 296
  and technology, 238–39
  trends in, 303, 339–42
  by type of job, 326–28
Oppression, 12, 121–22
Orgasm, 47
Overcrowding hypothesis of sex inequality, 185, 195–97

Pairing family, 149–50, 157
Patriarchy:
  in China, 400–402
  in family industry system, 61–63, 76
  and occupational segregation, 81–82
  origins of, 74, 77–78, 157–58
  and women's status, 150–51
Patrilineality, 150
Pay differential. See Earnings differential
People's Republic of China, 48–49, 173, 364, 392, 400–414
Personal life:
  created through proletarianization, 58, 67

distortion of by psychology and psychoanalysis, 58–59
  functions of, 265
  and private property, 59–60
  women as keepers of, 59
Physical barriers to job interchangeability, 322–23
Pluralist model of sex equality, 388
Polyandry, 157
Polygyny, 157
Poverty, 351–53, 374–85
Power, of women vs. men, 337–38. See also Authority in family
Preplow horticulture, 163
Preschool children, importance of reducing labor force participation among married women (fig.), 88
Private property:
  and consent for marriage, 152–53
  and patriarchy, 157–58
  and personal life, 59–60
Producer role:
  and capitalism, 56, 59, 67
  choice inherent in, 32–33
  effects of mother/wife role on, 13–14, 34
  in precapitalist societies, 57, 75–76, 130–34
  of women, 41, 174, 248–55
Productivity:
  in family industry system, 76–77
  in internal labor market approach, 204–5
  and occupational segregation, 196, 197
Proletarian family:
  Engels's view of, 159
  threatened by factories, 65
Promiscuity, 157, 161–62
Prostitution, 151–52, 167
Protective legislation, 66
  as barrier to job interchangeability, 323–24
  to remove competition from women, 81–82
Protestantism. See Religion
Punaluan, defined, 157

Race:
  and comparison of earnings (table), 342
  and educational attainment, 97–98
  effect of on labor force participation, 90–91

model for assessing effects of, 338–39
and occupational aspirations, 96–97
Race relations cycle:
defined, 144
similarity to sex relations cycle, 143–45
Radical economic approach, 183–84
and housework, 365–67
Rational administrative framework, 11
Reindeer Chukchee, division of labor among, 131–32
Religion:
and domestic labor, 63
and divorce, 159
subordination of women in, 41–42
Remarriage, 297–98, 354
Reproductive role of women, changes in, 174–75
Reserve army of labor, women as, 222–23
Resocialization, 183
Role complementarity, 237
Role reversal, 122
Romantic love, 237
Rucci v. *Rucci*, 292
Russian Revolution, 173

Sanitary facilities, and job interchangeability, 323
Scholarship, impact of feminism on, 6–8. *See also* Universities
Science, invisibility of women in, 3
Separatism, 391
Serial monogamy. *See* Pairing marriage
Service industries:
as alternative to housework, 224
women in, 91, 224
Sex differences approach to study of sexual inequality, 105–10
Sex equality:
assimilation model of, 388–89
hybrid model of, 390
pluralist model of, 388
Sex inequalities:
caste/class status approach to, 103–4, 111–13
and earnings differential (table), 342
gender role approach to, 102–3, 107–10
minority group status approach to, 103–4, 110–11

sex difference approach to, 102–3, 105–7
Sex relations cycle:
contravention in, 144
similarities to race relations cycle, 144–45
Sex role, distinguished from gender role, 114–15. *See also* gender role
Sexual freedom:
as bourgeois hobby, 176
and contraception, 45–46, 174–75
in People's Republic of China, 173, 410
Social distance between men and women, problems in measuring, 141–42
Social reality:
as basis of social science framework, 10–11
construction of, 6–7, 263
effect of on research, 6–7
and marriage, 262–71
of women, 19
Social relation, knowledge as, 16–17
Social services, 46
Social stratification, 7, 20–21, 73–74. *See also* Status of women
Socialist party, 210
Socialist theory, and women, 48, 65, 170–71
Socialization:
as basis of sex inequalities, 102–3
as function of nuclear family, 235–36
Sociological discourse:
effect of capitalism on, 18
male perspective of, 18–21
social organization of, 17–18
Sociology, as social relations, 16–17
Sociology for women, 12–13
and housework, 367
Status of men:
in matrilineal, matrilocal families, 148–50
in pairing family, 149–50
Status of women:
in bourgeois family, 63
under capitalism, 57–58, 218–19
in China, 400–414
conditions for change in, 176–79
Engels on origins of, 148–55
increases in, 43–49
and industrialization, 40–43, 402–3
and occupation, 229

as marginal, 145–46
as minority group, 137–46
myths about, 346–49
occupational competence of, 348
participation rates of (table), 95
productivity of (table), 375
proportion of planning to work
  (table), 95
as a reserve army of labor, 222–23
role confusion of, 145–46
in socialist theory, 48, 65, 170–72
subculture of, 139
as successful vs. unsuccessful
  person, 227–30

Women's Bureau, 381–85
Women's jobs, 326–28
Women's liberation, 223–24
Women's work life, changing
  patterns of (fig.), 86
Working wives. *See* Labor force
  participation of women
World War I, 45
World War II, 45

Yahgan, division of labor among,
  133–34